GW00601959

Certificate Paper C3

FUNDAMENTALS OF BUSINESS MATHEMATICS

For assessments under the 2006 new syllabus in 2006 and 2007

Study Text

In this June 2006 new edition

- A **user-friendly format** for easy navigation

- Regular **fast forward** summaries emphasising the key points in each chapter

- **Assessment focus points** showing you what the assessor will want you to do

- **Questions** and **quick quizzes** to test your understanding

- **Question bank** containing objective test questions with answers

- A full index

BPP's **i-Pass** product also supports this paper.

FOR ASSESSMENTS UNDER THE 2006 NEW SYLLABUS IN 2006 AND 2007

First edition June 2006

ISBN 0 7517 2649 4

British Library Cataloguing-in-Publication Data
A catalogue record for this book
is available from the British Library

Published by

BPP Professional Education
Aldine House, Aldine Place
London W12 8AW

Printed in Great Britain by
WM Print
45-47 Frederick Street
Walsall
WS2 9NE

We are grateful to the Chartered Institute of
Management Accountants for permission to reproduce
past examination questions. The suggested solutions
in the Answer bank have been prepared by BPP
Professional Education.

Contents

Computer-based learning products from BPP

If you want to reinforce your studies by **interactive** learning, try BPP's **i-Learn** product, covering major syllabus areas in an interactive format. For **self-testing**, try **i-Pass,** which offers a large number of **objective test questions**, particularly useful where objective test questions form part of the exam.

See the order form at the back of this text for details of these innovative learning tools.

Learn Online

Learn Online uses BPP's wealth of teaching experience to produce a fully **interactive** e-learning resource **delivered via the Internet**. The site offers comprehensive **tutor support** and features areas such as **study**, **practice**, **email service**, **revision** and **useful resources**.

Visit our website www.bpp.com/cima/learnonline to sample aspects of Learn Online free of charge.

Learning to Learn Accountancy

BPP's ground-breaking **Learning to Learn Accountancy** book is designed to be used both at the outset of your CIMA studies and throughout the process of learning accountancy. It challenges you to consider how you study and gives you helpful hints about how to approach the various types of paper which you will encounter. It can help you **focus your studies on the subject and exam**, enabling you to **acquire knowledge**, **practise and revise efficiently and effectively**.

The BPP Study Text

Aims of this Study Text

To provide you with the knowledge and understanding, skills and application techniques that you need if you are to be successful in your exams

This Study Text has been written around the **Business Mathematics** syllabus.

- It is **comprehensive**. It covers the syllabus content. No more, no less.

- It is written at the **right level**. Each chapter is written with CIMA's precise learning outcomes in mind.

- It is targeted to the **exam**. We have taken account of the pilot paper, guidance the examiner has given and the assessment methodology.

To allow you to study in the way that best suits your learning style and the time you have available, by following your personal Study Plan (see page (viii))

You may be studying at home on your own until the date of the exam, or you may be attending a full-time course. You may like to (and have time to) read every word, or you may prefer to (or only have time to) skim-read and devote the remainder of your time to question practice. Wherever you fall in the spectrum, you will find the BPP Study Text meets your needs in designing and following your personal Study Plan.

To tie in with the other components of the BPP Effective Study Package to ensure you have the best possible chance of passing the exam (see page (vi))

The BPP Effective Study Package

Recommended period of use	The BPP Effective Study Package
From the outset and throughout	**Learning to Learn Accountancy** Read this invaluable book as you begin your studies and refer to it as you work through the various elements of the BPP Effective Study Package. It will help you to acquire knowledge, practise and revise, efficiently and effectively.
Three to twelve months before the exam	**Study Text and i-Learn** Use the Study Text to acquire knowledge, understanding, skills and the ability to apply techniques. Use BPP's **i-Learn** product to reinforce your learning.
Throughout	**Learn Online** Study, practise, revise and take advantage of other useful resources with BPP's fully interactive e-learning site with comprehensive tutor support.
Throughout	**i-Pass** **i-Pass**, our computer-based testing package, provides objective test questions in a variety of formats and is ideal for self-assessment.
One to six months before the exam	**Practice & Revision Kit** Try the numerous examination-format questions, for which there are realistic suggested solutions prepared by BPP's own authors. Then attempt the two mock exams.
From three months before the exam until the last minute	**Passcards** Work through these short, memorable notes which are focused on what is most likely to come up in the exam you will be sitting.
One to six months before the exam	**Success CDs** The CDs cover the vital elements of your syllabus in less than 90 minutes per subject. They also contain exam hints to help you fine tune your strategy.

Help yourself study for your CIMA exams

Exams for professional bodies such as CIMA are very different from those you have taken at college or university. You will be under **greater time pressure before** the exam – as you may be combining your study with work. There are many different ways of learning and so the BPP Study Text offers you a number of different tools to help you through. Here are some hints and tips: they are not plucked out of the air, but **based on research and experience**. (You don't need to know that long-term memory is in the same part of the brain as emotions and feelings - but it's a fact anyway.)

The right approach

1   **The right attitude**

Believe in yourself	Yes, there is a lot to learn. Yes, it is a challenge. But thousands have succeeded before and you can too.
Remember why you're doing it	Studying might seem a grind at times, but you are doing it for a reason: to advance your career.

2   **The right focus**

Read through the Syllabus and learning outcomes	These tell you what you are expected to know and are supplemented by Exam focus points in the text.
Study the Assessment section	This will give you an indication of the style of questions you could encounter in the assessment.

3   **The right method**

The whole picture	You need to grasp the detail - but keeping in mind how everything fits into the whole picture will help you understand better. • The **Introduction** of each chapter puts the material in context. • The **Syllabus content, Learning outcomes** and **Exam focus points** show you what you need to **grasp**.
In your own words	To absorb the information (and to practise your written communication skills), it helps to **put it into your own words**. • **Take notes.** • Answer the **questions** in each chapter. You will practise your written communication skills, which become increasingly important as you progress through your CIMA exams. • Draw **mindmaps**. • Try **'teaching' a subject** to a colleague or friend.
Give yourself cues to jog your memory	The BPP Study Text uses **bold** to **highlight key points**. • Try **colour coding** with a highlighter pen. • Write **key points** on cards.

4   The right review

Review, review, review	It is a **fact** that regularly reviewing a topic in summary form can **fix it in your memory**. Because **review** is so important, the BPP Study Text helps you to do so in many ways.
	• **Chapter roundups** summarise the 'fast forward' key points in each chapter. Use them to recap each study session.
	• The **Quick quiz** is another review technique you can use to ensure that you have grasped the essentials.
	• Go through the **Examples** in each chapter a second or third time.

Developing your personal Study Plan

BPP's **Learning to Learn Accountancy** book emphasises the need to prepare (and use) a study plan. Planning and sticking to the plan are key elements of learning success.

There are four steps you should work through.

Step 1   How do you learn?

First you need to be aware of your style of learning. The BPP **Learning to Learn Accountancy** book commits a chapter to this **self-discovery**. What types of intelligence do you display when learning? You might be advised to brush up on certain study skills before launching into this Study Text.

BPP's **Learning to Learn Accountancy** book helps you to identify what intelligences you show more strongly and then details how you can tailor your study process to your preferences. It also includes handy hints on how to develop intelligences you exhibit less strongly, but which might be needed as you study accountancy.

Are you a **theorist** or are you more **practical**? If you would rather get to grips with a theory before trying to apply it in practice, you should follow the study sequence on page (ix). If the reverse is true (you like to know why you are learning theory before you do so), you might be advised to flick through Study Text chapters and look at examples, case studies and questions (Steps 8, 9 and 10 in the **suggested study sequence**) before reading through the detailed theory.

Step 2   How much time do you have?

Work out the time you have available per week, given the following.

- The standard you have set yourself
- The time you need to set aside later for work on the Practice & Revision Kit and Passcards
- The other exam(s) you are sitting
- Very importantly, practical matters such as work, travel, exercise, sleep and social life

Hours

Note your time available in box A.   A [   ]

BPP
PROFESSIONAL EDUCATION

Step 3   Allocate your time

- Take the time you have available per week for this Study Text shown in box A, multiply it by the number of weeks available and insert the result in box B.   B

- Divide the figure in box B by the number of chapters in this text and insert the result in box C.   C

Remember that this is only a rough guide. Some of the chapters in this book are longer and more complicated than others, and you will find some subjects easier to understand than others.

Step 4   Implement

Set about studying each chapter in the time shown in box C, following the key study steps in the order suggested by your particular learning style.

This is your personal **Study Plan**. You should try and combine it with the study sequence outlined below. You may want to modify the sequence a little (as has been suggested above) to adapt it to your **personal style**.

BPP's **Learning to Learn Accountancy** gives further guidance on developing a study plan, and deciding where and when to study.

Suggested study sequence

It is likely that the best way to approach this Study Text is to tackle the chapters in the order in which you find them. Taking into account your individual learning style, you could follow this sequence.

Key study steps	Activity
Step 1 **Topic list**	Each numbered topic is a numbered section in the chapter.
Step 2 **Introduction**	This gives you the big picture in terms of the context of the chapter, the learning outcomes the chapter covers, and the content you will read. In other words, it sets your objectives for study.
Step 3 **Knowledge brought forward boxes**	In these we highlight information and techniques that it is assumed you have 'brought forward' with you from your earlier studies. If there are topics which have changed recently due to legislation for example, these topics are explained in more detail.
Step 4 **Fast forward**	Fast forward boxes give you a quick summary of the content of each of the main chapter sections. They are listed together in the roundup at the end of each chapter to provide you with an overview of the contents of the whole chapter.
Step 5 **Explanations**	Proceed methodically through the chapter, reading each section thoroughly and making sure you understand.
Step 6 **Key terms and focus points**	<ul><li>Key terms can often earn you *easy marks* if you state them clearly and correctly in an appropriate exam answer (and they are highlighted in the index at the back of the text).</li><li>Exam focus points state how we think the examiner intends to examine certain topics.</li></ul>
Step 7 **Note taking**	Take brief notes, if you wish. Avoid the temptation to copy out too much. Remember that being able to put something into your own words is a sign of being able to understand it. If you find you cannot explain something you have read, read it again before you make the notes.

Key study steps	Activity
Step 8 **Examples**	Follow each through to its solution very carefully.
Step 9 **Case studies**	Study each one, and try to add flesh to them from your own experience. They are designed to show how the topics you are studying come alive (and often come unstuck) in the real world.
Step 10 **Questions**	Make a very good attempt at each one.
Step 11 **Answers**	Check yours against ours, and make sure you understand any discrepancies.
Step 12 **Chapter roundup**	Work through it carefully, to make sure you have grasped the significance of all the fast forward points.
Step 13 **Quick quiz**	When you are happy that you have covered the chapter, use the Quick quiz to check how much you have remembered of the topics covered and to practise questions in a variety of formats.
Step 14 **Question(s) in the question bank**	Either at this point, or later when you are thinking about revising, make a full attempt at the Question(s) suggested at the very end of the chapter. You can find these at the end of the Study Text, along with the Answers so you can see how you did.

Short of time: Skim study technique?

You may find you simply do not have the time available to follow all the key study steps for each chapter, however you adapt them for your particular learning style. If this is the case, follow the **skim study** technique below.

- Study the chapters in the order you find them in the Study Text.

- For each chapter:

    - Follow the key study steps 1-3

    - Skim-read through step 5, looking out for the points highlighted in the fast forward boxes (step 4)

    - Jump to step 12

    - Go back to step 6

    - Follow through steps 8 and 9

    - Prepare outline answers to questions (steps 10/11)

    - Try the Quick quiz (step 13), following up any items you can't answer

    - Do a plan for the Question (step 14), comparing it against our answers

    - You should probably still follow step 7 (note-taking), although you may decide simply to rely on the BPP Passcards for this.

Moving on...

However you study, when you are ready to embark on the practice and revision phase of the BPP Effective Study Package, you should still refer back to this Study Text, both as a source of **reference** (you should find the index particularly helpful for this) and as a way to **review** (the Fast forwards, Exam focus points, Chapter roundups and Quick quizzes help you here).

And remember to keep careful hold of this Study Text – you will find it invaluable in your work.

More advice on Study Skills can be found in BPP's **Learning to Learn Accountancy** book.

Learning outcomes and Syllabus

Syllabus overview

This is a foundation level study in mathematical and statistical concepts and techniques. The first and third sections, Basic Mathematics and Summarising and Analysing Data, include techniques which are fundamental to the work of the Management Accountant. The second section covers basic probability and is needed because Management Accountants need to be aware of and be able to estimate the risk and uncertainty involved in the decisions they make. In the fourth and fifth sections, there is an introduction to the mathematical techniques needed for forecasting, necessary in the area of business planning. The sixth section is an introduction to financial mathematics, a topic that is important to the study of financial management. Finally, there is a section covering how Chartered Management Accountants use spreadsheets in their day-to-day work.

Aims

This syllabus aims to test the student's ability to:

- Demonstrate the use of basic mathematics, including formulae and ratios

- Identify reasonableness in the calculation of answers

- Demonstrate the use of probability where risk and uncertainty exist

- Apply techniques for summarising and analysing data

- Calculate correlation coefficients for bivariate data and apply the technique of simple regression analysis

- Demonstrate techniques used for forecasting

- Apply financial mathematical techniques

- Use spreadsheets to facilitate the presentation of data, analysis of univariate and bivariate data and use of formulae

Assessment

There will be a computer based assessment of 2 hours duration, comprising 45 compulsory questions, each with one or more parts.

Learning outcomes and syllabus content

A Basic mathematics – 15%

Learning outcomes

On completion of their studies students should be able to:

(i)   Demonstrate the order of operations in formulae, including the use of brackets, powers and roots

(ii)   Calculate percentages and proportions

(iii)   Calculate answers to appropriate decimal places or significant figures

(iv)   Solve simple equations, including 2 variable simultaneous equations and quadratic equations

(v)   Prepare graphs of linear and quadratic equations

Syllabus content

		Covered in chapter
(1)	Use of formulae, including negative powers as in the formula for the learning curve	2
(2)	Percentages and ratios	1
(3)	Rounding of numbers	1
(4)	Basic algebraic techniques and the solution of equations – including simultaneous and quadratic equations	2
(5)	Manipulation of inequalities	2

B Probability – 15%

Learning outcomes

On completion of their studies students should be able to:

(i)   Calculate a simple probability
(ii)   Demonstrate the addition and multiplication rules of probability
(iii)   Calculate a simple conditional probability
(iv)   Calculate an expected value
(v)   Demonstrate the use of expected value tables in decision making
(vi)   Explain the limitations of expected values
(vii)   Explain the concepts of risk and uncertainty

Syllabus content

		Covered in chapter
(1)	The relationship between probability, proportion and percent	3
(2)	Addition and multiplication rules in probability theory	3
(3)	Venn diagrams	3
(4)	Expected values and expected value tables	3
(5)	Risk and uncertainty	3

C Summarising and analysing data - 15%

Learning outcomes

On completion of their studies students should be able to:

(i)   Explain the difference between data and information

(ii)   Identify the characteristics of good information

(iii)   Tabulate data and prepare histograms

(iv)   Calculate for both ungrouped and grouped data: arithmetic mean, median, mode, range, variance, standard deviation and coefficient of variation.

(v)   Explain the concept of a frequency distribution

(vi)   Prepare graphs/diagrams of normal distribution, explain its properties and use tables of normal distribution

(vii)   Apply the Pareto distribution and the '80:20 rule'

(viii) Explain how and why indices are used

(ix)   Calculate indices using either base or current weights

(x)   Apply indices to deflate a series

Syllabus content

		Covered in chapter
(1)	Data and information	4
(2)	Tabulation of data	5
(3)	Graphs and diagrams: bar charts, scatter diagrams, histograms and ogives	5
(4)	Summary measures of central tendency and dispersion for both grouped and ungrouped data	6, 7
(5)	Frequency distributions	5
(6)	Normal distribution, the Pareto distribution and the '80:20 rule'	8
(7)	Index numbers	9

D Inter-relationships between variables – 15%

Learning outcomes

On completion of their studies students should be able to:

(i)   Prepare a scatter diagram
(ii)   Calculate the correlation coefficient and the coefficient of determination between two variables
(iii) Calculate the regression equation between two variables
(iv) Apply the regression equation to predict the dependent variable, given a value of the independent variable

Syllabus content

		Covered in chapter
(1)	Scatter diagrams and the correlation coefficient	5, 10
(2)	Simple linear regression	10

E Forecasting – 15%

Learning outcomes

On completion of their studies students should be able to:

(i)   Prepare a time series graph
(ii)   Identify trends and patterns using an appropriate moving average
(iii) Identify the components of a time series model
(iv) Prepare a trend equation using either graphical means or regression analysis
(v)   Calculate seasonal factors for both additive and multiplicative models and explain when each is appropriate
(vi) Calculate predicted values given a time series model
(vii) Identify the limitations of forecasting models

Syllabus content

		Covered in chapter
(1)	Time series analysis – graphical analysis	11
(2)	Trends in time series – graphs, moving averages and linear regression	11
(3)	Seasonal variations using both additive and multiplicative models	11
(4)	Forecasting and its limitations	11

F Financial Mathematics - 15%

Learning outcomes

On completion of their studies students should be able to:

(i)   Calculate future values of an investment using both simple and compound interest

(ii)   Calculate an Annual Percentage Rate of interest given a quarterly or monthly rate

(iii)   Calculate the present value of a future cash sum, using both a formula and CIMA tables

(iv)   Calculate the present value of an annuity and a perpetuity using formula and CIMA tables

(v)   Calculate loan/mortgage repayments and the value of an outstanding loan/mortgage

(vi)   Calculate the future value of regular savings and/or the regular investment needed to generate a required future sum, using the formula for the sum of a geometric progression

(vii)   Calculate the NPV and IRR of a project and explain whether and why it should be accepted

Syllabus content

		Covered in chapter
(1)	Simple and compound interest	12
(2)	Annuities and perpetuities	13
(3)	Loans and mortgages	12, 13
(4)	Sinking funds and savings funds	12, 13
(5)	Discounting to find net present value and internal rate of return and interpretation of NPV and IRR	13

G Spreadsheets – 10%

Learning outcomes

On completion of their studies students should be able to:

(i)   Explain the features and functions of spreadsheet software
(ii)   Explain the use and limitations of spreadsheet software in business
(iii)   Apply spreadsheet software to the normal work of a Chartered Management Accountant

Indicative Syllabus content

		Covered in chapter
(1)	Features and functions of commonly-used spreadsheet software: workbook, worksheet, rows, columns, cells, data, text, formulae, formatting, printing, graphics and macros. Note: *Knowlegde of Microsoft Excel type spreadsheet vocabulary/formulae syntax is required. Formula tested will be that which is constructed by users rather than pre-programmed formulae*	14
(2)	Advantages and disadvantages of spreadsheet software, when compared to manual analysis and other types of software application packages	14
(3)	Use of spreadsheet software in the day-to-day work of the Chartered Management Accountant: budgeting, forecasting, reporting performance, variance analysis, what-if analysis, discounted cashflow calculations	14

The assessment

Format of computer-based assessment (CBA)

The CBA will not be divided into sections. There will be a total of 45 objective test questions and you will need to answer **ALL** of them in the time allowed, 2 hours.

Frequently asked questions about CBA

Q   What are the main advantages of CBA?

A
- Assessments can be offered on a continuing basis rather than at six-monthly intervals
- Instant feedback is provided for candidates by displaying their results on the computer screen

Q   Where can I take CBA?

A
- CBA must be taken at a 'CIMA Accredited CBA Centre'. For further information on CBA, you can email CIMA at cba@cimaglobal.com.

Q   How does CBA work?

A
- Questions are displayed on a monitor

- Candidates enter their answers directly onto a computer

- Candidates have 2 hours to complete the Business Mathematics examination

- The computer automatically marks the candidate's answers when the candidate has completed the examination

- Candidates are provided with some indicative feedback on areas of weakness if the candidate is unsuccessful

Q   What sort of questions can I expect to find in CBA?

Your assessment will consist entirely of a number of different types of **objective test question**. Here are some possible examples.

- **MCQs.** Read through the information on page (xxii) about MCQs and how to tackle them.

- **Data entry.** This type of OT requires you to provide figures such as the correct figure for creditors in a balance sheet.

- **Hot spots.** This question format might ask you to identify which cell on a spreadsheet contains a particular formula or where on a graph marginal revenue equals marginal cost.

- **Multiple response.** These questions provide you with a number of options and you have to identify those which fulfil certain criteria.

- **Matching.** This OT question format could ask you to classify particular costs into one of a range of cost classifications provided, to match descriptions of variances with one of a number of variances listed, and so on.

This text provides you with **plenty of opportunities to practise** these various question types. You will find OTs **within each chapter** in the text and the **Quick quizzes** at the end of each chapter are full of them. The Question Bank contains more than one hundred and twenty objective test questions similar to the ones that you are likely to meet in your CBA.

Further information relating to OTs is given on page (xix).

The **Practice and Revision Kit** for this paper was published in **June 2006** and is **full of OTs**, providing you with vital revision opportunities for the fundamental techniques and skills you will require in the assessment.

Tackling multiple choice questions

In a multiple choice question on your paper, you are given how many **incorrect** options?

A   Two
B   Three
C   Four
D   Five

The correct answer is B.

The MCQs in your exam contain four possible answers. You have to **choose the option that best answers the question**. The three incorrect options are called distracters. There is a skill in answering MCQs quickly and correctly. By practising MCQs you can develop this skill, giving you a better chance of passing the exam.

You may wish to follow the approach outlined below, or you may prefer to adapt it.

Step 1   **Skim read** all the MCQs and **identify** what appear to be the easier questions.

Step 2   Attempt each question – **starting with the easier questions** identified in Step 1. Read the question thoroughly. You may prefer to work out the answer before looking at the options, or you may prefer to look at the options at the beginning. Adopt the method that works best for you.

Step 3   Read the four options and see if one matches your own answer. **Be careful with numerical questions**, as the distracters are designed to match answers that incorporate common errors. Check that your calculation is correct. Have you followed the requirement exactly? Have you included every stage of the calculation?

Step 4   You may **find that none of the options matches your answer**.

- Re-read the question to ensure that you understand it and are answering the requirement.
- Eliminate any obviously wrong answers.
- Consider which of the remaining answers is the most likely to be correct and select the option.

Step 5   If you are still **unsure** make a note **and continue to the next question.**

Step 6   **Revisit unanswered** questions. When you come back to a question after a break you often find you are able to answer it correctly straight away. If you are still unsure have a guess. You are not penalised for incorrect answers, so **never leave a question unanswered!**

Exam focus. After extensive practice and revision of MCQs, you may find that you recognise a question when you sit the exam. Be aware that the detail and/or requirement may be different. If the question seems familiar read the requirement and options carefully – do not assume that it is identical.

BPP's i-Pass for this paper provides you with plenty of opportunity for further practice of MCQs.

Tackling objective test questions

Of the total marks available for the paper, objective test questions (OTs) comprise 20/50 per cent. Questions will be worth between 2 to 4 marks.

What is an objective test question?

An **OT** is made up of some form of **stimulus**, usually a question, and a **requirement** to do something.

(a)   Multiple choice questions
(b)   Filling in blanks or completing a sentence
(c)   Listing items, in any order or a specified order such as rank order
(d)   Stating a definition
(e)   Identifying a key issue, term, figure or item
(f)   Calculating a specific figure
(g)   Completing gaps in a set of data where the relevant numbers can be calculated from the information given
(h)   Identifying points/zones/ranges/areas on graphs or diagrams, labelling graphs or filling in lines on a graph
(i)   Matching items or statements
(j)   Stating whether statements are true or false
(k)   Writing brief (in a specified number of words) explanations
(l)   Deleting incorrect items
(m)   Choosing right words from a number of options
(n)   Complete an equation, or define what the symbols used in an equation mean

OT questions in CIMA exams

CIMA has offered the following **guidance** about OT questions in the exam.

- Credit may be given for **workings** where you are asked to calculate a specific figure.

- If you **exceed a specified limit on the number of words** you can use in an answer, you will **not be awarded any marks**.

- If you make **more than one attempt** at a question, clearly **cross through** any answers that you do not want to submit. If you don't do this, only your first answer will be marked.

Examples of OTs are included within each chapter, in the **quick quizzes** at the end of each chapter and in the **objective test question bank**.

> BPP's i-Pass for this paper provides you with plenty of opportunity for further practice of OTs.

Part A

Basic mathematics

1

Basic mathematical techniques

Introduction

Business mathematics is a certificate level paper which is designed to provide you with a number of mathematical and statistical concepts and techniques that you will need as you progress through your managerial and strategic level papers.

This Study Text is divided into the following seven sections.

PART A: BASIC MATHEMATICS

PART B: PROBABILITY

PART C: SUMMARISING AND ANALYSING DATA

PART D: INTER-RELATIONSHIPS BETWEEN VARIABLES

PART E: FORECASTING

PART F: FINANCIAL MATHEMATICS

PART G: SPREADSHEETS

Many students do not have a mathematical background and so this chapter is intended to cover the basic mathematics that you will need for the **Business Mathematics** assessment.

Even if you have done mathematics in the past don't ignore this chapter. Skim through it to make sure that you are aware of all the concepts and techniques covered. Since it provides the foundation for much of what is to follow it is an **extremely important chapter**.

Topic list	Syllabus references
1 Integers, fractions and decimals	A (iii) (3)
2 Using a scientific calculator	All
3 Order of operations	A (i)
4 Percentages and ratios	A (ii) (2)
5 Roots and powers	A (i)

1 Integers, fractions and decimals

FAST FORWARD

- An **integer** is a whole number and can be either positive or negatives.
- **Fractions** and **decimals** are ways of showing parts of a whole.

1.1 Integers

Examples of integers are …, −5, −4 , −3 , −2, −1, 0, 1, 2, 3, 4, 5, …

Examples of fractions are 1/2, 1/4, 19/35, 10/377 …

Examples of decimals are 0.1, 0.25, 0.3135, …

1.2 Negative numbers

FAST FORWARD

The **negative number rules** are as follows:

$$-p + q = q - p$$
$$q - (-p) = q + p$$
$$-p \times -q = pq \text{ and } \frac{-p}{-q} = \frac{p}{q}$$
$$-p \times q = -pq \text{ and } \frac{-p}{q} = -\frac{p}{q}$$

1.2.1 Adding and subtracting negative numbers

When a negative number (−p) is **added** to another number (q), the net effect is to **subtract** p from q.

(a) $10 + (-6) = 10 - 6 = 4$ (b) $-10 + (-6) = -10 - 6 = -16$

When a negative number (−p) is **subtracted** from another number (q), the net effect is to **add** p to q.

(a) $12 - (-8) = 12 + 8 = 20$ (b) $-12 - (-8) = -12 + 8 = -4$

1.2.2 Multiplying and dividing negative numbers

When a negative number is **multiplied** or **divided** by another negative number, the result is a **positive** number.

(a) $-8 \times (-4) = +32$ (b) $\frac{-18}{-3} = +6$

If there is only **one negative number** in a multiplication or division, the result is **negative**.

(a) $-8 \times 4 = -32$ (b) $3 \times (-2) = -6$ (c) $\frac{12}{-4} = -3$ (d) $\frac{-20}{5} = -4$

 **Question**

Work out the following.

(a) $(72 - 8) - (-2 + 1)$

(c) $8(2 - 5) - (4 - (-8))$

(b) $\dfrac{88 + 8}{12} + \dfrac{(29 - 11)}{-2}$

(d) $\dfrac{-36}{9 - 3} - \dfrac{84}{3 - 10} - \dfrac{-81}{3}$

Answer

(a) $64 - (-1) = 64 + 1 = 65$

(c) $-24 - (12) = -36$

(b) $8 + (-9) = -1$ (d) $-6 - (-12) - (-27) = -6 + 12 + 27 = 33$

1.3 Fractions

A fraction has a numerator (the number on the top line) and a denominator (the number on the bottom line).

$$\text{FRACTION} = \frac{\text{NUMERATOR}}{\text{DENOMINATOR}}$$

For example, the fraction 1/2 has a numerator equal to 1 and a denominator of 2.

1.4 Reciprocals

The reciprocal of a number is 1 divided by that number for example. For example, the reciprocal of 2 is 1 divided by 2 = 1/2. The reciprocal of 3 is 1 divided by 3 = 1/3.

1.5 Decimals

A fraction can be turned into a decimal by dividing the numerator by the denominator. For example, the fraction 1/2 equates to 0.5, and the fraction 1/4 equates to 0.25. When turning decimals into fractions, you need to remember that places after the decimal point stand for tenths, hundredths, thousandths and so on.

1.5.1 Decimal places

Sometimes a decimal number has too many figures in it for practical use. For example consider the fraction 6/9 which when turned into a decimal = 0.666666 recurring. This problem can be overcome by **rounding** the decimal number to a specific number of **decimal places** by discarding figures using the following rule.

If the first figure to be discarded is greater than or equal to five then add one to the previous figure. Otherwise the previous figure is unchanged.

1.5.2 Example: Decimal places

(a)   49.28723 correct to four decimal places is 49.2872
        Discarding a 3 causes nothing to be added to the 2.

(b)   49.28723 correct to three decimal places is 49.287
        Discarding a 2 causes nothing to be added to the 7.

(c)   49.28723 correct to two decimal places is 49.29
        Discarding the 7 causes 1 to be added to the 8.

(d)   49.28723 correct to one decimal place is 49.3
        Discarding the 8 causes 1 to be added to the 2.

1.6 Significant figures

Another method for giving an approximated answer is to round off using **significant** figures. Significant means important and the closer a digit is to the beginning of a number, the more significant it is.

For example, if we want to express 95,431 to 3 significant figures, '31' will be discarded, leaving 95,400 (3sf).

Zeros have specific rules. All zeros **between** non-zeros are significant. For example, 20,606 has 5 significant figures. Leading zeros in a decimal are **not** significant. For example, 0.025 has 2 significant figures.

Question   **Significant figures and decimal places**

(a)   Round off the number 37,649 to one significant figure
(b)   Round off the number 0.073184 to one significant figure
(c)   Round off the number 0.0073184 to four decimal places
(d)   Work out the answer to 974 × 586 on a calculator and round off the answer to three significant figures
(e)   Work out the answer to 23 ÷ 946 on a calculator and round off the answer to three decimal places

Answer

(a)   40,000

(b)   0.07

(c)   0.0073

(d)   974 × 586 = 570,764
                  = 571,000 (3 sf)

(e)   23 ÷ 946 = 0.02431289641
                  = 0.024 (3 dp)

Assessment focus point

It is vitally important that you are able to perform calculations correct to a given number of significant figures or decimal places as correct rounding is essential in computer based assessments. If you did not get all parts of the above question on significant figures and decimal places correct, work through Section 1 again and retry the question. Do not underestimate the importance of understanding significant figures and decimal places.

1.7 Extra symbols

We will come across several other mathematical signs in this book but there are five which you should learn **now**.

(a)   > means 'greater than'. So 46 > 29 is true, but 40 > 86 is false.
(b)   ≥ means 'is greater than or equal to'. So 4 ≥ 3 and 4 ≥ 4.
(c)   < means 'is less than'. So 29 < 46 is true, but 86 < 40 is false.
(d)   ≤ means 'is less than or equal to'. So 7 ≤ 8 and 7 ≤ 7.
(e)   ≠ means 'is not equal to'. So we could write 100.004 ≠ 100.

2 Using a scientific calculator

FAST FORWARD

Scientific calculators can make calculations quicker and easier.

2.1 The need for a scientific calculator

For this exam and for your future CIMA studies you will need to have an up to date scientific calculator. They are not expensive and if you spend time now getting to know what it can do for you, you will have a much better chance of succeeding in your studies. CIMA guidance states that you should be aware of what your calculator can do for you and that you should not take a new calculator into an exam without knowing how to use it.

The calculator can make calculations quicker and easier but it is very important that you show all your workings to numerical calculations. The marker will not award you marks where your final answer is wrong if they can't see your workings and how you arrived at your answer.

2.2 A typical scientific calculator

The illustration below shows a typical scientific calculator that is widely available. It has a natural textbook display which allows you to input and display fractions, square roots and other numeric expressions as they appear in your textbook and assessment. Your calculator may be slightly different and it is essential that you read its instruction leaflet and practice using it.

REPLAY
◀▶ This allows you to change any part of the series of keys you have pressed
▲ This lets you go back to previous calculations

COMP mode is the usual setting for calculations. STAT mode lets you do statistical calculations

RECIPROCAL
This recalculates the number displayed as 1 over that number $\left(\dfrac{1}{x}\right)$

SHIFT
Pressing this key followed by a second key performs the alternative function of the second key

POWER and ROOT
Press the SHIFT button before this button if you want to find a root. This is the same as $\wedge$, y^x or x^y

FRACTIONS
This lets you put a fraction into a calculation without having to convert it into a decimal

NEGATIVE
A very useful button for minus numbers

DELETE
Used with the replay button, this allows you to go back and correct your calculation

BRACKETS
These are used just like you write a calculation so that it is done in the right order

ANSWER
This stores the last calculation result

EQUALS
Input the calculation expressions as they are written then press = to execute it

Question

Using a scientific calculator

(a)   Put the following calculation into your calculator exactly as it is written

3 + 6 x 5 =

What does this tell you about how your calculator carries out the order of operation?

(b)   Calculate the following using the brackets buttons on your calculator

(3 + 5) x 2

What happens if you don't use brackets?

(c)   Use the fraction button to calculate the following:

$\frac{1}{2} + \frac{1}{4} + \frac{1}{8}$

(d)   What is $6^{2.75}$?

(e)   What is $\sqrt[7]{78,125}$?

(f)   What is $1/0.2 \times (3 - (1 + 0.7)^5)$?

(g)   What is $\dfrac{2.25^4 + 0.025^{-3}}{2.653}$?

Answer

(a)   33

This tells you that the calculator carries out mathematical operations in the correct order (see section 3 below).

(b)   16

If brackets are not used the answer is 13. The calculator has done the multiplication before the addition.

(c) $\frac{7}{8}$

(d)   138.0117105

(e)   1,956.55948

(f)   −55.99285

(g)   24,133.29397

3 Order of operations

3.1 Brackets

FAST FORWARD **Brackets** indicate a priority or an order in which calculations should be made.

Brackets are commonly used to indicate which parts of a mathematical expression should be grouped together, and calculated before other parts. The rule for using brackets is as follows.

(a)   Do things in brackets before doing things outside them.

(b)   Subject to rule (a), do things in this order.

(1)   Powers and roots
(2)   Multiplications and divisions, working from left to right
(3)   Additions and subtractions, working from left to right

3.1.1 Brackets – clarity

Brackets are used for the sake of clarity.

(a) $3 + 6 \times 8 = 51$. This is the same as writing $3 + (6 \times 8) = 51$.
(b) $(3 + 6) \times 8 = 72$. The brackets indicate that we wish to multiply the sum of 3 and 6 by 8.
(c) $12 - 4 \div 2 = 10$. This is the same as writing $12 - (4 \div 2) = 10$ or $12 - (4/2) = 10$.
(d) $(12 - 4) \div 2 = 4$. The brackets tell us to do the subtraction first.

A figure outside a bracket may be multiplied by two or more figures inside a bracket, linked by addition or subtraction signs. Here is an example.

$5(6 + 8) = 5 \times (6 + 8) = (5 \times 6) + (5 \times 8) = 70$

This is the same as $5(14) = 5 \times 14 = 70$

The multiplication sign after the 5 can be omitted, as shown here $(5(6 + 8))$, but there is no harm in putting it in $(5 \times (6 + 8))$ if you want to.

Similarly:

$5(8 - 6) = 5(2) = 10$; or
$(5 \times 8) - (5 \times 6) = 10$

3.1.2 Brackets – multiplication

When two sets of figures linked by addition or subtraction signs within brackets are multiplied together, each figure in one bracket is multiplied in turn by every figure in the second bracket. Thus:

$(8 + 4)(7 + 2) = (12)(9) = 108$ or
$(8 \times 7) + (8 \times 2) + (4 \times 7) + (4 \times 2) = 56 + 16 + 28 + 8 = 108$

3.1.3 Brackets on a calculator

A modern scientific calculator will let you do calculations with brackets in the same way they are written. Try doing the examples above using the brackets buttons.

Question

Four decimal places

Work out all answers to four decimal places, using a calculator.

(a) $(43 + 26.705) \times 9.3$

(b) $(844.2 \div 26) - 2.45$

(c) $\dfrac{45.6 - 13.92 + 823.1}{14.3 \times 112.5}$

(d) $\dfrac{303.3 + 7.06 \times 42.11}{1.03 \times 111.03}$

(e) $\dfrac{7.6 \times 1{,}010}{10.1 \times 76{,}000}$

(f) $(43.756 + 26.321) \div 171.036$

(g) $(43.756 + 26.321) \times 171.036$

(h) $171.45 + (-221.36) + 143.22$

(i) $66 - (-43.57) + (-212.36)$

(j) $\dfrac{10.1 \times 76{,}000}{7.6 \times 1{,}010}$

(k) $\dfrac{21.032 + (-31.476)}{3.27 \times 41.201}$

(l) $\dfrac{-33.33 - (-41.37)}{11.21 + (-24.32)}$

(m) $\dfrac{-10.75 \times (-15.44)}{-14.25 \times 17.15} + \left(\dfrac{16.23}{8.4 + 3.002} \right)$

(n) $\dfrac{-7.366 \times 921.3}{10{,}493 - 2{,}422.8} - \left(\dfrac{8.4 + 3.002}{16.23} \right)$

Answer

(a) 648.2565

(b) 30.0192

(c) 0.5313

(d) 5.2518

(e) 0.01

(f) 0.4097

(g) 11,985.6898

(h) 93.31

(i) –102.79

(j) 100 (Note that this question is the reciprocal of part (e), and so the answer is the reciprocal of the answer to part (e).)

(k) –0.0775

(l) –0.6133

(m) 0.7443

(n) –1.5434

4 Percentages and ratios

4.1 Percentages

FAST FORWARD

Percentages are used to indicate the **relative size** or **proportion** of items, rather than their **absolute** size.

If one office employs ten accountants, six secretaries and four supervisors, the **absolute** values of staff numbers and the **percentage** of the total work force in each type would be as follows.

	Accountants	Secretaries	Supervisors	Total
Absolute numbers	10	6	4	20
Percentages	50%	30%	20%	100%

The idea of percentages is that the whole of something can be thought of as 100%. The whole of a cake, for example, is 100%. If you share it out equally with a friend, you will get half each, or 100%/2 = 50% each.

FAST FORWARD To turn a percentage into a fraction or decimal you **divide by 100%**. To turn a fraction or decimal back into a percentage you **multiply by 100%**.

4.1.1 Percentages, fractions and decimals

Consider the following.

(a) $0.16 = 0.16 \times 100\% = 16\%$

(b) $\dfrac{4}{5} = 4/5 \times 100\% = \dfrac{400}{5\%} = 80\%$

(c) $40\% = \dfrac{40}{100\%} = \dfrac{2}{5} = 0.4$

4.2 Situations involving percentages

4.2.1 Find X% of Y

Question: What is 40% of $64?

Answer: 40% of $64 $= \dfrac{40}{100} \times \$64 = 0.4 \times \$64 = \$25.60$.

4.2.2 Express X as a percentage of Y

Question: What is $16 as a percentage of $64?

Answer: $16 as a percentage of $64 = 16/64 $\times 100\% = 1/4 \times 100\% = 25\%$

In other words, put the $16 as a fraction of the $64, and then multiply by 100%.

4.2.3 Find the original value of X, given that after a percentage increase of Y% it is equal to X₁

Question:

Fred Bloggs' salary is now $60,000 per annum after an annual increase of 20%. What was his annual salary before the increase?

Answer:

	%
Fred Bloggs' salary *before* increase (original)	100
Salary increase	20
Fred Bloggs' salary after increase (final)	120

We know that Fred's salary after the increase (final) also equals $60,000.

Therefore 120% = $60,000.

We need to find his salary *before* the increase (original), ie 100%.

We can do this as follows.

Step 1   Calculate 1%

If 120% = $60,000

$$1\% \;=\; \frac{£60,000}{120}$$

1% = $500

Step 2   Calculate 100% (original)

If   1% = $500

100% = $500 × 100

100% = $50,000

Therefore, Fred Bloggs' annual salary before the increase was $50,000.

4.2.4 Find the final value of A, given that after a percentage increase/decrease of B% it is equal to A_1

Question:

If sales receipts in year 1 are $500,000 and there was a percentage decrease of 10% in year 2, what are the sales receipts in year 2?

Answer:

Adopt the step-by-step approach used in paragraph 4.2.3 as follows.

	%
Sales receipts – year 1 (original)	100
Percentage decrease	10
Sales receipts – year 2 (final)	90

This question is slightly different to that in paragraph 4.2.3 because we have the original value (100%) and not the final value as in paragraph 4.2.3.

We know that sales receipts in year 1 (original) also equal $500,000.

We need to find the sales receipts in year 2 (final). We can do this as follows.

Step 1   Calculate 1%

If 100% = $500,000

1% = $5,000

Step 2   Calculate 90% (original)

If   1% = $5,000

90% = $5,000 × 90

90% = $450,000

Therefore, sales receipts in year 2 are $450,000.

4.2.5 Summary

You might think that the calculations involved in paragraphs 4.2.3 and 4.2.4 above are long-winded but it is vitally important that you understand how to perform these types of calculation. As you become more confident with calculating percentages you may not need to go through all of the steps that we have shown. The key to answering these types of question correctly is to be very clear about which values represent the **original** amount (100%) and which values represent the **final** amount (100 + x%).

	Increase %	Decrease %
ORIGINAL VALUE	100	100
INCREASE/(DECREASE)	X	−X
FINAL VALUE	100 + X	100 − X

4.3 Percentage changes

FAST FORWARD

A **percentage increase** or **reduction** is calculated as (change ÷ original) × 100%.

You might also be required to calculate the value of the **percentage change**, ie in paragraph 4.2.3 you may have been required to calculate the percentage increase in Fred Bloggs' salary, or in paragraph 4.2.4 you may have been required to calculate the percentage decrease of sales receipts in year 2 (as compared with year 1).

The formula required for calculating the **percentage change** is as follows.

$$\text{Percentage change} = \frac{\text{'Change'}}{\text{Original value}} \times 100\%$$

Note that it is the **original value** that the change is compared with and not the final value when calculating the percentage change.

Question	Percentage reduction

A television has been reduced from $490.99 to $340.99. What is the percentage reduction in price to three decimal places?

A	30.550	B	30.551	C	43.990	D	43.989

Answer

Difference in price = $(490.99 − 340.99) = $150.00

$$\text{Percentage reduction} = \frac{\text{change}}{\text{original price}} \times 100\% = \frac{150}{490.99} \times 100\% = 30.551\%$$

The correct answer is B.

4.3.1 Discounts

A business may offer a discount on a price to encourage sales. The calculation of discounts requires an ability to manipulate percentages. For example, a travel agent is offering a 17% discount on the brochure price of a particular holiday to America. The brochure price of the holiday is $795. What price is being offered by the travel agent?

Solution

Discount = 17% of $795 = $\frac{17}{100}$ × $795 = $135.15

Price offered = $(795 − 135.15) = $659.85

= ∴ 17% = 17 × 1% = 17 × $7.95 = $135.15

Alternatively, price offered = $795 × (100 − 17)% = $795 × 83% = $795 × 0.83 = $659.85

4.3.2 Quicker percentage change calculations

If something is increased by 10%, we can calculate the increased value by multiplying by (1 + 10%) = 1 +0.1 = 1.1. We are multiplying the number by itself plus 10% expressed as a decimal.

For example, a 15% increase to $1000 = $1000 × 1.15
= $1150

In the same way, a 10% decrease can be calculated by multiplying a number by (1 − 10%) = 1 − 0.1 = 0.9. With practice, this method will speed up your percentage calculations and will be very useful in your future studies.

Question   **Percentage price change**

Three years ago a retailer sold action man toys for $17.50 each. At the end of the first year he increased the price by 6% and at the end of the second year by a further 5%. At the end of the third year the selling price was $20.06. The percentage price change in year three was

| A | −3% | B | +3% | C | −6% | D | +9% |

Answer

Selling price at end of year 1 =	$17.50 × 1.06 =	$18.55
Selling price at end of year 2 =	$18.55 × 1.05 =	$19.48
Change in selling price in year 3 =	$(20.06 − 19.48) =	$0.58

∴ Percentage change in year 3 was $\frac{£0.58}{£19.48}$ × 100% = 2.97%, say 3%

The correct answer is B.

4.4 Profits

You may be required in your assessment to calculate profit, selling price or cost of sale of an item or number of items from certain information. To do this you need to remember the following crucial formula.

	%
Cost of sales	100
Plus Profit	25
Equals Sales	125

Profit may be expressed either as a percentage of **cost of sales** (such as 25% (25/100) mark-up) or as a percentage of **sales** (such as 20% (25/125) **margin**).

4.4.1 Profit margins

If profit is expressed as a percentage of sales (**margin**) the following formula is also useful.

	%
Selling price	100
Profit	20
Cost of sales	80

It is best to think of the selling price as 100% if profit is expressed as a **margin** (percentage of sales). On the other hand, if profit is expressed as a percentage of cost of sales (**mark-up**) it is best to think of the cost of sales as being 100%. The following examples should help to clarify this point.

4.4.2 Example: Margin

Delilah's Dresses sells a dress at a 10% margin. The dress cost the shop $100. Calculate the profit made by Delilah's Dresses.

Solution

The margin is 10% (ie 10/100)

$\therefore$ Let selling price = 100%

$\therefore$ Profit = 10%

$\therefore$ Cost = 90% = $100

$\therefore 1\% = \left(\dfrac{\$100}{90} \right)$

$\therefore 10\% = \text{profit} = \$\dfrac{100}{90} \times 10 = \$11.11$

4.4.3 Example: mark-up

Trevor's Trousers sells a pair of trousers for $80 at a 15% mark-up.

Required

Calculate the profit made by Trevor's Trousers.

Solution

The markup is 15%.

$\therefore$ Let cost of sales = 100%

$\therefore$ Profit = 15%

$\therefore$ Selling price = 115% = $80

$\therefore 1\% = \left(\dfrac{\$180}{115} \right)$

$\therefore 15\% = \text{profit} = \left(\dfrac{\$180}{115} \right) \times 15 = \$10.43$

Question   **Profits**

A skirt which cost the retailer $75 is sold at a profit of 25% on the selling price. The profit is therefore

A $18.75   B $20.00   C $25.00   D $30.00

Answer

Let selling price = 100%

Profit = 25% of selling price

∴ Cost = 75% of selling price

Cost = $75 = 75%

∴ 1% = $\dfrac{\$75}{75}$

∴ 25% = profit = $\dfrac{\$75}{75} \times 25 = \$25$

The correct answer is C.

4.5 Proportions

FAST FORWARD

A **proportion** means writing a percentage as a proportion of 1 (that is, as a decimal). 100% can be thought of as the whole, or 1. 50% is half of that, or 0.5.

4.5.1 Example: Proportions

Suppose there are 14 women in an audience of 70. What proportion of the audience are men?

Number of men = 70 − 14 = 56

Proportion of men = $\dfrac{56}{70} = \dfrac{8}{10}$ = 80% = 0.8

- The **fraction** of the audience made up of men is 8/10 or 4/5
- The **percentage** of the audience made up of men is 80%
- The **proportion** of the audience made up of men is 0.8

Question   **Proportions**

There are 30 students in a class room, 17 of whom have blonde hair. What proportion of the students (to four decimal places) do not have blonde hair (delete as appropriate).

0.5667	0.5666
0.4334	0.4333

Answer

0.5667	0.5666
0.4334	0.4333

$$\frac{(30-17)}{30} \times 100\% = 43.33\% = 0.4333$$

4.6 Ratios

FAST FORWARD

Ratios show relative shares of a whole.

Suppose Tom has $12 and Dick has $8. The **ratio** of Tom's cash to Dick's cash is 12:8. This can be cancelled down, just like a fraction, to 3:2. Study the following examples carefully.

4.6.1 Example: Ratios

Suppose Tom and Dick wish to share $20 out in the ratio 3:2. How much will each receive?

Solution

Because 3 + 2 = 5, we must divide the whole up into five equal parts, then give Tom three parts and Dick two parts.

$20 ÷ 5 = $4 (so each part is $4)

Tom's share = 3 × $4 = $12

Dick's share = 2 × $4 = $8

Check: $12 + $8 = $20 (adding up the two shares in the answer gets us back to the $20 in the question)

This method of calculating ratios as amounts works no matter how many ratios are involved.

4.6.2 Example: Ratios again

A, B, C and D wish to share $600 in the ratio 6:1:2:3. How much will each receive?

Solution

Number of parts = 6 + 1 + 2 + 3 = 12

Value of each part = $600 ÷ 12 = $50

A: 6 × $50 = $300
B: 1 × $50 = $50
C: 2 × $50 = $100
D: 3 × $50 = $150

Check: $300 + $50 + $100 + $150 = $600

Question

Tom, Dick and Harry wish to share out $800. Calculate how much each would receive if the ratio used was:

(a)   3 : 2 : 5
(b)   5 : 3 : 2
(c)   3 : 1 : 1

Answer

(a)   Total parts = 10

Each part is worth $800 ÷ 10 = $80

Tom gets   3 × $80 = $240
Dick gets   2 × $80 = $160
Harry gets 5 × $80 = $400

(b)   Same parts as (a) but in a different order.

Tom gets $400
Dick gets $240
Harry gets $160

(c)   Total parts = 5

Each part is worth $800 ÷ 5 = $160

Therefore Tom gets $480

Dick and Harry each get $160

5 Roots and powers

FAST FORWARD

The **nth root** of a number is a value which, when multiplied by itself $(n - 1)$ times, equals the original number. **Powers** work the other way round.

Key term

The **square root** of a number is a value which, when multiplied by itself, equals the original number. $\sqrt{9} = 3$, since $3 \times 3 = 9$

The **cube root** of a number is the value which, when multiplied by itself twice, equals the original number. $\sqrt[3]{64} = 4$, since $4 \times 4 \times 4 = 64$

5.1 Powers

A **power** is the result when equal numbers are multiplied together.

The 6th power of 2 = 2^6 = 2 × 2 × 2 × 2 × 2 × 2 = 64.

Similarly, 3^4 = 3 × 3 × 3 × 3 = 81.

Familiarise yourself with the power button on your calculator. ($x^\blacksquare$, $\wedge$, x^y or y^x). Most calculators will also have separate buttons to square (x^2) and cube a number (x^3).

5.2 Roots

A **root** is the reverse of a power. When 5 is squared, the answer is 25. That is 5^2 = 25. The reverse of this process is called finding the square root. $\sqrt[2]{25} = \sqrt{25} = 5$. Most calculators have a square root button $\sqrt{}$ or $\sqrt{\blacksquare}$. Higher roots eg $\sqrt[5]{7{,}776}$ can be found by using 'shift' before the power ($x^\blacksquare$, $\wedge$, x^y, y^x) button. On a modern scientific calculator, press 5 shift $x^\blacksquare$ 7,776 = to obtain the answer = 6.

5.3 Rules for powers

Use your calculator to enter each of the following examples to practice this very important topic.

5.3.1 Powers – Rule 1

When a number with a power is multiplied by the **same** number with the same or a different power, the result is that number to the power of the **sum** of the powers.

    (a) $5^2 \times 5 = 5^2 \times 5^1 = 5^{(2+1)} = 5^3 = 125$

    (b) $4^3 \times 4^3 = 4^{(3+3)} = 4^6 = 4{,}096$

5.3.2 Powers – Rule 2

Similarly, when a number with a power is divided by the **same** number with the same or a different power, the result is that number to the power of the first index **minus** the second power.

    (a) $6^4 \div 6^3 = 6^{(4-3)} = 6^1 = 6$

    (b) $7^8 \div 7^6 = 7^{(8-6)} = 7^2 = 49$

5.3.3 Powers – Rule 3

When a number x with a power is raised to the power y, the result is the number raised to the power xy.

The powers are simply multiplied together.

    (a) $(2^2)^3 = 2^{2 \times 3} = 2^6 = 64$

    (b) $(5^3)^3 = 5^{3 \times 3} = 5^9 = 1{,}953{,}125$

5.3.4 Powers – Rule 4

Any figure to the power of one always equals itself: 2^1 = 2, 3^1 = 3, 4^1 = 4 and so on.

5.3.5 Powers – Rule 5

Any figure to the power of **zero** always equals **one**. $1^0 = 1$, $2^0 = 1$, $3^0 = 1$, $4^0 = 1$ and so on.

5.3.6 Powers – Rule 6

One to any power always equals one. $1^2 = 1$, $1^3 = 1$, $1^4 = 1$ and so on.

5.3.7 Powers – Rule 7

A power can be a **fraction**, as in $16^{\frac{1}{2}}$. What $16^{\frac{1}{2}}$ means is the square root of $16\left(\sqrt{16} \text{ or } 4\right)$ If we multiply $16^{\frac{1}{2}}$ by $16^{\frac{1}{2}}$ we get $16^{\left(\frac{1}{2}+\frac{1}{2}\right)}$ which equals 16^1 and thus 16.

Similarly, $216^{\frac{1}{3}}$ is the cube root of 216 (which is 6) because $216^{\frac{1}{3}} \times 216^{\frac{1}{3}} \times 216^{\frac{1}{3}} = 216^{\left(\frac{1}{3}+\frac{1}{3}+\frac{1}{3}\right)} = 216^1 = 216$.

5.3.8 Powers – Rule 8

An power can be a **negative** value. The negative sign represents a **reciprocal**. Thus 2^{-1} is the reciprocal of, or one over, 2^1.

$$2^{-1} = \frac{1}{2^1} = \frac{1}{2}$$

Likewise $2^{-2} = \frac{1}{2^2} = \frac{1}{4}$

$$2^{-3} = \frac{1}{2^3} = \frac{1}{8}$$

$$5^{-6} = \frac{1}{5^6} = \frac{1}{15,625}$$

5.4 Example: Powers

When we multiply or divide by a number with a negative power, the rules previously stated still apply.

(a) $9^2 \times 9^{-2} = 9^{(2+(-2))} = 9^0 = 1$ (That is, $9^2 \times \frac{1}{9^2} = 1$)

(b) $4^5 \div 4^{-2} = 4^{(5-(-2))} = 4^7 = 16,384$

(c) $3^8 \times 3^{-5} = 3^{(8-5)} = 3^3 = 27$

(d) $3^{-5} \div 3^{-2} = 3^{-5-(-2)} = 3^{-3} = \frac{1}{3^3} = \frac{1}{27}$. (This could be re-expressed as $\frac{1}{3^3} \div \frac{1}{3^2} = \frac{1}{3^5} \times 3^2 = \frac{1}{3^3}$.)

A fraction might have a power applied to it. In this situation, the main point to remember is that the power must be applied to both the top and the bottom of the fraction.

(a) $\left(2\frac{1}{3}\right)^3 = \left(\frac{7}{3}\right)^3 = \frac{7^3}{3^3} = \frac{343}{27}$

(b) $\left(5\frac{2}{5}\right)^{-4} = \left(\frac{27}{5}\right)^4 = \frac{1}{\left(\frac{27}{5}\right)^4} = \frac{1}{\frac{27^4}{5^4}} = \frac{5^4}{27^4} = \frac{625}{531,441}$

FAST FORWARD

The **main rules** to apply when dealing with powers and roots are as follows.

- $2^x \times 2^y = 2^{x+y}$

- $2^x \div 2^y = 2^{x-y}$

- $(2^x)^y = 2^{x \times y} = 2^{xy}$

- $x^0 = 1$

- $x^1 = x$

- $1^x = 1$

- $2^{-x} = \dfrac{1}{2^x}$

- $\left(1\dfrac{1}{2}\right)^x = \left(\dfrac{3}{2}\right)^x = \dfrac{3_x}{2_x}$

Question

Powers

Work out the following, using your calculator as necessary.

(a) $(18.6)^{2.6}$

(b) $(18.6)^{-2.6}$

(c) $\sqrt[2.6]{18.6}$

(d) $(14.2)^4 \times (14.2)^{\frac{1}{4}}$

(e) $(14.2)^4 + (14.2)^{\frac{1}{4}}$

Answer

(a) $(18.6)^{2.6} = 1{,}998.6358$

(b) $(18.6)^{-2.6} = \left(\dfrac{1}{18.6}\right)^{2.6} = 0.0005$

(c) $\sqrt[2.6]{18.6} = 3.078$

(d) $(14.2)^4 \times (14.2)^{\frac{1}{4}} = (14.2)^{4.25} = 78{,}926.976$

(e) $(14.2)^4 + (14.2)^{\frac{1}{4}} = 40{,}658.6896 + 1.9412 = 40{,}660.6308$

Chapter Roundup

- An **integer** is a whole number and can be either positive or negative.

- **Fractions** and **decimals** are ways of showing parts of a whole.

- The **negative number rules** are as follows.

$$-p + q = q - p$$
$$q - (-p) = q + p$$
$$-p \times -q = pq \text{ and } \frac{-p}{-q} = \frac{p}{q}$$

$$-p \times q = -pq \text{ and } \frac{-p}{q} = -\frac{p}{q}$$

- Scientific calculators can make calculations quicker and easier.

- **Brackets** indicate a priority or an order in which calculations should be made.

- The **reciprocal** of a number is 1 divided by that number.

- **Percentages** are used to indicate the **relative size** or **proportion** of items, rather than their **absolute** size. To turn a percentage into a fraction or decimal you **divide by 100%**.

- To turn a fraction or decimal back into a percentage you **multiply by 100%**.

- A **percentage increase** or **reduction** is calculated as (change ÷ original value) × 100%.

- A **proportion** means writing a percentage as a proportion of 1 (that is, as a decimal). 100% can be thought of as the whole, or 1. 50% is half of that, or 0.5.

- **Ratios** show relative shares of a whole.

- The **nth root** of a number is a value which, when multiplied by itself (n−1) times, equals the original number. **Powers** work the other way round.

- The **main rules** to apply when dealing with powers and roots are as follows.

  - $2^x \times 2^y = 2^{x+y}$

  - $2^x \div 2^y = 2^{x-y}$

  - $(2^x)^y = 2^{x \times y} = 2^{xy}$

  - $x^0 = 1$

  - $x^1 = x$

  - $1^x = 1$

  - $2^{-x} = \dfrac{1}{2^x}$

  - $\left(1\dfrac{1}{2}\right)^x = \left(\dfrac{3}{2}\right)^x = \dfrac{3^x}{2^x}$

Quick Quiz

1   $3\frac{3}{4}$ is an integer/fraction/decimal

2   1004.002955 to nine significant figures is ....

3   The product of a negative number and a negative number is

    Positive   ☐

    Negative   ☐

4   $217 \leq 217$

    True   ☐

    False   ☐

5   To turn a percentage into a fraction or decimal you must

    A   Divide by 100%
    B   Multiply by 100%
    C   Divide by 100
    D   Multiply by 100

6   3^{-1} can also be written as

    A 3^{-1}
    B 3^{1}
    C $\frac{1}{3}$
    D -1^{3}

Answers to Quick Quiz

1   Fraction

2   1004.00296

3   Positive

4   True

5   A

6   $C = \frac{1}{3}$

Now try the questions below from the Exam Question Bank

Question numbers	Page
1–8	331

Formulae and equations

Introduction

You are over the moon. You have just been awarded a $1,000 pay rise. If the man on the Clapham omnibus asks you to explain your new salary in terms of your old salary, what would you say? You might say something like 'my new salary equals my old salary plus $1,000'. Easy. What would you say, on the other hand, to the mathematics professor who asks you to give a mathematical equation which describes your new salary in terms of your old salary? Like many students, you may be perfectly capable of answering the man on the omnibus, but not the professor. Your reply to the professor should be something like 'y = x + 1,000' but many students get completely confused when they have to deal with mathematical symbols and letters instead of simple words. There is, however, no need to worry about equations: they are simply a shorthand method of expressing words. Work through this chapter and it should help to make things clearer.

Topic list	Syllabus references
1 Formulae and equations	A, (i), (iv), (1)
2 Manipulating inequalities	A, (5)
3 Linear equations	A, (iv)
4 Linear equations and graphs	A, (v)
5 Simultaneous equations	A, (iv), (4)
6 Non-linear equations	A, (iv), (v), (4)

1 Formulae and equations

1.1 Formulae

So far all our problems have been formulated entirely in terms of specific numbers. However, we also need to be able to use letters to represent numbers in formulae and equations.

FAST FORWARD
> A formula enables us to calculate the value of one variable from the value(s) of one or more other variables.

1.1.1 Use of variables

The use of variables enables us to state general truths about mathematics and you will come across many formulae in your CIMA studies.

For example:

- $x = x$
- $x^2 = x \times x$
- If $y = 0.5 \times x$, then $x = 2 \times y$

These will be true **whatever** values x and y have. For example, let $y = 0.5 \times x$

- If $y = 3$, $x = 2 \times y = 6$
- If $y = 7$, $x = 2 \times y = 14$
- If $y = 1$, $x = 2 \times y = 2$, and so on for any other choice of a value for y.

We can use **variables** to build up useful **formulae**, we can then put in values for the variables, and get out a value for something we are interested in. It is usual when writing formulae to leave out multiplication signs between letters. Thus $p \times u - c$ can be written as $pu - c$. We will also write (for example) $2x$ instead of $2 \times x$.

1.1.2 Example: Variables

For a business, profit = revenue – costs. Since revenue = selling price × units sold, we can say that:

profit = (selling price × units sold) – costs.

'(Selling price × units sold) – costs' is a formula for profit.

Notice the use of brackets to help with the order of operations.

We can then use single letters to make the formula quicker to write.

Let   p   =   profit
      s   =   selling price
      u   =   units sold
      c   =   cost

Then $p = (s \times u) - c$.

If we are then told that in a particular month, s = \$5, u = 30 and c = \$118, we can find out the month's profit.

Profit   = $p = (s \times u) - c = (\$5 \times 30) - \$118$
         = $\$150 - \$118 = \$32$

1.1.3 Example: A more complicated formula

In your later CIMA studies, you will come across the learning curve formula, $Y = aX^b$ which shows how unit labour times tend to decrease at a constant rate as production increases.

Y = cumulative average time taken per unit

a = time taken for the first unit

X = total number of units

b = index of learning

What is the average time taken per unit if the time taken for the first unit is 10 minutes, the total number of units is 8 and the index of learning is $- 0.32$?

Solution

$Y = aX^b$

a = 10 minutes

X = 8

b = $- 0.32$

$Y = 10 \times 8^{-0.32} = 5.14$

On your calculator, press $10 \times 8\ X^{\blacksquare}\ (-)\ 0.32 =$

1.2 Equations

In the above example, $su - c$ was a formula for profit. If we write $p = su - c$, we have written an **equation**. It says that one thing (profit, p) is **equal** to another ($su - c$).

1.2.1 'Solving the equation'

Sometimes, we are given an equation with numbers filled in for all but one of the variables. The problem is then to find the number which should be filled in for the last variable. This is called **solving the equation**.

(a) Returning to $p = su - c$, we could be told that for a particular month s = \$4, u = 60 and c = \$208. We would then have the **equation** p = (\$4 × 60) − \$208. We can solve this easily by working out (\$4 × 60) − \$208 = \$240 − \$208 = \$32. Thus p = \$32.

(b) On the other hand, we might have been told that in a month when profits were \$172, 50 units were sold and the selling price was \$7. The thing we have not been told is the month's costs, c. We can work out c by writing out the equation.

$$\$172 = (\$7 \times 50) - c$$
$$\$172 = \$350 - c$$

(c) We need c to be such that when it is taken away from \$350 we have \$172 left. With a bit of trial and error, we can get to c = \$178.

1.2.2 The rule for solving equations

FAST FORWARD The **general rule for solving equations** is that you must always do the same thing to both sides of the equal sign so the 'scales' stay balanced.

(a) To solve an equation, we need to get it into the following form.

Unknown variable = something with just numbers in it, which we can work out.

We therefore want to get the unknown variable on one side of the = sign, and everything else on the other side.

(b) **The rule is that you must always do the same thing to both sides of the equal sign so the 'scales' stay balanced. The two sides are equal, and they will stay equal so long as you treat them in the same way.**

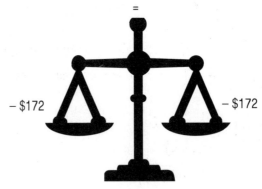

$$\$172 + c = \$350$$

Take $172 from both sides: $\$172 + c - \$172 = \$350 - \$172$

$$c = \$350 - \$172$$
$$c = \$178$$

1.2.3 Example: Solving the equation

For example, you can do any of the following: add 37 to both sides; subtract 3x from both sides; multiply both sides by −4.329; divide both sides by (x + 2); take the reciprocal of both sides; square both sides; take the cube root of both sides.

We can do any of these things to an equation either before or after filling in numbers for the variables for which we have values.

(a)

If $172	= $350 − c	(as in Paragraph 1.2.1) we can then get
$172 + c	= $350	(add c to each side)
c	= $350 − $172	(subtract $172 from each side)
c	= $178	(work out the right hand side)

(b)

450	= 3x + 72	(initial equation: x unknown)
450 − 72	= 3x	(subtract 72 from each side)
$\dfrac{450 - 72}{3}$	= x	(divide each side by 3)
126	= x	(work out the left hand side)

(c)
$$3y + 2 = 5y - 7 \quad \text{(initial equation: y unknown)}$$
$$3y + 9 = 5y \quad \text{(add 7 to each side)}$$
$$9 = 2y \quad \text{(subtract 3y from each side)}$$
$$4.5 = y \quad \text{(divide each side by 2)}$$

(d)
$$\frac{\sqrt{3x^2 + x}}{2\sqrt{x}} = 7 \quad \text{(initial equation: x unknown)}$$

$$\frac{3x^2 + x}{4x} = 49 \quad \text{(square each side)}$$

$$\frac{(3x + 1)}{4} = 49 \quad \text{(cancel x in the numerator and the denominator of the left hand side:}$$

this does not affect the value of the left hand side, so we do not need to change the right hand side)

$$3x + 1 = 196 \quad \text{(multiply each side by 4)}$$
$$3x = 195 \quad \text{(subtract 1 from each side)}$$
$$x = 65 \quad \text{(divide each side by 3)}$$

(e) Our example in Paragraph 1.2 was $p = su - c$. We could change this, so as to give a formula for s.

$$s = su - c$$
$$p + c = su \quad \text{(add c to each side)}$$
$$\frac{p + c}{u} = s \quad \text{(divide each side by u)}$$
$$s = \frac{p + c}{u} \quad \text{(swap the sides for ease of reading)}$$

Given values for p, c and u we can now find s. We have rearranged the equation to give s in terms of p, c and u.

(f) Given that $y = \sqrt{3x + 7}$, we can get an equation giving x in terms of y.

$$y = \sqrt{3x + 7}$$
$$y^2 = 3x + 7 \quad \text{(square each side)}$$
$$y^2 - 7 = 3x \quad \text{(subtract 7 from each side)}$$
$$x = \frac{y^2 - 7}{3} \quad \text{(divide each side by 3, and swap the sides for ease of reading)}$$

1.2.4 Solving the equation and brackets

In equations, you may come across expressions like $3(x + 4y - 2)$ (that is, $3 \times (x + 4y - 2)$). These can be re-written in separate bits without the brackets, simply by multiplying the number outside the brackets by each item inside them. Thus $3(x + 4y - 2) = 3x + 12y - 6$.

Question

(a)   If $47x + 256 = 52x$, then $x =$ ☐

(b)   If $4\sqrt{x} + 32 = 40.6718$, then $x =$ ☐

(c)   If $\dfrac{1}{3x + 4} = \dfrac{5}{2.7x - 2}$, then $x =$ ☐

Answer

(a) $\boxed{x = 51.2}$

$47x + 256 = 52x$

$256 = 5x$ (subtract 47x from each side)

$51.2 = x$ (divide each side by 5)

(b) $\boxed{x = 4.7}$

$4\sqrt{x} + 32 = 40.6718$

$4\sqrt{x} = 8.6718$ (subtract 32 from each side)

$\sqrt{x} = 2.16795$ (divide each side by 4)

$x = 4.7$ (square each side).

(c) $\boxed{x = -1.789}$

$\dfrac{1}{3x + 4} = \dfrac{5}{2.7x - 2}$

$3x + 4 = \dfrac{2.7x - 2}{5}$ (take the reciprocal of each side)

$15x + 20 = 2.7x - 2$ (multiply each side by 5)

$12.3x = -22$ (subtract 20 and subtract 2.7x from each side)

$x = -1.789$ (divide each side by 12.3).

Question

(a)   Rearrange $x = (3y - 20)^2$ to get an expression for y in terms of x.

(b)   Rearrange $2(y - 4) - 4(x^2 + 3) = 0$ to get an expression for x in terms of y.

Answer

(a)
$$x = (3y - 20)^2$$

$$\sqrt{x} = 3y - 20 \qquad \text{(take the square root of each side)}$$

$$20 + \sqrt{x} = 3y \qquad \text{(add 20 to each side)}$$

$$y = \frac{20 + \sqrt{x}}{3} \qquad \text{(divide each side by 3, and swap the sides for ease of reading)}$$

(b)
$$2(y - 4) - 4(x^2 + 3) = 0$$

$$2(y - 4) = 4(x^2 + 3) \qquad \text{(add } 4(x^2 + 3) \text{ to each side)}$$

$$0.5(y - 4) = x^2 + 3 \qquad \text{(divide each side by 4)}$$

$$0.5(y - 4) - 3 = x^2 \qquad \text{(subtract 3 from each side)}$$

$$x = \sqrt{0.5(y - 4) - 3} \qquad \text{(take the square root of each side, and swap the sides for ease of reading)}$$

$$x = \sqrt{0.5y - 5}$$

2 Manipulating inequalities

FAST FORWARD

An inequality is a statement that shows the relationship between two (or more) expressions with one of the following signs: $>, \geqslant, <, \leqslant$. We can solve inequalities in the same way that we can solve equations.

2.1 Inequality symbols

Equations are called inequalities when the '=' sign is replaced by one of the following.

    (a) $>$ means 'greater than'
    (b) $\geqslant$ means 'is greater than or equal to'
    (c) $<$ means 'is less than'
    (d) $\leqslant$ means 'is less than or equal to'+

2.2 Using inequalities

Inequalities are used in a short-term decision making technique called linear programming which you will come across in your managerial studies. It involves using inequalities to represent situations where resources are limited.

2.2.1 Example: Using inequalities 1

If a product needs 3kg of material and 700 kg is available, express this as an inequality

Solution

If the number of units of the product = X

$3X \leqslant 700$

2.2.2 Example: Using inequalities 2

Product Z needs 3 minutes of machining time and product Y needs 2 minutes of machining time. There are 10 hours of machining time available. Express this as an inequality.

Solution

10 hours of machining time = 600 minutes

The total machining time must be less than or equal to 600 minutes.

$3Z + 2Y \leqslant 600$

where Z = no of units of product Z
   Y = no of units of product Y

2.3 Solving inequalities

We can solve inequalities in the same way we can solve equations. For example, the inequality $7x - 2 > 0$ can be solved by getting x on its own, but the answer will be a range of values rather than a specific number.

$7x - 2 > 0$
   $7x > 2$ (add 2 to both sides)
   $x > \dfrac{2}{7}$ (divide both sides by 7)

2.4 Rules for manipulating inequalities

(i)   Adding or subtracting the same quantity from both sides of an inequality leaves the inequality symbol unchanged
(ii)   Multiplying or dividing both sides by a **positive** number leaves the inequality symbol unchanged
(iii) Multiplying or dividing both sides by a **negative** number **reverses** the inequality so < changes to >

2.5 Example: Solving inequalities

Find the range of values of x satisfying $x - 5 < 2x + 7$

$x - 5 < 2x + 7$
   $x < 2x + 12$ (add 5 to both sides)
   $-x < 12$ (subtract 2x from both sides)
   $x > -12$ (multiply both sides by -1 and so reverse the inequality)

Question

Solve the following inequalities

(a) $2x > 11$
(b) $x + 3 > 15$
(c) $-3x < 7$
(d) $7x + 11 > 2x + 5$
(e) $2(x + 3) < x + 1$

Answer

(a) $2x > 11$

$x > \dfrac{11}{2}$ (divide both sides by 2)

$x > 5.5$

(b) $x + 3 > 15$
$x > 12$ (subtract 3 from both sides)

(c) $-3x < 7$

$-x < \dfrac{7}{3}$ (divide both sides by 3)

$x > -\dfrac{7}{3}$ (multiply both sides by -1 and so reverse the inequality)

(d) $7x + 11 > 2x + 5$
$5x > -6$ (subtract 2x and 11 from both sides)

$x > -\dfrac{6}{5}$ (divide both sides by 5)

(e) $2(x + 3) < x + 1$
$2x + 6 < x + 1$ (multiply out the brackets)
$x < -5$ (subtract x and 6 from both sides)

3 Linear equations

FAST FORWARD

A **linear equation** has the general form y = a + bx

where y is the **dependent variable**, depending for its value on the value of x

   x is the **independent variable** whose value helps to determine the corresponding value of y

   a is a **constant**, that is, a fixed amount

   b is also a **constant**, being the **coefficient** of x (that is, the number by which the value of x should be multiplied to derive the value of y)

3.1 Example: Establishing basic linear equations

(a)   Let us establish some basic linear equations. Suppose that it takes Joe Bloggs 15 minutes to walk one mile. How long does it take Joe to walk two miles? Obviously it takes him 30 minutes. How did you calculate the time? You probably thought that if the distance is doubled then the time must be doubled. How do you explain (in words) the relationships between the distance walked and the time taken? One explanation would be that every mile walked takes 15 minutes. Now let us try to explain the relationship with an equation.

(b)   First you must decide which is the **dependent variable** and which is the **independent variable**. In other words, does the time taken depend on the number of miles walked or does the number of miles walked depend on the time it takes to walk a mile? Obviously the time depends on the distance. We can therefore let y be the dependent variable (time taken in minutes) and x be the independent variable (distance walked in miles).

(c)   We now need to determine the **constants a** and **b**. There is no fixed amount so a = 0. To ascertain b, we need to establish the number of times by which the value of x should be multiplied to derive the value of y. Obviously y = 15x where y is in minutes. If y were in hours then y = x/4.

3.2 Example: Deriving a linear equation

A salesman's weekly wage is made up of a basic weekly wage of $100 and commission of $5 for every item he sells. Derive an equation which describes this scenario.

Solution

x = number of items sold and y = weekly wage

a = $100 (fixed weekly wage paid however many items he sells) and b = $5 (variable element of wage, depends on how many items he sells)

∴ y = 5x + 100

Note that the letters used in an equation do not have to be x and y. It may be sensible to use other letters, for example we could use p and q if we are describing the relationship between the price of an item and the quantity demanded.

4 Linear equations and graphs

The **graph of a linear equation is a straight line**. The intercept of the line on the y axis is a in:

y = a + bx

where a = the incercept of the line on the y axis

and b = the slope of the line

One of the clearest ways of presenting the relationship between two variables is by plotting a **linear equation** as a **straight line** on a graph.

4.1 The rules for drawing graphs

A graph has a **horizontal axis**, the **x axis** and a **vertical axis**, the **y axis**. The x axis is used to represent the **independent variable** and the y axis is used to represent the **dependent variable**. If calendar time is one variable, it is always treated as the independent variable. When time is represented on the x axis of a graph, we have the graph of a **time series**.

(a)   If the data to be plotted are derived from calculations, rather than given in the question, make sure that there is a neat table in your workings.

(b)   The scales on each axis should be selected so as to use as much of the graph paper as possible. Do not cramp a graph into one corner.

(c)   In some cases it is best not to start a scale at zero so as to avoid having a large area of wasted paper. This is perfectly acceptable as long as the scale adopted is clearly shown on the axis. One way of avoiding confusion is to break the axis concerned, as shown below.

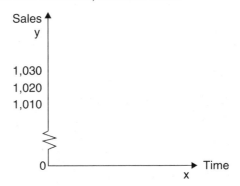

(d)   The scales on the x axis and the y axis should be marked. For example, if the y axis relates to amounts of money, the axis should be marked at every $1, or $100 or $1,000 interval or at whatever other interval is appropriate. The axes must be marked with values to give the reader an idea of how big the values on the graph are.

(e)   A graph should not be overcrowded with too many lines. Graphs should always give a clear, neat impression.

(f)   A graph must always be given a **title**, and where appropriate, a reference should be made to the **source** of data.

4.2 Example: Drawing graphs

Plot the graph for y = 4x + 5.

Consider the range of values from x = 0 to x = 10.

Solution

The first step is to draw up a table for the equation. Although the problem mentions x = 0 to x = 10, it is not necessary to calculate values of y for x = 1, 2, 3 etc. A graph of a linear equation can actually be drawn from just two (x, y) values but it is always best to calculate a number of values in case you make an arithmetical error. We have calculated five values, but three would be enough in your assessment.

x	y
0	5
2	13
4	21
6	29
8	37
10	45

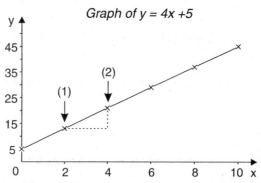

Graph of y = 4x +5

4.3 The intercept and the gradient

The graph of a linear equation is determined by two things.

- The gradient (or slope) of the straight line
- The point at which the straight line crosses the y axis

Key term

- The **intercept** is the point at which a straight line crosses the y-axis.

- The **gradient** of the graph of a linear equation is $\frac{\text{change in } y}{\text{change in } x}$ = $(y_2 - y_1)/(x_2 - x_1)$ where (x_1, y_1) and (x_2, y_2) are two points on the straight line.

4.3.1 The intercept

The intercept of y = 4x + 5 is where y = 5. It is no coincidence that the intercept is the same as the constant represented by a in the general form of the equation y = a + bx. a is the value y takes when x = 0, in other words a constant.

4.3.2 The gradient

If we take two points on the line (see graph in 4.2):

(1) $x = 2, y = 13$
(2) $x = 4, y = 21$

The gradient of $y = 4x + 5 = \dfrac{\text{change in } y}{\text{change in } x} = \dfrac{(21-13)}{(4-2)} = \dfrac{8}{2} = 4$

Notice that the gradient is also given by the number multiplied by x in the equation (b in the general form of the equation).

Question   **Gradient**

If $y = 10 - x$, the gradient = ⬜

Answer

The gradient = | −1 |

If $y = 10 - x$, then a = 10 and b = −1 (−1 × x = −x).

Therefore gradient = −1

4.3.3 Positive and negative gradients

Note that the gradient of $y = 4x + 5$ is positive whereas the gradient of $y = 10 - x$ is negative.

- A positive gradient slopes upwards from left to right
- A negative gradient slopes downwards from left to right
- The greater the value of the gradient, the steeper the slope

Question   **Intercept and gradient**

What is the intercept and gradient of the graph of $4y = 16x - 12$?

	Intercept	Gradient
A	−3	+4
B	−4	+3
C	+3	−4
D	+4	−3

Answer

$4y = 16x - 12$

Equation must be in the form $y = a + bx$

$y = 4x - 3$ (divide both sides by 4)

$y = -3 + 4x$ (rearrange the RHS)

Intercept = $a = -3$

Gradient = $b = 4$

Therefore the correct answer is A.

If you selected option D, you have obviously confused the intercept and the gradient. Remember that with an equation in the form $y = a + bx$, a = intercept (ie where the line of the graph crosses the y axis) and b = the slope or gradient of the line.

Question

Linear graphs

A company manufactures a product. The total fixed costs are $75 and the variable cost per unit is $5.

Required

(a)   Find an expression for total costs (c) in terms of q, the quantity produced.
(b)   Use your answer to (a) to determine the total costs if 100 units are produced.
(c)   Prepare a graph of the expression for total costs.
(d)   Use your graph to determine the total cost if 75 units are produced.

Answer

(a) Let C = total costs
         C = total variable costs + total fixed costs
         C = 5q + 75

(b) If q = 100, C = (5 × 100) + 75 = $575

(c) If q = 0,   C = $75
     If q = 100,   C = $575

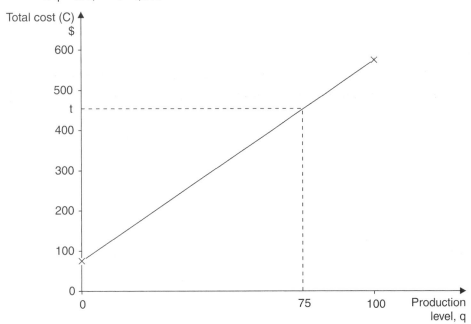

(d) From graph above, if q = 75, C = $450

5 Simultaneous equations

FAST FORWARD

Simultaneous equations are two or more equations which are satisfied by the same variable values. They can be solved graphically or algebraically.

5.1 Example: Simultaneous equations

The following two linear equations both involve the unknown values x and y. There are as many equations as there are unknowns and so we can find the values of x and y.

$$y = 3x + 16$$
$$2y = x + 72$$

5.1.1 Solution: Graphical approach

One way of finding a solution is by a **graph**. If both equations are satisfied together, the values of x and y must be those where the straight line graphs of the two equations **intersect**.

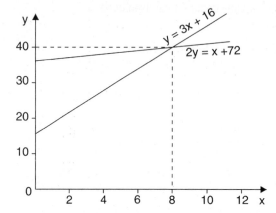

Since both equations are satisfied, the values of x and y must lie on both the lines. Since this happens only once, at the intersection of the lines, the value of x must be 8, and of y 40.

5.1.2 Solution: Algebraic approach

A more common method of solving simultaneous equations is by **algebra**.

(a)   Returning to the original equations, we have:

$y = 3x + 16$ (1)
$2y = x + 72$ (2)

(b)   Rearranging these, we have:

$y - 3x\ = 16$ (3)
$2y - x\ = 72$ (4)

(c)   If we now multiply equation (4) by 3, so that the coefficient for x becomes the same as in equation (3) we get:

$6y - 3x\ = 216$ (5)
$\ y - 3x\ = 16$ (3)

(d)   Subtracting (3) from (5) we get:

$5y\ = 200$
$\ y\ = 40$

(e)   Substituting 40 for y in any equation, we can derive a value for x. Thus substituting in equation (4) we get:

$2(40) - x\ = 72$
$80 - 72\ = x$
$8\ = x$

(f)   The solution is $y = 40$, $x = 8$.

Question

Solve the following simultaneous equations using algebra.

$5x + 2y = 34$

$x + 3y = 25$

Answer

$5x + 2y$	$= 34$		(1)
$x + 3y$	$= 25$		(2)

Multiply (2) × 5:

$5x + 15y = 125$		(3)

Subtract (1) from (3):

$13y = 91$

$y = 7$

Substitute into (2):

$x + 21 = 25$

$x = 25 - 21$

$x = 4$

The solution is $x = 4$, $y = 7$.

6 Non-linear equations

So far we have looked at equations in which the highest power of the unknown variable(s) is one (that is, the equation contains x, y but not x^2, y^3 and so on). We are now going to turn our attention to **non-linear equations**.

> **FAST FORWARD**
>
> In **non-linear equations**, one variable varies with the nth power of another, where n>1. The graph of a non-linear equation is *not* a straight line.

6.1 Examples – non-linear equations

(a) $y = x^2$; $y = 3x^3 + 2$; $2y = 5x^4 - 6$; $y = -x^{12} + 3$

(b)   It is common for a non-linear equation to include a number of terms, all to different powers. Here are some examples.

$y = x^2 + 6x + 10$ $y = -12x^9 + 3x^6 + 6x^3 + 3x^2 - 1$

$2y = 3x^3 - 4x^2 - 8x + 10$ $3y = 22x^8 + 7x^7 + 3x^4 - 12$

6.2 Graphing non-linear equations

The graph of a **linear equation**, as we saw earlier, is a **straight line**. The graph of a **non-linear equation**, on the other hand, **is not a straight line**. Let us consider an example.

6.2.1 Example: Graphing non-linear equations

Graph the equation $y = -2x^3 + x^2 - 2x + 10$.

Solution

The graph of this equation can be plotted in the same way as the graph of a linear equation is plotted. Take a selection of values of x, calculate the corresponding values of y, plot the pairs of values and join the points together. The joining must be done using as smooth a curve as possible.

x	−3	−2	−1	0	1	2	3
−2x	6	4	2	0	−2	−4	−6
x^2	9	4	1	0	1	4	9
$-2x^3$	54	16	2	0	−2	−16	−54
10	10	10	10	10	10	10	10
y	79	34	15	10	7	−6	−41

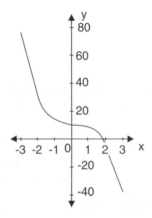

6.3 Quadratic equations

FAST FORWARD

Quadratic equations are a type of **non-linear equation** in which one variable varies with the square (or second power) of the other variable. They can be expressed in the form
$y = ax^2 + bx + c$.

A **quadratic equation** may include both a term involving the square and also a term involving the **first power** of a variable. Here are some examples.

$y = x^2$ $\qquad\qquad$ $y = x^2 + 6x + 10$ $\qquad\qquad$ $2y = 3x^2 - 4x - 8$ $\qquad\qquad$ $y = 5x^2 + 7$

In the equation $y = 3x^2 + 2x - 6$, $a = 3$, $b = 2$, $c = -6$.

6.3.1 Graphing a quadratic equation

The graph of a quadratic equation can be plotted using the same method as that illustrated in Paragraph 6.2.1.

6.3.2 Example: Graphing a quadratic equation

Graph the equation $y = -2x^2 + x - 3$

Solution

x	−3	−2	−1	0	1	2	3
−2x²	−18	−8	−2	0	−2	−8	−18
−3	−3	−3	−3	−3	−3	−3	−3
y	−24	−13	−6	−3	−4	−9	−18

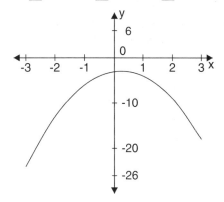

6.3.3 Parabolas

FAST FORWARD

The graphs of quadratic equations are **parabolas**, the sign of 'a' in the general form of the quadratic equation ($y = ax^2 + bx + c$) determining the way up the curve appears.

(a)   The constant term 'c' determines the value of y at the point where the curve crosses the y axis (the intercept). In the graph above, $c = -3$ and the curve crosses the y axis at $y = -3$.

(b)   The sign of 'a' determines the way up the curve appears.

- If 'a' is positive, the curve is shaped like a ditch
- If 'a' is negative, as in Paragraph 6.3.2, the curve is shaped like a bell

A ditch-shaped curve is said to have a **minimum point** whereas a bell-shaped curve is said to have a **maximum point**.

(c)   The graph enables us to find the values of x when $y = 0$ (if there are any). In other words the graph allows us to solve the quadratic equation $0 = ax^2 + bx + c$. For the curve in Paragraph 6.3.2 we see that there are no such values (that is, $0 = -2x^2 + x - 3$ cannot be solved).

6.4 Solving quadratic equations

The graphical method is not, in practice, the most efficient way to determine the solution of a quadratic equation. Many quadratic equations have two values of x (called **'solutions for x'** or **'roots of the equation'**) which satisfy the equation for any particular value of y.

FAST FORWARD

Quadratic equations can be solved by the formula:

$$x = \frac{-b \pm \sqrt{(b^2 - 4ac)}}{2a} \quad \text{when } ax^2 + bx + c = 0$$

You will be given this formula in your exam.

6.4.1 Example: Quadratic equations

Solve $x^2 + x - 2 = 0$.

Solution

For the equation $x^2 + x - 2 = 0$

a = 1
b = 1
c = −2

We can insert these values into the quadratic equation formula.

$$x = \frac{-b \pm \sqrt{(b^2 - 4ac)}}{2a}$$

$$x = \frac{-1 \pm \sqrt{(1^2 - (4 \times 1 \times (-2)))}}{2 \times 1} = \frac{-1 \pm \sqrt{(1+8)}}{2} = \frac{-1 \pm 3}{2}$$

$$\therefore \quad x = \frac{-4}{2} \quad \text{or} \quad \frac{2}{2} \quad \text{ie } x = -2 \text{ or } x = 1$$

6.5 Quadratic equations with a single value for x

Sometimes, $b^2 - 4ac = 0$, and so there is only one solution to the quadratic equation. Let us solve $x^2 + 2x + 1 = 0$ using the formula above where a = 1, b = 2 and c = 1.

$$x = \frac{-2 \pm \sqrt{(2^2 - (4 \times 1 \times 1))}}{2} = \frac{-2 \pm 0}{2} = -1$$

This quadratic equation can only be solved by one value of x.

Question   **Non-linear graphs**

A company manufactures a product, the total cost function for the product being given by $C = 25q - q^2$, where q is the quantity produced and C is in $.

Required

(a)   Calculate the total costs if 15 units are produced.
(b)   Draw a graph of the total cost function and use it to calculate the total cost if 23 units are produced.

Answer

(a) $C = 25q - q^2$

If $q = 15$, $C = (25 \times 15) - 15^2 = 375 - 225 = \$150$

(b)

q	C
0	0
5.0	100.00
10.0	150.00
12.5	156.25
15.0	150.00
20.0	100.00
25.0	0

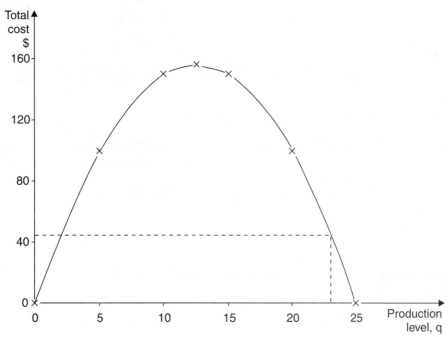

From the graph, if 23 units are produced the total cost is approximately \$45.

Chapter Roundup

- A formula enables us to calculate the value of one variable from the value(s) of one or more other variables.

- The **general rule for solving equations** is that you must always do the same thing to both sides of the equal sign so the scales stay balanced.

- An inequality is a statement that shows the relationship between two (or more) expressions with one of the following signs: $>$, $\geqslant$, $<$, $\leqslant$. We can solve inequalities in the same way that we can solve equations.

- A **linear equation** has the general form **y = a + bx**, where x is the independent variable and y the dependent variable, and a and b are fixed amounts.

- The **graph of a linear equation is a straight** line, where y = a + bx. The intercept of the line on the y axis = a and the gradient of the line = b.

- **Simultaneous equations** are two or more equations which are satisfied by the same variable values. They can be solved graphically or algebraically.

- In **non-linear equations**, one variable varies with the nth power of another, where n > 1. The graph of a non-linear equation is *not* a straight line.

- **Quadratic equations** are a type of **non-linear equation** in which one variable varies with the square (or second power) of the other variable. They can be expressed in the form $y = ax^2 + bx + c$.

- The graphs of quadratic equations are **parabolas**, the sign of 'a' in the general form of the quadratic equation ($y = ax^2 + bx + c$) determining the way up the curve appears.

- **Quadratic equations** can be solved by the formula

$$x = \frac{-b \pm \sqrt{(b^2 - 4ac)}}{2a} \text{ when } ax^2 + bx + c = 0$$

You will be given this formula in your exam.

Quick Quiz

1   A linear equation has the general form y = a + bx where

     y   independent variable

     x   ]   ?   [constant (fixed amount)

     b   constant (coefficient of x)

     a   dependent variable

2   The horizontal axis on a graph is known as the y axis.

     True   ☐

     False   ☐

3   The intercept is ....

                                                          True   *False*

4   (a)   A positive gradient slopes upwards from right to left   ☐   ☐

     (b)   A negative gradient slopes downwards from left to right   ☐   ☐

     (c)   The greater the value of the gradient, the steeper the slope ☐   ☐

5   What are simultaneous equations?

6   In what form are quadratic equations usually expressed?

7   Consider the equation $y = -4x^2 + 3x - 2$

     (a)   The graph of the equation is shaped like a ditch/bell
     (b)   The graph of the equation has a minimum/maximum point
     (c)   The point at which the curve crosses the y axis is ....

8   Use the symbols and numbers below to construct the formula for solving a quadratic equation.

     $x, -b, -4, a, a, \sqrt{}, =, \pm, b^2, c, 2$

Answers to Quick Quiz

1   y = dependent variable
       x = independent variable
       b = constant (coefficient of x)
       a = constant (fixed amount)

2   False

3   The point at which a straight line crosses the y-axis

4   (a)   False
       (b)   True
       (c)   True

5   Two or more equations which are satisfied by the same variable values

6      $y = ax^2 + bx + c$

7   (a)   bell
       (b)   maximum point
       (c)   −2

8      $x = \dfrac{-b \pm \sqrt{(b^2 - 4ac)}}{2a}$

Now try the questions below from the Exam Question Bank

Question numbers	Pages
9–18	331-332

Part B
Probability

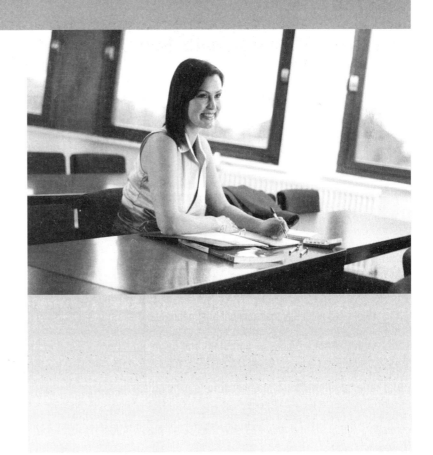

3

Probability

Introduction

'The likelihood of rain this afternoon is fifty percent' warns the weather report from your radio alarm clock. 'There's no chance of you catching that bus' grunts the helpful soul as you puff up the hill. The headline on your newspaper screams 'Odds of Rainbow Party winning the election rise to one in four'.

'**Likelihood**' and '**chance**' are expressions used in our everyday lives to denote a **level of uncertainty**. **Probability**, a word which often strikes fear into the hearts of students, is simply the mathematical term used when we need to imply a degree of **uncertainty**.

An understanding of the concept of probability is vital if you are to take account of uncertainty.

This chapter will therefore explain various techniques for assessing probability and look at how it can be applied in business decision making.

Topic list	Syllabus references
1 The concept of probability	(B), (i), (1)
2 The rules of probability	(B), (ii), (iii), (2), (3)
3 Expected values	(B), (iv), (4)
4 Expectation and decision making	(B), (v), (vi), (vii), (4), (5)

1 The concept of probability

1.1 Introducing probability

Probability is a measure of **likelihood** and can be stated as a percentage, a ratio, or more usually as a number from 0 to 1.

Consider the following.

- Probability = 0 = impossibility
- Probability = 1 = certainty
- Probability = 1/2 = a 50% chance of something happening
- Probability = 1/4 = a 1 in 4 chance of something happening

1.2 Expressing probabilities

In statistics, **probabilities** are more commonly expressed as **proportions** than as **percentages**. Consider the following possible outcomes.

Possible outcome	Probability as a percentage %	Probability as a proportion
A	15.0	0.150
B	20.0	0.200
C	32.5	0.325
D	7.5	0.075
E	12.5	0.125
F	12.5	0.125
	100.0	1.000

It is useful to consider how probability can be quantified. A businessman might estimate that if the selling price of a product is raised by 20p, there would be a 90% probability that demand would fall by 30%, but how would he have reached his estimate of 90% probability?

1.3 Assessing probabilities

There are several ways of assessing probabilities.

- They may be measurable with **mathematical certainty**.

    - If a coin is tossed, there is a 0.5 probability that it will come down heads, and a 0.5 probability that it will come down tails.

    - If a die is thrown, there is a one-sixth probability that a 6 will turn up.

- They may be measurable from an analysis of **past experience**.

- Probabilities can be estimated from **research** or **surveys**.

It is important to note that probability is a measure of the likelihood of an event happening in the long run, or over a large number of times.

The rules of probability in Section 2 will go through in detail how to calculate probabilities in various situations.

2 The rules of probability

2.1 Setting the scene

It is the year 2020 and examiners are extinct. A mighty but completely fair computer churns out examinations that are equally likely to be easy or difficult. There is no link between the number of questions on each paper, which is arrived at on a fair basis by the computer, and the standard of the paper. You are about to take five examinations.

2.2 Simple probability

It is vital that the first examination is easy as it covers a subject which you have tried, but unfortunately failed, to understand. What is the probability that it will be an easy examination?

Obviously (let us hope), the probability of an easy paper is 1/2 (or 50% or 0.5). This reveals a very important principle (which holds if each result is equally likely).

Formula to learn

$$\text{Probability of achieving the desired result} = \frac{\text{Number of ways of achieving desired result}}{\text{Total number of possible outcomes}}$$

Let us apply the principle to our example.

Total number of possible outcomes = 'easy' or 'difficult' = 2
Total number of ways of achieving the desired result (which is 'easy') = 1
The probability of an easy examination, or P(easy examination) = 1/2

2.2.1 Example: Simple probability

Suppose that a dice is rolled. What is the probability that it will show a six?

Solution

$$P(\text{heads}) = \frac{\text{Number of ways of achieving desired result}}{\text{Total number of possible outcomes}}$$

$$= \frac{1}{6} \text{ or } 16.7\% \text{ or } 0.167$$

2.3 Venn diagrams

A Venn diagram is a pictorial method of showing probability. We can show all the possible outcomes (E) and the outcome we are interested in (A).

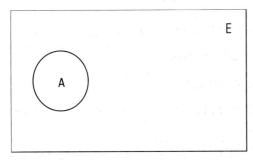

2.4 Complementary outcomes

You are desperate to pass more of the examinations than your sworn enemy but, unlike you, he is more likely to pass the first examination if it is difficult. (He is very strange!) What is the probability of the first examination being more suited to your enemy's requirements?

We know that the probability of certainty is one. The certainty in this scenario is that the examination will be easy or difficult.

P(easy or difficult examination)	=	1
From Paragraph 2.2, P(easy examination)	=	1/2
P(not easy examination)	=	P(difficult examination)
	=	1 – P(easy examination)
	=	1 – 1/2
	=	1/2

Formula to learn

$P(\overline{A}) = 1 - P(A)$, where $\overline{A}$ is 'not A'.

2.4.1 Venn diagram: Complementary outcomes

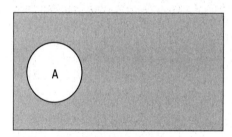

The probability of **not** A is shown by the shaded region.

2.4.2 Example: Complementary outcomes

If there is a 25 per cent chance of the Rainbow Party winning the next general election, use the law of complementary events to calculate the probability of the Rainbow Party *not* winning the next election.

Solution

P(winning) = 25% = 1/4
P(not winning) = 1 – P(winning) = 1 – 1/4 = 3/4

2.5 The simple addition or OR law

FAST FORWARD

The **simple addition law** for two mutually exclusive events, A and B, is as follows.

P(A or B) = P (A ∪ B) = P(A) + P(B)

The time pressure in the second examination is enormous. The computer will produce a paper which will have between five and nine questions. You know that, easy or difficult, the examination must have six questions at the most for you to have any hope of passing it.

What is the probability of the computer producing an examination with six or fewer questions? In other words, what is the probability of an examination with five *or* six questions?

Don't panic. Let us start by using the basic principle.

$$P(5 \text{ questions}) = \frac{\text{Total number of ways of achieving a five question examination}}{\text{Total number of possible outcomes} (= 5, 6, 7, 8 \text{ or } 9 \text{ questions})}$$

$$= \frac{1}{5}$$

Likewise $P(6 \text{ questions}) = \frac{1}{5}$

Either five questions or six questions would be acceptable, so the probability of you passing the examination must be greater than if just five questions or just six questions (but not both) were acceptable. We therefore add the two probabilities together so that the probability of passing the examination has increased.

So $P(5 \text{ or } 6 \text{ questions}) = P(5 \text{ questions}) + P(6 \text{ questions})$

$$= \frac{1}{5} + \frac{1}{5} = \frac{2}{5}$$

FAST FORWARD

Mutually exclusive outcomes are outcomes where the occurrence of one of the outcomes excludes the possibility of any of the others happening.

In the example the outcomes are **mutually exclusive** because it is impossible to have five questions *and* six questions in the same examination.

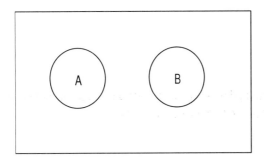

2.5.2 Example: Mutually exclusive outcomes

The delivery of an item of raw material from a supplier may take up to six weeks from the time the order is placed. The probabilities of various delivery times are as follows.

Delivery time	Probability
≤ 1 week	0.10
> 1, ≤ 2 weeks	0.25
> 2, ≤ 3 weeks	0.20
> 3, ≤ 4 weeks	0.20
> 4, ≤ 5 weeks	0.15
> 5, ≤ 6 weeks	0.10
	1.00

Required

Calculate the probability that a delivery will take the following times.

(a)   Two weeks or less
(b)   More than three weeks

Solution

(a)   P ($\leq$ 1 or > 1, $\leq$ 2 weeks)   =   P ($\leq$ 1 week) + P (>1, $\leq$ 2 weeks)
                                            =   0.10 + 0.25
                                            =   0.35

(b)   P (> 3, $\leq$ 6 weeks)   =   P (> 3, $\leq$ 4 weeks) + P (> 4, $\leq$ 5 weeks) + P (> 5, $\leq$ 6 weeks)
                                   =   0.20 + 0.15 + 0.10
                                   =   0.45

2.6 The simple multiplication or AND law

FAST FORWARD

The **simple multiplication law** for two independent events, A and B, is as follows.

P(A and B) = P (A $\cap$ B) = P(A)P(B)

Important!

P(A and B) = 0 when A and B have mutually exclusive outcomes.

You still have three examinations to sit: astrophysics, geography of the moon and computer art. Stupidly, you forgot to revise for the astrophysics examination, which will have between 15 and 20 questions. You think that you may scrape through this paper if it is easy *and* if there are only 15 questions.

What is the probability that the paper the computer produces will exactly match your needs? Do not forget that there is no link between the standard of the examination and the number of questions ie they are **independent** events.

The best way to approach this question is diagrammatically, showing all the possible outcomes.

Type of paper	Number of questions					
	15	16	17	18	19	20
Easy (E)	E and 15*	E and 16	E and 17	E and 18	E and 19	E and 20
Difficult (D)	D and 15	D and 16	D and 17	D and 18	D and 19	D and 20

The diagram shows us that, of the twelve possible outcomes, there is only one 'desired result' (which is asterisked). We can therefore calculate the probability as follows.

P(easy paper *and* 15 questions) =1/12.

The answer can be found more easily as follows.

P(easy paper *and* 15 questions) = P(easy paper) $\times$ P(15 questions) = 1/2 $\times$ 1/6 = 1/12.

The number of questions has no effect on, nor is it affected by whether it is an easy or difficult paper.

FAST FORWARD

Independent events are events where the outcome of one event in no way affects the outcome of the other events.

2.6.1 Example: Independent events

A die is thrown and a coin is tossed simultaneously. What is the probability of throwing a 5 and getting heads on the coin?

Solution

The probability of throwing a 5 on a die is 1/6
The probability of a tossed coin coming up heads is 1/2
The probability of throwing a 5 and getting heads on a coin is $1/2 \times 1/6 = 1/12$

2.7 The general rule of addition

FAST FORWARD

The **general rule of addition** for two events, A and B, which are not mutually exclusive, is as follows.

$P(A \text{ or } B) = P(A \cup B) = P(A) + P(B) - P(A \text{ and } B)$

The three examinations you still have to sit are placed face down in a line in front of you at the final examination sitting. There is an easy astrophysics paper, a difficult geography of the moon paper and a difficult computer art paper. Without turning over any of the papers you are told to choose one of them. What is the probability that the first paper that you select is difficult *or* is the geography of the moon paper?

Let us think about this carefully.

There are two difficult papers, so P(difficult) = 2/3

There is one geography of the moon paper, so P(geography of the moon) = 1/3

If we use the OR law and add the two probabilities then we will have double counted the difficult geography of the moon paper. It is included in the set of difficult papers *and* in the set of geography of the moon papers. In other words, we are *not* faced with mutually exclusive outcomes because the occurrence of a geography of the moon paper does not exclude the possibility of the occurrence of a difficult paper. We therefore need to take account of this **double counting**.

P(difficult paper or geography of the moon paper) = P(difficult paper) + P(geography of the moon paper) − P(difficult paper and geography of the moon paper).

Using the AND law, P(difficult paper or geography of the moon paper) = 2/3 + 1/3 − (1/3) = 2/3.

Since it is *not* impossible to have an examination which is difficult *and* about the geography of the moon, these two events are not mutually exclusive.

2.7.1 Venn diagram: General rule of addition

We can show how to calculate P(A ∪ B) from three diagrams.

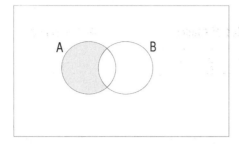

The shaded area is the probability of A and **not** B = P(A) − P(A ∩ B)

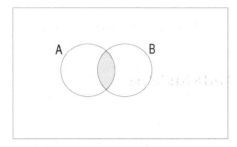

The shaded area is the probability of A **and** B = P (A ∩ B)

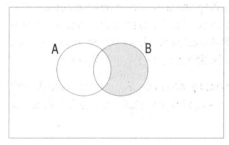

The shaded area is the probability of B and **not** A = P (B) − (A ∩ B)

If we add these three sections together we get the formula for the probability of A **or** B = P(A) + P(B) − P (A ∩ B)

Question   **General rule of addition**

If one card is drawn from a normal pack of 52 playing cards, what is the probability of getting an ace or a spade?

Probability

Ace	*Spade*	*Ace of spades*	*Ace or spade*

Answer

Probability

Ace	Spade	Ace of spades	Ace or spade
$\frac{4}{52}$	$\frac{13}{52}$	$\frac{1}{52}$	$\frac{4}{13}$

Working

$$P(\text{ace or spade}) = \frac{4}{52} + \frac{13}{52} - \frac{1}{52} = \frac{16}{52} = \frac{4}{13}$$

2.8 The general rule of multiplication

FAST FORWARD ▶▶

The **general rule of multiplication** for two dependent events, A and B is as follows.

$$\begin{aligned} P(A \text{ and } B) &= P(A \cap B) \, P(A) \times P(B/A) \\ &= P(B) \times P(A/B) \end{aligned}$$

Computer art is your last examination. Understandably you are very tired and you are uncertain whether you will be able to stay awake. You believe that there is a 70% chance of your falling asleep if it becomes too hot and stuffy in the examination hall. It is well known that the air conditioning system serving the examination hall was installed in the last millennium and is therefore extremely unreliable. There is a 1 in 4 chance of it breaking down during the examination, thereby causing the temperature in the hall to rise. What is the likelihood that you will drop off?

The scenario above has led us to face what is known as **conditional probability**. We can rephrase the information provided as 'the probability that you will fall asleep, given that it is too hot and stuffy, is equal to 70%' and we can write this as follows.

P(fall asleep/too hot and stuffy) = 70%.

FAST FORWARD ▶▶

Dependent or **conditional** events are events where the outcome of one event depends on the outcome of the others.

Whether you fall asleep is **conditional** upon whether the hall becomes too hot and stuffy. The events are not, therefore, independent and so we cannot use the simple multiplication law. So:

P(it becomes too hot and stuffy and you fall asleep)

$$\begin{aligned} &= P(\text{too hot and stuffy}) \times P(\text{fall asleep/too hot and stuffy}) \\ &= 25\% \times 70\% = 0.25 \times 0.7 = 0.175 = 17\tfrac{1}{2}\% \end{aligned}$$

Important!

> When A and B are independent events, then P(B/A) = P(B) since, by definition, the occurrence of B (and therefore P(B)) does not depend upon the occurrence of A. Similarly P(A/B) = P(A).

2.8.1 Example: Conditional probability

The board of directors of Shuttem Ltd has warned that there is a 60% probability that a factory will be closed down unless its workforce improves its productivity. The factory's manager has estimated that the probability of success in agreeing a productivity deal with the workforce is only 30%.

Required

Determine the likelihood that the factory will be closed.

Solution

If outcome A is the shutdown of the factory and outcome B is the failure to improve productivity:

$$
\begin{aligned}
P(A \text{ and } B) \ &= \ P(B) \times P(A/B) \\
&= \ 0.7 \times 0.6 \\
&= \ 0.42
\end{aligned}
$$

> **FAST FORWARD**
>
> **Contingency tables** can be useful for dealing with **conditional probability**.

2.8.2 Example: Contingency tables

A cosmetics company has developed a new anti-dandruff shampoo which is being tested on volunteers. Seventy percent of the volunteers have used the shampoo whereas others have used a normal shampoo, believing it to be the new anti-dandruff shampoo. Two sevenths of those using the new shampoo showed no improvement whereas one third of those using the normal shampoo had less dandruff.

Required

A volunteer shows no improvement. What is the probability that he used the normal shampoo?

Solution

The problem is solved by drawing a contingency table, showing 'improvement' and 'no improvement', volunteers using normal shampoo and volunteers using the new shampoo.

Let us suppose that there were 1,000 volunteers (we could use any number). We could depict the results of the test on the 1,000 volunteers as follows.

	New shampoo	Normal shampoo	Total
Improvement	***500	****100	600
No improvement	**200	200	400
	*700	***300	1,000

* 70% × 1,000   ** $\dfrac{2}{7} \times 700$

*** Balancing figure   **** $\dfrac{1}{3} \times 300$

We can now calculate P (shows no improvement)

$$P(\text{shows no improvement}) = \frac{400}{1,000}$$

$$P(\text{used normal shampoo/shows no improvement}) = \frac{200}{400} = \frac{1}{2}$$

Other probabilities are just as easy to calculate.

P (shows improvement/used new shampoo) = $\dfrac{500}{700}$ = $\dfrac{5}{7}$

P (used new shampoo/shows improvement) = $\dfrac{500}{600}$ = $\dfrac{5}{6}$

Question

Independent events

The independent probabilities that the three sections of a management accounting department will encounter one computer error in a week are respectively 0.1, 0.2 and 0.3. There is never more than one computer error encountered by any one section in a week. Calculate the probability that there will be the following number of errors encountered by the management accounting department next week.

(a)   At least one computer error
(b)   One and only one computer error

Answer

(a)   The probability of at least one computer error is 1 minus the probability of no error. The probability of no error is 0.9 × 0.8 × 0.7 = 0.504.

(Since the probability of an error is 0.1, 0.2 and 0.3 in each section, the probability of no error in each section must be 0.9, 0.8 and 0.7 respectively.)

The probability of at least one error is 1 − 0.504 = 0.496.

(b)   Y = yes, N = no

		Section 1	Section 2	Section 3
(i)	Error?	Y	N	N
(ii)	Error?	N	Y	N
(iii)	Error?	N	N	Y

			Probabilities
(i)	0.1 × 0.8 × 0.7	=	0.056
(ii)	0.9 × 0.2 × 0.7	=	0.126
(iii)	0.9 × 0.8 × 0.3	=	0.216
			Total 0.398

The probability of only one error only is 0.398.

Question

General rule of addition

In a student survey, 60% of the students are male and 75% are CIMA candidates. The probability that a student chosen at random is either female or a CIMA candidate is:

A   0.85
B   0.30
C   0.40
D   1.00

Answer

P(male) = 60% = 0.6
P(female) = 1 – 0.6 = 0.4
P(CIMA candidate) = 75% = 0.75

We need to use the general rule of addition to avoid double counting.

∴ P(female or CIMA candidate) = P(female) + P(CIMA candidate) – P(female *and* CIMA candidate)

$$= 0.4 + 0.75 - (0.4 \times 0.75)$$
$$= 1.15 - 0.3$$
$$= 0.85$$

The correct answer is A.

You should have been able to eliminate options C and D immediately. 0.4 is the probability that the candidate is female and 1.00 is the probability that something will definitely happen – neither of these options are likely to correspond to the probability that the candidate is either female or a CIMA candidate.

3 Expected values

An **expected value** (or **EV**) is a weighted average value, based on probabilities. The expected value for a single event can offer a helpful guide for management decisions.

3.1 How to calculate expected values

If the probability of an outcome of an event is p, then the expected number of times that this outcome will occur in n events (the expected value) is equal to n × p.

For example, suppose that the probability that a transistor is defective is 0.02. How many defectives would we expect to find in a batch of 4,000 transistors?

EV = 4,000 × 0.02
    = 80 defectives

3.2 Example: Expected values

The daily sales of Product T may be as follows.

Units	Probability
1,000	0.2
2,000	0.3
3,000	0.4
4,000	0.1
	1.0

Required

Calculate the expected daily sales.

Solution

The EV of daily sales may be calculated by multiplying each possible outcome (volume of daily sales) by the probability that this outcome will occur.

	Probability	Expected value
Units		Units
1,000	0.2	200
2,000	0.3	600
3,000	0.4	1,200
4,000	0.1	400
	EV of daily sales	2,400

In the long run the expected value should be approximately the actual average, if the event occurs many times over. In the example above, we do not expect sales on any one day to equal 2,400 units, but in the long run, over a large number of days, average sales should equal 2,400 units a day.

3.3 Expected values and single events

The point made in the preceding paragraph is an important one. An **expected value** can be calculated when the **event will only occur once or twice**, but it will not be a true long-run average of what will actually happen, because there is no long run.

3.4 Example: Expected values and single events

Suppose, for example, that a businessman is trying to decide whether to invest in a project. He estimates that there are three possible outcomes.

Outcome	Profit/(loss)	Probability
	$	
Success	10,000	0.2
Moderate success	2,000	0.7
Failure	(4,000)	0.1

The expected value of profit may be calculated as follows.

Profit/(loss)	Probability	Expected value
$		$
10,000	0.2	2,000
2,000	0.7	1,400
(4,000)	0.1	(400)
	Expected value of profit	3,000

In this example, the project is a one-off event, and as far as we are aware, it will not be repeated. The actual profit or loss will be $10,000, $2,000 or $(4,000), and the average value of $3,000 will not actually happen. There is no long-run average of a single event.

Nevertheless, the expected value can be used to help the manager decide whether or not to invest in the project.

✎ Question

A company manufactures and sells product D. The selling price of the product is $6 per unit, and estimates of demand and variable costs of sales are as follows.

Probability	Demand Units	Probability	Variable cost per unit $
0.3	5,000	0.1	3.00
0.6	6,000	0.3	3.50
0.1	8,000	0.5	4.00
		0.1	4.50

The unit variable costs do not depend on the volume of sales.

Fixed costs will be $10,000.

Required

Calculate the expected profit.

Answer

The EV of demand is as follows.

Demand Units	Probability	Expected value Units
5,000	0.3	1,500
6,000	0.6	3,600
8,000	0.1	800
		EV of demand 5,900

The EV of the variable cost per unit is as follows.

Variable costs $	Probability	Expected value $
3.00	0.1	0.30
3.50	0.3	1.05
4.00	0.5	2.00
4.50	0.1	0.45
		EV of unit variable costs 3.80

		$
Sales	5,900 units × $6.00	35,400
Less: variable costs	5,900 units × $3.80	22,420
Contribution		12,980
Less: fixed costs		10,000
Expected profit		2,980

3.5 The expected value equation

The expected value is summarised in equation form as follows.

$E(x) = \sum xP(x)$

This is read as 'the expected value of a particular outcome "x" is equal to the sum of the products of each value of x and the corresponding probability of that value of x occurring'.

4 Expectation and decision making

4.1 Decision making

FAST FORWARD

Probability and expectation should be seen as an aid to decision making.

The concepts of probability and expected value are vital in **business decision making**. The expected values for single events can offer a helpful guide for management decisions.

- A project with a positive EV should be accepted
- A project with a negative EV should be rejected

Another decision rule involving expected values that you are likely to come across is the choice of an option or alternative which has the **highest EV of profit** (or the **lowest EV of cost**).

Choosing the option with the highest EV of profit is a decision rule that has both merits and drawbacks, as the following simple example will show.

4.2 Example: The expected value criterion

Suppose that there are two mutually exclusive projects with the following possible profits.

Project A		Project B	
Probability	Profit	Probability	Profit/(loss)
	$		$
0.8	5,000	0.1	(2,000)
0.2	6,000	0.2	5,000
		0.6	7,000
		0.1	8,000

Required

Determine which project should be chosen.

Solution

The EV of profit for each project is as follows.

			$
(a)	Project A $(0.8 \times 5,000) + (0.2 \times 6,000)$	=	5,200
(b)	Project B $(0.1 \times (2,000)) + (0.2 \times 5,000) + (0.6 \times 7,000) + (0.1 \times 8,000)$	=	5,800

Project B has a higher EV of profit. This means that on the balance of probabilities, it could offer a better return than A, and so is arguably a better choice.

On the other hand, the minimum return from project A would be $5,000 whereas with B there is a 0.1 chance of a loss of $2,000. So project A might be a safer choice.

Question

Expected values

A company is deciding whether to invest in a project. There are three possible outcomes of the investment:

Outcome	Profit/(Loss)
	$'000
Optimistic	19.2
Most likely	12.5
Pessimistic	(6.7)

There is a 30% chance of the optimistic outcome, and a 60% chance of the most likely outcome arising. The expected value of profit from the project is

A $7,500
B $12,590
C $13,930
D $25,000

Answer

B   Since the probabilities must total 100%, the probability of the pessimistic outcome = 100% − 60% − 30% = 10%.

Outcome	Profit/(Loss)	Probability	Expected value
	$		$
Optimistic	19,200	0.3	5,760
Most likely	12,500	0.6	7,500
Pessimistic	(6,700)	0.1	(670)
		1.0	12,590

If you selected option A, you calculated the expected value of the most likely outcome instead of the entire project.

If you selected option C, you forgot to treat the 6,700 as a loss, ie as a negative value.

If you selected option D, you forgot to take into account the probabilities of the various outcomes arising.

4.3 Payoff tables

Decisions have to be taken about a wide variety of matters (capital investment, controls on production, project scheduling and so on) and under a wide variety of conditions from **virtual certainty** to **complete uncertainty**.

There are, however, certain common factors in many business decisions.

(a)   When a decision has to be made, there will be a range of possible **actions**.

(b)   Each action will have certain **consequences**, or **payoffs** (for example, profits, costs, time).

(c)   The payoff from any given action will depend on the **circumstances** (for example, high demand or low demand), which may or may not be known when the decision is taken. Frequently each circumstance will be assigned a probability of occurrence. The circumstances are *not* dependent on the action taken.

For a decision with these elements, a **payoff table** can be prepared.

FAST FORWARD

A payoff table is simply a table with **rows for circumstances** and **columns for actions** (or vice versa), and the payoffs in the cells of the table.

For example, a decision on the level of advertising expenditure to be undertaken given different states of the economy, would have payoffs in $'000 of profit after advertising expenditure as follows.

		High	*Medium*	*Low*
		Actions: expenditure		
Circumstances:	Boom	+50	+30	+15
the state of the	Stable	+20	+25	+5
economy	Recession	0	−10	−35

4.4 Example: Payoff table

A cinema has to decide how many programmes to print for a premiere of a film. From previous experience of similar events, it is expected that the probability of sales will be as follows.

Number of programmes demanded	*Probability of demand*
250	0.1
500	0.2
750	0.4
1,000	0.1
1,250	0.2

The best print quotation received is $2,000 plus 20 pence per copy. Advertising revenue from advertisements placed in the programme totals $2,500. Programmes are sold for $2 each. Unsold programmes are worthless.

Required

(a)   Construct a payoff table.
(b)   Find the most profitable number of programmes to print.

Solution

(a)

Actions: print levels

		250	*500*	*750*	*1,000*	*1,250*
	250 (p = 0.1)	950	900	850	800	750
Circumstances:	500 (p = 0.2)	950	1,400	1,350	1,300	1,250
demand levels	750 (p = 0.4)	950	1,400	1,850	1,800	1,750
	1,000 (p = 0.1)	950	1,400	1,850	2,300	2,250
	1,250 (p = 0.2)	950	1,400	1,850	2,300	2,750

These figures are calculated as the profit under each set of circumstances. For example, if the cinema produces 1,000 programmes and 1,000 are demanded, the profit is calculated as follows.

Total revenue = advertising revenue + sale of programmes
$$= \$2,500 + \$(1,000 \times 2)$$
$$= \$4,500$$

Total costs = $2,000 + $(0.20 × 1,000)
$$= \$2,000 + \$200$$
$$= \$2,200$$

Profit = total revenue − total costs = $4,500 − $2,200 = $2,300

Similarly, if the cinema produces 750 programmes, but only 500 are demanded, the profit is calculated as follows.

Total revenue = $2,500 + $(500 × 2)
= $2,500 + $1,000 = $3,500

Total costs = $2,000 + $(0.20 × 750)
= $2,000 + $150
= $2,150

Profit = total revenue – total costs = $3,500 – $2,150 = $1,350

Note that whatever the print level, the maximum profit that can be earned is determined by the demand. This means that when 250 programmes are printed, the profit is $950 when demand is 250. Profit is also $950 when demand is 500, 750, 1,000 or 1,250.

(b) The expected profits from each of the possible print levels are as follows.

Print 250

Expected profit = $((950 × 0.1) + (950 × 0.2) + (950 × 0.4) + (950 × 0.1) + (950 × 0.2)) = $950

Print 500

Expected profit = $((900 × 0.1) + (1,400 × (0.2 + 0.4 + 0.1 + 0.2))) = $1,350

Print 750

Expected profit = $((850 × 0.1) + (1,350 × 0.2) + (1,850 × 0.7)) = $1,650

Print 1,000

Expected profit = $((800 × 0.1) + (1,300 × 0.2) + (1,800 × 0.4) + (2,300 × 0.3)) = $1,750

Print 1,250

Expected profit = $((750 × 0.1) + (1,250 × 0.2) + (1,750 × 0.4) + (2,250 × 0.1) + (2,750 × 0.2)) = $1,800

1,250 programmes should therefore be printed in order to **maximise expected profit**.

Assessment formula

E(X) = Expected value = Probability × Pay off

Question   **Payoff tables**

In a restaurant there is a 30% chance of five apple pies being ordered a day and a 70% chance of ten being ordered. Each apple pie sells for $2. It costs $1 to make an apple pie. Using a payoff table, decide how many apple pies the restaurant should prepare each day, bearing in mind that unsold apple pies must be thrown away at the end of each day.

Answer

		Prepared	
		Five	*Ten*
Demand	Five (P = 0.3)	5	0
	Ten (P = 0.7)	5	10

Prepare five, profit = ($5 × 0.3) + ($5 × 0.7) = $5
Prepare ten, profit = ($0 × 0.3) + ($10 × 0.7) = $7

Ten pies should be prepared.

4.5 Limitations of expected values

Evaluating decisions by using expected values have a number of limitations.

(a) The **probabilities** used when calculating expected values are likely to be estimates. They may therefore be **unreliable** or **inaccurate**.

(b) Expected values are **long-term averages** and may not be suitable for use in situations involving **one-off decisions**. They may therefore be useful as a **guide** to decision making.

(c) Expected values do not consider the **attitudes to risk of** the people involved in the decision-making process. They do not, therefore, take into account all of the factors involved in the decision.

(d) The time value of money may not be taken into account: $100 now is worth more than $100 in ten years' time. We shall study the time value of money in Section F of this Study Text.

4.6 Risk and uncertainty

FAST FORWARD

Probability is used to help to calculate **risk** in decision making.

Risk involves situations or events which may or may not occur, but whose probability of occurrence can be calculated statistically and the frequency predicted.

Uncertainty involves situations or events whose outcome cannot be predicted with statistical confidence.

Assessment focus point

Do not underestimate the importance of probability in the **Business Mathematics** assessment – this topic accounts for 15% of the syllabus. The key to being able to answer probability questions is lots of practice.

Chapter Roundup

- Probability is a measure of **likelihood** and can be stated as a percentage, a ratio, or more usually as a number from 0 to 1.

- The **simple addition law** for two mutually exclusive events, A and B is as follows.

  P(A or B) = P(A) + P(B)

- **Mutually exclusive outcomes** are outcomes where the occurrence of one of the outcomes excludes the possibility of any of the others happening.

- The **simple multiplication law** for two independent events A and B, is as follows.

  P(A and B) = P(A) P(B)

- **Independent events** are events where the outcome of one event in no way affects the outcome of the other events.

- The **general rule of addition** for two events, A and B, which are not mutually exclusive, is as follows.

  P(A or B) = P(A) + P(B) − P(A and B)

- The **general rule of multiplication** for two dependent events, A and B, is as follows.

  P(A and B) = P(A) × P(B/A)
               = P(B) × P(A/B)

- **Dependent** or **conditional** events are events where the outcome of one event depends on the outcome of the others.

- **Contingency tables** can be useful for dealing with **conditional probability**.

- An **expected value (or EV)** is a weighted average, based on probabilities. The expected value for a single event can offer a helpful guide for management decisions: **a project with a positive EV should be accepted** and a **project with a negative EV should be rejected**.

- **Probability and expectation should be seen as an aid to decision making**.

- A payoff table is simply a table with **rows for circumstances** and **columns for actions** (or vice versa), and the payoffs in the cells of the table.

- Probability is used to help to calculate **risk** in decision making.

Quick Quiz

1   Complete the following equations

    (a) $P(\overline{X})$ = 1 − ....

    (b)   Simple addition/OR law

            P(A or B or C) = ...

            where A, B and C are ....

    (c)   Simple multiplication/AND law

            P(A and B) = ...

            where A and B are ....

(d)   General rule of addition

P(A or B) = ...

where A and B are ....

(e)   General rule of multiplication

P(A and B) = ...

where A and B are ....

2   1 | Mutually exclusive outcomes |

    2 | Independent events |

    3 | Conditional events |

A   The occurrence of one of the outcomes excludes the possibility of any of the others happening

B   Events where the outcome of one event depends on the outcome of the others

C   Events where the outcome of one event in no way affects the outcome of the other events

1	2	3
1	2	3
1	2	3

3   An analysis of 480 working days in a factory shows that on 360 days there were no machine breakdowns. Assuming that this pattern will continue, what is the probability that there will be a machine breakdown on a particular day?

A   0%

B   25%

C   35%

D   75%

4   A production director is responsible for overseeing the operations of three factories – North, South and West. He visits one factory per week. He visits the West factory as often as he visits the North factory, but he visits the South factory twice as often as he visits the West factory.

What is the probability that in any one week he will visit the North factory?

A   0.17

B   0.20

C   0.25

D   0.33

5   What is an expected value?

6   Expected values can be used to help managers decide whether or not to invest in a project. Generally, a project with a .... EV should be rejected, and one with a .... EV should be ....

Answers to Quick Quiz

1   (a) $1 - P(X)$

    (b) $P(A) + P(B) + P(C)$ Mutually exclusive outcomes

    (c) $P(A) \times P(B)$ Independent events

    (d) $P(A) + P(B) - P(A \text{ and } B)$ Not mutually exclusive outcomes

    (e) $P(A) \times P(B/A) = P(B) \times P(A/B)$ Dependent events

2   A = 1

    B = 3

    C = 2

3   B   The data tells us that there was a machine breakdown on 120 days (480 – 360) out of a total of 480.

        P(machine breakdown) = 120/480 × 100%

                     = 25%

        You should have been able to eliminate option A immediately since a probability of 0% = impossibility.

        If you selected option C, you calculated the probability of a machine breakdown as 120 out of a possible 365 days instead of 480 days.

        If you selected option D, you incorrectly calculated the probability that there was **not** a machine breakdown on any particular day.

4

Factory	Ratio of visits
North	1
South	2
West	$\frac{1}{4}$

    Pr(visiting North factory) = 1/4 = 0.25

    If you didn't select the correct option, make sure that you are clear about how the correct answer has been arrived at. Remember to look at the **ratio** of visits since no actual numbers of visits are given.

5   A weighted average value based on probabilities.

6   Generally, a project with a negative EV should be rejected, and one with a positive EV should be accepted.

Now try the questions below from the Exam Question Bank

Question numbers	Pages
20-28	333-335

Part C
Summarising and analysing data

Data and information

Introduction

The words 'quantitative methods' often strike terror into the hearts of students. They conjure up images of complicated mathematical formulae, scientific analysis of reams of computer output and the drawing of strange graphs and diagrams. Such images are wrong. Quantitative methods simply involves.

- **Collecting data**
- **Presenting the data in a useful form**
- **Inspecting the data**

A study of the subject will demonstrate that quantitative methods is nothing to be afraid of and that a knowledge of it is extremely advantageous in your working environment.

We will start our study of quantitative methods by looking at **data collection**. In Chapter 5 we will consider how to **present data** once they have been collected

Topic list	Syllabus references
1 Data and information	C, (i), (1)
2 Characteristics of good information	C, (ii), (1)
3 Data types	C, (i), (1)

1 Data and information

FAST FORWARD

Data are the raw materials for data processing. **Information** is data that has been processed.

1.1 Examples of data

- The number of tourists who visit Hong Kong each year
- The sales turnovers of all restaurants in Salisbury
- The number of people (with black hair) who pass their driving test each year

Information is sometimes referred to as processed data. The terms 'information' and 'data' are often used interchangeably. Let us consider the following situation in which data is **collected** and then **processed** in order to produce meaningful information.

1.2 Example: Data and information

Many companies providing a product or service like to research consumer opinion, and employ market research organisations to do so. A typical market research survey employs a number of researchers who request a sample of the public to answer questions relating to the product. Several hundred questionnaires may be completed. The questionnaires are input to a system. Once every questionnaire has been input, a number of processing operations are performed on the data. A report which summarises the results and discusses their significance is sent to the company that commissioned the survey.

Individually, a completed questionnaire would not tell the company very much, only the views of one consumer. In this case, the individual questionnaires are **data**. Once they have been processed, and analysed, the resulting report is **information**. The company will use it to inform its decisions regarding the product. If the report revealed that consumers disliked the product, the company would scrap or alter it.

The **quality of source data** affects the value of information. Information is worthless if the source data is flawed. If the researchers filled in questionnaires themselves, inventing the answers, then the conclusions drawn from the processed data would be wrong, and poor decisions would be made.

1.3 Quantitative and qualitative data

FAST FORWARD

Quantitative data are data that can be measured. A **'variable'** is something which can be measured.

Qualitative data cannot be measured, but have **attributes** (an attribute is something an object either has or does not have).

Examples of quantitative data include the following.

- The temperature on each day of January in Singapore. This can be **measured** in degrees Fahrenheit or Celsius.

- The time it takes you to swim 50 lengths. This can be **measured** in hours and minutes.

An example of **qualitative data** is whether someone is male or female. Whether you are male or female is an **attribute** because the sex of a person cannot be measured.

1.4 Quantitative and qualitative information

Just as data may be quantitative or qualitative, so too may information.

Key term

- **Quantitative information** is information which is capable of being expressed in numbers.

- **Qualitative information** is information which may not be expressed very easily in terms of numbers. Information of this nature is more likely to reflect the quality of something.

An example of **quantitative information** is 'The Chairman of the company has announced that the turnover for the year is **$4 million.**' You can see how this information is easily expressed in numerical terms.

An example of **qualitative information** is 'The standard of the books produced was **very high.**' This information cannot easily be expressed in terms of numbers, as the standard of something is usually described as being very high, quite low, or average and so on.

2 Characteristics of good information

FAST FORWARD

The main characteristics of good information are as follows.

- It should be **relevant** for its purpose
- It should be **complete** for its purpose
- It should be sufficiently **accurate** for its purpose
- It should be **clear** to the user
- The user should have **confidence** in it
- It should be **communicated** to the right person
- It should not be excessive – its **volume** should be manageable
- It should be **timely** – in other words communicated at the most appropriate time
- It should be communicated by an appropriate **channel** of communication
- It should be provided at a **cost** which is less than the value of its benefits

Let us look at these characteristics in more detail.

(a) **Relevance**. Information must be relevant to the purpose for which a manager wants to use it. In practice, far too many reports fail to 'keep to the point' and contain purposeless, irritating paragraphs which only serve to vex the managers reading them.

(b) **Completeness**. An information user should have all the information needed to do a job properly. An incomplete picture of the situation could result in bad decisions.

(c) **Accuracy**. Information should obviously be accurate because using incorrect information could have serious and damaging consequences. However, information should only be accurate enough for its purpose and there is no need to go into unnecessary detail for pointless accuracy.

(d) **Clarity**. Information must be clear to the user. If the user does not understand it properly it cannot be used properly. Lack of clarity is one of the causes of a breakdown in communication. It is therefore important to choose the most appropriate presentation medium or channel of communication.

(e) **Confidence**. Information must be trusted by the managers who are expected to use it. However not all information is certain. Some information has to be certain, especially operating information, for example, related to a production process. Strategic information, especially relating to the environment, is uncertain.

However, if the assumptions underlying it are clearly stated, this might enhance the confidence with which the information is perceived.

(f) **Communication**. Within any organisation, individuals are given the authority to do certain tasks, and they must be given the information they need to do them. An office manager might be made responsible for controlling expenditures in his office, and given a budget expenditure limit for the year. As the year progresses, he might try to keep expenditure in check but unless he is told throughout the year what is his current total expenditure to date, he will find it difficult to judge whether he is keeping within budget or not.

(g) **Volume**. There are physical and mental limitations to what a person can read, absorb and understand properly before taking action. An enormous mountain of information, even if it is all relevant, cannot be handled. Reports to management must therefore be **clear** and **concise** and in many systems, control action works basically on the 'exception' principle.

(h) **Timing**. Information which is not available until after a decision is made will be useful only for comparisons and longer-term control, and may serve no purpose even then. Information prepared too frequently can also be a problem. If, for example, a decision is taken at a monthly meeting about a certain aspect of a company's operations, information to make the decision is only required once a month, so weekly reports would be a time-consuming waste of effort.

(i) **Channel of communication**. There are occasions when using one particular method of communication will be better than others. For example, job vacancies should be announced in a medium where they will be brought to the attention of the people most likely to be interested. The channel of communication might be the company's in-house journal, a national or local newspaper, a professional magazine, a job centre or school careers office. Some internal memoranda may be better sent by 'electronic mail'. Some information is best communicated informally by telephone or word-of-mouth, whereas other information ought to be formally communicated in writing or figures.

(j) **Cost**. Information should have some value, otherwise it would not be worth the cost of collecting and filing it. The benefits obtainable from the information must exceed the costs of acquiring it.

3 Data types

3.1 Classifying data

We have already seen how data can be classified as being **quantitative** (can be measured (variables)) or qualitative (cannot be measured, has an **attribute**). We shall now consider the ways in which data may be further classified as follows.

- Primary and secondary data
- Discrete and continuous data

3.2 Primary and secondary data

FAST FORWARD

Data may be **primary** (collected specifically for the purpose of a survey) or **secondary** (collected for some other purpose).

(a) **Primary data** are data collected especially for the purpose of whatever survey is being conducted. Raw data are primary data which have not been processed at all, and which are still just a list of numbers.

(b) **Secondary data** are data which have already been collected elsewhere, for some other purpose, but which can be used or adapted for the survey being conducted.

3.3 Discrete and continuous data

Quantitative data may be further classified as being **discrete** or **continuous.**

FAST FORWARD

> **Discrete** data/variables can only take on a countable number of values. **Continuous** data/variables can take on any value.

(a) **Discrete data** are the number of goals scored by Arsenal against Chelsea in the FA Cup Final: Arsenal could score 0, 1, 2, 3 or even 4 goals (**discrete variables** = 0, 1, 2, 3, 4), but they cannot score $1\frac{1}{2}$ or $2\frac{1}{2}$ goals.

(b) **Continuous data** include the heights of all the members of your family, as these can take on any value: 1.542m, 1.639m and 1.492m for example. **Continuous variables** = 1.542, 1.639, 1.492.

The following diagram should help you to remember the ways in which data may be classified.

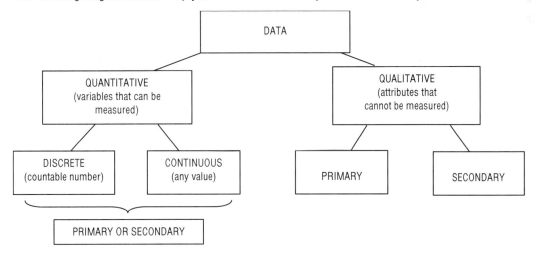

Question

Quantitative and qualitative data

Look through the following list of surveys and decide whether each is collecting qualitative data or quantitative data. If you think the data is quantitative, indicate whether it is discrete or continuous.

(a) A survey of accountancy textbooks, to determine how many diagrams they contain.

(b) A survey of greetings cards on a newsagent's shelf, to determine whether or not each has a price sticker on it.

(c) A survey of the results in a cost accounting assessment, to determine what percentage of marks the students obtained.

(d) A survey of heights of telegraph poles in Papua New Guinea, to find out if there is any variation across the country.

(e) A survey of swimmers to find out how long they take to swim a kilometre.

Answer

(a) The number of diagrams in an accountancy text book is an example of **quantitative** data, because it can be measured. Because the number of diagrams can only be counted in whole number steps, the resulting data is **discrete.** You cannot for example have $42\frac{1}{2}$ diagrams, but you can have 42 or 43 diagrams.

(b) Whether or not a greetings card has a price sticker on it is not something that can be measured. This is therefore an example of **qualitative** data, as a greetings card either has a price sticker on it, or it does not have a price sticker on it.

(c) The results of a cost accounting assessment can be measured, and are therefore an example of **quantitative** data. The assessment results can only take on whole number values between 0% and 100%, and the data are therefore **discrete.** (It may be possible to score $62\frac{1}{2}$ %, or $64\frac{1}{2}$ %, but it is not possible to score 62.41%, so the variable is not continuous.)

(d) The heights of telegraph poles is an example of **quantitative** data as they can be measured. Since the telegraph poles may take on any height, the data is said to be **continuous.**

(e) The time taken to swim a kilometre may be measured and is therefore **quantitative** data. Because the time recorded can take on any value, in theory, the data is said to be **continuous.**

Chapter Roundup

- **Data** are the raw materials for data processing. **Information** is data that has been processed.

- **Quantitative data** are data that can be measured. A 'variable' is something which can be measured.

- **Qualitative data** cannot be measured, but have **attributes** (an attribute is something an object either has or does not have).

- The main **characteristics of good information** are as follows.
    - It should be **relevant** for its purpose.
    - It should be **complete** for its purpose.
    - It should be sufficiently **accurate** for its purpose.
    - It should be **clear** to the user.
    - The user should have **confidence** in it.
    - It should be **communicated** to the right person.
    - It should not be excessive – its **volume** should be manageable.
    - It should be **timely** – in other words communicated at the most appropriate time.
    - It should be communicated by an appropriate **channel** of communication.
    - It should be provided at a **cost** which is less than the value of its benefits.

- Data may be **primary** (collected specifically for the purpose of a survey) or **secondary** (collected for some other purpose).

- **Discrete** data/variables can only take on a countable number of values. **Continuous** data/ variables can take on any value.

Quick Quiz

1 **Fill in the blanks** in the statements below using the words in the box.

Data can be either (1) .... (have variables) or (2) .... (have (3) ....).
Variables can be either (4) .... (eg 0, 1, 2, 3) or (5) .... (eg 0.54, 0.612, 0.117). Data may
also be classified as (6) .... (collected for a specific survey) or (7) .... (collected for some
other purpose).

• Quantitative	• Continuous	• Attributes	• Primary
• Secondary	• Qualitative	• Discrete	

2 List ten characteristics of good information.

Answers to Quick Quiz

1 (1) Quantitative   (2) Qualitative   (3) Attributes
   (4) Discrete   (5) Continuous   (6) Primary
   (7) Secondary

2 • Relevant
   • Complete
   • Accurate
   • Clear
   • User has confidence in it
   • Communicated to the right person
   • Manageable volume
   • Timely
   • Appropriate channel of communication
   • Cost is less than benefits obtained

Now try the questions below from the Exam Question Bank

Question numbers	Pages
19	332

Data presentation

Introduction

We now have to **present** the data we have collected so that they can be of use. This chapter begins by looking at how data can be presented in **tables** and **charts**. Such methods are helpful in presenting key data in a **concise** and **easy to understand way**.

Data that are a mass of numbers can usefully be summarised into a **frequency distribution**. **Histograms** and **ogives** are the **pictorial representation** of grouped and cumulative frequency distributions.

Topic list	Syllabus references
1 Tables	C, (iii), (2)
2 Charts	C, (iii), (3)
3 Frequency distributions	C, (v), (5)
4 Histograms	C, (iii), (3)
5 Ogives	C, (3)
6 Scatter diagrams	C, (3)

1 Tables

1.1 Tables and tabulation

FAST FORWARD

Tables are a simple way of presenting information about two variables.

Raw data (for example a list of results from a survey) need to be **summarised** and **analysed**, to give them meaning. One of the most basic ways is the preparation of a **table**.

Key term

- **Tabulation** means putting data into tables.
- A **table** is a matrix of data in rows and columns, with the rows and the columns having titles.

Since a table is **two-dimensional**, it can only show **two variables**. To tabulate data, you need to recognise what the two dimensions should represent, prepare **rows** and **columns** accordingly with suitable **titles**, and then **insert the data** into the appropriate places in the table.

1.2 Example: Tables

The total number of employees in a certain trading company is 1,000. They are employed in three departments: production, administration and sales. 600 people are employed in the production department and 300 in administration. There are 110 males under 21 in employment, 110 females under 21, and 290 females aged 21 years and over. The remaining employees are males aged 21 and over.

In the production department there are 350 males aged 21 and over, 150 females aged 21 and over and 50 males under 21, whilst in the administration department there are 100 males aged 21 and over, 110 females aged 21 and over and 50 males aged under 21.

Draw up a table to show all the details of employment in the company and its departments and provide suitable secondary statistics to describe the distribution of people in departments.

Solution

The basic table required has the following two dimensions.

- Departments
- Age/sex analysis

In this example we are going to show the percentage of the total workforce in each department.

Analysis of employees

| | \multicolumn{8}{c}{Department} | | | | | | | |
| | Production | | Administration | | Sales | | Total | |
	No	%	No	%	No	%	No	%
Males 21 yrs +	350	58.4	100	33.3	40 **	40.0	490 *	49.0
Females 21 yrs +	150	25.0	110	36.7	30 **	30.0	290	29.0
Subtotals 21 yrs +	500	83.4	210	70.0	70	70.0	780	78.0
Males under 21	50	8.3	50	16.7	10 **	10.0	110	11.0
Females under 21	50 *	8.3	40 *	13.3	20 **	20.0	110	11.0
Subtotals under 21	100	16.6	90	30.0	30	30.0	220	22.0
Total	600	100.0	300	100.0	100	100.0	1,000	100.0

*   Balancing figure to make up the column total
** Balancing figure then needed to make up the row total

1.3 Guidelines for tabulation

The example above illustrates certain guidelines which you should apply when presenting data in tabular form. These are as follows.

- The table should be given a **clear title**
- All columns should be **clearly labelled**
- Where appropriate, there should be **clear sub-totals**
- A **total column** may be presented; this would usually be the right-hand column
- A **total figure** is often advisable at the bottom of each column of figures
- Tables should not be packed with so much data that reading information is difficult
- Non-essential information should be eliminated
- Consider ordering columns/rows by order of importance/magnitude

2 Charts

2.1 Visual display

FAST FORWARD

Charts often convey the meaning or significance of data more clearly than would a table.

Instead of presenting data in a table, it might be preferable to give a **visual display** in the form of a **chart**. The purpose of a chart is to convey the data in a way that will demonstrate its meaning more clearly than a table of data would. Charts are not always more appropriate than tables, and the most suitable way of presenting data will depend on the following.

(a) **What the data are intended to show.** Visual displays usually make one or two points quite forcefully, whereas tables usually give more detailed information.

(b) **Who is going to use the data**. Some individuals might understand visual displays more readily than tabulated data.

2.2 Bar charts

Key term

The **bar chart** is one of the most common methods of presenting data in a visual form. It is a chart in which quantities are shown in the form of bars.

FAST FORWARD

There are three main **types of bar chart**: **simple**, **component** (including **percentage component**) and **multiple** (or **compound**).

Key term

A **simple bar chart** is a chart consisting of one or more bars, in which the length of each bar indicates the magnitude of the corresponding data item.

2.2.1 Example: A simple bar chart

A company's total sales for the years from 20X1 to 20X6 are as follows.

Year	Sales
	$'000
20X1	800
20X2	1,200
20X3	1,100
20X4	1,400
20X5	1,600
20X6	1,700

The data could be shown on a simple bar chart as follows:

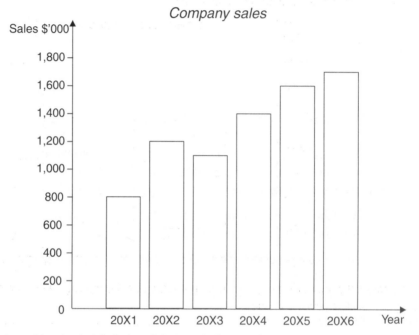

Each axis of the chart must be clearly labelled, and there must be a scale to indicate the magnitude of the data. Here, the y axis includes a scale for the amount of sales, and so readers of the bar chart can see not only that sales have been rising year by year (with 20X3 being an exception), but also what the actual sales have been each year.

2.2.2 Purposes of simple bar charts

Simple bar charts serve two purposes.

- The actual magnitude of each item is shown
- The lengths of bars on the chart allow magnitudes to be compared

Key term

> A **component bar chart** is a bar chart that gives a breakdown of each total into its components. The total length of each bar and each component on a component bar chart indicates magnitude (a bigger amount is shown by a longer bar).

2.2.3 Example: A component bar chart

Charbart plc's sales for the years from 20X7 to 20X9 are as follows.

	20X7	20X8	20X9
	$'000	$'000	$'000
Product A	1,000	1,200	1,700
Product B	900	1,000	1,000
Product C	500	600	700
Total	2,400	2,800	3,400

A component bar chart would show the following.

- How total sales have changed from year to year
- The components of each year's total

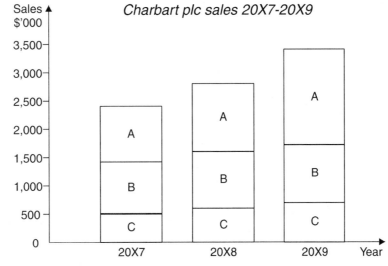

In this diagram the growth in sales is illustrated and the significance of growth in product A sales as the reason for the total sales growth is also fairly clear.

Key term

> A **percentage component bar chart** is a component bar chart which does not show **total magnitudes** – if one or more bars are drawn on the chart, the total length of each bar is the same. The lengths of the sections of the bar however, do vary, and it is these lengths that indicate the **relative sizes** of the components.

2.2.4 Example: A percentage component bar chart

The information in the previous example of sales of Charbart plc could have been shown in a **percentage component bar chart** as follows.

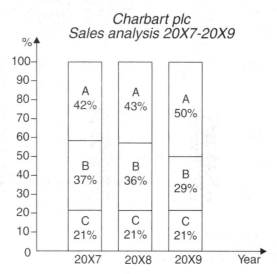

Charbart plc
Sales analysis 20X7-20X9

Working

	20X7		20X8		20X9	
	$'000	%	$'000	%	$'000	%
Product A	1,000	42	1,200	43	1,700	50
Product B	900	37	1,000	36	1,000	29
Product C	500	21	600	21	700	21
Total	2,400	100	2,800	100	3,400	100

This chart shows that sales of C have remained a steady proportion of total sales, but the proportion of A in total sales has gone up quite considerably, while the proportion of B has fallen correspondingly.

Key term

> A **multiple bar chart** (or **compound bar chart**) is a bar chart in which two or more separate bars are used to present subdivisions of data.

2.2.5 Example: A multiple bar chart

The data on Charbart plc's sales could be shown in a multiple bar chart as follows.

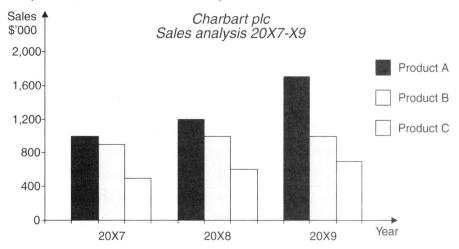

A multiple bar chart uses several bars for each total. In this multiple bar chart, the sales in each year are shown as three separate bars, one for each product, A, B and C.

2.2.6 Information presented by multiple bar charts

Multiple bar charts present similar information to component bar charts, except for the following.

(a)   Multiple bar charts do not show the grand total whereas component bar charts do.

(b)   Multiple bar charts illustrate the comparative magnitudes of the components more clearly than component bar charts.

Multiple bar charts are sometimes drawn with the bars horizontal instead of vertical.

Question

Income for Canary Bank in 20X0, 20X1 and 20X2 is made up as follows.

	20X0 $'000	20X1 $'000	20X2 $'000
Interest income	3,579	2,961	2,192
Commission income	857	893	917
Other income	62	59	70

Using the above data complete the following graphs.

(a)   *A simple bar chart*

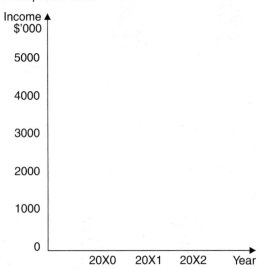

(b)   *A multiple bar chart*

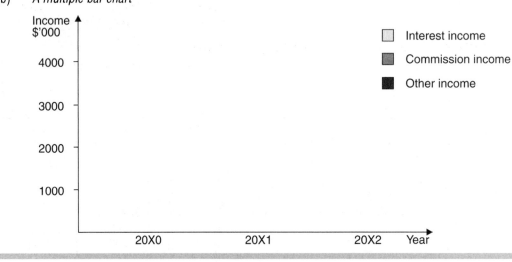

Answer

Workings

	20X0	*20X1*	*20X2*
	$'000	$'000	$'000
	3,579	2,961	2,192
	857	893	917
	62	59	70
	4,498	3,913	3,179

(a) *A simple bar chart*

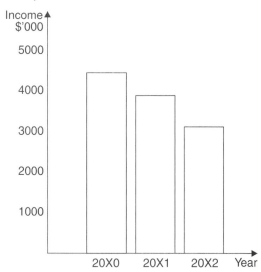

(b) *A multiple bar chart*

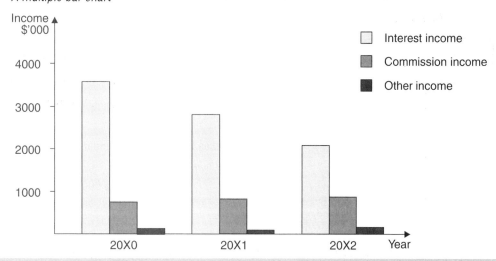

2.3 Pie charts

Key term

> A **pie chart** is a chart which is used to show pictorially the relative size of component elements of a total.

It is called a pie chart because it is **circular**, and so has the **shape of a pie** in a round pie dish. The 'pie' is then cut into slices with each slice representing part of the total.

Pie charts have sectors of varying sizes, and you need to be able to draw sectors fairly accurately. To do this, you need a **protractor**. Working out sector sizes involves converting parts of the total into **equivalent degrees of a circle**. A complete 'pie' = 360°: the number of degrees in a circle = 100% of whatever you are showing. An element which is 50% of your total will therefore occupy a segment of 180°, and so on.

2.3.1 Using shading and colour

Two pie charts are shown as follows.

Breakdown of air and noise pollution complaints, 1

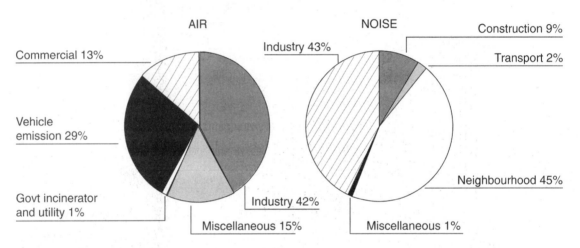

- • **Shading** distinguishes the segments from each other
- • **Colour** can also be used to distinguish segments

2.3.2 Example: Pie charts

The costs of materials at the Cardiff Factory and the Swansea Factory during January 20X0 were as follows.

	Cardiff factory		Swansea factory	
	$'000	%	$'000	%
Material W	70	35	50	20
Material A	30	15	125	50
Material L	90	45	50	20
Material E	10	5	25	10
	200	100	250	100

Show the costs for the factories in pie charts.

Solution

To convert the components into degrees of a circle, we can use either the **percentage figures** or the **actual cost figures**.

Using the percentage figures

The total percentage is 100%, and the total number of degrees in a circle is 360°. To convert from one to the other, we multiply each percentage value by 360/100% = 3.6.

	Cardiff factory		Swansea factory	
	%	Degrees	%	Degrees
Material W	35	126	20	72
Material A	15	54	50	180
Material L	45	162	20	72
Material E	5	18	10	36
	100	360	100	360

Using the actual cost figures

	Cardiff factory		Swansea factory	
	$'000	Degrees	$'000	Degrees
Material W (70/200 × 360°)	70	126	50	72
Material A	30	54	125	180
Material L	90	162	50	72
Material E	10	18	25	36
	200	360	250	360

A pie chart could be drawn for each factory.

Cardiff Factory

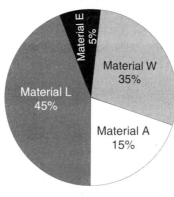

Swansea Factory

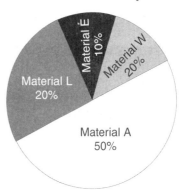

(a) If the pie chart is drawn manually, a protractor must be used to measure the degrees accurately to obtain the correct sector sizes.

(b) Using a computer makes the process much simpler, especially using a spreadsheet. You just draw up the data in a spreadsheet and click on the chart button to create a visual representation of what you want. Note that you can only use colour effectively if you have a colour printer!

2.3.3 Advantages of pie charts

- They give a simple pictorial display of the relative sizes of elements of a total
- They show clearly when one element is much bigger than others
- They can clearly show differences in the elements of two different totals

2.3.4 Disadvantages of pie charts

(a) They only show the relative sizes of elements. In the example of the two factories, for instance, the pie charts do not show that costs at the Swansea factory were $50,000 higher in total than at the Cardiff factory.

(b) They involve **calculating degrees of a circle** and drawing sectors accurately, and this can be time consuming unless computer software is used.

(c) It is often **difficult to compare sector sizes** easily. For example, suppose that the following two pie charts are used to show the elements of a company's sales.

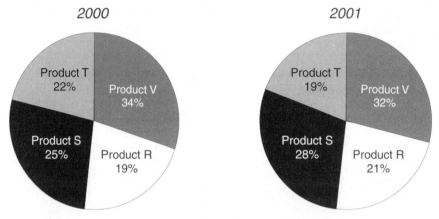

2000   *2001*

Without the percentage figures, it would not be easy to see how the distribution of sales had changed between 2000 and 2001.

| Question | **Pie charts** |

The European division of Scent to You Ltd, a flower delivery service has just published its accounts for the year ended 30 June 20X0. The sales director made the following comments.

'Our total sales for the year were $1,751,000, of which $787,000 were made in the United Kingdom, $219,000 in Italy, $285,000 in France and $92,000 in Germany. Sales in Spain and Holland amounted to $189,000 and $34,000 respectively, whilst the rest of Europe collectively had sales of $145,000 in the twelve months to 30 June 20X0.'

Required

Present the above information in the form of a pie chart. Show all of your workings.

Answer

Workings

	Sales $'000		Degrees
United Kingdom	787	(787/1,751 × 360)	162
Italy	219		45
France	285		58
Germany	92		19
Spain	189		39
Rest of Europe	145		30
Holland	34		7
	1,751		360

Scent to You Ltd
Sales for the year ended 30 June 20X0

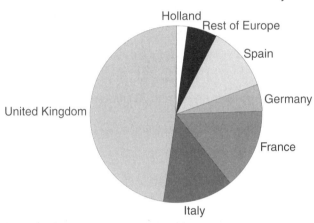

3 Frequency distributions

3.1 Introduction to frequency distributions

FAST FORWARD

Frequency distributions are used if values of particular variables occur more than once.

Frequently the data collected from a statistical survey or investigation is simply a mass of numbers.

65	69	70	71	70	68	69	67	70	68
72	71	69	74	70	73	71	67	69	70

The raw data above yields little information as it stands; imagine how much more difficult it would be if there were hundreds or even thousands of data items. The data could, of course, be arranged in **order size** (an **array**) and the lowest and highest data items, as well as typical items, could be identified.

3.2 Example: Frequency distribution

Many sets of data, however, contain a limited number of data values, even though there may be many occurrences of each value. It can therefore be useful to organise the data into what is known as a **frequency distribution** (or **frequency table**) which records the number of times each value occurs (the **frequency**). A frequency distribution for the data in Paragraph 3.1 (the output in units of 20 employees during one week) is as follows.

Output of employees in one week in units

Output Units	Number of employees (frequency)
65	1
66	0
67	2
68	2
69	4
70	5
71	3
72	1
73	1
74	1
	20

When the data are arranged in this way it is immediately obvious that 69 and 70 units are the most common volumes of output per employee per week.

3.3 Grouped frequency distributions

If there is a large set of data or if every (or nearly every) data item is different, it is often convenient to group frequencies together into **bands** or **classes**. For example, suppose that the output produced by another group of 20 employees during one week was as follows, in units.

1,087	850	1,084	792
924	1,226	1,012	1,205
1,265	1,028	1,230	1,182
1,086	1,130	989	1,155
1,134	1,166	1,129	1,160

3.4 Class intervals

The range of output from the lowest to the highest producer is 792 to 1,265, a **range** of 473 units. This range could be divided into classes of say, 100 units (the **class width** or **class interval**), and the number of employees producing output within each class could then be grouped into a single frequency, as follows.

Output Units	Number of employees (frequency)
700 – 799	1
800 – 899	1
900 – 999	2
1,000 – 1,099	5
1,100 – 1,199	7
1,200 – 1,299	4
	20

Note, however, that once items have been 'grouped' in this way their individual values are lost.

As well as being used for **discrete variables** (as above), grouped frequency distributions (or grouped frequency tables) can be used to present data for **continuous variables**.

3.5 Example: A grouped frequency distribution for a continuous variable

Suppose we wish to record the heights of 50 different individuals. The information might be presented as a grouped frequency distribution, as follows.

Height cm	Number of individuals (frequency)
Up to and including 154	1
Over 154, up to and including 163	3
Over 163, up to and including 172	8
Over 172, up to and including 181	16
Over 181, up to and including 190	18
Over 190	4
	50

Note the following points.

(a)   It would be wrong to show the ranges as 0 – 154, 154 – 163, 163 – 172 and so on, because 154 cm and 163 cm would then be values in two classes, which is not permissible. Although each value should only be in one class, we have to make sure that each possible value can be included. Classes such as 154–162, 163–172 would not be suitable since a height of 162.5 cm would not belong in either class. Such classes could be used for discrete variables, however.

(b)   **There is an open ended class at each end of the range**. This is because heights up to 154 cm and over 190 cm are thought to be uncommon, so that a single 'open ended' class is used to group all the frequencies together.

3.6 Guidelines for preparing grouped frequency distributions

To prepare a grouped frequency distribution, a decision must be made about how wide each class should be. You should observe the following guidelines if you are not told how many classes to use or what the class interval should be.

(a)   The size of each class should be appropriate to the nature of the data being recorded, and the most appropriate class interval varies according to circumstances.

(b)   The upper and lower limits of each class interval should be suitable 'round' numbers for class intervals which are in multiples of 5, 10, 100, 1,000 and so on. For example, if the class interval is 10, and data items range in value from 23 to 62 (discrete values), the class intervals should be 20–29, 30–39, 40–49, 50–59 and 60–69, rather than 23–32, 33–42, 43–52 and 53–62.

(c)   With **continuous variables**, either:

(i)   the **upper limit** of a class should be **'up to and including ...'** and the **lower limit** of the next class should be **'over ...'**

(ii)   the **upper limit** of a class should be **'less than...'**, and the **lower limit** of the next class should be **'at least ...'**

Grouped frequency distributions

The commission earnings for May 20X0 of the assistants in a department store were as follows (in dollars).

60	35	53	47	25	44	55	58	47	71
63	67	57	44	61	48	50	56	61	42
43	38	41	39	61	51	27	56	57	50
55	68	55	50	25	48	44	43	49	73
53	35	36	41	45	71	56	40	69	52
36	47	66	52	32	46	44	32	52	58
49	41	45	45	48	36	46	42	52	33
31	36	40	66	53	58	60	52	66	51
51	44	59	53	51	57	35	45	46	54
46	54	51	39	64	43	54	47	60	45

Required

Prepare a grouped frequency distribution classifying the commission earnings into categories of $5 commencing with '$25 and under $30'

We are told what classes to use, so the first step is to identify the lowest and highest values in the data. The lowest value is $25 (in the first row) and the highest value is $73 (in the fourth row). This means that the class intervals must go up to '$70 and under $75'.

We can now set out the classes in a column, and then count the number of items in each class using tally marks.

Class interval	Tally marks	Total
$25 and less than $30	///	3
$30 and less than $35	////	4
$35 and less than $40	### ###	10
$40 and less than $45	### ### ###	15
$45 and less than $50	### ### ### ///	18
$50 and less than $55	### ### ### ###	20
$55 and less than $60	### ### ///	13
$60 and less than $65	### ///	8
$65 and less than $70	### /	6
$70 and less than $75	///	3
	Total	100

3.7 Cumulative frequency distributions

A cumulative frequency distribution (or cumulative frequency table) can be used to show the total number of times that a value above or below a certain amount occurs.

There are two possible cumulative frequency distributions for the grouped frequency distribution in Paragraph 3.4.

	Cumulative frequency		Cumulative frequency
$\geq$ 700	20	< 800	1
$\geq$ 800	19	< 900	2
$\geq$ 900	18	<1,000	4
$\geq$1,000	16	<1,100	9
$\geq$1,100	11	<1,200	16
$\geq$1,200	4	<1,300	20

(a) The symbol > means 'greater than' and $\geq$ means 'greater than or equal to'. The symbol < means 'less than' and $\leq$ means 'less than or equal to'. These symbols provide a convenient method of stating classes.

(b) The first cumulative frequency distribution shows that of the total of 20 employees, 19 produced 800 units or more, 18 produced 900 units or more, 16 produced 1,000 units or more and so on.

(c) The second cumulative frequency distribution shows that, of the total of 20 employees, one produced under 800 units, two produced under 900 units, four produced under 1,000 units and so on.

3.8 Frequency distributions – a summary

Students often find frequency distributions tricky. The following summary might help to clarify the different types of frequency distribution we have covered in this section.

(a) **Frequency distribution**. Individual data items are arranged in a table showing the frequency each **individual** data item occurs.

(b) **Grouped frequency distribution – discrete variables**. Data items which are discrete variables, (eg the number of marks obtained in an examination) are divided into classes of say 10 marks. The numbers of students (frequencies) scoring marks within each band are then grouped into a single frequency.

(c) **Grouped frequency distribution – continuous variables**. These are similar to the grouped frequency distributions for discrete variables (above.) However, as they are concerned with **continuous** variables note the following points.

   (i) There is an open-ended class at the end of the range.

   (ii) Class intervals must be carefully considered so that they capture all of the data once (and only once!).

(d) **Cumulative frequency distribution**. These distributions are used to show the number of times that a value above or below a certain amount occurs. Cumulative frequencies are obtained by adding the individual frequencies together.

4 Histograms

FAST FORWARD

A **frequency distribution** can be represented pictorially by means of a **histogram**. The number of observations in a class is represented by the **area** covered by the bar, rather than by its height.

4.1 Histograms of frequency distributions with equal class intervals

If all the class intervals are the same, as in the frequency distribution in Paragraph 3.4, **the bars of the histogram all have the same width and the heights will be proportional to the frequencies.** The histogram looks almost identical to a bar chart except that **the bars are joined together.** Because the bars are joined together, when presenting discrete data the data must be treated as continuous so that there are no gaps between class intervals. For example, for a cricketer's scores in various games the classes would have to be ≥ 0 but < 10, ≥ 10 but < 20 and so on, instead of 0–9, 10–19 and so on.

A histogram of the distribution in Paragraph 3.4 would be drawn as follows.

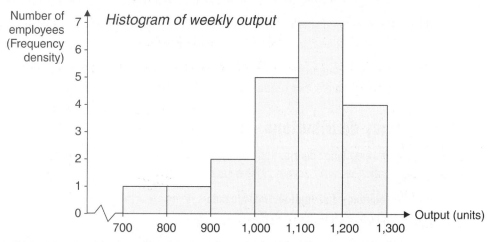

Note that the discrete data have been treated as continuous, the intervals being changed to >700 but ≤ 800, >800 but ≤ 900 and so on.

4.2 Histograms of frequency distributions with unequal class intervals

If a distribution has **unequal class intervals,** the **heights** of the bars have to be **adjusted** for the fact that the bars do not have the same width.

4.2.1 Example: A histogram with unequal class intervals

The weekly wages of employees of Salt Lake Company are as follows.

Wages per employee	Number of employees
Up to and including $60	4
> $60 ≤ $80	6
> $80 ≤ $90	6
> $90 ≤ $120	6
More than $120	3

The class intervals for wages per employee are not all the same, and range from $10 to $30.

Solution

A histogram is drawn as follows.

(a) **The width of each bar on the chart must be proportionate to the corresponding class interval**. In other words, the bar representing wages of > $60 ≤ $80, a range of $20, will be twice as wide as the bar representing wages of > $80 ≤ $90, a range of only $10.

(b) **A standard width of bar must be selected**. This should be the size of class interval which occurs most frequently. In our example, class intervals $10, $20 and $30 each occur once. An interval of $20 will be selected as the standard width.

(c) **Open-ended classes must be closed off**. It is usual for the width of such classes to be the same as that of the adjoining class. In this example, the class 'up to and including $60' will become >$40 ≤ $60 and the class 'more than $120' will become >$120 ≤ $150.

(d) **Each frequency is then multiplied by (standard class width ÷ actual class width)** to obtain the height of the bar in the histogram.

(e) The height of bars no longer corresponds to **frequency** but rather to **frequency density** and hence the vertical axis should be labelled **frequency density**.

(f) Note that the data is considered to be **continuous** since the gap between, for example, $79.99 and $80.00 is very, very small.

Class interval	Size of interval	Frequency	Adjustment	Height of bar
> $40 ≤ $60	20	4	× 20/20	4
> $60 ≤ $80	20	6	× 20/20	6
> $80 ≤ $90	10	6	× 20/10	12
> $90 ≤ $120	30	6	× 20/30	4
> $120 ≤ $150	30	3	× 20/30	2

(a) The first two bars will be of normal height.

(b) The third bar will be twice as high as the class frequency (6) would suggest, to compensate for the fact that the class interval, $10, is only half the standard size.

(c) The fourth and fifth bars will be two thirds as high as the class frequencies (6 and 3) would suggest, to compensate for the fact that the class interval, $30, is 150% of the standard size.

Histogram of weekly earnings: Salt Lake

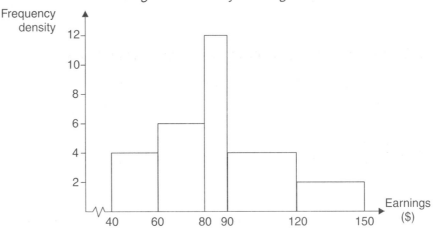

Question

Histogram (1)

In a histogram in which one class interval is one and a half times as wide as the remaining classes, the height to be plotted in relation to the frequency for that class is

A   × 1.5
B   × 1.00
C   × 0.75
D   × 0.67

Answer

If a distribution has unequal class intervals, the heights of the bars have to be adjusted for the fact that the bars do not have the same width. If the width of one bar is one and a half times the standard width, we must divide the frequency by one and a half, ie multiply by 0.67 (1/1.5 = 2/3 = 0.67).

The correct answer is D.

Question

Histogram (2)

The following grouped frequency distribution shows the performances of individual sales staff in one month.

Sales	Number of sales staff
Up to $10,000	1
> $10,000 ≤ $12,000	10
> $12,000 ≤ $14,000	12
> $14,000 ≤ $18,000	8
> $18,000 ≤ $22,000	4
> $22,000	1

Required

Draw a histogram from this information

Answer

This is a grouped frequency distribution for continuous variables.

Before drawing the histogram, we must decide on the following.

(a)   A **standard class width**: $2,000 will be chosen.

(b)   An **open-ended class width**. In this example, the open-ended class width will therefore be $2,000 for class 'up to $10,000' and $4,000 for the class '> $22,000'.

Class interval	Size of interval $	Frequency	Adjustment	Height of bar
Up to $10,000	2,000	1	× 2/2	1
> $10,000 ≤ $12,000	2,000	10	× 2/2	10
> $12,000 ≤ $14,000	2,000	12	× 2/2	12
> $14,000 ≤ $18,000	4,000	8	× 2/4	4
> $18,000 ≤ $22,000	4,000	4	× 2/4	2
> $22,000	4,000	1	× 2/4	½

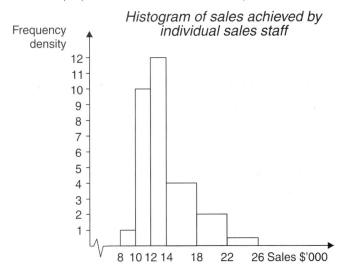

Histogram of sales achieved by individual sales staff

4.3 Frequency polygons

Frequency polygons and **frequency curves** are perhaps more accurate methods of data presentation than the standard histogram.

A histogram is not a particularly accurate method of presenting a frequency distribution because, in grouping frequencies together in a class interval, it is assumed that these frequencies occur evenly throughout the class interval, which is unlikely. To overcome this criticism, we can convert a histogram into a **frequency polygon**, which is drawn on the assumption that, within each class interval, the frequency of occurrence of data items is not evenly spread. There will be more values at the end of each class interval nearer the histogram's peak (if any), and so the flat top on a histogram bar should be converted into a rising or falling line.

4.3.1 Drawing a frequency polygon

A frequency polygon is drawn from a histogram, in the following way.

Step 1   Mark the mid-point of the top of each bar in the histogram.

Step 2   Join up all these points with straight lines.

Step 3   The ends of the diagram (the mid-points of the two end bars) should be joined to the base line at the mid-points of the next class intervals outside the range of observed data. These intervals should be taken to be of the same size as the last class intervals for observed data.

4.3.2 Example: A frequency polygon

The following grouped frequency distribution relates to the number of occasions during the past 40 weeks that a particular cost has been a given amount.

Cost $	Number of occasions
> 800 ≤ 1,000	4
> 1,000 ≤ 1,200	10
> 1,200 ≤ 1,400	12
> 1,400 ≤ 1,600	10
> 1,600 ≤ 1,800	4
	40

Required

Prepare a frequency polygon.

Solution

A histogram is first drawn, in the way described earlier. All classes are of the same width.

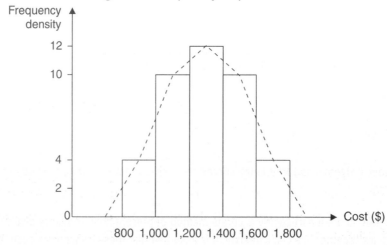

Histogram of frequency of particular costs

The mid-points of the class intervals outside the range of observed data are 700 and 1,900.

4.4 Frequency curves

Because a frequency polygon has straight lines between points, it too can be seen as an inaccurate way of presenting data. One method of obtaining greater accuracy would be to make the class intervals smaller. If the class intervals of a distribution were made small enough the frequency polygon would become very smooth. It would become a curve.

5 Ogives

Just as a grouped frequency distribution can be graphed as a histogram, a cumulative frequency distribution can be graphed as an ogive.

FAST FORWARD

An **ogive** shows the cumulative number of items with a value less than or equal to, or alternatively greater than or equal to, a certain amount.

5.1 Example: Ogives

Consider the following frequency distribution.

Number of faulty units rejected on inspection	Frequency	Cumulative frequency
$> 0, \leq 1$	5	5
$> 1, \leq 2$	5	10
$> 2, \leq 3$	3	13
$> 3, \leq 4$	1	14
	14	

An ogive would be drawn as follows.

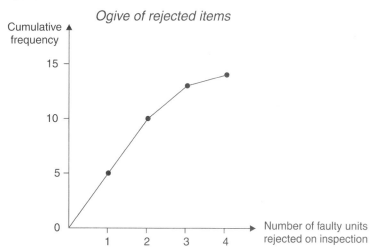

Ogive of rejected items

The ogive is drawn by plotting the cumulative frequencies on the graph, and joining them with straight lines. Although many ogives are more accurately curved lines, you can use straight lines to make them easier to draw. **An ogive drawn with straight lines may be referred to as a cumulative frequency polygon (or cumulative frequency diagram) whereas one drawn as a curve may be referred to as a cumulative frequency curve.**

For grouped frequency distributions, where we work up through values of the variable, the cumulative frequencies are plotted against the **upper limits** of the classes. For example, for the class 'over 2, up to and including 3', the cumulative frequency should be plotted against 3.

Question

A grouped frequency distribution for the volume of output produced at a factory over a period of 40 weeks is as follows.

Output (units)	Number of times output achieved
> 0 ≤ 200	4
> 200 ≤ 400	8
> 400 ≤ 600	12
> 600 ≤ 800	10
> 800 ≤ 1,000	6
	40

Required

Draw an appropriate ogive, and estimate the number of weeks in which output was 550 units or less.

Answer

Upper limit of interval	Frequency	Cumulative frequency
200	4	4
400	8	12
600	12	24
800	10	34
1,000	6	40

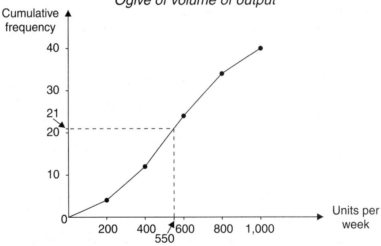

Ogive of volume of output

The dotted lines indicate that output of up to 550 units was achieved in 21 out of the 40 weeks.

5.2 Downward-sloping ogives

We can also draw ogives to show the cumulative number of items with values greater than or equal to some given value.

5.3 Example: Downward-sloping ogives

Output at a factory over a period of 80 weeks is shown by the following frequency distribution.

Output per week Units	Number of times output achieved
> 0 ≤ 100	10
> 100 ≤ 200	20
> 200 ≤ 300	25
> 300 ≤ 400	15
> 400 ≤ 500	10
	80

Required

Present this information in the form of a downward-sloping ogive.

Solution

If we want to draw an ogive to show the number of weeks in which output **exceeded** a certain value, the cumulative total should begin at 80 and drop to 0. In drawing an ogive when we work down through values of the variable, the **descending cumulative frequency** should be plotted against the **lower limit** of each class interval.

Lower limit of interval	Frequency	Cumulative ('more than') frequency
0	10	80
100	20	70
200	25	50
300	15	25
400	10	10
500	0	0

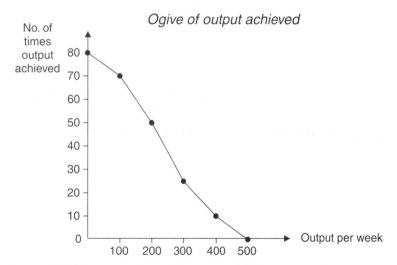

Ogive of output achieved

Make sure that you understand what this curve shows. For example, 350 on the x axis corresponds with about 18 on the y axis. This means that output of 350 units or more was achieved 18 times out of the 80 weeks.

6 Scatter diagrams

Scatter diagrams are graphs which are used to exhibit data, (rather than equations) in order to compare the way in which two variables vary with each other.

6.1 Constructing a scatter diagram

The x axis of a scatter diagram is used to represent the independent variable and the y axis represents the dependent variable.

To construct a scatter diagram or scattergraph, we must have several pairs of data, with each pair showing the value of one variable and the corresponding value of the other variable. Each pair is plotted on a graph. The resulting graph will show a number of pairs, scattered over the graph. The scattered points might or might not appear to follow a trend.

6.2 Example: Scatter diagram

The output at a factory each week for the last ten weeks, and the cost of that output, were as follows.

Week	1	2	3	4	5	6	7	8	9	10
Output (units)	10	12	10	8	9	11	7	12	9	14
Cost ($)	42	44	38	34	38	43	30	47	37	50

Required

Plot the data given on a scatter diagram.

Solution

The data could be shown on a scatter diagram as follows.

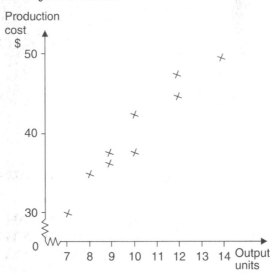

(a) The cost depends on the volume of output: volume is the independent variable and is shown on the x axis.

(b) You will notice from the graph that the plotted data, although scattered, lie approximately on a rising trend line, with higher total costs at higher output volumes. (The lower part of the axes have been omitted, so as not to waste space. The break in the axes is indicated by the jagged lines.)

6.3 The trend line

For the most part, scatter diagrams are used to try to identify **trend lines**.

If a trend can be seen in a scatter diagram, the next step is to try to draw a trend line.

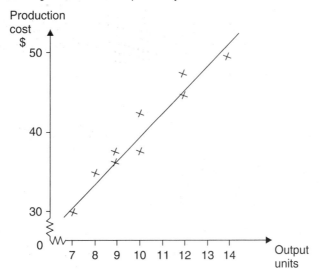

6.3.1 Using trend lines to make predictions

(a) In the previous example, we have drawn a trend line from the scatter diagram of output units and production cost. This trend line might turn out to be, say, $y = 10 + 3x$. We could then use this trend line to establish what we think costs ought to be, approximately, if output were, say, 10 units or 15 units in any week. (These 'expected' costs could subsequently be compared with the actual costs, so that managers could judge whether actual costs were higher or lower than they ought to be.)

(b) If a scatter diagram is used to record sales over time, we could draw a trend line, and use this to forecast sales for next year.

6.3.2 Adding trend lines to scatter diagrams

The trend line could be a straight line, or a curved line. The simplest technique for drawing a trend line is to make a visual judgement about what the closest-fitting trend line seems to be, the 'line of best fit'.

Here is another example of a scatter diagram with a trend line added.

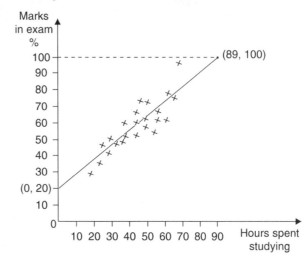

The equation of a straight line is given by y = a + bx, where a is the intercept on the y axis and b is the gradient.

The line passes through the point x = 0, y = 20, so a = 20. The line also passes through x = 89, y = 100, so:

$$100 = 20 + (b \times 89)$$

$$b = \frac{(100 - 20)}{89}$$

$$= 0.9.$$

The line is y = 20 + 0.9x.

Question

The quantities of widgets produced by WDG Ltd during the year ended 31 October 20X9 and the related costs were as follows.

Month	Production Thousands	Factory cost $'000
20X8		
November	7	45
December	10	59
20X9		
January	13	75
February	14	80
March	11	65
April	7	46
May	5	35
June	4	30
July	3	25
August	2	20
September	1	15
October	5	35

You may assume that the value of money remained stable throughout the year.

Required

(a)   Draw a scatter diagram related to the data provided above, and plot on it the line of best fit.

(b)   Now answer the following questions.

(i)   What would you expect the factory cost to have been if 12,000 widgets had been produced in a particular month?

(ii)   What is your estimate of WDG's monthly fixed cost?

Answer

Your answers to parts (b)(i) and (ii) may have been slightly different from those given here, but they should not have been very different, because the data points lay very nearly along a straight line.

(a)   WDG Ltd – Scatter diagram of production and factory costs, November 20X8-October 20X9

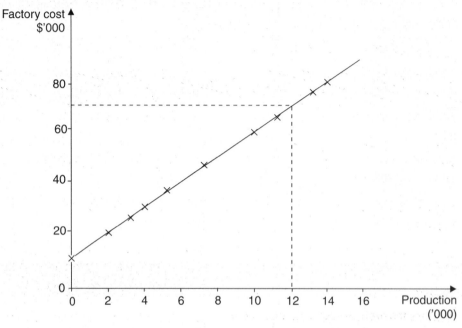

(b)   (i)   The estimated factory cost for a production of 12,000 widgets is $70,000.

   (ii)   The monthly fixed costs are indicated by the point where the line of best fit meets the vertical axis (costs at zero production). The fixed costs are estimated as $10,000 a month.

Chapter Roundup

- **Tables** are a simple way of presenting information about two variables.

- **Charts** often convey the meaning or significance of data more clearly than would a table.

- There are three main **types of bar chart**: **simple**, **component** (including **percentage component**) and **multiple** (or **compound**).

- **Frequency distributions** are used if values of particular variables occur more than once.

- A **frequency distribution** can be represented pictorially by means of a **histogram**. The number of observations in a class is represented by the **area** covered by the bar, rather than by its height.

- **Frequency polygons** and **frequency curves** are perhaps more accurate methods of data presentation than the standard histogram.

- An **ogive** shows the cumulative number of items with a value less than or equal to, or alternatively greater than or equal to, a certain amount.

- **Scatter diagrams** are graphs which are used to exhibit data, (rather than equations) in order to compare the way in which two variables vary with each other.

Quick Quiz

1   What are the main guidelines for tabulation?

2   What are the two purposes served by simple bar charts?

3   When selecting a standard width of bar when calculating the heights of the bars in a histogram you would select the size of the class interval which occurs most frequently.

   True   ☐

   False   ☐

4   The steps involved in drawing a frequency polygon from a histogram are

   Step 1 ....

   Step 2 ....

   Step 3 ....

5   A grouped frequency distribution can be drawn as a(n) histogram/ogive, whereas a cumulative frequency distribution can be graphed as a(n) ogive/histogram.

6   A scatter diagram has an x axis and a y axis which represent dependent and independent variables as follows.

   x axis ⎤   ⎡ independent variable
           ⎥   ?   ⎢
   y axis ⎦   ⎣ dependent variable

7   How do downward-sloping ogives differ from upward-sloping ogives?

Answers to Quick Quiz

1   •   The table should have a clear title
       •   All columns should be clearly labelled
       •   Clear sub-totals should be included
       •   Columns should be totalled showing a total figure
       •   Tables should be spaced out so information presented may be read easily

2   •   The magnitude of each item is shown
       •   The lengths of bars on the chart allow magnitudes to be compared

3   True

4   **Step 1**   Mark mid-points of each bar at the top

       Step 2   Join all these points with straight lines

       Step 3   Estimate the mid-points of the class intervals outside the range of observed data and join up with the midpoints of the two end bars

5   A grouped frequency distribution can be drawn as a **histogram**, whereas a cumulative frequency distribution can be graphed as an **ogive**.

6   x axis   ⟶   independent variable
       y axis   ⟶   dependent variable

7   **Upward-sloping ogive**

       •   Work up through grouped frequency distributions

       •   Plot ascending cumulative frequency distributions against upper limits of each class interval

    Downward-sloping ogive

       •   Work down through grouped frequency distributions

       •   Plot descending cumulative frequency distributions against lower limits of each class interval

Now try the questions below from the Exam Question Bank

Question numbers	Pages
29-35	336-338

PROFESSIONAL EDUCATION

6

Averages

Introduction

In Chapter 5 we saw how data can be summarised and presented in tabular, chart and graphical formats. Sometimes you might need more information than that provided by diagrammatic representations of data. In such circumstances you may need to apply some sort of numerical analysis, for example you might wish to calculate a **measure of centrality** and a **measure of dispersion**. In Chapter 7 we will look at measures of dispersion, in this chapter measures of centrality, or averages.

An **average** is a representative figure that is used to give some impression of the size of all the items in the population. There are three main types of average.

- Arithmetic mean
- Mode
- Median

We will be looking at each of these averages in turn, their calculation, advantages and disadvantages. In the next chapter we will move on to the second type of numerical measure, measures of dispersion.

Topic list	Syllabus references
1 The arithmetic mean	C, (iv), (4)
2 The mode	C, (iv), (4)
3 The median	C, (iv), (4)

1 The arithmetic mean

1.1 Arithmetic mean of ungrouped data

The **arithmetic mean** is the best known type of average and is widely understood. It is used for further statistical analysis.

$$\text{Arithmetic mean of ungrouped data} = \frac{\text{Sum of values of items}}{\text{Number of items}}$$

The arithmetic mean of a variable x is shown as $\bar{x}$ ('x bar').

1.1.1 Example: The arithmetic mean

The demand for a product on each of 20 days was as follows (in units).

3   12   7   17   3   14   9   6   11   10   1   4   19   7   15   6   9   12   12   8

The arithmetic mean of daily demand is $\bar{x}$.

$$\bar{x} = \frac{\text{Sum of demand}}{\text{Number of days}} = \frac{185}{20} = 9.25 \text{ units}$$

In this example, demand on any one day is never actually 9.25 units. The arithmetic mean is merely an **average representation** of demand on each of the 20 days.

1.2 Arithmetic mean of data in a frequency distribution

It is more likely in an assessment that you will be asked to calculate the arithmetic mean of a **frequency distribution**. In our previous example, the frequency distribution would be shown as follows.

Daily demand	Frequency	Demand × frequency
x	f	fx
1	1	1
3	2	6
4	1	4
6	2	12
7	2	14
8	1	8
9	2	18
10	1	10
11	1	11
12	3	36
14	1	14
15	1	15
17	1	17
19	1	19
	20	185

$$\bar{x} = \frac{185}{20} = 9.25$$

1.3 Sigma, Σ

Σ means 'the sum of' and is used as shorthand to mean 'the sum of a set of values'.

In the previous example:

(a) Σf would mean the sum of all the frequencies, which is 20

(b) Σfx would mean the sum of all the values of 'frequency multiplied by daily demand', that is, all 14 values of fx, so $\Sigma fx = 185$

1.4 Arithmetic mean of grouped data in class intervals

FAST FORWARD

The **arithmetic mean of grouped data**, $\bar{x} = \dfrac{\Sigma fx}{n}$ or $\dfrac{\Sigma fx}{\Sigma f}$ where n is the number of values recorded, or the number of items measured.

This formula will be given to you in your exam.

You might also be asked to calculate (or at least approximate) the arithmetic mean of a frequency distribution, where the frequencies are shown in class intervals.

1.4.1 Example: The arithmetic mean of grouped data

Using the example in Paragraph 1.2, the frequency distribution might have been shown as follows.

Daily demand	Frequency
$> 0 \leq 5$	4
$> 5 \leq 10$	8
$>10 \leq 15$	6
$>15 \leq 20$	2
	20

There is, of course, an extra difficulty with finding the average now; as the data have been collected into classes, a **certain amount of detail has been lost** and the values of the variables to be used in the calculation of the mean are **not clearly specified**.

1.4.2 The mid-point of class intervals

To calculate the arithmetic mean of grouped data we therefore need to decide on **a value which best represents all of the values in a particular class interval**. This value is known as the **mid-point**.

The **mid-point** of each class interval is conventionally taken, on the assumption that the frequencies occur **evenly** over the class interval range. In the example above, the variable is **discrete**, so the first class includes 1, 2, 3, 4 and 5, giving a mid-point of 3. With a **continuous** variable, the mid-points would have been 2.5, 7.5 and so on. Once the value of x has been decided, the mean is calculated using the formula for the arithmetic mean of grouped data.

Daily demand	Mid point x	Frequency f	fx
> 0 ≤ 5	3	4	12
> 5 ≤ 10	8	8	64
>10 ≤ 15	13	6	78
>15 ≤ 20	18	2	36
		$\sum f = 20$	$\sum fx = 190$

Arithmetic mean $\bar{x} = \dfrac{\sum fx}{\sum f} = \dfrac{190}{20} = 9.5$ units

Because the assumption that frequencies occur evenly within each class interval is not quite correct in this example, our approximate mean of 9.5 is not exactly correct, and is in error by 0.25 (9.5 – 9.25). **As the frequencies become larger, the size of this approximating error should become smaller.**

1.5 Example: The arithmetic mean of combined data

Suppose that the mean age of a group of five people is 27 and the mean age of another group of eight people is 32. How would we find the mean age of the whole group of 13 people?

Arithmetic mean $= \dfrac{\text{Sum of values of items}}{\text{Number of items}}$

The sum of the ages in the first group is $5 \times 27 = 135$

The sum of the ages in the second group is $8 \times 32 = 256$

The sum of all 13 ages is $135 + 256 = 391$

The mean age is therefore $\dfrac{391}{13} = 30.08$ years.

Question   **Mean**

The mean weight of 10 units at 5 kgs, 10 units at 7 kgs and 20 units at X kgs is 8 kgs.

The value of X is ☐

Answer

The value of X is | 10 |

Workings

$$\text{Mean} = \frac{\text{Sum of values of items}}{\text{Number of items}}$$

Sum of first 10 units = 5 × 10 = 50 kgs

Sum of second 10 units = 7 × 10 = 70 kgs

Sum of third 20 units = 20 × X = 20X

Sum of all 40 units = 50 + 70 + 20X = 120 + 20X

$$\therefore \text{Arithmetic mean} \quad = \quad 8 = \frac{120 + 20X}{40}$$

$$\therefore 8 \times 40 \quad = \quad 120 + 20X$$

$$320 \quad = \quad 120 + 20X \text{ (subtract 120 from both sides)}$$

$$320 - 120 \quad = \quad 20X$$

$$200 \quad = \quad 20X$$

$$10 \quad = \quad X \text{ (divide both sides by 20)}$$

1.6 The advantages and disadvantages of the arithmetic mean

Advantages of the arithmetic mean

- It is easy to calculate
- It is widely understood
- It is representative of the whole set of data
- It is supported by mathematical theory and is suited to further statistical analysis

Disadvantages of the arithmetic mean

- **Its value may not correspond to any actual value**. For example, the 'average' family might have 2.3 children, but no family has exactly 2.3 children.

- **An arithmetic mean might be distorted by extremely high or low values**. For example, the mean of 3, 4, 4 and 6 is 4.25, but the mean of 3, 4, 4, 6 and 15 is 6.4. The high value, 15, distorts the average and in some circumstances the mean would be a misleading and inappropriate figure.

Question

For the week ended 15 November, the wages earned by the 69 operators employed in the machine shop of Mermaid Ltd were as follows.

Wages	Number of operatives
under $60	3
$60 and under $70	11
$70 and under $80	16
$80 and under $90	15
$90 and under $100	10
$100 and under $110	8
Over $110	6
	69

Required

Calculate the arithmetic mean wage of the machine operators of Mermaid Ltd for the week ended 15 November.

Answer

The mid point of the range 'under $60' is assumed to be $55 and that of the range over $110 to be $115, since all other class intervals are $10. This is obviously an approximation which might result in a loss of accuracy, but there is no better alternative assumption to use. Because wages can vary in steps of 1c, they are virtually a continuous variable and hence the mid-points of the classes are halfway between their end points.

Mid-point of class x $	Frequency f	fx
55	3	165
65	11	715
75	16	1,200
85	15	1,275
95	10	950
105	8	840
115	6	690
	69	5,835

$$\text{Arithmetic mean} = \frac{\sum fx}{\sum f} = \frac{5,835}{69} = \$84.57$$

2 The mode

2.1 The modal value

FAST FORWARD

The **mode** or **modal value** is an average which means 'the most frequently occurring value'.

2.2 Example: The mode

The daily demand for stock in a ten day period is as follows.

Demand Units	Number of days
6	3
7	6
8	1
	10

The mode is 7 units, because it is the value which occurs most frequently.

2.3 The mode of a grouped frequency distribution

FAST FORWARD

The **mode of a grouped frequency distribution** can be calculated from a histogram.

2.4 Example: Finding the mode from a histogram

Consider the following grouped frequency distribution

	Class interval			Frequency
0	and less than	10		0
10	and less than	20		50
20	and less than	30		150
30	and less than	40		100

(a) The modal class (the one with the highest frequency) is '20 and less than 30'. But how can we find a single value to represent the mode?

(b) What we need to do is draw a histogram of the frequency distribution.

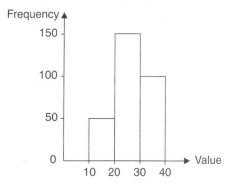

The modal class is always the class with the tallest bar. This may not be the class with the highest frequency if the classes do not all have the same width.

(c)   We can estimate the mode graphically as follows.

Step 1   Join with a straight line the top left hand corner of the bar for the modal class and the top left hand corner of the next bar to the right.

Step 2   Join with a straight line the top right hand corner of the bar for the modal class and the top right hand corner of the next bar to the left.

(d)   Where these two lines intersect, we find the **estimated modal value**. In this example it is approximately 26.7.

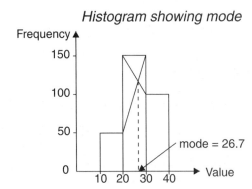

Histogram showing mode

(e)   We are assuming that the frequencies occur evenly within each class interval but this may not always be correct. It is unlikely that the 150 values in the modal class occur evenly. Hence **the mode in a grouped frequency distribution is only an estimate.**

2.5 The advantages and disadvantages of the mode

Advantages of the mode

- It is easy to find
- It is not influenced by a few extreme values
- It can be used for data which are not even numerical (unlike the mean and median)
- It can be the value of an actual item in the distribution

Disadvantages of the mode

- It may be unrepresentative; it takes no account of a high proportion of the data, only representing the most common value

- It does not take every value into account

- There can be two or more modes within a set of data

- If the modal class is only very slightly bigger than another class, just a few more items in this other class could mean a substantially different result, suggesting some instability in the measure

3 The median

3.1 The middle item of a distribution

The median of a set of ungrouped data is found by arranging the items in ascending or descending order of value, and selecting the item in the middle of the range. **A list of items in order of value is called an array**.

FAST FORWARD

The **median** is the value of the middle member of an array. The middle item of an odd number of items is calculated as the $\frac{(n+1)^{th}}{2}$ item.

3.2 Example: The median

(a) The median of the following nine values:

8   6   9   12   15   6   3   20   11

is found by taking the middle item (the fifth one) in the array:

3   6   6   8   9   11   12   15   20

The median is 9.

(b) Consider the following array.

1   2   2   2   3   5   6   7   8   11

The median is 4 because, with an even number of items, we have to take the arithmetic mean of the two middle ones (in this example, (3 + 5)/2 = 4).

Question   **Median (1)**

The following times taken to produce a batch of 100 units of Product X have been noted.

21 mins,	17 mins,	24 mins,	11 mins,	37 mins,	27 mins,
20 mins,	15 mins,	17 mins,	23 mins,	29 mins,	30 mins
24 mins,	18 mins,	17 mins,	21 mins,	24 mins,	20 mins

What is the median time?

Answer

The times can be arranged as follows.

11,   15,   17,   17,   17,   18,   20,   20,   21,   21,   23,   24,   24,
24,   27,   29   30,   37

There are eighteen items which is an even number, therefore the median is the arithmetic mean of the two middle items (ie ninth and tenth items) = 21 mins.

Question

The following scores are observed for the times taken to complete a task, in minutes.

12,   34,   14,   15,   21,   24,   9,   17,   11,   8

What is the median score?

A   14.00
B   14.10
C   14.50
D   14.60

Answer

The first thing to do is to arrange the scores in order of magnitude.

8,   9,   11,   12,   14,   15,   17,   21,   24,   34

There are ten items, and so median is the arithmetic mean of the 5th and 6th items.

$$= \frac{14 + 15}{2} = \frac{29}{2} = 14.50$$

The correct answer is therefore C.

You could have eliminated options B and D straight away. Since there are ten items, and they are all whole numbers, the average of the 5th and 6th items is either going to be a whole number (14.00) or 'something and a half' (14.50).

3.3 Finding the median of an ungrouped frequency distribution

The median of an ungrouped frequency distribution is found in a similar way. Consider the following distribution.

Value x	Frequency f	Cumulative frequency
8	3	3
12	7	10
16	12	22
17	8	30
19	5	35
	35	

The median would be the $(35 + 1)/2 = 18^{th}$ item. The 18th item has a value of 16, as we can see from the cumulative frequencies in the right hand column of the above table.

3.4 Finding the median of a grouped frequency distribution

FAST FORWARD

The median of a grouped frequency distribution can be established from an ogive.

Finding the median of a grouped frequency distribution from an ogive is best explained by means of an example.

BPP
PROFESSIONAL EDUCATION

3.5 Example: The median from an ogive

Construct an ogive of the following frequency distribution and hence establish the median.

Class $	Frequency	Cumulative frequency
$\geq 340, < 370$	17	17
$\geq 370, < 400$	9	26
$\geq 400, < 430$	9	35
$\geq 430, < 460$	3	38
$\geq 460, < 490$	2	40
	40	

Solution

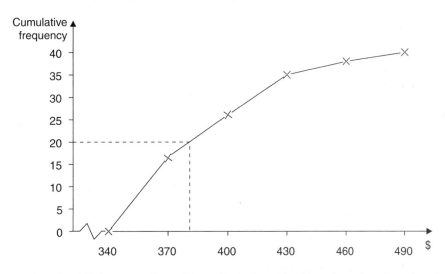

The median is at the $1/2 \times 40 = 20^{th}$ item. Reading off from the horizontal axis on the ogive, the value of the median is approximately $380.

Note that, **because we are assuming that the values are spread evenly within each class, the median calculated is only approximate.**

3.6 The advantages and disadvantages of the median

Advantages of the median

- It is easy to understand
- It is unaffected by extremely high or low values
- It can be the value of an actual item in the distribution

Disadvantages of the median

- It fails to reflect the full range of values
- It is unsuitable for further statistical analysis
- Arranging data into order of size can be tedious

Assessment focus point

If you are asked to find the median of a set of ungrouped data, remember to arrange the items in order of value first and then to count the number of items in the array. If you have an even number of items, the median may not be the value of one of the items in the data set. The median of an even number of items is found by calculating the arithmetic mean of the two middle items.

Important!

- The arithmetic mean, mode and median of a grouped frequency distribution can only be estimated approximately

- Each type of average has a number of advantages and disadvantages that you need to be aware of

Chapter Roundup

- The **arithmetic mean** is the best known type of average and is widely understood. It is used for further statistical analysis.

- The **arithmetic mean of ungrouped data** = sum of items ÷ number of items.

- The **arithmetic mean of grouped data**, $\bar{x} = \dfrac{\sum fx}{n}$ or $\dfrac{\sum fx}{\sum f}$ where n is the number of values recorded, or the number of items measured.

- The **mode or modal value** is an average which means 'the most frequently occurring value'.

- The **mode of a grouped frequency distribution** can be calculated from a histogram.

- The **median** is the value of the middle member of an array. The middle item of an odd number of items is calculated as the $\dfrac{(n+1)^{th}}{2}$ item.

- The **median of a grouped frequency distribution** can be established from an ogive.

Quick Quiz

1   Insert the formulae in the box below into the correct position.

(a)   The arithmetic mean of ungrouped data =

(b)   The arithmetic mean of grouped data =   or

$$\bullet \quad \frac{\sum x}{n}$$

$$\bullet \quad \frac{\sum fx}{n}$$

$$\bullet \quad \frac{\sum fx}{\sum f}$$

2   What is the name given to the average which means 'the most frequently occurring value'?

| Arithmetic mean |
| Median |
| Mode |

3   List four advantages of the arithmetic mean.

4   Calculate the mid-points for both discrete and continuous variables in the table below.

Class interval	Mid-point (Discrete data)	Mid-point (Continuous data)
25 < 30		
30 < 35		
35 < 40		
40 < 45		
45 < 50		
50 < 55		
55 < 60		
60 < 65		

5   (a)   The mode of a grouped frequency distribution can be found from a(n) histogram/ogive.
    (b)   The median of a grouped frequency distribution can be found from a(n) histogram/ogive.

6   List four advantages of the mode.

7   List three disadvantages of the median.

Answers to Quick Quiz

1 (a) $\dfrac{\sum x}{n}$

   (b) $\dfrac{\sum fx}{n}$ or $\dfrac{\sum fx}{\sum f}$

2 Mode

3 • It is easy to calculate
   • It is widely understood
   • It is representative of the whole set of data
   • It is suited to further statistical analysis

4

Class interval	Mid-point (Discrete data)	Mid-point (Continuous data)
25 < 30	27	27.5
30 < 35	32	32.5
35 < 40	37	37.5
40 < 45	42	42.5
45 < 50	47	47.5
50 < 55	52	52.5
55 < 60	57	57.5
60 < 65	62	62.5

5 (a) Histogram
   (b) Ogive

6 • It is easy to find
   • It is not influenced by a few extreme values
   • It can be used for non-numerical data (unlike the mean and the median)
   • It can be the value of an actual item in the distribution

7 • It fails to reflect the full range of values (unrepresentative)
   • It is unsuitable for further statistical analysis
   • Arranging data into order size can be tedious

Now try the questions below from the Exam Question Bank

Question numbers	Pages
36-40	338-339

7

Dispersion

Introduction

In Chapter 6 we introduced the first type of statistic that can be used to describe certain aspects of a set of data – **averages**. Averages are a method of determining the '**location**' or **central point** of a distribution, but they give no information about the **dispersion** of values in the distribution.

Measures of dispersion give some idea of the **spread of a variable about its average**. The main measures are as follows.

- The range
- The semi-interquartile range
- The standard deviation
- The variance
- The coefficient of variation

Topic list	Syllabus references
1 The range	C, (iv), (4)
2 Quartiles and the semi-interquartile range	C, (iv), (4)
3 The mean deviation	C, (iv), (4)
4 The variance and the standard deviation	C, (iv), (4)
5 The coefficient of variation	C, (iv), (4)
6 Skewness	C, (iv), (4)

1 The range

The **range** is the difference between the highest and lowest observations.

1.1 Main properties of the range as a measure of spread

- It is easy to find and to understand
- It is easily affected by one or two extreme values
- It gives no indication of spread between the extremes
- It is not suitable for further statistical analysis

Question

Mean and range

Calculate the mean and the range of the following set of data.

4   8   7   3   5   16   24   5

Mean	Range

Answer

Mean	Range
9	21

Workings

Mean, $\bar{x} = \dfrac{72}{8} = 9$

Range = 24 − 3 = 21.

2 Quartiles and the semi-interquartile range

2.1 Quartiles

The **quartiles** and the **median** divide the population into four groups of equal size.

Key term

Quartiles are one means of identifying the range within which most of the values in the population occur.

- The **lower quartile** (Q_1) is the value below which 25% of the population fall
- The **upper quartile** (Q_3) is the value above which 25% of the population fall
- The **median** (Q_2) is the value of the middle member of an array

2.1.1 Example: Quartiles

If we had 11 data items:

- $Q_1 = 11 \times 1/4 = 2.75 = 3^{rd}$ item
- $Q_3 = 11 \times 3/4 = 8.25 = 9^{th}$ item
- $Q_2 = 11 \times 1/2 = 5.5 = 6^{th}$ item

2.2 The semi-interquartile range

FAST FORWARD

The **semi-interquartile range** is half the difference between the upper and lower quartiles.

The lower and upper quartiles can be used to calculate a measure of spread called the **semi-interquartile range.**

Key term

The **semi-interquartile range** is half the difference between the lower and upper quartiles and is sometimes called the quartile deviation, $\dfrac{(Q_3 - Q_1)}{2}$.

For example, if the lower and upper quartiles of a frequency distribution were 6 and 11, the semi-interquartile range of the distribution would be $(11 - 6)/2 = 2.5$ units. This shows that the average distance of a quartile from the median is 2.5. The smaller the quartile deviation, the less dispersed is the distribution.

As with the range, the quartile deviation may be misleading as a measure of spread. If the majority of the data are towards the lower end of the range then the third quartile will be considerably further above the median than the first quartile is below it, and when the two distances from the median are averaged the difference is disguised. Therefore it is often better to quote the actual values of the two quartiles, rather than the quartile deviation.

2.3 The inter-quartile range

FAST FORWARD

The **inter-quartile range** is the difference between the values of the upper and lower quartiles ($Q_3 - Q_1$) and hence shows the range of values of the middle half of the population.

2.4 Example: Using ogives to find the semi-interquartile range

Construct an ogive of the following frequency distribution and hence establish the semi-interquartile range.

Class $	Frequency	Cumulative frequency
≥ 340, < 370	17	17
≥ 370, < 400	9	26
≥ 400, < 430	9	35
≥ 430, < 460	3	38
≥ 460, < 490	2	40
	40	

Solution

Establish which items are Q_1 and Q_3 (the lower and upper quartiles respectively).

Upper quartile (Q_3) = $3/4 \times 40 = 30^{th}$ value

Lower quartile (Q_1) = $3/4 \times 40 = 10^{th}$ value

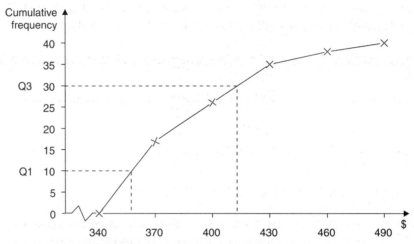

Reading off the values from the ogive, approximate values are as follows.

Q_3 (upper quartile) = $412

Q_1 (lower quartile) = $358

Semi-interquartile range $= \dfrac{Q_3 - Q_1}{2}$

$$= \dfrac{\$(412 - 358)}{2}$$

$$= \dfrac{\$54}{2}$$

$$= \$27$$

Assessment focus point

> Remember that the median is equal to Q_2 (the point above which, and below which, 50% of the population fall). In the example in Paragraph 2.4 the median would be the $40/2 = 20^{th}$ item which could be found from reading off the ogive (approximately 385).

3 The mean deviation

3.1 Measuring dispersion

Because it only uses the middle 50% of the population, the inter-quartile range is a useful measure of dispersion if there are **extreme values** in the distribution. If there are no extreme values which could potentially distort a measure of dispersion, however, it seems unreasonable to exclude 50% of the data. The mean deviation (the topic of this section), and the standard deviation (the topic of Section 4) are often more useful measures.

FAST FORWARD

The **mean deviation** is a measure of the average amount by which the values in a distribution differ from the arithmetic mean.

Formula to learn

$$\text{Mean deviation} = \frac{\sum f\,|x - \bar{x}|}{n}$$

3.2 Explaining the mean deviation formula

(a) $|x - \bar{x}|$ is the difference between each value (x) in the distribution and the arithmetic mean $\bar{x}$ of the distribution. When calculating the mean deviation for grouped data the deviations should be measured to the midpoint of each class: that is, x is the midpoint of the class interval. The vertical bars mean that all differences are taken as positive since the total of all of the differences, if this is not done, will always equal zero. Thus if x = 3 and $\bar{x}$ = 5, then $x - \bar{x}$ = –2 but $|x - \bar{x}|$ = 2.

(b) $f\,|x - \bar{x}|$ is the value in (a) above, multiplied by the frequency for the class.

(c) $\sum f\,|x - \bar{x}|$ is the sum of the results of all the calculations in (b) above.

(d)   n (which equals $\sum f$) is the number of items in the distribution.

3.3 Example: The mean deviation

The hours of overtime worked in a particular quarter by the 60 employees of ABC Ltd are as follows.

Hours		Frequency
More than	*Not more than*	
0	10	3
10	20	6
20	30	11
30	40	15
40	50	12
50	60	7
60	70	6
		60

Required

Calculate the mean deviation of the frequency distribution shown above.

Solution

Midpoint

x	f	fx	$\lvert x - \bar{x} \rvert$	$f\lvert x - \bar{x} \rvert$
5	3	15	32	96
15	6	90	22	132
25	11	275	12	132
35	15	525	2	30
45	12	540	8	96
55	7	385	18	126
65	6	390	28	168
$\Sigma f = 60$		$\Sigma fx = 2{,}220$		780

Arithmetic mean $\bar{x} = \dfrac{\Sigma fx}{\Sigma f} = \dfrac{2{,}220}{60} = 37$

Mean deviation $= \dfrac{780}{60} = 13$ hours

Question	Mean deviation

Complete the following table and then calculate the arithmetic mean and the mean deviation of the following frequency distribution (to one decimal place).

Value	Frequency of occurrence
5	4
15	6
25	8
35	20
45	6
55	6
	50

x	f	fx	$\lvert x - \bar{x} \rvert$	$f\lvert x - \bar{x} \rvert$
5				
15				
25				
35				
45				
55				

Arithmetic mean $\bar{x} = \boxed{} = \boxed{}$

Mean deviation $= \boxed{} = \boxed{}$

Answer

x	f	fx	$|x - \bar{x}|$	$f|x - \bar{x}|$
5	4	20	27.2	108.8
15	6	90	17.2	103.2
25	8	200	7.2	57.6
35	20	700	2.8	56.0
45	6	270	12.8	76.8
55	6	330	22.8	136.8
	50	1,610		539.2

Arithmetic mean $\bar{x}$ = $\dfrac{1,610}{50}$ = 32.2

Mean deviation = $\dfrac{539.2}{50}$ = 10.8

3.4 Summary of the mean deviation

(a)   It is a measure of dispersion which shows by how much, on average, each item in the distribution differs in value from the arithmetic mean of the distribution.

(b)   Unlike quartiles, it uses all values in the distribution to measure the dispersion, but it is not greatly affected by a few extreme values because an average is taken.

(c)   It is not, however, suitable for further statistical analysis.

4 The variance and the standard deviation

4.1 The variance

FAST FORWARD

The **variance**, σ^2, is the average of the squared mean deviation for each value in a distribution.

σ is the Greek letter sigma (in lower case). The variance is therefore called 'sigma squared'.

4.2 Calculation of the variance for ungrouped data

Step 1	Difference between value and mean	$x - \bar{x}$
Step 2	Square of the difference	$(x - \bar{x})^2$
Step 3	Sum of the squares of the difference	$\sum(x - \bar{x})^2$
Step 4	Average of the sum (= variance = σ^2)	$\dfrac{\sum(x - \bar{x})^2}{n}$

4.3 Calculation of the variance for grouped data

Step 1	Difference between value and mean	$(x - \bar{x})$
Step 2	Square of the difference	$(x - \bar{x})^2$
Step 3	Sum of the squares of the difference	$\sum f(x - \bar{x})^2$
Step 4	Average of the sum (= variance = σ^2)	$\dfrac{\sum f(x - \bar{x})^2}{\sum f}$

4.4 The standard deviation

The units of the variance are the square of those in the original data because we squared the differences. We therefore need to take the square root to get back to the units of the original data. **The standard deviation = square root of the variance.**

The standard deviation measures the spread of data around the mean. In general, the larger the standard deviation value in relation to the mean, the more dispersed the data.

FAST FORWARD

The **standard deviation**, which is the square root of the variance, is the most important measure of spread used in statistics. Make sure you understand how to calculate the standard deviation of a set of data.

There are a number of formulae which you may use to calculate the standard deviation; use whichever one you feel comfortable with. The standard deviation formulae provided in your assessment are shown as follows.

Assessment formula

$$\text{Standard deviation (for ungrouped data)} = \sqrt{\frac{\sum(x - \bar{x})^2}{n}} = \sqrt{\frac{\sum x^2}{n} - \bar{x}^2}$$

$$\text{Standard deviation (for grouped data)} = \sqrt{\frac{\sum f(x - \bar{x})^2}{\sum f}} = \sqrt{\frac{\sum fx^2}{\sum f} - \left(\frac{\sum fx}{\sum f}\right)^2}$$

The key to these calculations is to set up a table with totals as shown below and then use the totals in the formulae given to you.

4.5 Example: The variance and the standard deviation

Calculate the variance and the standard deviation of the frequency distribution in Paragraph 3.3

Solution

Using the formula provided in the assessment, the calculation is as follows.

Midpoint x	f	fx	x^2	fx^2
5	3	15	25	75
15	6	90	225	1,350
25	11	275	625	6,875
35	15	525	1,225	18,375
45	12	540	2,025	24,300
55	7	385	3,025	21,175
65	6	390	4,225	25,350
	$\Sigma f = 60$	$\Sigma fx = 2{,}220$		$\Sigma fx^2 = 97{,}500$

$$\text{Mean} = \frac{\Sigma fx}{\Sigma f} = \frac{2{,}220}{60} = 37$$

$$\text{Variance} = \frac{\Sigma fx^2}{\Sigma f} - \left(\frac{\Sigma fx}{\Sigma f}\right)^2 = \frac{97{,}500}{60} - (37)^2 = 256 \text{ hours}$$

$$\text{Standard deviation} = \sqrt{256} = 16 \text{ hours}$$

Question

Variance and standard deviation

Calculate the variance and the standard deviation of the frequency distribution in the question entitled: mean deviation.

Answer

x	f	fx	x^2	fx^2
5	4	20	25	100
15	6	90	225	1,350
25	8	200	625	5,000
35	20	700	1,225	24,500
45	6	270	2,025	12,150
55	6	330	3,025	18,150
	$\Sigma f = 50$	$\Sigma fx = 1610$		$\Sigma fx^2 = 61{,}250$

$$\text{Mean} = \frac{1{,}610}{50} = 32.2$$

$$\text{Variance} = \frac{61{,}250}{50} - (32.2)^2 = 188.16$$

$$\text{Standard deviation} = \sqrt{188.16} = 13.72$$

4.6 The main properties of the standard deviation

The standard deviation's main properties are as follows.

(a) It is based on **all the values in the distribution** and so is more comprehensive than dispersion measures based on quartiles, such as the quartile deviation.

(b) It is suitable for **further statistical analysis**.

(c) It is **more difficult to understand** than some other measures of dispersion.

The importance of the standard deviation lies in its suitability for further statistical analysis (we shall consider this further when we study the normal distribution in Chapter 8).

4.7 The variance and the standard deviation of several items together

You may need to calculate the variance and standard deviation for n items together, given the variance and standard deviation for one item alone.

4.8 Example: Several items together

The daily demand for an item of stock has a mean of 6 units, with a variance of 4 and a standard deviation of 2 units. Demand on any one day is unaffected by demand on previous days or subsequent days.

Required

Calculate the arithmetic mean, the variance and the standard deviation of demand for a five day week.

Solution

If we let

- Arithmetic mean = $\bar{x}$ = 6
- Variance = σ^2 = 4
- Standard deviation = σ = 2
- Number of days in week = n = 5

The following rules apply to $\bar{x}$, σ^2 and σ when we have several items together.

- **Arithmetic mean** = $n\bar{x}$ = 5 × 6 = 30 units
- **Variance** = $n\sigma^2$ = 5 × 4 = 20 units
- **Standard deviation** = $\sqrt{n\sigma^2}$ = $\sqrt{20}$ = 4.47 units

5 The coefficient of variation

5.1 Comparing the spreads of two distributions

FAST FORWARD

The spreads of two distributions can be compared using the **coefficient of variation**.

Formula to learn

> **Coefficient of variation** (coefficient of relative spread) = $\dfrac{\text{Standard deviation}}{\text{mean}}$

The bigger the coefficient of variation, the wider the spread. For example, suppose that two sets of data, A and B, have the following means and standard deviations.

	A		B
Mean	120		125
Standard deviation	50		51
Coefficient of variation (50/120)	0.417	(51/125)	0.408

Although B has a higher standard deviation in absolute terms (51 compared to 50) its relative spread is less than A's since the coefficient of variation is smaller.

Question	Coefficient of variation

Calculate the coefficient of variation of the distribution in the questions on pages 134 and 137.

Answer

Coefficient of variation = $\dfrac{\text{standard deviation}}{\text{mean}} = \dfrac{13.72}{32.2} = 0.426$

Question	Variance

The number of new orders received by five salesmen last week is: 1, 3, 5, 7, 9. The variance of the number of new orders received is:

A   2.40
B   2.83
C   6.67
D   8.00

Answer

x	$(x - \bar{x})^2$
1	16
3	4
5	0
7	4
9	16
$\sum x = 25$	$\sum(x - \bar{x})^2 = 40$

$$X \ \bar{x} = \frac{25}{5} = 5$$

$$\frac{\sum(x - \bar{x})^2}{n} = \frac{40}{5} = 8$$

The correct answer is therefore D.

6 Skewness

6.1 Skewed distributions

As well as being able to calculate the average and spread of a frequency distribution, you should be aware of the **skewness** of a distribution.

FAST FORWARD

Skewness is the asymmetry of a frequency distribution curve.

6.2 Symmetrical frequency distributions

A **symmetrical frequency distribution** (a normal distribution) can be drawn as follows.

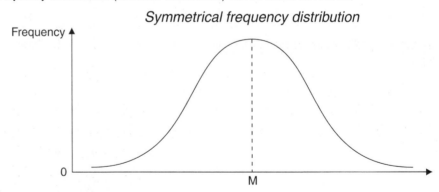

Symmetrical frequency distribution

Properties of a symmetrical distribution

- Its mean, mode and median all have the same value, M
- Its two halves are mirror images of each other

6.3 Positively skewed distributions

A **positively skewed** distribution's graph will lean towards the **left hand side**, with a tail stretching out to the right, and can be drawn as follows.

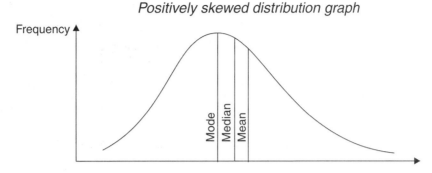

Positively skewed distribution graph

Properties of a positively skewed distribution

- Its mean, mode and median all have different values
- The mode will have a lower value than the median
- Its mean will have a higher value than the median (and than most of the distribution)
- It does not have two halves which are mirror images of each other

6.4 Negatively skewed distributions

A **negatively skewed distribution's** graph will lean towards the **right hand side**, with a tail stretching out to the left, and can be drawn as follows.

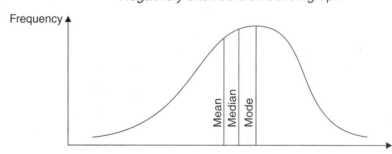

Negatively skewed distribution graph

Properties of a negatively skewed distribution

- Its mean, median and mode all have different values
- The mode will be higher than the median
- The mean will have a lower value than the median (and than most of the distribution)

Since the mean is affected by extreme values, it may not be representative of the items in a very skewed distribution.

6.5 Example: Skewness

In a quality control test, the weights of standard packages were measured to give the following grouped frequency table.

Weights in grams	Number of packages
198 and less than 199	3
199 and less than 200	8
200 and less than 201	93
201 and less than 202	148
202 and less than 203	48

Required

(a)   Calculate the mean, standard deviation and median of the weights of the packages.
(b)   Explain whether or not you think that the distribution is symmetrical.

Solution

(a)

	Weight	Mid point				
	g	*x*	*f*	*fx*	$x - \bar{x}$	$f(x - \bar{x})^2$
	198 and less than 199	198.5	3	595.5	−2.77	23.0187
	199 and less than 200	199.5	8	1,596.0	−1.77	25.0632
	200 and less than 201	200.5	93	18,646.5	−0.77	55.1397
	201 and less than 202	201.5	148	29,822.0	0.23	7.8292
	202 and less than 203	202.5	48	9,720.0	1.23	72.6192
			300	60,380.0		183.6700

$$\text{Mean} = \frac{\Sigma fx}{\Sigma f} = \frac{60,380}{300} = 201.27g$$

$$\text{Standard deviation} = \sqrt{\frac{183.67}{300}} = 0.78g$$

The **median** (the 150th item) could be estimated as

$$201 + \frac{(150 - 93 - 8 - 3)}{148} = 201.31g$$

(b)   The distribution appears not to be symmetrical, but negatively skewed.

The mean is in the higher end of the range of values at 201.27 g.

The median has a higher value than the mean, and the mode has a higher value than the median. This suggests that the frequency distribution is negatively skewed.

Important!

> Measures of spread are valuable in giving a full picture of a frequency distribution. We would nearly always want to be told an average for a distribution, but just one more number, a measure of spread, can be very informative.

Chapter Roundup

- The **range** is the difference between the highest and lowest observations.

- The **quartiles** and the **median** divide the population into four groups of equal size.

- The **semi-interquartile range** is half the difference between the upper and lower quartiles.

- The **inter-quartile range** is the difference between the upper and lower quartiles ($Q_3 - Q_1$) and hence shows the range of values of the middle half of the population.

- The **mean deviation** is a measure of the average amount by which the values in a distribution differ from the arithmetic mean.

- The **variance**, σ^2, is the average of the squared mean deviation for each value in a distribution.

- The **standard deviation**, which is the square root of the variance, is the most important measure of spread used in statistics. Make sure you understand how to calculate the standard deviation of a set of data.

- The spreads of two distributions can be compared using the **coefficient of variation**.

- **Skewness** is the asymmetry of a frequency distribution curve.

Quick Quiz

1   What is the range?

2   Fill in the blanks in the statements below using the words in the box.

   (a)   .... quartile = Q_1 = value .... which 25% of the population fall.
   (b)   .... quartile = Q_3 = value .... which 25% of the population fall.

Upper	Above	Below	Lower

3   (a)   The formula for the semi-interquartile range is ....
    (b)   The semi-interquartile range is also known as the ....

4   What are the main properties of the standard deviation?

Answers to Quick Quiz

1   The difference between the highest and lowest observations.

2   (a)   **Lower** quartile = Q_1 = value **below** which 25% of the population fall
     (b)   **Upper** quartile = Q_3 = value **above** which 25% of the population fall

3   (a) $$\frac{Q_3 - Q_1}{2}$$
     (b)   Quartile deviation

4   •   It is based on all values in the distribution
     •   It is suitable for further statistical analysis
     •   It is more difficult to understand than some other measures of dispersion

Now try the questions below from the Exam Question Bank

Question numbers	Pages
41-43	339-340

Distributions

Introduction

This chapter will build on many of the statistical topics already covered. We saw in Chapter 7 that a frequency distribution of continuous data can be drawn as a symmetrical bell-shaped curve called the **normal distribution**. This can be linked with the calculation of probabilities studied in Chapter 3 and is a useful business decision making tool. We will also be looking at the Pareto Distribution which demonstrates that 80% of value is concentrated in 20% of items.

Topic list	Syllabus references
1 Probability distributions	C, (vi), (6)
2 The normal distribution	C, (vi), (6)
3 The standard normal distribution	C, (vi), (6)
4 Using the normal distribution to calculate probabilities	C, (vi), (6)
5 The Pareto distribution and '80:20 rule'	C, (vii), (6)

1 Probability distributions

1.1 Converting frequency distributions into probability distributions

FAST FORWARD

If we convert the frequencies in a frequency distribution table into proportions, we get a **probability distribution**.

Marks out of 10 (statistics test)	Number of students (frequency distribution)	Proportion or probability (probability distribution)
0	0	0.00
1	0	0.00
2	1	0.02*
3	2	0.04
4	4	0.08
5	10	0.20
6	15	0.30
7	10	0.20
8	6	0.12
9	2	0.04
10	0	0.00
	50	1.00

* 1/50 = 0.02

Key term

A **probability distribution** is an analysis of the proportion of times each particular value occurs in a set of items.

1.2 Graphing probability distributions

A graph of the probability distribution would be the same as the graph of the frequency distribution, but with the **vertical axis marked in proportions** rather than in numbers.

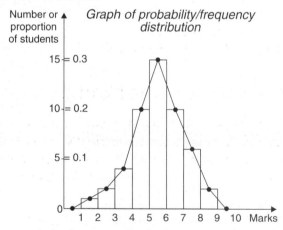

Graph of probability/frequency distribution

(a)   The area under the curve in the frequency distribution represents the total number of students whose marks have been recorded, 50 people.

(b)   **The area under the curve in a probability distribution is 100%, or 1** (the total of all the probabilities).

There are a number of different probability distributions but the only one that you need to know about for the *Business Mathematics* assessment is the **normal distribution**.

2 The normal distribution

FAST FORWARD

The **normal distribution** is a probability distribution which usually applies to **continuous variables**, such as distance and time.

2.1 Introduction

In calculating P(x), x can be any value, and does not have to be a whole number.

The normal distribution can also apply to **discrete variables** which can take **many possible values**. For example, the volume of sales, in units, of a product might be any whole number in the range 100 – 5,000 units. There are so many possibilities within this range that the variable is for all practical purposes **continuous**.

2.2 Graphing the normal distribution

The normal distribution can be drawn as a graph, and it would be a **bell-shaped curve**.

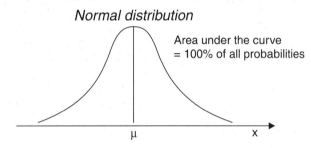

2.3 Properties of the normal distribution

FAST FORWARD

Properties of the normal distribution are as follows.

- It is symmetrical and bell-shaped
- It has a mean, μ (pronounced mew)
- The area under the curve totals exactly 1
- The area to the left of μ = area to the right of μ = 0.5

2.4 Importance of the normal distribution

The normal distribution is important because in the practical application of statistics, it has been found that **many probability distributions are close enough to a normal distribution** to be treated as one without any significant loss of accuracy. This means that the normal distribution can be used as a tool in business decision making involving probabilities.

3 The standard normal distribution

3.1 Introduction

For any normal distribution, the **dispersion** around the mean (μ) of the frequency of occurrences can be measured exactly in terms of the **standard deviation** (σ) (a concept we covered in Chapter 7).

The **standard** normal distribution has a mean (μ) of 0 and a standard deviation (σ) of 1.

(a) The entire frequency curve represents all the possible outcomes and their frequencies of occurrence. Since the normal curve is **symmetrical**, 50% of occurrences have a value greater than the mean value (μ), and 50% of occurrences have a value less than the mean value (μ).

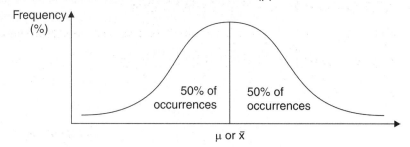

(b) About 68% of frequencies have a value within one standard deviation either side of the mean.

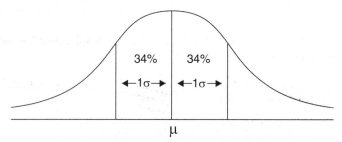

(c) 95% of the frequencies in a normal distribution occur in the range ± 1.96 standard deviations from the mean.

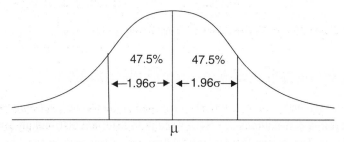

You will not need to remember these precise figures as a **normal distribution table** can be used to find the relevant proportions and this will be given to you in the exam.

3.2 Normal distribution tables

Although there is an infinite number of normal distributions, depending on values of the mean μ and the standard deviation σ, **the relative dispersion of frequencies around the mean, measured as proportions of the total population, is exactly the same for all normal distributions**. In other words, whatever the normal distribution, 47.5% of outcomes will always be in the range between the mean and 1.96 standard deviations below the mean, 49.5% of outcomes will always be in the range between the mean and 2.58 standard deviations below the mean and so on.

A **normal distribution table**, shown at the end of this Study Text, gives the proportion of the total between the mean and a point above or below the mean for any multiple of the standard deviation.

3.2.1 Example: Normal distribution tables

What is the probability that a randomly picked item will be in the shaded area of the diagram below?

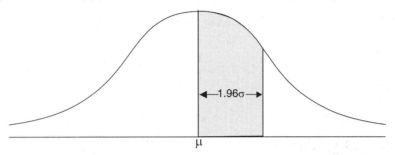

Look up 1.96 in the normal distribution table and you will obtain the value .475. This means there is a 47.5% probability that the item will be in the shaded area.

Since the normal distribution is symmetrical 1.96σ below the mean will also correspond to an area of 47.5%.

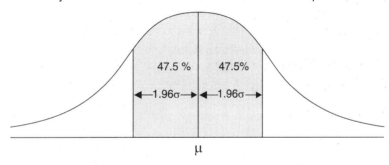

The total shaded area = 47.5% $\times$ 2 = 95%

In Paragraph 3.1(c) we said that 95% of the frequencies in a normal distribution lie in the range $\pm$ 1.96 standard deviations from the mean but we did not say what this figure was based on. It was of course based on the corresponding value in the normal distribution tables (when z = 1.96) as shown above.

We can also show that 99% of the frequencies occur in the range ± 2.58 standard deviation from the mean. Using the normal distribution table, a z score of 2.58 corresponds to an area of 0.4949 (or 49.5%). Remember, the normal distribution is symmetrical.

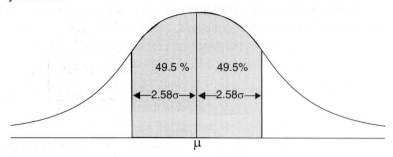

$49.5\% \times 2 = 99\%$

If mean, $\mu + 2.58\sigma$	=	49.5% and
mean, $\mu - 2.58\sigma$	=	49.5%
Range = mean $\pm 2.58\sigma$	=	99.0%

Therefore, 99% of frequencies occur in the range mean (μ) $\pm$ 2.58 standard deviations (σ), as proved by using normal distribution tables.

Question   68% of frequencies

Prove that approximately 68% of frequencies have a value within one standard deviation either side of the mean, μ.

Answer

One standard deviation corresponds to z = 1

If z = 1, we can look this value up in normal distribution tables to get a value (area) of 0.3413. One standard deviation above the mean can be shown on a graph as follows.

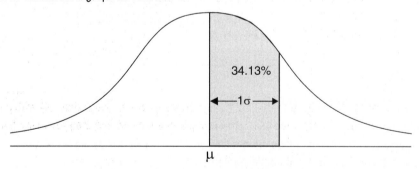

The normal distribution is symmetrical, and we must therefore show the area corresponding to one standard deviation below the mean on the graph also.

① The area one standard deviation *below* the mean

② The area one standard deviation *above* the mean

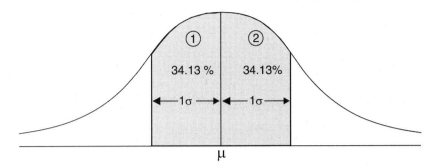

Area one standard deviation above *and* below the mean

= ① + ②

= 34.13% + 34.13%

= 68.26% ≃ 68%

4 Using the normal distribution to calculate probabilities

FAST FORWARD

The normal distribution can be used to calculate probabilities. Sketching a graph of a normal distribution curve often helps in normal distribution problems.

$$z = \frac{x - \mu}{\sigma}$$

where z = the number of standard deviations above or below the mean (z score)
       x = the value of the variable under consideration
       μ = the mean
       σ = the standard deviation.

4.1 Introduction

In order to calculate probabilities, we need to **convert** a normal distribution (X) with a mean μ and standard deviation σ to the standard normal distribution (z) before using the table to find the probability figure.

4.2 Example: Calculating z

Calculate the following z scores and identify the corresponding proportions using normal distribution tables.

(a)   x = 100, μ = 200, σ = 50
(b)   x = 1,000, μ = 1,200, σ = 200
(c)   x = 25, μ = 30, σ = 6

Solution

(a) $z = \dfrac{x - \mu}{\sigma}$

$= \dfrac{100 - 200}{50}$

$= 2$

A z score of 2 corresponds to a proportion of 0.4772 or 47.72%.

(b) $z = \dfrac{x - \mu}{\sigma}$

$= \dfrac{1{,}000 - 1{,}200}{200}$

$= 1$

A z score of 1 corresponds to a proportion of 0.3413 or 34.13%.

(c) $z = \dfrac{x - \mu}{\sigma}$

$= \dfrac{25 - 30}{6}$

$= 0.8333$

0.8333 corresponds to a proportion of 0.2967 or 29.67%

4.3 Example: Using the normal distribution to calculate probabilities

A frequency distribution is normal, with a mean of 100 and a standard deviation of 10.

Required

Calculate the proportion of the total frequencies which will be:

(a)   above 80
(b)   above 90
(c)   above 100
(d)   above 115
(e)   below 85
(f)   below 95
(g)   below 108
(h)   in the range 80 – 110
(i)   in the range 90 – 95

Solution

(a)   If the value (x) is **below** the mean (μ), the total proportion is 0.5 plus proportion between the value and the mean (area (a)).

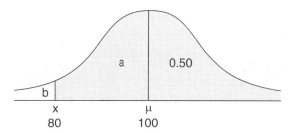

The proportion of the total frequencies which will be above 80 is calculated as follows.

$\dfrac{80 - 100}{10}$ = 2 standard deviations **below** the mean.

From the tables, where z = 2 the proportion is 0.4772.

The proportion of frequencies above 80 is 0.5 + 0.4772 = 0.9772.

(b)   The proportion of the total frequencies which will be above 90 is calculated as follows.

$\dfrac{90 - 100}{10}$ = 1 standard deviation **below** the mean.

From the tables, when z = 1, the proportion is 0.3413.

The proportion of frequencies above 90 is 0.5 + 0.3413 = 0.8413.

(c)   100 is the mean. The proportion above this is 0.5. (The normal curve is symmetrical and 50% of occurrences have a value greater than the mean, and 50% of occurrences have a value less than the mean.)

(d)   If the value is **above** the mean, the proportion (b) is 0.5 minus the proportion between the value and the mean (area (a)).

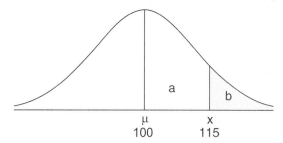

The proportion of the total frequencies which will be above 115 is calculated as follows.

$\dfrac{115 - 100}{10}$ = 1.5 standard deviations **above** the mean.

From the tables, where z = 1.5, the proportion is 0.4332.

The proportion of frequencies above 115 is therefore 0.5 − 0.4332 = 0.0668.

(e)   If the value is **below** the mean, the proportion (b) is 0.5 minus the proportion between the value and the mean (area (a)).

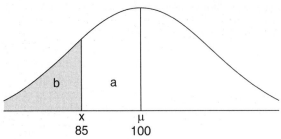

The proportion of the total frequencies which will be below 85 is calculated as follows.

$$\frac{85 - 100}{10} = 1.5 \text{ standard deviations } \textbf{below} \text{ the mean.}$$

The proportion of frequencies below 85 is therefore the same as the proportion above 115 = 0.0668.

(f)   The proportion of the total frequencies which will be below 95 is calculated as follows.

$$\frac{95 - 100}{10} = 0.5 \text{ standard deviations } \textbf{below} \text{ the mean.}$$

When z = 0.5, the proportion from the tables is 0.1915. The proportion of frequencies below 95 is therefore 0.5 – 0.1915 = 0.3085.

(g)   If the value is **above** the mean, the proportion required is 0.5 plus the proportion between the value and the mean (area (a)).

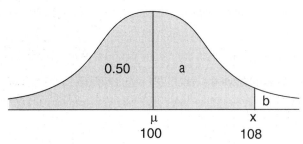

The proportion of the total frequencies which will be below 108 is calculated as follows.

$$\frac{108 - 100}{10} = 0.8 \text{ standard deviations } \textbf{above} \text{ the mean.}$$

From the tables for z = 0.8 the proportion is 0.2881.

The proportion of frequencies below 108 is 0.5 + 0.2881 = 0.7881.

(h) The proportion of the total frequencies which will be in the range 80–110 is calculated as follows. The range 80 to 110 may be divided into two parts:

(i) 80 to 100 (the mean);
(ii) 100 to 110.

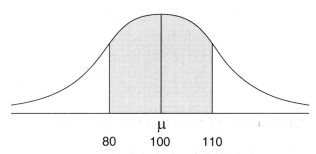

The proportion in the range 80 to 100 is (2 standard deviations) 0.4772

The proportion in the range 100 to 110 is (1 standard deviation) 0.3413

The proportion in the total range 80 to 110 is 0.4772 + 0.3413 = 0.8185.

(i) The range 90 to 95 may be analysed as:

(i) the proportion above 90 and below the mean
(ii) minus the proportion above 95 and below the mean

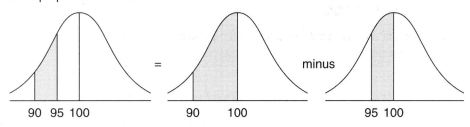

Proportion above 90 and below the mean (1 standard deviation)	0.3413
Proportion above 95 and below the mean (0.5 standard deviations)	0.1915
Proportion between 90 and 95	0.1498

Question

Normal distribution and proportions

The salaries of employees in an industry are normally distributed, with a mean of $14,000 and a standard deviation of $2,700.

Required

(a) Calculate the proportion of employees who earn less than $12,000.
(b) Calculate the proportion of employees who earn between $11,000 and $19,000.

Answer

(a)

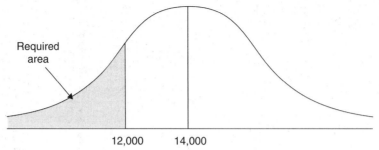

$$z = \frac{12,000 - 14,000}{2,700}$$

$$= -0.74$$

From normal distribution tables, the proportion of salaries between $12,000 and $14,000 is 0.2704 (from tables). The proportion of salaries less than $12,000 is therefore 0.5 − 0.2704 = 0.2296.

(b)

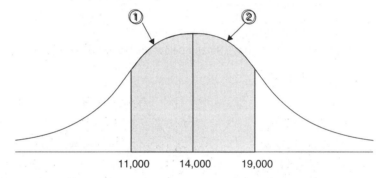

① $z = \dfrac{11,000 - 14,000}{2,700}$

$= 1.11$

② $z = \dfrac{19,000 - 14,000}{2,700}$

$= 1.85$

The proportion with earnings between $11,000 and $14,000 is 0.3665 (from tables where z = 1.11).

The proportion with earnings between $14,000 and $19,000 is 0.4678 (from tables where z = 1.85).

The required proportion is therefore 0.3665 + 0.4678 = 0.8343.

Note that **the normal distribution is, in fact, a way of calculating probabilities**. In this question, for example, the **probability** that an employee earns less than $12,000 (part (a)) is 0.2296 (or 22.96%) and the probability that an employee earns between $11,000 and $19,000 is 0.8343 (or 83.43%).

FAST FORWARD

If you are given the **variance** of a distribution, remember to first calculate the standard deviation by taking its square root.

Question

The specification for the width of a widget is a minimum of 42mm and a maximum of 46.2mm. A normally distributed batch of widgets is produced with a mean of 45mm and a variance of 4mm.

Required

(a) Calculate the percentage of parts that are too small
(b) Calculate the percentage of parts that are too big

Answer

(a)

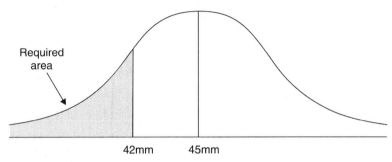

$$\sigma = \sqrt{4} = 2$$

$$z = \frac{42 - 45}{2} = -1.5$$

Proportion of widgets between 42mm and 45mm = 0.4332.
Proportion of widgets smaller than 42mm = 0.5 − 0.4332 = 0.0668
= 6.68%

(b)

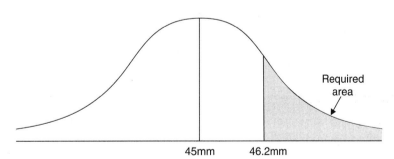

$$z = \frac{46.2 - 45}{2} = 0.6$$

Proportion of widgets between 45mm and 46.2mm = 0.2257.
Proportion of widgets bigger than 46.2mm = 0.5 − 0.2257 = 0.2743
= 27.43%

Assessment
focus point

> Make sure that you always draw a sketch of a normal distribution to identify the areas that you are concerned with when using the normal distribution to calculate probabilities. You should also make sure that you are confident with reading normal distribution tables – marks may be allocated in the assessment for correctly reading values from the tables.

5 The Pareto distribution and the '80:20 rule'

FAST FORWARD

> **Pareto analysis** is used to highlight the general principle that 80% of value (inventory value, wealth, profit and so on) is concentrated in 20% of the items in a particular population.

Key term

> **Pareto analysis** is based on the observations of the economist Vilfredo Pareto, who suggested that 80% of a nation's wealth is held by 20% of its population (and so the remaining 80% of the population holds only 20% of the nation's wealth).

Pareto analysis is the 80/20 rule and it has been applied to many other situations.

- In inventory control, where 20% of inventory items might represent 80% of the value
- In product analysis, where 80% of company profit is earned by 20% of the products

5.1 Example: Pareto analysis and products

(a)   A company produces ten products which it sells in various markets. The revenue from each product is as follows.

Product	Revenue
	$'000
A	231
B	593
C	150
D	32
E	74
F	17
G	1,440
H	12
I	2
J	19
	2,570

(b) Rearranging revenue in descending order and calculating cumulative figures and percentages gives us the following analysis.

Product	Revenue	Cumulative revenue (W1)	% (W2)
	$'000	$'000	
G	1,440	1,440	56.0
B	593	2,033	79.1
A	231	2,264	88.1
C	150	2,414	93.9
E	74	2,488	96.8
D	32	2,520	98.1
J	19	2,539	98.8
F	17	2,556	99.5
H	12	2,568	99.9
I	2	2,570	100.0
	2,570		

Workings

1   This is calculated as follows:

1,440 + 593 = 2,033
2,033 + 231 = 2,264   and so on.

2   $(1/2,570 \times 1,440 \times 100)\% = 56.0\%$
$(1/2,570 \times 2,033 \times 100)\% = 79.1\%$ and so on.

(c) In this case the Pareto rule applies – almost 80% of revenue is brought in by just two products, G and B. The point of Pareto analysis is to highlight the fact that the effort that is put into a company's products is often barely worth the trouble in terms of the sales revenue generated.

(d) We can illustrate a pareto distribution on a graph, plotting cumulative revenue against each product.

Revenue information presented as a pareto curve

Question

In Pareto analysis, what is the 80:20 rule?

(i)   An approximate rule to the effect that 20% of the products will provide 80% of sales.

(ii)   An approximate rule to the effect that an increase of 80% in costs will be reflected by a 20% decline in sales

(iii)   An approximate rule that 80% of wealth is held by 20% of the population.

(iv)   An approximate rule to the effect that the wealth of the richest 20% of the population equals that of the other 80%.

A   (ii) and (iii)

B   (ii) only

C   (i) only

D   (i) and (iii)

Answer

D   **Rule (i)** was first suggested by the economist Pareto in the context of the distribution of wealth.

There is no such general guidance to the effect of **rule (ii)**.

Rule (iii) was initially suggested by Pareto on the basis of his observations of social inequality.

Rule (iv) is incorrect.

Chapter Roundup

- If we convert the frequencies in a frequency distribution table into proportions, we get a **probability distribution.**

- The **normal distribution** is a probability distribution which usually applies to **continuous variables,** such as distance and time.

- Properties of the normal distribution are as follows.

  - It is symmetrical
  - It has a mean, μ (pronounced mew)
  - The area under the curve totals exactly 1
  - The area to the left of μ = area to right of μ
  - It is a bell shaped curve

- Distances above or below the mean of a normal distribution are expressed in numbers of **standard deviations, z.**

$$z = \frac{x - \mu}{\sigma}$$

Where z =   the number of standard deviations above or below the mean
       x =   the value of the variable under consideration
      μ =   the mean
      σ =   the standard deviation

- The normal distribution can be used to calculate probabilities. Sketching a graph of a normal distribution curve often helps in normal distribution problems.

- If you are given the **variance** of a distribution, remember to first calculate the standard deviation by taking its square root.

- Pareto analysis is used to highlight the general principle that 80% of value (inventory value, wealth, profit and so on) is concentrated in 20% of the items in a particular population.

Quick Quiz

1   The normal distribution is a type of .... distribution.

2   The area under the curve of a normal distribution = ... which represents ....% of all probabilities.

3   The mean of a normal distribution = σ

True   ☐

False   ☐

4   Use the following symbols to create a formula for calculating the 'z score'.

X	μ	z	σ

5   What proportions/percentages do the following z scores represent?

(a)   1.45
(b)   2.93
(c)   0.955

6   What are the corresponding z scores for the following proportions/percentages?

(a)   0.4382
(b)   0.4750
(c)   0.4747

7   On the axes below, sketch and label correctly a Pareto curve to demonstrate a situation where 80% of an organisation's profit is derived from 20% of its retail outlets.

Answers to Quick Quiz

1   Probability

2   1, 100%

3   False. The mean of a normal distribution = μ

4    $z = \dfrac{x - \mu}{\sigma}$

5   (a)   0.4265 = 42.65%
     (b)   0.4983 = 49.83%
     (c)   0.3302 = 33.02% (Take average of 0.95 and 0.96 = (0.3289 + 0.3315) ÷ 2 = 0.3302.)

6   (a)   1.54
     (b)   1.96
     (c)   1.955

7

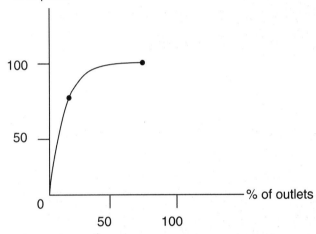

Now try the questions below from the Exam Question Bank

Question numbers	Pages
44-49	340-341

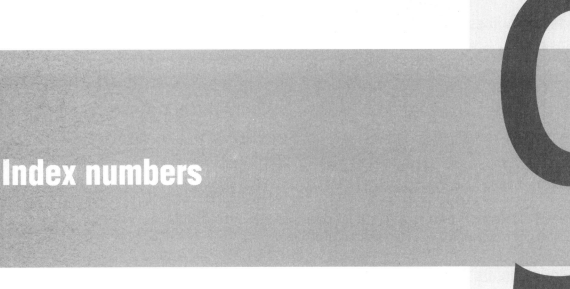

Index numbers

Introduction

A number of methods of data presentation looked at in Chapter 5 can be used to identify visually the **trends** in data over a period of time. It may also be useful, however, to identify trends using statistical rather than visual means. This is frequently achieved by constructing a set of **index numbers**.

Index numbers provide a **standardised way of comparing the values**, over time, of prices, wages, volume of output and so on. They are used extensively in business, government and commerce.

Topic list	Syllabus references
1 Basic terminology	C, (viii), (7)
2 Index relatives	C, (viii), (7)
3 Time series of index relatives	C, (viii), (7)
4 Time series deflation	C, (x), (7)
5 Composite index numbers	C, (viii), (7)
6 Weighted index numbers	C, (ix), (7)
7 The Retail Prices Index for the United Kingdom	C, (xiii), (x), (7)

1 Basic terminology

1.1 Price indices and quantity indices

An **index** is a measure, over time, of the average changes in the values (price or quantity) of a group of items.

> An index comprises a series of index numbers and may be a price index or a quantity index.
>
> - A **price index** measures the change in the money value of a group of items over time.
>
> - A **quantity index** (also called a volume index) measures the change in the non-monetary values of a group of items over time.

It is possible to prepare an index for a single item, but such an index would probably be unnecessary. An index is a most useful measure of comparison when there is a **group of items**.

1.2 Index points

The term **'points'** refers to the difference between the index values in two years.

1.3 Example: Index points

For example, suppose that the index of food prices in 20X1 – 20X6 was as follows.

20X1	180
20X2	200
20X3	230
20X4	250
20X5	300
20X6	336

The index has risen 156 points between 20X1 and 20X6 (336 – 180). This is an increase of:

$$\left(\frac{156}{180}\right) \times 100 = 86.7\%.$$

Similarly, the index rose 36 points between 20X5 and 20X6 (336 – 300), a rise of 12%.

1.4 The base period, or base year

Index numbers normally take the value for a **base date as 100**. The base period is usually the starting point of the series, though this is not always the case.

2 Index relatives

2.1 Assessment formulae

An **index relative** (sometimes just called a relative) is the name given to an index number which measures the change in a single distinct commodity.

Assessment formula

- A **price relative** is calculated as $100 \times \dfrac{P_1}{P_0}$

- A **quantity relative** is calculated as $100 \times \dfrac{Q_1}{Q_0}$

2.2 Example: Single-item indices

(a) **Price index number**

If the price of a cup of coffee was 40c in 20X0, 50c in 20X1 and 76c in 20X2, then using 20X0 as a base year the **price index numbers** for 20X1 and 20X2 would be as follows.

20X1 price index $= 100 \times \dfrac{50}{40} = 125$

20X2 price index $= 100 \times \dfrac{76}{40} = 190$

(b) **Quantity index number**

If the number of cups of coffee sold in 20X0 was 500,000, in 20X1 700,000 and in 20X2 600,000, then using 20X0 as a base year, the **quantity index numbers** for 20X1 and 20X2 would be as follows.

20X1 quantity index $= 100 \times \dfrac{700,000}{500,000} = 140$

20X2 quantity index $= 100 \times \dfrac{600,000}{500,000} = 120$

Question   **Price index**

The price of a kilogram of raw material was $80 in year 1 and $120 in year 2. Using year 1 as a base year, the price index number for year 2 is

A   67
B   140
C   150
D   167

Answer

C   Year 2 price index = 120/80 × 100 = 150

Option C is therefore correct.

If you selected option A, you have confused the numerator with the denominator and calculated 80/120 instead of 120/80.

If you selected option B, you simply took the price difference of $40 ($120 − $80 = $40) and added this to 100.

If you selected option D, you added 80/120 × 100% = 67% to 100 which equals 167 which is incorrect.

Question   **Quantity index**

A company used 20,000 litres of a raw material in year 1. In year 5 the usage of the same raw material amounted to 25,000 litres. Using year 1 as a base year, the quantity index number for year 5 is

A   105
B   120
C   125
D   180

Answer

C   Year 5 quantity index = $\dfrac{25,000}{20,000}$ × 100 = 125

If you selected option A, you took the difference in litres (25,000 − 20,000 = 5,000) and interpreted this as a five point increase, ie 100 + 5 = 105.

If you selected option D you calculated $\dfrac{20,000}{25,000}$ × 100 = 80 and added this to 100 which is not the correct method to use.

3 Time series of index relatives

FAST FORWARD

Index relatives can be calculated using the **fixed base method** or the **chain base method**.

(a)   The **fixed base method**. A base year is selected (index 100), and all subsequent changes are measured against this base. Such an approach should only be used if **the basic nature of the commodity is unchanged over time**.

(b)   The **chain base method**. Changes are calculated with respect to the value of the commodity in the period immediately before. This approach can be used for any set of commodity values but must be used if **the basic nature of the commodity is changing over time**.

3.1 Example: Fixed base method

The price of a commodity was $2.70 in 20X0, $3.11 in 20X1, $3.42 in 20X2 and $3.83 in 20X3. Construct a **fixed base index** for the years 20X0 to 20X3 using 20X0 as the base year.

Solution

Fixed base index	20X0	100	
	20X1	115	(3.11/2.70 × 100)
	20X2	127	(3.42/2.70 × 100)
	20X3	142	(3.83/2.70 × 100)

3.2 Example: Chain base method

Using the information in Paragraph 3.1 construct a chain base index for the years 20X0 to 20X3 using 20X0 as the base year.

Solution

Chain base index	20X0	100	
	20X1	115	(3.11/2.70 × 100)
	20X2	110	(3.42/3.11 × 100)
	20X3	112	(3.83/3.42 × 100)

Important!

The chain base relatives show the rate of change in prices from year to year, whereas the fixed base relatives show changes relative to prices in the base year.

3.3 Changing the base of fixed base relatives

FAST FORWARD

In order to compare two time series of relatives, each series should have the same base period and hence one (or both) may need **rebasing**.

It is sometimes necessary to change the base of a time series (to **rebase**) of fixed base relatives, perhaps because the **base time point is too far in the past**. The following time series has a base date of 1970 which would probably be considered too out of date.

	1990	1991	1992	1993	1994	1995
Index (1970 = 100)	451	463	472	490	499	505

To change the base date, divide each relative by the relative corresponding to the new base time point and multiply the result by 100.

Question   **Rebasing**

Rebase the index in Paragraph 3.3 to 1993.

Answer

	1990	1991	1992	1993	1994	1995
Index (1993 = 100)	92*	94	96	100	102**	103

* $\dfrac{451}{490} \times 100$

** $\dfrac{499}{490} \times 100$

3.4 Comparing sets of fixed base relatives

(a) You may be required to compare two sets of time series relatives. For example, an index of the annual number of advertisements placed by an organisation in the press and the index of the number of the organisation's product sold per annum might be compared. If the base years of the two indices differ, however, comparison is extremely difficult (as the illustration below shows).

	20W8	20W9	20X0	20X1	20X2	20X3	20X4
Number of advertisements Placed (20X0 = 100)	90	96	100	115	128	140	160
Volumes of sales (20W0 = 100)	340	347	355	420	472	515	572

(b) From the figures above it is impossible to determine whether sales are increasing at a greater rate than the number of advertisements placed, or vice versa. This difficulty can be overcome by **rebasing** one set of relatives so that the **base dates are the same**. For example, we could rebase the index of volume of sales to 20X0.

	20W8	20W9	20X0	20X1	20X2	20X3	20X4
Number of advertisements Placed (20X0 = 100)	90	96	100	115	128	140	160
Volumes of sales (20X0 = 100)	96	98*	100	118	133*ʲ	145	161

* $\dfrac{347}{355} \times 100$

** $\dfrac{472}{355} \times 100$

(c) The two sets of relatives are now much easier to compare. They show that volume of sales is increasing at a slightly faster rate, in general, than the number of advertisements placed.

4 Time series deflation

4.1 Real value of a commodity

The real value of a commodity can only be measured in terms of some **'indicator'** such as the **rate of inflation** (normally represented by the Retail Prices Index (RPI)).

For example the cost of a commodity may have been $10 in 20X0 and $11 in 20X1, representing an increase of 10%. However, if we are told the prices **in general** (as measured by the RPI) increased by 12% between 20X0 and 20X1, we can argue that the **real** cost of the commodity has decreased.

Time series deflation is a technique used to obtain a set of index relatives that measure the changes in the real value of some commodity with respect to some given indicator.

4.2 Example: Deflation

Mack Johnson works for Pound of Flesh Ltd. Over the last five years he has received an annual salary increase of $500. Despite his employer assuring him that $500 is a reasonable annual salary increase, Mack is unhappy because, although he agrees $500 is a lot of money, he finds it difficult to maintain the standard of living he had when he first joined the company.

Consider the figures below.

Year	(a) Wages $	(b) RPI	(c) Real wages $
1	12,000	250	12,000
2	12,500	260	12,019
3	13,000	275	11,818
4	13,500	295	11,441
5	14,000	315	11,111

(a)   This column shows Mack's wages over the five-year period.

(b)   This column shows the current RPI.

(c)   This column shows what Mack's wages are worth taking prices, as represented by the RPI, into account. The wages have been deflated relative to the new base period (year 1). Economists call these deflated wage figures **real wages**. The real wages for years 2 and 4, for example, are calculated as follows.

$$\text{Year 2: } \$12,500 \times \frac{250}{260} = \$12,019$$

$$\text{Year 4: } \$13,500 \times \frac{250}{295} = \$11,441$$

Conclusion

The real wages index shows that the real value of Mack's wages has fallen by 7.4% over the five-year period

$$(= \frac{12,000 - 11,111}{12,000} \times 100\%).$$ In real terms he is now earning $11,111 compared to $12,000 in year 1. He is probably justified, therefore, in being unhappy.

5 Composite index numbers

FAST FORWARD

Composite index numbers cover more than one item.

5.1 Example: Composite index numbers

Suppose that the cost of living index is calculated from only three commodities: bread, tea and caviar, and that the prices for 20X1 and 20X2 were as follows.

	20X1	20X2
Bread	20c a loaf	40c a loaf
Tea	25c a packet	30c a packet
Caviar	450c a jar	405c a jar

(a)   A simple index could be calculated by adding the prices for single items in 20X2 and dividing by the corresponding sum relating to 20X1 (if 20X1 is the base year). In general, if the sum of the prices in the base year is $\sum P_0$ and the sum of the prices in the new year is $\sum P_1$, the index is $100 \times \dfrac{\sum P_1}{\sum P_0}$. The index, known as a **simple aggregate price index**, would therefore be calculated as follows.

	P_0 20X1 $\$$	P_1 20X2 $\$$
Bread	0.20	0.40
Tea	0.25	0.30
Caviar	4.50	4.05
	$\sum P_0 = 4.95$	$\sum P_1 = 4.75$

Year	$\dfrac{\sum P_1}{\sum P_0}$	Simple aggregate price index
20X1	$\dfrac{4.95}{4.95} = 1.00$	100
20X2	$\dfrac{4.75}{4.95} = 0.96$	96

(b)   The simple aggregate price index has a number of **disadvantages**.

(i)   It ignores the **amounts** of bread, tea and caviar consumed (and hence the importance of each item).

(ii)   It ignores the **units** to which the prices refer. If, for example, we had been given the price of a cup of tea rather than a packet of tea, the index would have been different.

5.2 Average relatives indices

To overcome the problem of different units we consider the changes in prices as **ratios** rather than absolutes so that all price movements, whatever their absolute values, are treated as equally important. Price changes are considered as ratios rather than absolutes by using the **average price relatives index**. Quantity changes are considered as ratios by using the **average quantity relatives index**.

- **Average price relatives index** $= 100 \times \dfrac{1}{n} \times \Sigma \left(\dfrac{P_1}{P_0} \right)$

- **Average quantity relatives index** $= 100 \times \dfrac{1}{n} \times \Sigma \left(\dfrac{Q_1}{Q_0} \right)$

where n is the number of goods.

The price relative P_1/P_0 (so called because it gives the new price level of each item relative to the base year price) for a particular commodity will have the same value whatever the unit for which the price is quoted.

5.3 Example: Average relatives indices

Using the information in the example in Paragraph 5.1, we can construct the **average price relatives index** as follows.

Commodity	P_0	P_1	$\dfrac{P_1}{P_0}$
	\$	\$	
Bread	0.20	0.40	2.00
Tea	0.25	0.30	1.20
Caviar	4.50	4.05	0.90
			4.10

Year	$\dfrac{1}{n} \Sigma \left(\dfrac{P_1}{P_0} \right)$	Average price relatives index
20X1	$\dfrac{1}{3} \times 3.00 = 1.00$	100
20X2	$\dfrac{1}{3} \times 4.10 = 1.37$	137

There has therefore been an average price increase of 37% between 20X1 and 20X2.

No account has been taken of the **relative importance** of each item in this index. Bread is probably more important than caviar. To overcome both the problem of quantities in different units and the need to attach importance to each item, we can use **weighting** which reflects the **importance of each item**. To decide the weightings of different items in an index, it is necessary to obtain information, perhaps by market research, about the **relative importance** of each item. The next section of this chapter looks at **weighted index numbers**.

6 Weighted index numbers

6.1 Weighting

FAST FORWARD

Weighting is used to reflect the importance of each item in the index.

There are two types of index which give different weights to different items.

- Weighted average of relatives indices
- Weighted aggregate indices

The weighted average of relatives index is the one that you need to be able to calculate in your assessment.

6.2 Weighted average of relatives indices

FAST FORWARD

Weighted average of relatives indices are found by calculating indices and then applying weights.

Assessment formula

- Weighted average of price relative index = $\dfrac{\sum W \times P_1 / P_0}{\sum W} \times 100$

- Weighted average of quantity relative index = $\dfrac{\sum W \times Q_1 / Q_0}{\sum W} \times 100$

  where W = the weighting factor

6.3 Example: Weighted average of relatives indices

Use both the information in Paragraph 5.1 and the following details about quantities purchased by each household in a week in 20X1 to determine a weighted average of price relatives index number for 20X2 using 20X1 as the base year.

	Quantity
Bread	12
Tea	5
Caviar	3

Solution

Price relatives (P_1 / P_0)	Bread	$\dfrac{40}{20} =$	2.00
	Tea	$\dfrac{30}{25} =$	1.20
	Caviar	$\dfrac{405}{450} =$	0.90

Weightings (W)	Bread		12.00
	Tea		5.00
	Caviar		3.00
		$\sum W =$	20.00

Index	Bread	$2 \times 12 =$	24.00
	Tea	$1.2 \times 5 =$	6.00
	Caviar	$0.9 \times 3 =$	2.70
		$\sum W \times P_1 / P_0 =$	32.70

Index number = $\dfrac{32.7}{20.0} \times 100 =$ 163.5

The average prices of three commodities and the number of units used annually by a company are given below.

Commodity	20X1 Price per unit (P_0) $	20X2 Price per unit(P_1) $	Quantity Units
X	20	22	20
Y	40	48	2
Z	100	104	10

The price for 20X2 based on 20X1, calculated using the weighted average of relatives method is (to the nearest whole number)

A   107
B   108
C   109
D   110

Answer

Commodity	Price P_1 / P_0	Weight (W)	Relative weight $(W \times P_1 / P_0)$
X	$\frac{22}{20} = 1.1$	20	22.0
Y	$\frac{48}{40} = 1.2$	2	2.4
Z	$\frac{104}{100} = 1.04$	10	10.4
		$\sum W = 32$	34.8

$$\text{Index} = \frac{34.8}{32} \times 100 = 108.75 = 109$$

The correct answer is therefore C.

Assessment focus point

The above question is indicative of the way in which index numbers could be assessed using objective test questions. Make sure you understand how to arrive at the correct answer.

7 The retail prices index for the United Kingdom

7.1 Items included in the RPI calculation

We will conclude our study of index numbers by looking at the construction of the UK Retail Prices Index (RPI). On one particular day of each month, data are collected about prices of the following groups of items.

- Food
- Alcoholic drink
- Tobacco
- Housing
- Fuel and light
- Durable household goods
- Clothing and footwear
- Transport and vehicles
- Miscellaneous goods
- Services
- Meals bought and consumed outside the home

(a) Each group is sub-divided into sections: for example 'food' will be sub-divided into bread, butter, potatoes and so on. These sections may in turn be sub-divided into more specific items. The groups do not cover every item of expenditure (for example they exclude income tax, pension fund contributions and lottery tickets).

(b) The weightings given to each group, section and sub-section are based on information provided by the *Family Expenditure Survey* which is based on a survey of over 10,000 households, spread evenly over the year.

Each member of the selected households (aged 16 or over) is asked to keep a detailed record of their expenditure over a period of 14 days, and to provide information about longer-term payments (such as insurance premiums). Information is also obtained about their income.

(c) The weightings used in the construction of the RPI are not revised every year, but are revised from time to time using information in the Family Expenditure Survey of the previous year.

Attention!

> **Index numbers** are a very useful way of summarising a large amount of data in a single series of numbers. They do, however, have a number of **limitations**.

Chapter Roundup

- An **index** is a measure, over time, of the average changes in the value (price or quantity) of a group of items.

- An **index relative** (sometimes just called a relative) is the name given to an index number which measures the change in a single distinct commodity.

- Index relatives can be calculated using the **fixed base method** or the **chain base method**.

- In order to compare two time series of relatives, each series should have the same base period and hence one (or both) may need **rebasing**.

- The **real value** of a commodity can only be measured in terms of some '**indicator**', such as the **rate of inflation** (normally represented by the Retail Prices Index (RPI)).

- **Time series deflation** is a technique used to obtain a set of index relatives that measure the changes in the real value of some commodity with respect to some given indicator.

- **Composite index numbers** cover more than one item.

- **Weighting** is used to reflect the importance of each item in the index.

- **Weighted average of relatives indices** are found by calculating indices and then applying weights.

Quick Quiz

1 What does a price index measure?

2 What does a quantity index measure?

3 Complete the following equations using the symbols in the box below.

    (a)   **Price index =** $\times 100$

    (b)   **Quantity index =** $\times 100$

P_1	P_0
Q_1	Q_0

4 An index relative is the name given to an index number which measures the change in a group of items.

    True   ☐

    False   ☐

5 Fixed base method   **] ? [**   Changes are measured against base period

    Chain base method   Changes are measured against the previous period

6 What is a composite index number?

7 How are problems of quantities different units and the need to attach importance to each item overcome?

8 There are two types of index which give different weights to different items.

- Weighted average of relatives indices
- Weighted aggregate indices

What is the general form of a weighted average of quantity relative index number?

Answers to Quick Quiz

1   The change in the money value of a group of items over time.

2   The change in the non-monetary values of a group of items over time.

3   (a)   Price index = $\dfrac{P_1}{P_0} \times 100$

   (b)   Quantity index = $\dfrac{Q_1}{Q_0} \times 100$

4   False. An index relative is an index number which measures the change in a **single distinct commodity.**

5   Fixed base method $\longrightarrow$ Changes are measured against the base period

   Chain base method $\longrightarrow$ Changes are measured against the previous period

6   A composite index number is an index covering more than one item.

7   By using weightings and calculating weighted index numbers.

8    $\dfrac{\sum W \times \dfrac{Q_1}{Q_0}}{\sum W}$

   Where   W   = the weighing factor

   $\dfrac{Q_1}{Q_0}$ = the index relative

Now try the questions below from the Exam Question Bank

Question numbers	Pages
50-52	342-343

Part D
Inter-relationship between variables

Correlation and regression

Introduction

We looked at scatter diagrams in Chapter 5. We are now going to look at how the inter-relationship shown between variables in a scatter diagram can be described and calculated. The first three sections deal with **correlation**, which is concerned with assessing the strength of the relationship between two variables.

We will then see how, if we assume that there is a **linear relationship** between two variables (such as selling costs and sales volume) we can determine the equation of a straight line to represent the relationship between the variables and use that equation to make **forecasts** or **predictions**.

Topic list	Syllabus references
1 Correlation	D, (i), (ii), (1)
2 The correlation coefficient and the coefficient of determination	D, (ii), (1)
3 Spearman's rank correlation coefficient	D, (ii)
4 Lines of best fit	D, (i), (1)
5 The scattergraph method	D, (i), (1)
6 Linear regression analysis	D, (iii), (2)

1 Correlation

When the value of one variable is related to the value of another, they are said to be **correlated**.

Key term

> Two variables are said to be correlated if a change in the value of one variable is accompanied by a change in the value of another variable. This is what is meant by **correlation**.

1.1 Examples of variables which might be correlated

- A person's height and weight
- The distance of a journey and the time it takes to make it

1.2 Scatter diagrams

One way of showing the correlation between two related variables is on a **scatter diagram**, plotting a number of pairs of data on the graph. For example, a scatter diagram showing monthly selling costs against the volume of sales for a 12-month period might be as follows.

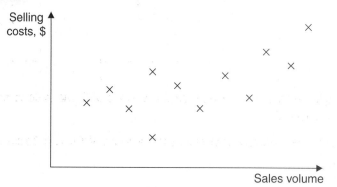

The **independent** variable (the cause) is plotted on the **horizontal** (x) axis and the **dependent** variable (the effect) is plotted on the **vertical** (y) axis.

This scattergraph suggests that there is some correlation between selling costs and sales volume, so that as sales volume rises, selling costs tend to rise as well.

1.3 Degrees of correlation

Two variables might be perfectly correlated, partly correlated or uncorrelated. Correlation can be positive or negative.

These differing degrees of correlation can be illustrated by scatter diagrams.

Perfect correlation

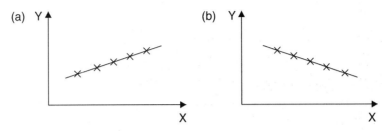

All the pairs of values lie on a straight line. An exact **linear relationship** exists between the two variables.

Partial correlation

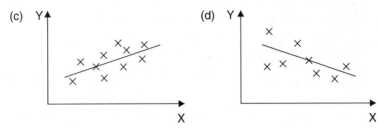

In (c), although there is no exact relationship, low values of X tend to be associated with low values of Y, and high values of X with high values of Y.

In (d) again, there is no exact relationship, but low values of X tend to be associated with high values of Y and vice versa.

No correlation

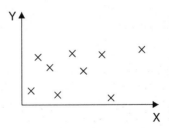

The values of these two variables are not correlated with each other.

1.4 Positive and negative correlation

Correlation, whether perfect or partial, can be **positive** or **negative**.

- **Positive correlation** means that low values of one variable are associated with low values of the other, and high values of one variable are associated with high values of the other.

- **Negative correlation** means that low values of one variable are associated with high values of the other, and high values of one variable with low values of the other.

2 The correlation coefficient and the coefficient of determination

The **degree of correlation** between two variables is measured by **Pearson's correlation coefficient, r**. The nearer r is to +1 or −1, the stronger the relationship.

2.1 The correlation coefficient

Pearson's correlation coefficient, r is used to measure how strong the connection is between two variables, known as the degree of correlation.

It is calculated using a formula which will be given to you in the assessment. It looks complicated but with a systematic approach and plenty of practice, you will be able to answer correlation questions in the assessment.

Assessment formula

$$\text{Correlation coefficient}, r = \frac{n\sum XY - \sum X \sum Y}{\sqrt{[n\sum X^2 - (\sum X)^2][n\sum Y^2 - (\sum Y)^2]}}$$

Where X and Y represent pairs of data for two variables X and Y

n = the number of pairs of data used in the analysis

2.2 The correlation coefficient range

The correlation coefficient, r must always fall between −1 and +1. If you get a value outside this range you have made a mistake.

- r = +1 means that the variables are **perfectly positively correlated**
- r = −1 means that the variables are **perfectly negatively correlated**
- r = 0 means that the variables are **uncorrelated**

2.3 Example: The correlation coefficient

The cost of output at a factory is thought to depend on the number of units produced. Data have been collected for the number of units produced each month in the last six months, and the associated costs, as follows.

Month	Output '000s of units X	Cost $'000 Y
1	2	9
2	3	11
3	1	7
4	4	13
5	3	11
6	5	15

Required

Assess whether there is there any correlation between output and cost.

Solution

$$r = \frac{n\sum XY - \sum X \sum Y}{\sqrt{[n\sum X^2 - (\sum X)^2][n\sum Y^2 - (\sum Y)^2]}}$$

We need to find the values for the following.

(a) $\sum XY$ Multiply each value of X by its corresponding Y value, so that there are six values for XY. Add up the six values to get the total.

(b) $\sum X$ Add up the six values of X to get a total. $(\sum X)^2$ will be the square of this total.

(c) $\sum Y$ Add up the six values of Y to get a total. $(\sum Y)^2$ will be the square of this total.

(d) $\sum X^2$ Find the square of each value of X, so that there are six values for X^2. Add up these values to get a total.

(e) $\sum Y^2$ Find the square of each value of Y, so that there are six values for Y^2. Add up these values to get a total.

Set out your workings in a table.

Workings

X	Y	XY	X^2	Y^2
2	9	18	4	81
3	11	33	9	121
1	7	7	1	49
4	13	52	16	169
3	11	33	9	121
5	15	75	25	225
$\sum X = 18$	$\sum Y = 66$	$\sum XY = 218$	$\sum X^2 = 64$	$\sum Y^2 = 766$

$(\sum X)^2 = 18^2 = 324$

$(\sum Y)^2 = 66^2 = 4,356$

$n = 6$

$$r = \frac{(6 \times 218) - (18 \times 66)}{\sqrt{[(6 \times 64) - 324] \times [(6 \times 766) - 4,356]}}$$

$$= \frac{1,308 - 1,188}{\sqrt{(384 - 324) \times (4,596 - 4,356)}}$$

$$= \frac{120}{\sqrt{60 \times 240}} = \frac{120}{\sqrt{14,400}} = \frac{120}{120} = 1$$

There is **perfect positive correlation** between the volume of output at the factory and costs which means that there is a perfect linear relationship between output and costs.

Question

A company wants to know if the money they spend on advertising is effective in creating sales. The following data have been collected.

Monthly advertising expenditure $'000	Sales in following month $'000
1.2	132.5
0.9	98.5
1.6	154.3
2.1	201.4
1.6	161.0

Required

Calculate Pearson's correlation' coefficient for the data and explain the result.

Answer

Monthly advertising Expenditure	Sales			
X	Y	X^2	Y^2	XY
1.2	132.5	1.44	17,556.25	159.00
0.9	98.5	0.81	9,702.25	88.65
1.6	154.3	2.56	23,808.49	246.88
2.1	201.4	4.41	40,561.96	422.94
1.6	161.0	2.56	25,921.00	257.60
7.4	747.7	11.78	117,549.95	1175.07

$(\sum X)^2 = 7.4^2 = 54.76$

$(\sum Y)^2 = 747.7^2 = 559,055.29$

$$r = \frac{(5 \times 1,175.07) - (7.4 \times 747.7)}{\sqrt{[(5 \times 11.78) - 54.76] \times [5 \times 117,549.95) - 559,055.29]}}$$

$$= \frac{5,875.35 - 5,532.98}{\sqrt{4.14 \times 28,694.46}}$$

$$= \frac{342.37}{\sqrt{118,795.06}}$$

$$= \frac{342.37}{344.67} = 0.993$$

0.993 is very close to 1, therefore there is a strong positive correlation and sales are dependent on advertising expenditure.

2.4 The coefficient of determination, r^2

FAST FORWARD

The **coefficient of determination**, r^2 measures the proportion of the total variation in the value of one variable that can be explained by variations in the value of the other variable.

Unless the correlation coefficient r is exactly or very nearly +1, −1 or 0, its meaning or significance is a little unclear. For example, if the correlation coefficient for two variables is +0.8, this would tell us that the variables are positively correlated, but the correlation is not perfect. It would not really tell us much else. A more meaningful analysis is available from **the square of the correlation coefficient, r**, which is called the **coefficient of determination**, r^2

2.5 Interpreting r^2

In the question above, r = −0.992, therefore r^2 = 0.984. This means that over 98% of variations in sales can be explained by the passage of time, leaving 0.016 (less than 2%) of variations to be explained by other factors.

Similarly, if the correlation coefficient between a company's output volume and maintenance costs was 0.9, r^2 would be 0.81, meaning that 81% of variations in maintenance costs could be explained by variations in output volume, leaving only 19% of variations to be explained by other factors (such as the age of the equipment).

Note, however, that if r^2 = 0.81, we would say that 81% of **the variations in y can be explained by variations in x**. We do not necessarily conclude that 81% of variations in y are *caused* by the variations in x. We must beware of reading too much significance into our statistical analysis.

2.6 Correlation and causation

If two variables are well correlated, either positively or negatively, this may be due to **pure chance** or there may be a **reason** for it. The larger the number of pairs of data collected, the less likely it is that the correlation is due to chance, though that possibility should never be ignored entirely.

If there is a reason, it may not be **causal**. For example, monthly net income is well correlated with monthly credit to a person's bank account, for the logical (rather than causal) reason that for most people the one equals the other.

Even if there is a causal explanation for a correlation, it does not follow that variations in the value of one variable cause variations in the value of the other. For example, sales of ice cream and of sunglasses are well correlated, not because of a direct causal link but because the weather influences both variables.

3 Spearman's rank correlation coefficient

3.1 Coefficient of rank correlation

In the examples considered above, the data were given in terms of the values of the relevant variables, such as the number of hours. Sometimes however, they are given in terms of order or **rank** rather than actual values.

FAST FORWARD

Spearman's rank correlation coefficient is used when data is given in terms of order or rank, rather than actual values.

Assessment formula

Coefficient of rank correlation, $R = 1 - \left[\dfrac{6 \sum d^2}{n(n^2 - 1)} \right]$

Where n = number of pairs of data

d = the difference between the rankings in each set of data.

The coefficient of rank correlation can be **interpreted** in exactly the same way as the ordinary correlation coefficient. Its value can range from –1 to +1.

3.2 Example: The rank correlation coefficient

The examination placings of seven students were as follows.

Student	Statistics placing	Economics placing
A	2	1
B	1	3
C	4	7
D	6	5
E	5	6
F	3	2
G	7	4

Required

Judge whether the placings of the students in statistics correlate with their placings in economics.

Solution

Correlation must be measured by **Spearman's coefficient** because we are given the **placings** of students, and not their actual marks.

$$R = 1 - \frac{6 \sum d^2}{n(n^2 - 1)}$$

where d is the difference between the rank in statistics and the rank in economics for each student.

Student	Rank Statistics	Rank Economics	d	d^2
A	2	1	1	1
B	1	3	2	4
C	4	7	3	9
D	6	5	1	1
E	5	6	1	1
F	3	2	1	1
G	7	4	3	9
			$\sum d^2 =$	26

$$R = 1 - \frac{6 \times 26}{7 \times (49 - 1)} = 1 - \frac{156}{336} = 0.536$$

The correlation is **positive**, 0.536, but the correlation is **not strong**.

3.3 Tied ranks

If in a problem some of the items **tie for a particular ranking**, these must be given an **average place** before the coefficient of rank correlation is calculated. Here is an example.

Position of students in examination		Express as
A	1 = average of 1 and 2	1.5
B	1 =	1.5
C	3	3
D	4	4
E	5 =	6
F	5 = average of 5, 6 and 7	6
G	5 =	6
H	8	8

Question	Spearman's coefficient

Five artists were placed in order of merit by two different judges as follows.

Artist	Judge P Rank	Judge Q Rank
A	1	4 =
B	2 =	1
C	4	3
D	5	2
E	2 =	4 =

Required

Assess how the two sets of rankings are correlated.

Answer

	Judge P Rank	Judge Q Rank	d	d^2
A	1.0	4.5	3.5	12.25
B	2.5	1.0	1.5	2.25
C	4.0	3.0	1.0	1.00
D	5.0	2.0	3.0	9.00
E	2.5	4.5	2.0	4.00
				28.50

$$R = 1 - \frac{6 \times 28.5}{5 \times (25 - 1)} = -0.425$$

There is a **slight negative correlation** between the rankings.

4 Lines of best fit

4.1 Strength of a relationship

Correlation enables us to determine the **strength of any relationship between two variables** but it does not offer us any method of **forecasting** values for one variable, Y, given values of another variable, X.

4.2 Equation of a straight line

If we assume that there is a **linear relationship** between the two variables and we determine the **equation of a straight line (Y = a + bX)** which is a good fit for the available data plotted on a scattergraph, we can use the equation for forecasting. We do this by substituting values for X into the equation and deriving values for Y.

4.3 Estimating the equation

There are a number of techniques for estimating the equation of a line of best fit. We will be looking at the **scattergraph method** and **simple linear regression analysis**. Both provide a technique for estimating values for a and b in the equation, y = a + bx.

5 The scattergraph method

FAST FORWARD

> The scattergraph method involves the use of judgement to draw what seems to be a line of best fit through plotted data.

5.1 Example: The scattergraph method

Suppose we have the following pairs of data about output and costs.

Month	Output '000 units	Costs $'000
1	20	82
2	16	70
3	24	90
4	22	85
5	18	73

(a)   These pairs of data can be plotted on a **scattergraph** (the **horizontal** axis representing the **independent** variable and the **vertical** axis the **dependent**) and a line of best fit might be judged as the one shown below. It is drawn to pass through the middle of the data points, thereby having as many data points below the line as above it.

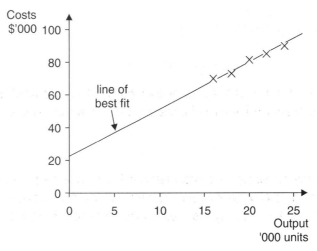

(b)   A **formula for the line of best fit** can be found. In our example, suppose that we read the following data from the graph.

(i)   When X = 0, Y = 22,000. This must be the value of **a** in the formula Y = a + bX.

(ii)   When X = 20,000, Y = 82,000. Since Y = a + bX, and a = 22,000, 82,000 = 22,000 + (b × 20,000)

b × 20,000 = 60,000

b = 3

(c)   In this example the estimated equation from the scattergraph is Y = 22,000 + 3X.

5.2 Forecasting and scattergraphs

If the company to which the data in Paragraph 5.1 relates wanted to predict costs at a certain level of output (say 13,000 units), the value of 13,000 could be substituted into the equation Y = 22,000 + 2.95X and an estimate of costs made.

If X = 13, Y = 22,000 + (3 × 13,000)

∴ Y = $61,000

Predictions can be made directly from the scattergraph, but this will usually be less accurate.

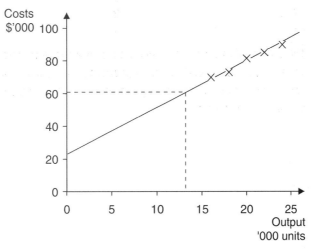

The prediction of the cost of producing 13,000 units from the scattergraph is $61,000.

6 Linear regression analysis

FAST FORWARD

Linear regression analysis (the **least squares method**) is one technique for estimating a line of best fit. Once an equation for a line of best fit has been determined, forecasts can be made.

Assessment formula

The **least squares method of linear regression analysis** involves using the following formulae for a and b in Y = a + bX.

$$b = \frac{n\sum XY - \sum X \sum Y}{n\sum X^2 - (\sum X)^2}$$

$$a = \overline{Y} - b\overline{X}$$

Where n   is the number of pairs of data

$\overline{X}$ is the mean X value of all the pairs of data

$\overline{Y}$ is the mean Y value of all the pairs of data

6.1 Some helpful hints

(a)   The value of b must be calculated first as it is needed to calculate a.

(b) $\overline{X}$ is the mean of the X values = $\dfrac{\sum X}{n}$

$\overline{Y}$ is the mean of the Y values = $\dfrac{\sum Y}{n}$

(c)   Remember that X is the independent variable and Y is the dependent variable

(d)   Set your workings out in a table to find the figures to put into the formulae.

6.2 Example: Linear regression analysis

(a)   Given that there is a fairly high degree of correlation between the output and the costs detailed in Paragraph 5.1 (so that a linear relationship can be assumed), calculate an equation to determine the expected level of costs, for any given volume of output, using the least squares method.

(b)   Prepare a budget for total costs if output is 22,000 units.

(c)   Confirm that the degree of correlation between output and costs is high by calculating the correlation coefficient.

Solution

(a) *Workings*

X	Y	XY	X^2	Y^2
20	82	1,640	400	6,724
16	70	1,120	256	4,900
24	90	2,160	576	8,100
22	85	1,870	484	7,225
18	73	1,314	324	5,329
$\sum X = 100$	$\sum Y = 400$	$\sum XY = 8,104$	$\sum X^2 = 2,040$	$\sum Y^2 = 32,278$

n = 5 (There are five pairs of data for x and y values)

$$b = \frac{n\sum XY - \sum X \sum Y}{n\sum X^2 - (\sum X)^2} = \frac{(5 \times 8,104) - (100 \times 400)}{(5 \times 2,040) - 100^2}$$

$$= \frac{40,520 - 40,000}{10,200 - 10,000} = \frac{520}{200} = 2.6$$

$$a = \overline{Y} - b\overline{X} = \frac{400}{5} - 2.6 \times \left(\frac{100}{5}\right) = 28$$

$$Y = 28 + 2.6X$$

Where Y = total cost, in thousands of pounds
　　　 X = output, in thousands of units

Compare this equation to that determined in Paragraph 5.1.

Note that the fixed costs are $28,000 (when X = 0 costs are $28,000) and the variable cost per unit is $2.60.

(b) If the output is 22,000 units, we would expect costs to be

28 + (2.6 × 22) = 85.2 = $85,200.

(c) $$r = \frac{520}{\sqrt{200 \times (5 \times 32,278 - 400^2)}} = \frac{520}{\sqrt{200 \times 1,390}} = \frac{520}{527.3} = +0.986$$

Assessment focus point

In an assessment, you might be required to use the linear regression analysis technique to calculate the values of a and b in the equation y = a + bx. This type of task is ideally tested by objective test questions.

Question

Linear regression analysis

If $\Sigma x = 79$, $\Sigma y = 1,466$, $\Sigma x^2 = 1,083$, $\Sigma y^2 = 363,076$, $\Sigma xy = 19,736$ and $n = 6$, then the value of b, the gradient, to two decimal places, is:

A   10.12
B   111.03
C   13.62
D   -8.53

Answer

A

$$r = \frac{(6 \times 19,736) - (79 \times 1,466)}{(6 \times 1,083) - 79^2}$$

$$= \frac{118,416 - 115,814}{6,498 - 6,241} = \frac{2,602}{257} = 10.12$$

Question

Forecasting

In a forecasting model based on $y = a + bx$, the intercept is $262. If the value of y is $503 and x is 23, then the value of the gradient, to two decimal places, is:

A   −20.96
B   −10.48
C   10.48
D   20.96

Answer

C $y = a + bx$
     $503 = 262 + (b \times 23)$
     $241 = b \times 23$

     $b = 10.48$

Chapter Roundup

- When the value of one variable is related to the value of another, they are said to be **correlated**.

- Two variables might be **perfectly correlated**, **partly correlated** or **uncorrelated**. Correlation can be **positive** or **negative**.

- The **degree of correlation** between two variables is measured by the **Pearson's correlation coefficient, r**. The nearer r is to +1 or −1, the stronger the relationship.

- The **coefficient of determination, r^2**, measures the proportion of the total variation in the value of one variable that can be explained by variations in the value of the other variable.

- **Spearman's rank correlation coefficient** is used when data is given in terms of order or rank, rather than actual values.

- The **scattergraph method** involves the use of judgement to draw what seems to be a line of best fit through plotted data.

- **Linear regression analysis** (the **least squares method**) is one technique for estimating a line of best fit. Once an equation for a line of best fit has been determined, forecasts can be made.

Quick Quiz

1 ………………..………….. means that low values of one variable are associated with low values of the other, and high values of one variable are associated with high values of the other.

2 ………………..………….. means that low values of one variable are associated with high values of the other, and high values of one variable with low values of the other.

3
- Perfect positive correlation, r = …………….…………...
- Perfect negative correlation, r = …………….…………...
- No correlation, r = …………….…………...

The correlation coefficient, r, must always fall within the range …………….……….. to …………….………...

4 If the correlation coefficient of a set of data is 0.95, what is the coefficient of determination and how is it interpreted?

5 Complete the following formula.

Coefficient of rank correlation, $R = 1 - \left[\dfrac{6\sum}{n(\quad)} \right]$

Where n = …………….…………...
       d = …………….…………...

6 When should Spearman's rank correlation coefficient be used?

7 (a) The equation of a straight line is given as Y = a + bX. Give two methods used for estimating the above equation.

(b) If Y = a + bX, it is best to use the regression of Y upon X where X is the dependent variable and Y is the independent variable.

True ☐

False ☐

Answers to Quick Quiz

1 Positive correlation

2 Negative correlation

3 • r = +1
• r = −1
• r = 0

The correlation coefficient, r, must always fall within the range −1 to +1.

4 Correlation coefficient = r = 0.95

Coefficient of determination = $r^2 = 0.95^2 = 0.9025$ or 90.25%

This tells us that over 90% of the variations in the dependent variable (Y) can be explained by variations in the independent variable, X.

5 $$R = 1 - \left[\frac{6 \sum d^2}{n(n^2 - 1)} \right]$$

where n = number of pairs of data
d = difference between the rankings in each set of data

6 When values of the relevant variables are given in terms of order or rank.

7 (a) • Scattergraph method (line of best fit)
• Simple linear regression analysis

(b) False. When using the regression of Y upon X, X is the independent variable and Y is the dependent variable (the value of Y will depend upon the value of X).

Now try the questions below from the Exam Question Bank

Question numbers	Pages
53-62	343-346

Part E
Forecasting

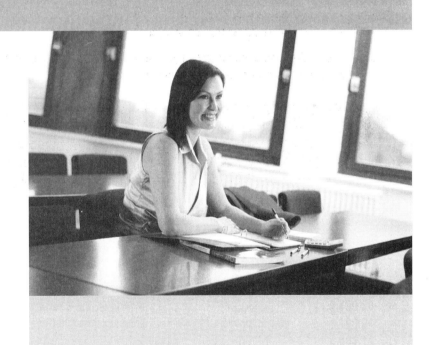

11

Forecasting

Introduction

In some situations, there are no independent variables from which to forecast a dependent variable. In this chapter we will be looking at a technique called **time series analysis**. With this **forecasting** method we look at **past data** about the variable which we want to forecast (such as sales levels) to see if there are **any patterns**. We then assume that these patterns will continue into the future. We are then able to forecast what we believe will be the value of a variable at some particular point of time in the future.

We will also use **linear regression analysis** (from Chapter 10) to make forecasts.

Topic list	Syllabus references
1 The components of time series	E, (i), (iii), (1)
2 Finding the trend	E, (ii), (2)
3 Finding the seasonal variations	E, (v), (3)
4 Forecasting	E, (iv), (vi), (vii), (4), D, (iv)
5 The limitations of forecasting models	E, (vii), (4)

1 The components of time series

A **time series** is a series of figures or values recorded over time. Any pattern found in the data is then assumed to continue into the future and an **extrapolative forecast** is produced.

1.1 Examples of time series

- Output at a factory each day for the last month
- Monthly sales over the last two years
- Total annual costs for the last ten years
- The Retail Prices Index each month for the last ten years
- The number of people employed by a company each year for the last 20 years

There are four components of a time series: trend, seasonal variations, cyclical variations and random variations.

1.2 The trend

The **trend** is the underlying long-term movement over time in the values of the data recorded.

1.3 Example: Preparing time series graphs and identifying trends

	Output per labour hour Units	Cost per unit $	Number of employees
20X4	30	1.00	100
20X5	24	1.08	103
20X6	26	1.20	96
20X7	22	1.15	102
20X8	21	1.18	103
20X9	17	1.25	98
	(A)	(B)	(C)

(a)   In time series (A) there is a **downward trend** in the output per labour hour. Output per labour hour did not fall every year, because it went up between 20X5 and 20X6, but the long-term movement is clearly a downward one.

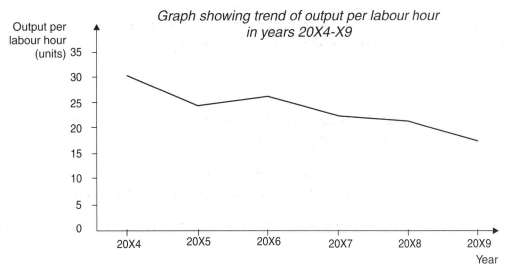

Graph showing trend of output per labour hour in years 20X4-X9

(b)   In time series (B) there is an **upward trend** in the cost per unit. Although unit costs went down in 20X7 from a higher level in 20X6, the basic movement over time is one of rising costs.

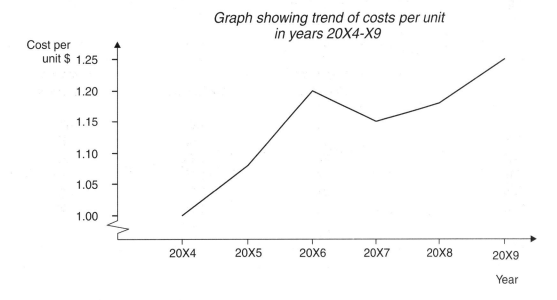

Graph showing trend of costs per unit in years 20X4-X9

(c)   In time series (C) there is no clear movement up or down, and the number of employees remained fairly constant around 100. The trend is therefore a **static**, or **level** one.

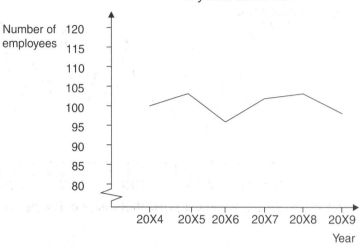

Graph showing trend of number of employees in years 20X4-X9

1.4 Seasonal variations

Key term

> **Seasonal variations** are short-term fluctuations in recorded values, due to different circumstances which affect results at different times of the year, on different days of the week or at different times of day etc.

1.5 Examples of seasonal variations

(a)   Sales of ice cream will be higher in summer than in winter, and sales of overcoats will be higher in autumn than in spring.

(b)   Shops might expect higher sales shortly before Christmas, or in their winter and summer sales.

(c)   Sales might be higher on Friday and Saturday than on Monday.

(d)   The telephone network may be heavily used at certain times of the day (such as mid-morning and mid-afternoon) and much less used at other times (such as in the middle of the night).

1.6 Example: The trend and seasonal variations

The number of customers served by a company of travel agents over the past four years is shown in the following **historigram** (time series graph).

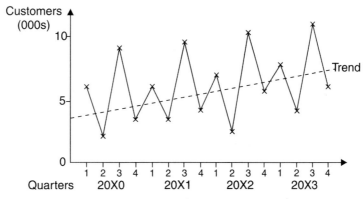

In this example, there would appear to be large **seasonal fluctuations in demand,** but there is also a basic **upward trend.**

1.7 Cyclical variations

Cyclical variations are medium-term changes in results caused by circumstances which repeat in cycles.

In business, cyclical variations are commonly associated with **economic cycles**, successive **booms** and **slumps** in the economy. Economic cycles may last a few years. Cyclical variations are **longer** term than seasonal variations.

Though you should be aware of the cyclical component, you will not be expected to carry out any calculation connected with isolating it. The mathematical models which we will use, therefore exclude any reference to C.

1.8 Summarising the components

The components of a time series **combine** to produce a variable in one of two ways.

Assessment formulae

Additive model: Series = Trend + Seasonal + Random
             Y = T + S + R

Multiplicative model: Series = Trend × Seasonal × Random
             Y = T × S × R

2 Finding the trend

2.1 Methods of finding the trend

The main problem we are concerned with in time series analysis is how to **identify the trend** and **seasonal variations.**

Main methods of finding a trend

(a)   A **line of best fit** (the **trend line**) can be drawn by eye on a graph.
(b)   **Linear regression analysis** can be used. (We covered this in Chapter 10)
(c)   A technique known as **moving averages** can be used.

2.2 Finding the trend by moving averages

One method of finding the trend is by the use of **moving averages**.

Key terms

- A **moving average** is an average of the results of a fixed number of periods

- The **moving averages method** attempts to remove seasonal variations from actual data by a process of averaging

2.3 Example: Moving averages of an odd number of results

Year	Sales Units
20X0	390
20X1	380
20X2	460
20X3	450
20X4	470
20X5	440
20X6	500

Required

Take a moving average of the annual sales over a period of three years.

Solution

(a)   Average sales in the three year period 20X0 – 20X2 were

$$\left(\frac{390 + 380 + 460}{3} \right) = \frac{1,230}{3} = 410$$

This average relates to the middle year of the period, 20X1.

(b)   Similarly, average sales in the three year period 20X1 – 20X3 were

$$\left(\frac{380 + 460 + 450}{3} \right) = \frac{1,290}{3} = 430$$

This average relates to the middle year of the period, 20X2.

(c)   The average sales can also be found for the periods 20X2–20X4, 20X3–20X5 and 20X4–20X6, to give the following.

Year	Sales	Moving total of 3 years' sales	Moving average of 3 years' sales (÷ 3)
20X0	390		
20X1	380	1,230	410
20X2	460	1,290	430
20X3	450	1,380	460
20X4	470	1,360	453
20X5	440	1,410	470
20X6	500		

Note the following points.

(i)   The moving average series has five figures relating to the years from 20X1 to 20X5. The original series had seven figures for the years from 20X0 to 20X6.

(ii)   There is an upward trend in sales, which is more noticeable from the series of moving averages than from the original series of actual sales each year.

2.4 Over what period should a moving average be taken?

The above example averaged over a three-year period. Over what period should a moving average be taken? The answer to this question is that **the moving average which is most appropriate will depend on the circumstances and the nature of the time series**. Note the following points.

(a)   A moving average which takes an average of the results in many time periods will represent results over a longer term than a moving average of two or three periods.

(b)   On the other hand, with a moving average of results in many time periods, the last figure in the series will be out of date by several periods. In our example, the most recent average related to 20X5. With a moving average of five years' results, the final figure in the series would relate to 20X4.

(c)   When there is a known cycle over which seasonal variations occur, such as all the days in the week or all the seasons in the year, the most suitable moving average would be one which covers one full cycle.

Question   **Three-month moving average**

Using the following data, complete the following table in order to determine the three-month moving average for the period January-June.

Month	No of new houses finished	Moving total 3 months new houses finished	Moving average of 3 months new houses finished
January	500		
February	450		
March	700		
April	900		
May	1,250		
June	1,000		

Answer

Month	No of new houses finished	Moving total 3 months new houses finished	Moving average of 3 months new houses finished
January	500		
February	450	1,650	550
March	700	2,050	683
April	900	2,850	950
May	1,250	3,150	1,050
June	1,000		

2.5 Moving averages of an even number of results

When finding the moving average of an **even number of results**, a second moving average has to be calculated so that trend values can relate to specific actual figures.

In the previous example, moving averages were taken of the results in an **odd number of time periods**, and the average then related to the **mid-point of the overall period**. If a moving average were taken of results in an **even number of time periods**, the basic technique would be the same, but **the mid-point of the overall period would not relate to a single period**. For example, suppose an average were taken of the following four results.

Spring	120	
Summer	90	average 115
Autumn	180	
Winter	70	

The average would relate to the mid-point of the period, between summer and autumn. The trend line average figures need to relate to a particular time period; otherwise, seasonal variations cannot be calculated. To overcome this difficulty, we take a **moving average of the moving average**. An example will illustrate this technique.

2.6 Example: Moving averages over an even number of periods

Calculate a moving average trend line of the following results.

Year	Quarter	Volume of sales '000 units
20X5	1	600
	2	840
	3	420
	4	720
20X6	1	640
	2	860
	3	420
	4	740
20X7	1	670
	2	900
	3	430
	4	760

Solution

A moving average of **four** will be used, since the volume of sales would appear to depend on the season of the year, and each year has four **quarterly** results.

The moving average of four does not relate to any specific period of time; therefore a second moving average of two will be calculated on the first moving average trend line.

Year	Quarter	Actual volume of sales '000 units (A)	Moving total of 4 quarters' sales '000 units (B)	Moving average of 4 quarters' sales '000 units (B ÷ 4)	Mid-point of 2 moving averages Trend line '000 units (C)
20X5	1	600			
	2	840			
	3	420	2,580	645.0	650.00
	4	720	2,620	655.0	657.50
20X6	1	640	2,640	660.0	660.00
	2	860	2,640	660.0	662.50
	3	420	2,660	665.0	668.75
	4	740	2,690	672.5	677.50
20X7	1	670	2,730	682.5	683.75
	2	900	2,740	685.0	687.50
	3	430	2,760	690.0	
	4	760			

By taking **a mid point** (a moving average of two) of the original moving averages, we can relate the results **to specific quarters** (from the third quarter of 20X5 to the second quarter of 20X7).

The time series information and moving average trend can be shown on a graph.

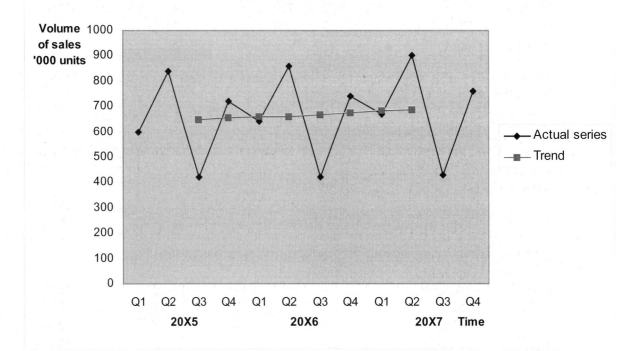

Time series graph and moving average trend

3 Finding the seasonal variations

Seasonal variations are the difference between actual and trend figures. An average of the seasonal variations for each time period within the cycle must be determined and then adjusted so that the total of the seasonal variations sums to zero. Seasonal variations can be estimated using the **additive model**.
($Y = T + S + R$, with seasonal variations = $Y - T$) or the multiplicative model ($Y = T \times S \times R$, with seasonal variations = $Y \div T$).

3.1 Finding the seasonal component using the additive model

Once a trend has been established, by whatever method, we can find the **seasonal variations**.

Step 1   The additive model for time series analysis is $Y = T + S + R$.

Step 2   If we deduct the trend from the additive model, we get $Y - T = S + R$.

Step 3   If we assume that R, the random, component of the time series is relatively small and therefore negligible, then $S = Y - T$.

Therefore, the seasonal component, $S = Y - T$ (the de-trended series).

3.2 Example: The trend and seasonal variations

Output at a factory appears to vary with the day of the week. Output over the last three weeks has been as follows.

	Week 1 '000 units	Week 2 '000 units	Week 3 '000 units
Monday	80	82	84
Tuesday	104	110	116
Wednesday	94	97	100
Thursday	120	125	130
Friday	62	64	66

Required

Find the seasonal variation for each of the 15 days, and the average seasonal variation for each day of the week using the moving averages method.

Solution

Actual results fluctuate up and down according to the day of the week and so a **moving average of five** will be used. The **difference** between the actual result on any one day (Y) and the trend figure for that day (T) will be the **seasonal variation (S)** for the day. The seasonal variations for the 15 days are as follows.

		Actual (Y)	Moving total of five days' output	Trend (T)	Seasonal variation (Y–T)
Week 1	Monday	80			
	Tuesday	104			
	Wednesday	94	460	92.0	+2.0
	Thursday	120	462	92.4	+27.6
	Friday	62	468	93.6	−31.6
Week 2	Monday	82	471	94.2	−12.2
	Tuesday	110	476	95.2	+14.8
	Wednesday	97	478	95.6	+1.4
	Thursday	125	480	96.0	+29.0
	Friday	64	486	97.2	−33.2
Week 3	Monday	84	489	97.8	−13.8
	Tuesday	116	494	98.8	+17.2
	Wednesday	100	496	99.2	+0.8
	Thursday	130			
	Friday	66			

You will notice that the variation between the actual results on any one particular day and the trend line average is not the same from week to week. This is because Y − T contains not only seasonal variations but **random** variations, and an **average** of these variations can be taken.

	Monday	Tuesday	Wednesday	Thursday	Friday
Week 1			+2.0	+27.6	−31.6
Week 2	−12.2	+14.8	+1.4	+29.0	−33.2
Week 3	−13.8	+17.2	+0.8		
Average	−13.0	+16.0	+1.4	+28.3	−32.4

Variations around the basic trend line should cancel each other out, and **add up to 0.** At the moment they do not. **The average seasonal estimates must therefore be corrected so that they add up to zero** and so we spread the total of the daily variations (0.30) across the five days (0.3 ÷ 5) so that the final total of the daily variations goes to zero.

	Monday	Tuesday	Wednesday	Thursday	Friday	Total
Estimated average daily variation	−13.00	+16.00	+1.40	+28.30	−32.40	0.30
Adjustment to reduce total variation to 0	−0.06	−0.06	−0.06	−0.06	−0.06	−0.30
Final estimate of average daily variation	−13.06	+15.94	+1.34	+28.24	−32.46	0.00

These might be rounded up or down as follows.

Monday −13; Tuesday +16; Wednesday +1; Thursday +28; Friday −32; Total 0.

Question

Four-quarter moving average trend

Calculate a four-quarter moving average trend centred on actual quarters and then find seasonal variations from the following.

			Sales in $'000		
		Spring	Summer	Autumn	Winter
20X7		200	120	160	280
20X8		220	140	140	300
20X9		200	120	180	320

Answer

		Sales (Y)	4-quarter total	8-quarter total	Moving average (T)	Seasonal variation (Y−T)
20X7	Spring	200				
	Summer	120				
			760			
	Autumn	160		1,540	192.5	−32.5
			780			
	Winter	280		1,580	197.5	+82.5
			800			
20X8	Spring	220		1,580	197.5	+22.5
			780			
	Summer	140		1,580	197.5	−57.5
			800			
	Autumn	140		1,580	197.5	−57.5
			780			
	Winter	300		1,540	192.5	+107.5
			760			

20X9	Spring	200		1,560	195.0	+5.0
			800			
	Summer	120		1,620	202.5	−82.5
			820			
	Autumn	180				
	Winter	320				

We can now average the seasonal variations.

	Spring	Summer	Autumn	Winter	Total
20X7			−32.5	+82.5	
20X8	+22.5	−57.5	−57.5	+107.5	
20X9	+5.0	−82.5			
	+27.5	−140.0	−90.0	+190.0	
Average variations (in $'000)	+13.75	−70.00	−45.00	+95.00	−6.25
Adjustment so sum is zero	+1.5625	+1.5625	+1.5625	+1.5625	+6.25
Adjusted average variations	+15.3125	−68.4375	−43.4375	+96.5625	0

These might be rounded up or down to:

Spring $15,000, Summer −$68,000, Autumn −$43,000, Winter $97,000

3.3 Finding the seasonal component using the multiplicative model

The method of estimating the seasonal variations in the additive model is to use the differences between the trend and actual data. **The additive model assumes that the components of the series are independent of each other**, an increasing trend not affecting the seasonal variations for example.

The alternative is to use the **multiplicative model** whereby **each actual figure is expressed as a proportion of the trend**. Sometimes this method is called the **proportional model**.

3.4 Example: Multiplicative model

The additive model example above (in Paragraph 3.2) can be reworked on this alternative basis. The trend is calculated in exactly the same way as before but we need a different approach for the seasonal variations.

The multiplicative model is $Y = T \times S \times R$ and, just as we calculated $S = Y - T$ for the additive model we can calculate **$S = Y/T$** for the multiplicative model.

		Actual (Y)	Trend (T)	Seasonal variation (Y/T)
Week 1	Monday	80		
	Tuesday	104		
	Wednesday	94	92.0	1.022
	Thursday	120	92.4	1.299
	Friday	62	93.6	0.662

Week 2	Monday	82	94.2	0.870
	Tuesday	110	95.2	1.155
	Wednesday	97	95.6	1.015
	Thursday	125	96.0	1.302
	Friday	64	97.2	0.658
Week 3	Monday	84	97.8	0.859
	Tuesday	116	98.8	1.174
	Wednesday	100	99.2	1.008
	Thursday	130		
	Friday	66		

The summary of the seasonal variations expressed in **proportional terms** is as follows.

	Monday	Tuesday	Wednesday	Thursday	Friday
Week 1			1.022	1.299	0.662
Week 2	0.870	1.155	1.015	1.302	0.658
Week 3	0.859	1.174	1.008		
Total	1.729	2.329	3.045	2.601	1.320
Average	0.8645	1.1645	1.0150	1.3005	0.6600

Instead of summing to zero, as with the absolute approach, these should **sum** (in this case) **to 5 (an average of 1)**.

They actually sum to 5.0045 so 0.0009 has to be deducted from each one. This is too small to make a difference to the figures above, so we should deduct 0.002 and 0.0025 to each of two seasonal variations. We could arbitrarily decrease Monday's variation to 0.8625 and Tuesday's to 1.162.

3.5 When to use the multiplicative model

The multiplicative model is better than the additive model for forecasting when the trend is increasing or decreasing over time. In such circumstances, seasonal variations are likely to be increasing or decreasing too. The additive model simply adds absolute and unchanging seasonal variations to the trend figures whereas the multiplicative model, by multiplying increasing or decreasing trend values by a constant seasonal variation factor, takes account of changing seasonal variations.

3.6 Summary

We can summarise the steps to be carried out when calculating the seasonal variation as follows.

Step 1   Calculate the moving total for an appropriate period.

Step 2   Calculate the moving average (the trend) for the period. (Calculate the mid-point of two moving averages if there are an even number of periods.)

Step 3   Calculate the seasonal variation. For an additive model, this is $Y - T$. For a multiplicative model, this is Y/T.

Step 4   Calculate an average of the seasonal variations.

Step 5   Adjust the average seasonal variations so that they add up to **zero** for an **additive model**. When using the **multiplicative model**, the average seasonal variations should add up to an **average of 1**.

Question

Average seasonal variations

Find the average seasonal variations for the sales data in the previous question (entitled: Four-quarter moving average trend) using the **multiplicative** model.

Answer

	Spring	Summer	Autumn	Winter	Total
20X7			0.83*	1.42	
20X8	1.11	0.71	0.71	1.56	
20X9	1.03	0.59			
	2.14	1.30	1.54	2.98	

	Spring	Summer	Autumn	Winter	Total
Average variations	1.070	0.650	0.770	1.490	3.980
Adjustment to sum to 4	+ 0.005	+ 0.005	+ 0.005	+ 0.005	0.020
Adjusted average variations	1.075	0.655	0.775	1.495	4.000

* Seasonal variation $Y/T = \dfrac{160}{192.5} = 0.83$

Question

Multiplicative model

In a time series analysis, the multiplicative model is used to forecast sales and the following seasonal variations apply.

Quarter	1	2	3	4
Seasonal variation	0.8	1.9	0.75	?

The actual sales value for the last two quarters of 20X1 were:

Quarter 3:	$250,000
Quarter 4:	$260,000

(a) The seasonal variation for the fourth quarter is:

    A   0.55

    B   −3.45

    C   1.00

    D   1.45

(b) The trend line for sales:

    A   remained constant between quarter 3 and quarter 4

    B   increased between quarter 3 and quarter 4

    C   decreased between quarter 3 and quarter 4

    D   cannot be determined from the information given

Answer

(a)   **The correct answer is A.**

As this is a multiplicative model, the seasonal variations should sum (in this case) to 4 (an average of 1) as there are four quarters.

Let x = seasonal variation in quarter 4.

0.8 + 1.9 + 0.75 + x = 4

$\therefore$ 3.45 + x = 4

x = 4 − 3.45

x = 0.55

(b)   **The correct answer is B.**

For a multiplicative model, the seasonal component is as follows.

S = Y/T

$\therefore$ T = Y/S

	Quarter	
	3	*4*
Seasonal component (S)	0.75	0.55
Actual sales (Y)	$250,000	$260,000
Trend (T) (= Y/S)	$333,333	$472,727

The trend line for sales has therefore increased between quarter 3 and quarter 4.

3.7 Seasonally-adjusted data

Key term

> **Seasonally-adjusted data (deseasonalised)** are data which have had any seasonal variations taken out, so leaving a figure which might indicate the trend. Seasonally-adjusted data should indicate whether the overall trend is rising, falling or stationary.

3.8 Example: Seasonally-adjusted data

Actual sales figures for four quarters, together with appropriate seasonal adjustment factors derived from previous data, are as follows.

		Seasonal adjustments	
Quarter	*Actual sales*	*Additive model*	*Multiplicative model*
	$'000	$'000	
1	150	+3	1.02
2	160	+4	1.05
3	164	−2	0.98
4	170	−5	0.95

Required

Deseasonalise these data.

BPP
PROFESSIONAL EDUCATION

Solution

We are reversing the normal process of applying seasonal variations to trend figures.

The rules for deseasonalising data are as follows.

- **Additive model** – subtract positive seasonal variations from and add negative seasonal variations to actual results.

- **Multiplicative model** – divide the actual results by the seasonal variation factors.

		Deseasonalised sales	
Quarter	Actual sales	Additive model	Multiplicative model
	$'000	$'000	$'000
1	150	147	147
2	160	156	152
3	164	166	167
4	170	175	179

Question   **Seasonally-adjusted figures**

Unemployment numbers actually recorded in a town for the first quarter of 20X9 were 4,700. The underlying trend at this point was 4,400 people and the seasonal factor is 0.85. Using the multiplicative model for seasonal adjustment, the seasonally-adjusted figure (in whole numbers) for the quarter is

A   5,529
B   5,176
C   3,995
D   3,740

Answer

The correct answer is A.

If you remembered the ruling that you need to **divide** by the seasonal variation factor to obtain seasonally-adjusted figures (using the multiplicative model), then you should have been able to eliminate options C and D. This might have been what you did if you weren't sure whether you divided the **actual results** or the **trend** by the seasonal variation factor.

$$\text{Seasonally adjusted data} = \frac{\text{Actual results}}{\text{Seasonal factor}} = \frac{4,700}{0.85} = 5,529$$

4 Forecasting

Forecasts can be made by **extrapolating the trend** and **adjusting for seasonal variations**. Remember, however, that all forecasts are subject to error.

4.1 Making a forecast

Step 1   **Plot a trend line**: use the line of best fit method, linear regression analysis or the moving averages method.

Step 2   **Extrapolate the trend line**. This means extending the trend line outside the range of known data and forecasting future results from historical data.

Step 3   **Adjust forecast trends** by the applicable average seasonal variation to obtain the actual forecast.

(a)   **Additive model** – add positive variations to and subtract negative variations from the forecast trends.

(b)   **Multiplicative model** – multiply the forecast trends by the seasonal variation.

4.2 Example: Forecasting

Use the trend values and the estimates of seasonal variations calculated in Paragraph 3.2 to forecast sales in week 4.

Solution

We begin by plotting the trend values on a graph and extrapolating the trend line.

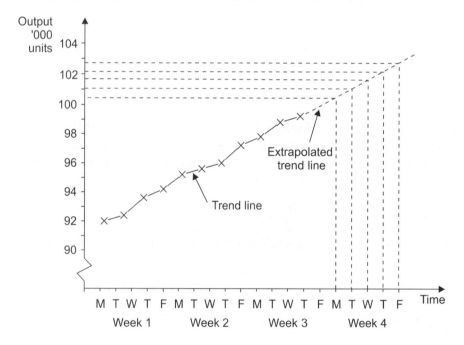

From the extrapolated trend line we can take the following readings and adjust them by the seasonal variations.

Week 4	Trend line readings	Seasonal variations	Forecast
Monday	100.5	−13	87.5
Tuesday	101.5	+16	117.1
Wednesday	101.7	+1	102.7
Thursday	102.2	+28	130.2
Friday	102.8	−32	70.8

If we had been using the multiplicative model the forecast for Tuesday, for example, would be $101.1 \times 1.1645 = 117.7$ (from Paragraph 3.4).

4.3 Forecasting using linear regression analysis

Correlation exists in a time series if there is a relationship between the period of time and the recorded value for that period of time. Time is the X variable and **simplified values for X are used** instead of year numbers.

For example, instead of having a series of years 20X1 to 20X5, we could have values for X from 0 (20X1) to 4 (20X5).

Using linear regression analysis, a trend line is found to be $y = 20 - 2.2X$ where X = 0 in 20X1 and Y = sales level in thousands of units. Using the trend line, predicted sales in 20X6 (X = 5) would be:

$20 - (2.2 \times 5) = 9$ ie 9,000 units

Predicted sales in 20X7 (year 6) would be:

$20 - (2.2 \times 6) = 6.8$ ie 6,800 units

Question   **Forecast sales**

Suppose that a trend line, found using linear regression analysis, is $Y = 300 - 4.7X$ where X is time (in quarters) and Y = sales level in thousands of units. Given that X = 0 represents 20X0 quarter 1 and that the seasonal variations are as set out below.

	Q_1	Q_2	Q_3	Q_4
Seasonal variations ('000 units)	−20	−8	+4	+15

The forecast sales level for 20X5 quarter 4 is ☐ units

Answer

☐ 206,900 ☐ units

Working

X = 0 corresponds to 20X0 quarter 1

∴ X = 23 corresponds to 20X5 quarter 4

Trend sales level = $300 - (4.7 \times 23) = 191.9$ ie 191,900 units

Seasonally-adjusted sales level = $191.9 + 15 = 206.9$ ie 206,900 units

Question

Over a 36-month period, sales have been found to have an underlying linear trend of Y = 14.224 + 7.898X, where Y is the number of items sold and X represents the month. Monthly deviations from trend have been calculated and month 37 is expected to be 1.28 times the trend value.

The forecast number of items to be sold in month 37 is approximately

A   389
B   390
C   391
D   392

Answer

This is typical of multiple choice questions that you must work through fully if you are to get the right answer.

Y = 14.224 + 7.898X

If X = 37, trend in sales for month 37 = 14.224 + (7.898 × 37)
                                                                 = 306.45

∴ Seasonally-adjusted trend value = 306.45 × 1.28
                                                           = 392.256

∴ The correct answer is 392, option D.

4.4 Residuals

Key term

> A **residual** is the difference between the results which would have been predicted (for a past period for which we already have data) by the trend line adjusted for the average seasonal variation and the actual results.

The residual is therefore the difference which is not explained by the trend line and the average seasonal variation. The residual gives some indication of how much actual results were affected by other factors. Large residuals suggest that any forecast is likely to be unreliable.

In the example in Paragraph 3.2, the 'prediction' for Wednesday of week 2 would have been 95.6 + 1 = 96.6. As the actual value was 97, the residual was only 97 – 96.6 = 0.4.

5 The limitations of forecasting models

FAST FORWARD

> Remember that all forecasts are subject to error. There are a number of factors which will affect the reliability of forecasts.

5.1 The reliability of time series analysis forecasts

All forecasts are subject to error, but the likely errors vary from case to case.

(a)   The further into the future the forecast is for, the more unreliable it is likely to be.

(b)   The less data available on which to base the forecast, the less reliable the forecast.

(c)   The pattern of trend and seasonal variations cannot be guaranteed to continue in the future.

(d)   There is always the danger of random variations upsetting the pattern of trend and seasonal variation.

(e)   The extrapolation of the trend line is done by judgement and can introduce error.

5.2 The reliability of regression analysis forecasts

There are a number of factors which affect the reliability of forecasts made using regression analysis.

(a)   **It assumes a linear relationship exists between the two variables** (since linear regression analysis produces an equation in the linear format) whereas a non-linear relationship might exist.

(b)   It **assumes that the value of one variable, Y, can be predicted or estimated from the value of one other variable, X**. In reality the value of Y might depend on several other variables, not just X.

(c)   When it is used for forecasting, **it assumes that what has happened in the past will provide a reliable guide to the future**.

(d)   When calculating a line of best fit, there will be a range of values for X. In the example in Paragraph 6.2, Chapter 10, the line $Y = 28 + 2.6X$ was predicted from data with output values ranging from $X = 16$ to $X = 24$. Depending on the degree of correlation between X and Y, we might safely use the estimated line of best fit to predict values for Y in the future, provided that the value of X remains within the range 16 to 24. We would be on less safe ground if we used the formula to predict a value for Y when $X = 10$, or 30, or any other value outside the range 16 to 24, because we would have to **assume that the trend line applies outside the range of X values used to establish the line in the first place**.

(e)   As with any forecasting process, **the amount of data available is very important**. Even if correlation is high, if we have fewer than about ten pairs of values, we must regard any forecast as being somewhat unreliable. (It is likely to provide more reliable forecasts than the scattergraph method, however, since it uses all of the available data.)

(f)   **The reliability of a forecast will depend on the reliability of the data collected to determine the regression analysis equation**. If the data is not collected accurately or if data used is false, forecasts are unlikely to be acceptable.

Chapter Roundup

- A **time series** is a series of figures or values recorded over time. Any pattern found in the data is then assumed to continue into the future and an **extrapolative forecast** is produced.

- There are four components of a time series: **trend**, **seasonal variations**, **cyclical variations** and **random variations**.

- The **trend** is the underlying long-term movement over time in the values of the data recorded.

- **Seasonal variations** are short-term fluctuations in recorded values, due to different circumstances which affect results at different times of the year, on different days of the week or at different times of the day etc.

- **Cyclical variations** are medium-term changes in results caused by circumstances which repeat in cycles.

- One method of finding the trend is by the use of **moving averages**.

- When finding the moving average of an **even number of results**, a second moving average has to be calculated so that trend values can relate to specific actual figures.

- **Seasonal variations are the difference between actual and trend figures**. An average of the seasonal variations for each time period within the cycle must be determined and then adjusted so that the total of the seasonal variations sums to zero. Seasonal variations can be estimated using the **additive model (Y = T + S + R, with seasonal variations = Y – T)** or the **multiplicative model (Y = T × S × R, with seasonal variations = Y/T)**.

- **Forecasts** can be made by **extrapolating the trend** and **adjusting for seasonal variations**.

- There are a number of factors which will affect the reliability of forecasts. Remember that all forecasts are subject to error.

Quick Quiz

1   What are the four main components of a time series?

2   **Additive model**

Y = T + S + R

Where Y =
           T =
           S =
           R =

3   What is the formula for the multiplicative model?

4   If the trend is increasing or decreasing over time, it is better to use the additive model for forecasting.

True   ☐

False   ☐

5   List three methods for finding trend lines.

BPP
PROFESSIONAL EDUCATION

6   **Results**   **Method**

Odd number of time periods   **?**   Calculate 1 moving average

Even number of time periods   Calculate 2 moving averages

7    $A = Y - T$

    $B = Y/T$

Seasonal variation:

Multiplicative model =
Additive model =

8   When calculating seasonal variations, adjust the average seasonal variations so that they add up to zero for a(n) additive/multiplicative model. When using the additive/multiplicative model, the average seasonal variations should add up to an average of 1.

9   When deseasonalising data, the following rules apply to the additive model.

    I   Add positive seasonal variations
    II   Subtract positive seasonal variations
    III   Add negative seasonal variations
    IV   Subtract negative seasonal variations

    A   I and II
    B   II and III
    C   II and IV
    D   I only

10   Time series analysis data can be used to make forecasts by **extrapolating** the trend line. What does extrapolation mean?

11   Cyclical variation is the term used for the difference which is not explained by the trend line and the average seasonal variation.

    True   ☐

    False   ☐

12   List the factors that might explain why time series analysis forecasts may not be 100% reliable.

Answers to Quick Quiz

1. • Trend
   • Seasonal variation (fluctuation)
   • Cyclical variations
   • Random variations

2. Y = the actual time series
   T = the trend series
   S = the seasonal component
   R = the random/irregular component

3. $Y = T \times S \times R$

4. False

5. • Line of best fit
   • Linear regression
   • Moving averages

6. Odd number of time periods = calculate 1 moving average

   Even number of time periods = calculate 2 moving averages

7. Multiplicative model = B = Y/T

   Additive model = A = Y – T

8. When calculating seasonal variations, adjust the average seasonal variations so that they add up to **zero** for an **additive model**. When using the **multiplicative model**, the average seasonal variations should add up to an average of **1**.

9. B

10. Extending the trend line outside the range of known data and forecasting future results from historical data.

11. False. The residual is the term used to explain the difference which is not explained by the trend line and the average seasonal variation.

12. (a) The further into the future a forecast is made, the more unreliable it is likely to be.
    (b) The less data available for forecasting, the less reliable the forecast.
    (c) The trend and seasonal variation patterns identified may not continue in the future.
    (d) Random variations may upset the pattern of trend and seasonal variation.
    (e) The extrapolation of the trend line is done by judgement and may not be accurate.

Now try the questions below from the Exam Question Bank

Question numbers	Pages
63-73	347-353

Part F
Financial mathematics

Interest

Introduction

The previous chapters introduced a variety of quantitative methods relevant to business analysis. This chapter and the next extend the use of mathematics and look at aspects of financial analysis typically undertaken in a business organisation.

In general, financial mathematics deals with problems of **investing money**, or **capital**. If a company (or an individual investor) puts some capital into an investment, a financial return will be expected.

The two major techniques of financial mathematics are **compounding** and **discounting**. This chapter will describe compounding and the next will introduce discounting

Topic list	Syllabus references
1 Simple interest	F, (i), (1)
2 Compound interest	F, (i), (1)
3 Regular savings and sinking funds	F, (vi), (4)
4 Loans and mortgages	F, (vi), (3)
5 Annual percentage rate (APR) of interest	F, (ii)

1 Simple interest

1.1 Interest

Interest is the amount of money which an investment earns over time.

Simple interest is interest which is earned in equal amounts every year (or month) and which is a given proportion of the original investment (the principal). The simple interest formula is **S = X + nrX**.

If a sum of money is invested for a period of time, then the amount of simple interest which accrues is equal to the number of periods × the interest rate × the amount invested. We can write this as a formula.

Formula to learn

The formula for **simple interest** is as follows.

$S = X + nrX$

Where X =   the original sum invested

         r =   the interest rate (expressed as a proportion, so 10% = 0.1)

         n =   the number of periods (normally years)

         S =   the sum invested after n periods, consisting of the original capital (X) plus interest earned.

1.2 Example: Simple interest

How much will an investor have after five years if he invests $1,000 at 10% simple interest per annum?

Solution

Using the formula $S = X + nrX$

where X = $1,000

       r = 10%

       n = 5

$\therefore S = \$1,000 + (5 \times 0.1 \times \$1,000) = \$1,500$

1.3 Investment periods

If , for example, the sum of money is invested for 3 months and the interest rate is a rate per annum, then n =3/12 = 1/4. If the investment period is 197 days and the rate is an annual rate, then n = 197/365.

2 Compound interest

2.1 Compounding

Interest is normally calculated by means of **compounding**.

FAST FORWARD

> **Compounding** means that, as interest is earned, it is added to the original investment and starts to earn interest itself. The basic formula for compound interest is $S = X(1 + r)^n$.

If a sum of money, the principal, is invested at a fixed rate of interest such that the interest is added to the principal and no withdrawals are made, then the amount invested will grow by an increasing number of pounds in each successive time period, because **interest earned in earlier periods will itself earn interest in later periods**.

2.2 Example: Compound interest

Suppose that $2,000 is invested at 10% interest. After one year, the original principal plus interest will amount to $2,200.

	$
Original investment	2,000
Interest in the first year (10%)	200
Total investment at the end of one year	2,200

(a) After two years the total investment will be $2,420.

	$
Investment at end of one year	2,200
Interest in the second year (10%)	220
Total investment at the end of two years	2,420

The second year interest of $220 represents 10% of the original investment, and 10% of the interest earned in the first year.

(b) Similarly, after three years, the total investment will be $2,662.

	$
Investment at the end of two years	2,420
Interest in the third year (10%)	242
Total investment at the end of three years	2,662

Instead of performing the calculations shown above, we could have used the following formula.

Assessment formula

> The basic formula for **compound interest** is $S = X(1 + r)^n$
>
> Where X $=$ the original sum invested
> r $=$ the interest rate, expressed as a proportion (so 5% = 0.05)
> n $=$ the number of periods
> S $=$ the sum invested after n periods

Using the formula for compound interest, $S = X(1 + r)^n$

where X = $2,000
       r = 10% = 0.1
       n = 3

       S = $2,000 × 1.10^3
           = $2,000 × 1.331
           = $2,662.

The interest earned over three years is $662, which is the same answer that was calculated above.

You will need to be familiar with the use of the power button on your calculator ($x^\blacksquare$, $x^\wedge$, x^y or y^x).

Question
Simple interest

Simon invests $5,000 now. To what value would this sum have grown after the following periods using the given interest rates? State your answer to two decimal places.

Value now	Investment period	Interest rate	Final value
$	Years	%	$
5,000	3	20	
5,000	4	15	
5,000	3	6	

Answer

Value now	Investment period	Interest rate	Final value
$	Years	%	$
5,000	3	20	8,640.00 [1]
5,000	4	15	8,745.03 [2]
5,000	3	6	5,955.08 [3]

Workings

(1) $5,000 × 1.20^3 = $8,640.00
(2) $5,000 × 1.15^4 = $8,745.03
(3) $5,000 × 1.06^3 = $5,955.08

Question
Compound interest

At what annual rate of compound interest will $2,000 grow to $2,721 after four years?

A   7%
B   8%
C   9%
D   10%

Answer

Using the formula for compound interest, $S = X(1 + r)^n$, we know that X = $2,000, S = $2,721 and n = 4. We need to find r. It is essential that you are able to rearrange equations confidently when faced with this type of multiple choice question - there is not a lot of room for guessing!

$$\$2,721 = \$2,000 \times (1 + r)^4$$

$$(1 + r)^4 = \frac{£2,721}{£2,000} = 1.3605$$

$$1 + r = \sqrt[4]{1.3605} = 1.08$$

$$r = 0.08 = 8\%$$

The correct answer is B.

2.3 Inflation

The same compounding formula can be used to **predict future prices** after allowing for **inflation**. For example, if we wish to predict the salary of an employee in five years' time, given that he earns $8,000 now and wage inflation is expected to be 10% per annum, the compound interest formula would be applied as follows.

$$S = X(1 + r)^n$$
$$= \$8,000 \times 1.10^5$$
$$= \$12,884.08$$

say, $12,900.

2.4 Withdrawals of capital or interest

If an investor takes money out of an investment, it will cease to earn interest. Thus, if an investor puts $3,000 into a bank deposit account which pays interest at 8% per annum, and makes no withdrawals except at the end of year 2, when he takes out $1,000, what would be the balance in his account after four years?

	$
Original investment	3,000.00
Interest in year 1 (8%)	240.00
Investment at end of year 1	3,240.00
Interest in year 2 (8%)	259.20
Investment at end of year 2	3,499.20
Less withdrawal	1,000.00
Net investment at start of year 3	2,499.20
Interest in year 3 (8%)	199.94
Investment at end of year 3	2,699.14
Interest in year 4 (8%)	215.93
Investment at end of year 4	2,915.07

A quicker approach would be as follows.

	$
$3,000 invested for 2 years at 8% would increase in value to $3,000 × 1.08² =	3,499.20
Less withdrawal	1,000.00
	2,499.20

$2,499.20 invested for a further two years at 8% would increase in value to

$2,499.20 × 1.08² = $2,915.07

2.5 Reverse compounding

The basic principle of compounding can be applied in a number of different situations.

- Reducing balance depreciation
- Falling prices
- Changes in the rate of interest

2.6 Reducing balance depreciation

FAST FORWARD

> The basic compound interest formula can be used to calculate the net book value of an asset depreciated using the **reducing balance method of depreciation** by using a negative rate of 'interest' (reverse compounding).

The basic compound interest formula can be used to deal with one method of **depreciation** (as you should already know, depreciation is an accounting technique whereby the cost of a capital asset is spread over a number of different accounting periods as a charge against profit in each of the periods).

The reducing balance method of depreciation is a kind of **reverse compounding** in which **the value of the asset goes down at a certain rate**. The **rate of 'interest'** is therefore **negative**.

2.7 Example: Reducing balance depreciation

An item of equipment is bought for $1,000 and is to be depreciated at a fixed rate of 40% per annum. What will be its value at the end of four years?

Solution

A depreciation rate of 40% equates to a **negative rate of interest**, therefore r = –40% = –0.4. We are told that X = $1,000 and that n = 4. Using the formula for compound interest we can calculate the value of S, the value of the equipment at the end of four years.

$S = X(1 + r)^n = 1,000(1 + (-0.4))^4 = \$129.60$.

2.8 Falling prices

As well as rising at a compound rate, perhaps because of inflation, costs can also **fall at a compound rate**.

2.9 Example: Falling prices

Suppose that the cost of product X is currently $10.80. It is estimated that over the next five years its cost will **fall by 10% pa compound**. The cost of product X at the end of five years is therefore calculated as follows, using the formula for compound interest, $S = X(1 + r)^n$.

$X = \$10.80$

$r = -10\% = -0.1$

$n = 5$

$\therefore S = \$10.80 \times (1 + (-0.1))^5 = \$6.38$

2.10 Changes in the rate of interest

FAST FORWARD

If the **rate of interest changes during the period** of an investment, the compounding formula must be amended slightly to $S = X(1 + r_1)^y (1 + r_2)^{n-y}$.

Formula to learn

The formula for **compound interest** when there are changes in the rate of interest is as follows.

$S = X(1 + r_1)^y (1 + r_2)^{n-y}$

Where	r_1	=	the initial rate of interest
	y	=	the number of years in which the interest rate r_1 applies
	r_2	=	the next rate of interest
	$n - y$	=	the (balancing) number of years in which the interest rate r_2 applies.

Question

Investments

(a) If $8,000 is invested now, to earn 10% interest for three years and 8% thereafter, what would be the size of the total investment at the end of five years?

(b) An investor puts $10,000 into an investment for ten years. The annual rate of interest earned is 15% for the first four years, 12% for the next four years and 9% for the final two years. How much will the investment be worth at the end of ten years?

(c) An item of equipment costs $6,000 now. The annual rates of inflation over the next four years are expected to be 16%, 20%, 15% and 10%. How much would the equipment cost after four years?

Answer

(a) $8,000 \times 1.10^3 \times 1.08^2 = \$12,419.83$

(b) $10,000 \times 1.15^4 \times 1.12^4 \times 1.09^2 = \$32,697.64$

(c) $6,000 \times 1.16 \times 1.20 \times 1.15 \times 1.10 = \$10,565.28$

3 Regular savings and sinking funds

3.1 Final value or terminal value

An investor may decide to add to his investment from time to time, and you may be asked to calculate the **final value** (or **terminal value**) of an investment to which equal annual amounts will be added. An example might be an individual or a company making annual payments into a pension fund: we may wish to know the value of the fund after n years.

3.2 Example: Regular savings

A person invests $400 now, and a further $400 each year for three more years. How much would the total investment be worth after four years, if interest is earned at the rate of 10% per annum?

Solution

In problems such as this, we call **now 'Year 0'**, the time **one year from now 'Year 1'** and so on. It is also a good idea to draw a time line in order to establish exactly when payments are made.

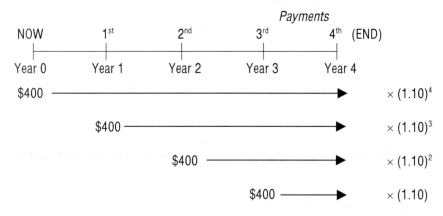

		$
(Year 0)	The first year's investment will grow to $400 (1.10)^4	585.64
(Year 1)	The second year's investment will grow to $400 (1.10)^3	532.40
(Year 2)	The third year's investment will grow to $400 (1.10)^2	484.00
(Year 3)	The fourth year's investment will grow to $400 (1.10)	440.00
		2,042.04

3.3 Geometric progressions

The example above was straightforward to calculate but if the time period was much longer, for example the endowment element of a mortgage, it is easier to use the **geometric progression formula** to find the sum of the terms

FAST FORWARD

A **geometric progression** is a sequence of numbers in which there is a common or constant ratio between adjacent terms.

Key term	An algebraic representation of a **geometric progression** is as follows.
	
	A, AR, AR^2, AR^3, AR^4,..., AR^{n-1}
	
	where A is the first term
	        R is the common ratio
	        n is the number of terms

3.3.1 Geometric progression examples

Examples of geometric progressions are as follows.

(a)   2, 4, 8, 16, 32, where there is a common ratio of 2.

(b)   121, 110, 100, 90.91, 82.64, where (allowing for rounding differences in the fourth and fifth terms) there is a common ratio of 1/1.1 = 0.9091.

Formula to learn	The sum of a **geometric progression**, $S = \dfrac{A(R^n - 1)}{R - 1}$
	
	Where A = the first term
	       R = the common ratio
	       n = the number of terms

3.4 Terminal value calculations

FAST FORWARD

The **final value** (or **terminal value**), S, of an investment to which equal annual amounts will be added is found using the following formula.

$$S = \frac{(R^n - 1)}{(R - 1)}$$ (the formula for a geometric progression).

The solution to the example above can be written as $(400 \times 1.1) + (400 \times 1.1^2) + (400 \times 1.1^3) + (400 \times 1.1^4)$ with the values placed in reverse order for convenience. This is a **geometric progression** with A (the first term) = (400×1.1), R = 1.1 and n = 4.

Using the geometric progression formula:

$$S = \frac{A(R^n - 1)}{R - 1}$$

$$= \frac{(400 \times 1.1) \times (1.1^4 - 1)}{1.1 - 1} = \frac{440 \times 0.4641}{0.1}$$

$$= \$2,042.04$$

3.5 Example: Investments at the ends of years

(a)   If, in the previous example, the investments had been made at the end of each of the first, second, third and fourth years, so that the last $400 invested had no time to earn interest, we can show this situation on the following time line.

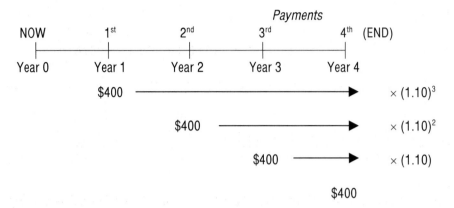

(Year 0)   No payment
(Year 1)   The first year's investment will grow to $400 $\times (1.10)^3$
(Year 2)   The second year's investment will grow to $400 $\times (1.10)^2$
(Year 3)   The third year's investment will grow to $400 $\times (1.10)$
(Year 4)   The fourth year's investment remains at $400

The value of the fund at the end of the four years is as follows.

$$400 + (400 \times 1.1) + (400 \times 1.1^2) + (400 \times 1.1^3)$$

This is a **geometric progression** with

A   = $400
R   =   1.1
n   =   4

If $S = \dfrac{A(R^n - 1)}{R - 1}$

$S = \dfrac{400\,(1.1^4 - 1)}{1.1 - 1}$

= $1,856.40

(b)   If our investor made investments as in (a) above, but also put in a $2,500 lump sum one year from now, the value of the fund after four years would be

$1,856.40 + $2,500 $\times 1.1^3$

= $1,856.40 + $3,327.50 = $5,183.90

That is, we **can compound parts of investments separately, and add up the results**.

Question

A man invests $1,000 now, and a further $1,000 each year for five more years. How much would the total investment be worth after six years, if interest is earned at the rate of 8% per annum?

Answer

This is a geometric progression with A (the first term) = $1,000 × 1.08, R = 1.08 and n = 6.

If $S = \dfrac{A(R^n - 1)}{R - 1}$

$$S = \frac{(\$1{,}000 \times 1.08) \times (1.08^6 - 1)}{1.08 - 1} = \frac{1080 \times 0.5869}{0.08}$$

$$= \quad \$7{,}923.15$$

3.6 Sinking funds

FAST FORWARD

A **sinking fund** is an investment into which equal annual instalments are paid in order to earn interest, so that by the end of a given number of years, the investment is large enough to pay off a known commitment at that time. Commitments include the replacement of an asset and the repayment of a mortgage.

With mortgages, the total of the constant annual payments (which are usually paid in equal monthly instalments) plus the interest they earn over the term of the mortgage must be sufficient to pay off the initial loan plus accrued interest. We shall be looking at mortgages later on in this chapter.

When replacing an asset at the end of its life, a company might decide to invest cash in a sinking fund during the course of the life of the existing asset to ensure that the money is available to buy a replacement.

3.7 Example: Sinking funds

A company has just bought an asset with a life of four years. At the end of four years, a replacement asset will cost $12,000, and the company has decided to provide for this future commitment by setting up a sinking fund into which equal annual investments will be made, starting at year 1 (one year from now). The fund will earn interest at 12%.

Required

Calculate the annual investment.

Solution

Let us start by drawing a time line where $A = equal annual investments.

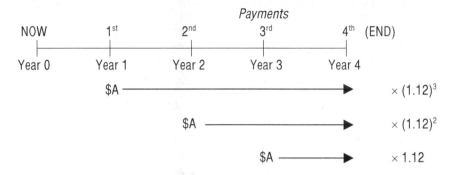

(Year 0)   No payment
(Year 1)   The first year's investment will grow to $A × (1.12)³
(Year 2)   The second year's investment will grow to $A × (1.12)²
(Year 3)   The third year's investment will grow to $A × (1.12)
(Year 4)   The fourth year's investment will remain at $A.

The value of the fund at the end of four years is as follows.

$$A + A(1.12) + A(1.12^2) + A(1.12^3)$$

This is a geometric progression with

A = A
R = 1.12
n = 4

The value of the sinking fund at the end of year 4 is $12,000 (given in the question) therefore

$$\$12,000 \ = \ \frac{A(1.12^4 - 1)}{1.12 - 1}$$

$12,000 = 4.779328A

$$\therefore A \ = \ \frac{\$12,000}{4.779328}$$

$$= \ \$2,510.81$$

Therefore, four investments, each of $2,510.81 should therefore be enough to allow the company to replace the asset.

 Question

Sinking funds

A farmer has just bought a combine harvester which has a life of ten years. At the end of ten years a replacement combine harvester will cost $100,000 and the farmer would like to provide for this future commitment by setting up a sinking fund into which equal annual investments will be made, starting *now*. The fund will earn interest at 10% per annum.

Answer

The value of the fund at the end of ten years is a geometric progression with:

A = $A × 1.1
R = 1.1
n = 10

Therefore the value of the sinking fund at the end of ten years is $100,000.

$$\therefore \$100,000 \; = \; \frac{A \times 1.1(1.1^{10} - 1)}{1.1 - 1}$$

$$100,000 \times 0.1 = A \times 1.1 \, (1.1^{10} - 1)$$

$$A \; = \; \frac{\$100,000 \times 0.1}{1.1(1.1^{10} - 1)}$$

$$= \; \frac{\$10,000}{1.753116706}$$

$$= \; \$5,704.13$$

4 Loans and mortgages

4.1 Loans

Most people will be familiar with the repayment of loans. The repayment of loans is best illustrated by means of an example.

4.2 Example: Loans

Timothy Lakeside borrows $50,000 now at an interest rate of 8 percent per annum. The loan has to be repaid through five equal instalments *after* each of the next five years. What is the annual repayment?

Solution

Let us start by calculating the final value of the loan (at the end of year 5).

Using the formula $S = X(1 + r)^n$

Where X = $50,000
       r = 8% = 0.08
       n = 5
       S = the sum invested after 5 years
∴   S = $50,000 (1 + 0.08)^5
          = $73,466.40

The value of the initial loan after 5 years ($73,466.40) must equal the sum of the repayments.

A time line will clarify when each of the repayments are made. Let \$A = the annual repayments which start a year from now, ie at year 1.

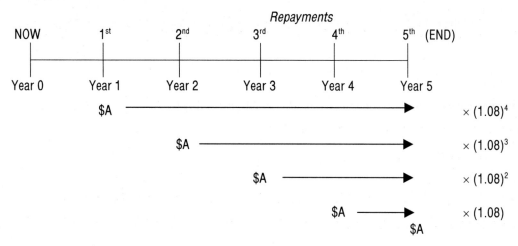

(Year 0)   No payment
(Year 1)   The first year's investment will grow to $\$A \times (1.08)^4$
(Year 2)   The second year's investment will grow to $\$A \times (1.08)^3$
(Year 3)   The third year's investment will grow to $\$A \times (1.08)^2$
(Year 4)   The fourth year's investment will grow to $\$A \times (1.08)$
(Year 5)   The fourth year's investment remains at $\$A$.

The value of the repayments at the end of five years is as follows.

$A + (A \times 1.08) + (A \times 1.08^2) + (A \times 1.08^3) + (A \times 1.08^4)$

This is a geometric progression with

A = A
R = 1.08
n = 5

The sum of this geometric progression, $S = \dfrac{A(R^n - 1)}{R - 1}$ = \$73,466.40 since the sum of repayments must **equal** the final value of the loan (ie \$73,466.40).

$S = \$73,466.40 = \dfrac{A(1.08^5 - 1)}{1.08 - 1}$

$\$73,466.40 = A \times 5.86660096$

$A = \dfrac{\$73,466.40}{5.86660096}$

$\quad = \$12,522.82$

The annual repayments are therefore \$12,522.82.

Question

John Johnstone borrows $50,000 now at an interest rate of 7% per annum. The loan has to be repaid through ten equal instalments after each of the next ten years. What is the annual repayment?

Answer

The final value of the loan (at the end of year 10) is

$$S = \$50,000 (1+ 0.07)^{10}$$
$$= \$98,357.57$$

The value of the initial loan after 10 years ($98,357.57) must equal the sum of the repayments.

The sum of the repayments is a geometric progression with

$A = A$
$R = 1.07$
$n = 10$

The sum of the repayments = $98,357.57

$$S = \$98,357.57 = \frac{A(R^n - 1)}{R - 1}$$

$$= \frac{A(1.07^{10} - 1)}{1.07 - 1}$$

$$= 13.816448A$$

$$\therefore A = \frac{\$98,357.57}{13.816448}$$

$$= \$7,118.88 \text{ per annum}$$

4.3 Sinking funds and loans compared

(a) **Sinking funds**. The sum of the **regular savings**, $A per period at r% over n periods *must* equal the sinking fund required at the end of n periods.

(b) **Loan repayments**. The sum of the **regular repayments** of $A per period at r% over n periods *must* equal the final value of the loan at the end of n periods.

The final value of a loan can therefore be seen to be equivalent to a sinking fund.

4.4 Mortgages

As you are probably aware, when a mortgage is taken out on a property over a number of years, there are several ways in which the loan can be repaid. One such way is the **repayment mortgage** which has the following features.

- A certain amount, S, is borrowed to be paid back over n years
- Interest, at a rate r, is added to the loan retrospectively at the end of each year
- A constant amount A is paid back each year

Income tax relief affects repayments but, for simplicity, we will ignore it here.

4.5 Mortgage repayments

Consider the repayments on a mortgage as follows.

(a) At the end of one year A has been repaid.

(b) At the end of two years the initial repayment of A has earned interest and so has a value of A(1 + r) and another A has been repaid. The value of the amount repaid is therefore A(1 + r) + A.

(c) At the end of three years, the initial repayment will have a value of $A(1 + r)^2$, the second repayment a value of A (1 + r) and a third repayment of A will have been made. The value of the amount repaid is therefore $A(1 + r)^2 + (1 + r) + A$.

(d) At the end of n years the value of the repayments is therefore $A (1 + r)^{n-1} + A(1 + r)^{n-2} + ... + A(1 + r)^2 + A(1 + r) + A$.

This is a **geometric progression** with 'A' = A, 'R' = (1 + r) and 'n' = n and hence the **sum of the repayments** =

$$\frac{A[(1+r)^n - 1]}{r} = \frac{A(R^n - 1)}{R - 1}$$

4.6 Sum of repayments = final value of mortgage

During the time the repayments have been made, the initial loan has accrued interest.

The repayments must, at the end of n years, repay the initial loan plus the accrued interest.

Therefore the **sum of the repayments** must equal the **final value of the mortgage**.

Sum of repayments = final value of mortgage

$$\frac{A(R^n - 1)}{R - 1} = SR^n$$

$$\therefore A = \frac{SR^n \times (R - 1)}{(R^n - 1)}$$

4.7 Example: Mortgages

(a) Sam has taken out a $30,000 mortgage over 25 years. Interest is to be charged at 12%. Calculate the monthly repayment.

(b) After nine years, the interest rate changes to 10%. What is the new monthly repayment?

Solution

(a) **Final value of mortgage** = $30,000 \times (1.12)^{25}$

                                     = $510,002

Sum of repayments, S

Where   A = annual repayment
          R = 1.12
          n = 25

$$\therefore S = \frac{A(1.12^{25} - 1)}{1.12 - 1}$$

       = 133.334A

Sum of repayments = final value of mortgage

133.334A = $510,002

$$A = \frac{\$510,002}{133.334}$$

A = $3,825

If annual repayment = $3,825

$$\text{Monthly repayment} = \frac{\$3,825}{12}$$

                            = $318.75

(b) After 9 years, the **value of the loan** = $30,000 \times (1.12)^9$
                                                      = $83,192

After 9 years, the **sum of the repayments** $= \dfrac{A(R^n - 1)}{R - 1}$

Where   A = $3,825
          R = 1.12
          n = 9

$$\therefore \text{Sum of repayments} = \frac{\$3,825(1.12^9 - 1)}{1.12 - 1}$$

                              = $56,517

	$
Value of loan at year 9	83,192
Sum of repayments at year 9	56,517
Loan outstanding at year 9	26,675

A new interest rate of 10% is to be charged on the outstanding loan of $26,675 for 16 years (25 − 9).

Final value of loan = $26,675 \times (1.1)^{16}$
                        = $122,571

Sum of repayments $= \dfrac{A(R^n - 1)}{R - 1}$

Where R $=$ 1.1

n $=$ 16

A $=$ annual repayment

$\therefore$ Sum of repayments $= \dfrac{A(1.1^{16} - 1)}{1.1 - 1}$

$= 35.94973A$

Final value of loan = sum of repayments

$\$122{,}571 = 35.94973A$

$\therefore A = \dfrac{\$122{,}571}{35.94973}$

A $= \$3{,}410$

$\therefore$ monthly repayment $= \dfrac{\$3{,}410}{12}$

$= \$284.17$

Important! | The final value of a loan/mortgage can be likened to a sinking fund also, since the final value must equate to the sum of the periodic repayments (compare this with a sinking fund where the sum of the regular savings must equal the fund required at some point in the future).

Question | **Monthly repayment**

Nicky Eastlacker has taken out a $200,000 mortgage over 25 years. Interest is to be charged at 9%. Calculate the monthly repayment.

Answer

Final value of mortgage $= \$200{,}000 \times (1.09)^{25}$

$ = \$1{,}724{,}616$

Sum of repayments, $S = \dfrac{A(R^n - 1)}{R - 1}$

Where A = Annual repayment

 R = 1.09

 n = 25

$\therefore \$1{,}724{,}616 = \dfrac{A(1.09^{25} - 1)}{1.09 - 1}$

$\therefore A = \$20{,}361.25$ per annum

If annual repayment = $\$20{,}361.25$

Monthly repayment $= \dfrac{\$20{,}361.25}{12}$

$ = \$1{,}696.77$

5 Annual Percentage Rate (APR) of Interest

5.1 Effective annual rate of interest

> **FAST FORWARD**
>
> An **effective annual rate of interest** is the corresponding annual rate when interest is compounded at intervals shorter than a year.

In the previous examples, interest has been calculated **annually**, but this isn't always the case. Interest may be compounded **daily**, **weekly**, **monthly** or **quarterly**.

The effective **equivalent annual** rate of interest, when interest is compounded at shorter intervals, is known as an **annual rate of interest**.

Formula to learn

Effective Annual Rate of Interest $= [(1+r)^{12/n} - 1]$ or $[(1+r)^{365/y} - 1]$

where r is the rate of interest for each time period

 n is the number of months in the time period

 y is the number of days in the time period

5.2 Example: The effective annual rate of interest

Calculate the effective annual rate of interest of:

(a)   1.5% per month, compound
(b)   4.5% per quarter, compound
(c)   9% per half year, compound

Solution

(a) $(1.015)^{12} - 1$ $= 0.1956 = 19.56\%$
(b) $(1.045)^4 - 1$ $= 0.1925 = 19.25\%$
(c) $(1.09)^2 - 1$ $= 0.1881 = 18.81\%$

5.3 Nominal rates of interest and the annual percentage rate

FAST FORWARD

> A **nominal rate** of interest is an interest rate expressed as a per annum figure although the interest is compounded over a period of less than one year. The corresponding effective rate of interest shortened to one decimal place is the **annual percentage rate (APR)** (sometimes called the compound annual rate, CAR).

Most interest rates are expressed as per annum figures even when the interest is compounded over periods of less than one year. In such cases, the given interest rate is called a **nominal rate**. We can, however, also work out the **effective rate** (**APR** or CAR).

Assessment focus point

Students often become seriously confused about the various rates of interest.

- The **NOMINAL RATE** is the interest rate expressed as a per annum figure, eg 12% pa nominal even though interest may be compounded over periods of less than one year.

- Adjusted nominal rate = **EQUIVALENT ANNUAL RATE**

- Equivalent annual rate (the rate per day or per month adjusted to give an annual rate) = **EFFECTIVE ANNUAL RATE**

- Effective annual rate = **ANNUAL PERCENTAGE RATE (APR)** = **COMPOUND ANNUAL RATE (CAR)**

5.4 Example: Nominal and effective rates of interest

A building society may offer investors 10% per annum interest payable half-yearly. If the 10% is a nominal rate of interest, the building society would in fact pay 5% every six months, compounded so that the effective annual rate of interest would be

$[(1.05)^2 - 1] = 0.1025 = 10.25\%$ per annum.

Similarly, if a bank offers depositors a nominal 12% per annum, with interest payable quarterly, the effective rate of interest would be 3% compound every three months, which is

$[(1.03)^4 - 1] = 0.1255 = 12.55\%$ per annum.

Effective rate of interest

A bank adds interest monthly to investors' accounts even though interest rates are expressed in annual terms. The current rate of interest is 12%. Fred deposits $2,000 on 1 July. How much interest will have been earned by 31 December (to the nearest $)?

A $123.00
B $60.00
C $240.00
D $120.00

Answer

The nominal rate is 12% pa payable monthly.

$\therefore$ The effective rate = $\dfrac{12\%}{12 \text{ months}}$ = 1% compound monthly.

$\therefore$ In the six months from July to December, the interest earned = ($2,000 $\times$ (1.01)^6) – $2,000 = $123.04.

The correct answer is A.

---

ssessment ocus point

You will probably find it useful to draw a time line to identify the time periods and interest rates involved when answering questions on financial mathematics. Don't be afraid to include a quick sketch of a time line in an assessment – it should help to clarify exactly when investments are made in saving funds or repayments are made on a loan.

Chapter Roundup

- **Simple interest** is interest which is earned in equal amounts every year (or month) and which is a given proportion of the original investment (the principal). The simple interest formula is **S = X + nrX**.

- **Compounding** means that, as interest is earned, it is added to the original investment and starts to earn interest itself. The basic formula for compound interest is **S = X(1 + r)^n**.

- The basic compound interest formula can be used to calculate the net book value of an asset depreciated using the **reducing balance method of depreciation** by using a negative rate of 'interest' (reverse compounding).

- If the **rate of interest changes during the period** of an investment, the compounding formula must be amended slightly to **S = X(1+r$_1$)^y(1 + r$_2$)$^{n-y}$**

- A **geometric progression** is a sequence of numbers in which there is a common or constant ratio between adjacent terms.

- The **final value** (or **terminal value**), S, of an investment to which equal annual amounts will be added is found using the following formula.

$$S = \frac{A\left(R^n - 1\right)}{(R-1)} \text{ (the formula for a geometric progression).}$$

- A **sinking fund** is an investment into which equal annual instalments are paid in order to earn interest, so that by the end of a given number of years, the investment is large enough to pay off a known commitment at that time. Commitments include the replacement of an asset and the repayment of a mortgage.

- An **effective annual rate of interest** is the corresponding annual rate when interest is compounded at intervals shorter than a year.

- A **nominal rate** of interest is an interest rate expressed as a per annum figure although the interest is compounded over a period of less than one year. The corresponding effective rate of interest shortened to one decimal place is the **annual percentage rate (APR)** (sometimes called the compound annual rate, CAR).

Quick Quiz

1   The formula for simple interest is ....

Where X = ...
        r = ...
        n = ...
        S = ...

2   The basic formula for compound interest is ....

Where X = ...
        r = ...
        n = ...
        S = ...

BPP
PROFESSIONAL EDUCATION

3   A depreciation rate of 20% equates to a value for r of

> A   + 20%
> B   −20%
> C   +0.2
> D   −0.2

4   If Smita Smitten invests $250 *now* and a further $250 each year for five more years at an interest rate of 20%, which of the following are true if the final investment is calculated using the formula for the sum of a geometric progression?

	A =	n =
A	$250 × 1.2	5
B	$250 × 1.2	4
C	$250	5
D	$250	4

5   A shopkeeper wishes to refurbish his store in five years' time. At the end of five years, the refurbishment will cost $50,000, and the storekeeper has decided to provide for this future refurbishment by setting up a sinking fund into which equal annual investments will be made, starting one year from now. The fund will earn interest at 10%. Using the formula for the sum of a geometric progression, calculate the annual investment.

6   What is the formula used for calculating the sum of the repayments of a mortgage?

7   The effective annual rate of interest is the same as the annual percentage rate which is the same as the compound annual rate.

True   ☐

False   ☐

8   What is the formula used to calculate the APR?

Answers to Quick Quiz

1    $S = X + nrX$

Where X = the original sum invested
       r = the rate of interest (as a proportion)
       n = the number of periods
       S = the sum invested after n periods

2    $S = X(1 + r)^n$

Where X = the original sum invested
       r = the rate of interest (as a proportion)
       n = the number of periods
       S = the sum invested after n periods

3   D   A depreciation rate of 20% equates to a negative rate of interest of −20% where r = −0.2.

4   A $S = \dfrac{A(R^n - 1)}{R - 1}$

Where A = the first term

   = $\$250 \times 1.2$ (as investment is made *now*)

   n = 5 years (the number of periods)

5   Using $S = \dfrac{A(R^n - 1)}{R - 1}$

Where S = final value of fund = $50,000

   A = annual investment = ?

   R = common ratio = 1.1

   n = number of periods = 5

$\$50,000 = \dfrac{A(1.1^5 - 1)}{1.1 - 1}$

$\therefore A = \dfrac{\$50,000 \times (1.1 - 1)}{(1.1^5 - 1)}$

   = $8,189.87

6   $S = \dfrac{A(R^n - 1)}{R - 1}$ (the sum of a geometric progression formula)

7   True. Effective annual rate = APR = CAR

8   APR = $[(1 + r^{12/n}) - 1]$ or $[(1 + r)^{365/y} - 1]$

Where r = the rate of interest for each time period

   n = the number of months in the time period

   y = the number of days in the time period

Now try the questions below from the Exam Question Bank

Question numbers	Pages
74-80	353-354

13

Discounting

Introduction

Discounting is the reverse of compounding, the topic of the previous chapter. Its major application in business is in the **evaluation of investments**, to decide whether they offer a satisfactory return to the investor. We will be looking at two methods of using discounting to appraise investments, the **net present value (NPV) method** and the **internal rate of return (IRR) method**.

1 The concept of discounting

1.1 Present value

The concept of **present value** can be thought of in two ways.

- It is the value today of an amount to be received some time in the future
- It is the amount which would be invested today to produce a given amount at some future date

Key term

The term '**present value**' simply means the amount of money which must be invested now for n years at an interest rate of r%, to earn a given future sum of money at the time it will be due.

1.2 The basic principles of discounting

Discounting is the reverse of compounding. The discounting formula is $X = S \times \dfrac{1}{(1+r)^n}$

The **basic principle of compounding** is that if we invest $X now for n years at r% interest per annum, we should obtain $X(1 + r)^n$ in n years' time.

Thus if we invest $10,000 now for four years at 10% interest per annum, we will have a total investment worth $10,000 \times 1.10^4 = \$14,641$ at the end of four years (that is, at year 4 if it is now year 0).

Key term

The basic principle of **discounting** is that if we wish to have $S in n years' time, we need to invest a certain sum *now* (year 0) at an interest rate of r% in order to obtain the required sum of money in the future.

1.3 Example: Discounting formula

For example, if we wish to have $14,641 in four years' time, how much money would we need to invest now at 10% interest per annum? This is the reverse of the situation described in Paragraph 1.2.

Using our corresponding formula, $S = X(1 + r)^n$

Where X = the original sum invested
        r = 10%
        n = 4
        S = $14,641

$\$14,641 = X(1 + 0.1)^4$

$\$14,641 = X \times 1.4641$

$\therefore X = \dfrac{\$14,641}{1.4641} = \$10,000$

$10,000 now, with the capacity to earn a return of 10% per annum, is the equivalent in value of $14,641 after four years. We can therefore say that **$10,000 is the present value of $14,641 at year 4, at an interest rate of 10%**.

Formula to learn

The **discounting formula** is:

$$X = S \times \frac{1}{(1+r)^n}$$

Where S   is the sum to be received after n time periods

X   is the present value (PV) of that sum

r   is the rate of return, expressed as a proportion

n   is the number of time periods (usually years)

The rate r is sometimes called a cost of capital.

Note that this equation is just a rearrangement of the compounding formula.

1.4 Example: Discounting

(a)   Calculate the present value of $60,000 at year 6, if a return of 15% per annum is obtainable.

(b)   Calculate the present value of $100,000 at year 5, if a return of 6% per annum is obtainable.

(c)   How much would a person need to invest now at 12% to earn $4,000 at year 2 and $4,000 at year 3?

Solution

The discounting formula, $X = S \times \dfrac{1}{(1+r)^n}$ is required.

(a)   S   = $60,000

n   = 6

r   = 0.15

PV = $60,000 \times \dfrac{1}{1.15^6}$ = $25,939.66

(b)   S   = $100,000

n   = 5

r   = 0.06

PV = $100,000 \times \dfrac{1}{1.06^5}$ = $74,725.82

(c)   S   = $4,000

n   = 2 or 3

r   = 0.12

PV = $\left(4,000 \times \dfrac{1}{1.12^2}\right) + \left(4,000 \times \dfrac{1}{1.12^3}\right)$

= 3,188.78 + 2,847.12

= $6,035.90

This calculation can be checked as follows.

	$
Year 0	6,036.00
Interest for the first year (12%)	724.32
	6,760.32
Interest for the second year (12%)	811.24
	7,571.56
Less: withdrawal	(4,000.00)
	3,571.56
Interest for the third year (12%)	428.59
	4,000.15
Less: withdrawal	(4,000.00)
Rounding error	0.15

1.5 Present value tables

Present value tables are provided in your exam (and at the end of this study text), and give the present value factor or **discount factor** for given values of n and r. They can only be used for whole numbers up to 20% and are rounded so lose some accuracy, but they simplify and speed up your calculations.

Look up the discount factor in the table and multiply the value of 'S' by the discount factor.

1.6 Example: Discounting and present value tables

Calculate the present values in (a) and (b) in example 1.4 using present value tables.

Solution

(a)   Present value = 60,000 × 0.432
                 = $25,920

(b)   Present value = 100,000 × 0.747
                 = $74,700

Question   **Present value**

The present value at 7% interest of $16,000 at year 12 is $ ☐ rounded to the nearest whole number.

Answer

£7,104

Working

Using the discounting formula, $X = S \times \dfrac{1}{(1+r)^n}$

Where S = \$16,000
n = 12
r = 0.07
X = Present Value

$X = \$16,000 \times \dfrac{1}{1.07^{12}} = \$7,104$

1.7 Capital expenditure appraisal

FAST FORWARD

Discounted cash flow techniques can be used to evaluate capital expenditure projects. There are two methods: the **NPV method** and the **IRR method**.

Key term

Discounted cash flow (DCF) involves the application of discounting arithmetic to the estimated future cash flows (receipts and expenditures) from a project in order to decide whether the project is expected to earn a satisfactory rate of return.

2 The Net Present Value (NPV) method

FAST FORWARD

The **Net Present Value (NPV) method** works out the present values of all items of income and expenditure related to an investment at a given rate of return, and then works out a net total. If it is **positive**, the investment is considered to be **acceptable**. If it is **negative**, the investment is considered to be **unacceptable**.

2.1 Example: The net present value of a project

Dog Ltd is considering whether to spend \$5,000 on an item of equipment. The 'cash profits', the excess of income over cash expenditure, from the project would be \$3,000 in the first year and \$4,000 in the second year.

The company will not invest in any project unless it offers a return in excess of 15% per annum.

Required

Assess whether the investment is worthwhile, or 'viable'.

Solution

(a) In this example, an outlay of $5,000 now promises a return of $3,000 **during** the first year and $4,000 **during** the second year. It is a convention in DCF, however, that cash flows spread over a year are assumed to occur **at the end of the year**, so that the cash flows of the project are as follows.

	$
Year 0 (now)	(5,000)
Year 1 (at the end of the year)	3,000
Year 2 (at the end of the year)	4,000

The NPV method takes the following approach.

(i) The project offers $3,000 at year 1 and $4,000 at year 2, for an outlay of $5,000 now.

(ii) The company might invest elsewhere to earn a return of 15% per annum.

(iii) If the company did invest at exactly 15% per annum, how much would it need to invest now, at 15%, to earn $3,000 at the end of year 1 plus $4,000 at the end of year 2?

(iv) Is it cheaper to invest $5,000 in the project, or to invest elsewhere at 15%, in order to obtain these future cash flows?

(b) If the company did invest elsewhere at 15% per annum, the amount required to earn $3,000 in year 1 and $4,000 in year 2 would be as follows.

Year	Cash flow	Discount factor	Present value
	$	15%	$
1	3,000	0.870	2,610
2	4,000	0.756	3,024
			5,634

(c) The choice is to invest $5,000 in the project, or $5,634 elsewhere at 15%, in order to obtain these future cash flows. We can therefore reach the following conclusion.

- It is cheaper to invest in the project, by $634
- The project offers a return of over 15% per annum

(d) The net present value is the difference between the present value of cash inflows from the project ($5,634) and the present value of future cash outflows (in this example, $5,000 \times 1/1.15^0 = $5,000$).

(e) An NPV statement could be drawn up as follows.

Year	Cash flow	Discount factor	Present value
	$	15%	$
0	(5,000)	1.000	(5,000)
1	3,000	0.870	2,610
2	4,000	0.756	3,024
		Net present value	+634

The project has a positive net present value, so it is acceptable.

NPV method

A company is wondering whether to spend $18,000 on an item of equipment, in order to obtain cash profits as follows.

Year	$
1	6,000
2	8,000
3	5,000
4	1,000

The company requires a return of 10% per annum.

Required

Use the NPV method to assess whether the project is viable.

Answer

Year	Cash flow	Discount factor	Present value
	$	10%	$
0	(18,000)	1.000	(18,000)
1	6,000	0.909	5,454
2	8,000	0.826	6,608
3	5,000	0.751	3,755
4	1,000	0.683	683
		Net present value	(1,500)

The NPV is negative. We can therefore draw the following conclusions.

(a)   It is cheaper to invest elsewhere at 10% than to invest in the project
(b)   The project would earn a return of less than 10%
(c)   The project is not viable (since the PV of the costs is greater than the PV of the benefits)

2.2 Project comparison

The NPV method can also be used to compare two or more investment options. For example, suppose a business can choose between the investment outlined in the previous question above *or* a second investment, which costs $28,000 but which would earn $6,500 in the first year, $7,500 in the second, $8,500 in the third, $9,500 in the fourth and $10,500 in the fifth. Which one should the business choose?

The decision rule is to choose the option with the highest NPV. We therefore need to calculate the NPV of the second option.

Year	Cash flow	Discount factor	Present value
	$	11%	$
0	(28,000)	1.000	(28,000)
1	6,500	0.901	5,857
2	7,500	0.812	6,090
3	8,500	0.731	6,214
4	9,500	0.659	6,261
5	10,500	0.593	6,227
			NPV = 2,649

The business should therefore invest in the second option since it has the higher NPV.

2.3 Expected values and discounting

Future cash flows cannot be predicted with complete accuracy. To take account of this uncertainty an **expected net present value** can be calculated which is a **weighted average net present value based on the probabilities of different sets of circumstances occurring**. Let us have a look at an example.

2.4 Example: Expected net present value

An organisation with a cost of capital of 5% is contemplating investing $340,000 in a project which has a 25% chance of being a big success and producing cash inflows of $210,000 after one and two years. There is, however, a 75% chance of the project not being quite so successful, in which case the cash inflows will be $162,000 after one year and $174,000 after two years.

Required

Calculate an NPV and hence advise the organisation.

Solution

Year	Discount factor	Success Cash flow	PV	Failure Cash flow	PV
	5%	$'000	$'000	$'000	$'000
0	1.000	(340)	(340.00)	(340)	(340.000)
1	0.952	210	199.92	162	154.224
2	0.907	210	190.47	174	157.818
			50.39		(27.958)

NPV = (25% × 50.39) + (75% × −27.958) = −8.371

The NPV is −$8,371 and hence the organisation should not invest in the project.

2.5 Limitations of using the NPV method

There are a number of problems associated with using the NPV method in practice.

(a) **The future discount factors** (or interest rates) which are used in calculating NPVs can only be **estimated** and are not known with certainty. Discount rates that are estimated for time periods far into the future are therefore less likely to be accurate, thereby leading to less accurate NPV values.

(b) Similarly, NPV calculations make use of estimated **future cash flows**. As with future discount factors, cash flows which are estimated for cash flows several years into the future cannot really be predicted with any real certainty.

(c) When using the NPV method it is common to assume that all cash flows occur **at the end of the year**. However, this assumption is also likely to give rise to less accurate NPV values.

There are a number of computer programs available these days which enable a range of NPVs to be calculated for a number of different circumstances (best-case and worst-case situations and so on). Such programs allow some of the limitations mentioned above to be alleviated.

3 The Internal Rate of Return (IRR) method

3.1 IRR method

FAST FORWARD

The **IRR method** determines the rate of interest (the IRR) at which the NPV is 0. Interpolation, using the following formula, is often necessary. **The project is viable if the IRR exceeds the minimum acceptable return**.

$$IRR = a\% + \left[\frac{A}{A-B} \times (b-a) \right] \%$$

The **internal rate of return (IRR) method** of evaluating investments is an alternative to the NPV method. The NPV method of discounted cash flow determines whether an investment earns a **positive or a negative NPV when discounted at a given rate of interest**. If the NPV is zero (that is, the present values of costs and benefits are equal) the return from the project would be exactly the rate used for discounting.

The IRR method will indicate that a project is viable **if the IRR exceeds the minimum acceptable rate of return**. Thus if the company expects a minimum return of, say, 15%, a project would be viable if its IRR is more than 15%.

3.2 Example: The IRR method over one year

If $500 is invested today and generates $600 in one year's time, the internal rate of return (r) can be calculated as follows.

PV of cost = PV of benefits

$$500 = \frac{600}{(1+r)}$$

$$500 (1 + r) = 600$$

$$1 + r = \frac{600}{500} = 1.2$$

$$r = 0.2 = 20\%$$

3.3 Interpolation method

The arithmetic for calculating the IRR is more complicated for investments and cash flows extending over a period of time longer than one year. A technique known as the **interpolation method** can be used to calculate an approximate IRR.

3.4 Example: Interpolation

A project costing $800 in year 0 is expected to earn $400 in year 1, $300 in year 2 and $200 in year 3.

Required

Calculate the internal rate of return.

Solution

The IRR is calculated by first of all finding the NPV at each of two interest rates. Ideally, one interest rate should give a small positive NPV and the other a small negative NPV. The IRR would then be somewhere between these two interest rates: above the rate where the NPV is positive, but below the rate where the NPV is negative.

A very rough guideline for estimating at what interest rate the NPV might be close to zero, is to take

$$\frac{2}{3} \times \left(\frac{profit}{cost\ of\ the\ project} \right)$$

In our example, the total profit over three years is $(400 + 300 + 200 − 800) = $100. An approximate IRR is therefore calculated as:

$$\frac{2}{3} \times \frac{100}{800} = 0.08\ approx.$$

A starting point is to try 8%.

(a)   Try 8%

Year	Cash flow	Discount factor	Present value
	$	8%	$
0	(800)	1.000	(800.0)
1	400	0.926	370.4
2	300	0.857	257.1
3	200	0.794	158.8
		NPV	(13.7)

The NPV is negative, therefore the project fails to earn 8% and the IRR must be less than 8%.

(b)   Try 6%

Year	Cash flow	Discount factor	Present value
	$	6%	$
0	(800)	1.000	(800.0)
1	400	0.943	377.2
2	300	0.890	267.0
3	200	0.840	168.0
		NPV	12.2

The NPV is positive, therefore the project earns more than 6% and less than 8%.

The **IRR is now calculated by interpolation**. The result will not be exact, but it will be a close approximation. Interpolation assumes that the NPV falls in a straight line from +12.2 at 6% to −13.7 at 8%.

Graph to show IRR calculation by interpolation

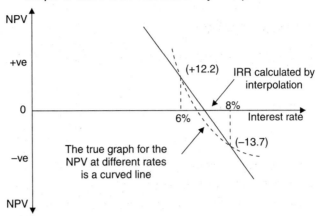

Formula to learn

The IRR, where the NPV is zero, can be calculated as follows.

$$IRR = a\% + \left[\frac{A}{A-B} \times (b-a) \right]\%$$

Where a is one interest rate

b is the other interest rate

A is the NPV at rate a

B is the NPV at rate b

(c)   Thus, in our example, IRR $= 6\% + \left[\dfrac{12.2}{(12.2+13.7)} \times (8-6) \right]\%$

$= 6\% + 0.942\%$

$= 6.942\%$ approx

(d)   The answer is only an **approximation** because the NPV falls in a slightly curved line and not a straight line between +12.2 and −13.7. Provided that NPVs close to zero are used, the linear assumption used in the interpolation method is nevertheless fairly accurate.

(e)   Note that the formula will still work if A and B are both positive, or both negative, and even if a and b are a long way from the true IRR, but the results will be less accurate.

Question

Internal rate of return

The net present value of an investment at 15% is $50,000 and at 20% is - $10,000. The internal rate of return of this investment (to the nearest whole number) is:

A   16%

B   17%

C   18%

D   19%

Answer

$$IRR = a\% + \left(\frac{A}{A-B} \times (b-a) \right)\%$$

Where a = one interest rate = 15%
    b = other interest rate = 20%
    A = NPV at rate a = $50,000
    B = NPV at rate b = –$10,000

$$IRR = 15\% + \left[\frac{£50,000}{£50,000 - (-£10,000)} \times (20-15) \right]\%$$

   = 15% + 4.17%

   = 19.17%

   = 19%

The correct answer is therefore D.

Assessment focus point

The IRR of a project can be estimated by plotting NPVs and their corresponding discount rates **accurately** on a graph. When all of the points are joined together, the approximate IRR value can be read off the graph at the point at which the line plotted crosses the x-axis.

4 Annuities and perpetuities

4.1 Annuities

FAST FORWARD

An **annuity** is a constant sum of money received or paid each year for a given number of years.

Many individuals nowadays may invest in **annuities** which can be purchased either through a single payment or a number of payments. For example, individuals planning for their retirement might make regular payments into a pension fund over a number of years. Over the years, the pension fund should (hopefully) grow and the final value of the fund can be used to buy an annuity.

An **annuity** might run until the recipient's death, or it might run for a guaranteed term of n years.

4.2 The annuity formula

The syllabus for *Business Mathematics* states that you need to be able to calculate the present value of an annuity using both a formula and CIMA Tables. Let's have a look at the formula you need to be able to use when calculating the PV of an annuity.

The **present value of an annuity** of *$1* per annum receivable or payable for n years commencing in one year, discounted at r% per annum, can be calculated using the following formula.

$$PV = \frac{1}{r}\left(1 - \frac{1}{(1+r)^n}\right)$$

Note that it is the PV of an annuity of *$1* and so you need to multiply it by the actual value of the annuity.

4.3 Example: The annuity formula

What is the present value of $4,000 per annum for years 1 to 4, at a discount rate of 10% per annum?

Solution

Using the annuity formula with r = 0.1 and n = 4.

$$PV = \$4,000 \times \left(\frac{1}{0.1}\left(1 - \frac{1}{(1+0.1)^4}\right)\right)$$

$$= \$4,000 \times 3.170 = \$12,680$$

4.4 Calculating a required annuity

If PV of $1 $= \frac{1}{r}\left(1 - \frac{1}{(1+r)^n}\right)$, then PV of $a $= a\left(\frac{1}{r}\left(1 - \frac{1}{(1+r)^n}\right)\right)$

$$\therefore a = \frac{PV \text{ of } \pounds a}{\left(\frac{1}{r}\left(1 - \frac{1}{(1+r)^n}\right)\right)}$$

This enables us to calculate the annuity required to yield a given rate of return (r) on a given investment (P).

4.5 Example: required annuity

The present value of a ten-year receivable annuity which begins in one year's time at 7% per annum compound is $3,000. What is the annual amount of the annuity?

Solution

$$\begin{aligned} PV \text{ of } \$a &= \$3,000 \\ r &= 0.07 \\ t &= 10 \end{aligned}$$

$$a = \frac{\$3,000}{\left(\frac{1}{0.07}\left(1 - \frac{1}{(1.07)^{10}}\right)\right)}$$

$$= \frac{\$3,000}{7.024} = 427.11$$

Question _____ **Annuity formula (1)**

(a) It is important to practise using the annuity factor formula. Calculate annuity factors in the following cases.

    (i)   n = 4, r = 10%

    (ii)   n = 3, r = 9.5%

    (iii)   For twenty years at a rate of 25%

(b) What is the present value of $4,000 per annum for four years, **years 2 to 5**, at a discount rate of 10% per annum? Use the annuity formula.

Answer

(a)   (i) $\dfrac{1}{0.1}\left(1-\dfrac{1}{(1+0.1)^4}\right)=3.170$

      (ii) $\dfrac{1}{0.095}\left(1-\dfrac{1}{(1+0.095)^3}\right)=2.509$

      (iii) $\dfrac{1}{0.25}\left(1-\dfrac{1}{(1+0.25)^{20}}\right)=3.954$

(b) The formula will give the value of $4,000 at 10% per annum, not as a year 0 present value, but as a value at the year preceding the first annuity cash flow, that is, at year (2 - 1) = year 1. We must therefore discount our solution in paragraph 4.3 further, from a year 1 to a year 0 value.

$$PV = \$12,680 \times \frac{1}{1.10} = \$11,527.27$$

Question _____ **Annuity formula (2)**

In the formula

$$PV = \frac{1}{r}\left(1-\frac{1}{(1+r)^n}\right)$$

  r = 0.04

  n = 10

What is the PV?

A   6.41

B   7.32

C   8.11

D   9.22

Answer

$$PV = \frac{1}{0.04}\left(1 - \frac{1}{(1+0.04)^{10}}\right)$$

$$= 8.11$$

The correct answer is therefore C.

4.6 Annuity tables

To calculate the present value of a constant annual cash flow, or annuity, we can multiply the annual cash flows by the sum of the discount factors for the relevant years. These total factors are known as **cumulative present value factors** or **annuity factors**. As with 'present value factors of $1 in year n', there are tables for annuity factors, which are shown at the end of this text. (For example, the cumulative present value factor of $1 per annum for five years at 11% per annum is in the column for 11% and the year 5 row, and is 3.696).

4.7 The use of annuity tables to calculate a required annuity

FAST FORWARD

The present value of an annuity can also be calculated using the annuity factors found in annuity tables.

Annuity (a) = $\dfrac{\text{Present value of an annuity}}{\text{Annuity factor}}$

4.8 Example: Annuity tables

A bank grants a loan of $3,000 at 7% per annum. The borrower is to repay the loan in ten annual instalments. How much must she pay each year?

Solution

Since the bank pays out the loan money *now*, the present value (PV) of the loan is $3,000. The annual repayment on the loan can be thought of as an annuity. We can therefore use the annuity formula

Annuity = $\dfrac{\text{PV}}{\text{annuity factor}}$

in order to calculate the loan repayments. The annuity factor is found by looking in the cumulative present value tables under n = 10 and r = 7%. The corresponding factor = 7.024.

Therefore, annuity = $\dfrac{\$3,000}{7.024}$

$$= \$427.11$$

The loan repayments are therefore $427.11 per annum.

4.9 Perpetuities

A **perpetuity** is an annuity which lasts for ever, instead of stopping after n years. The **present value of a perpetuity** is PV = a/r where r is the cost of capital as a proportion.

Assessment formula

The present value of $1 per annum, payable or receivable in perpetuity, commencing in one year, discounted at r% per annum

$$PV = \frac{1}{r}$$

4.10 Example: A perpetuity

How much should be invested *now* (to the nearest $) to receive $35,000 per annum in perpetuity if the annual rate of interest is 9%?

Solution

$$PV = \frac{a}{r}$$

Where a = $35,000

r = 9%

$$\therefore PV = \frac{£35,000}{0.09}$$

$$= \$388,889$$

4.11 Example: A perpetuity again

Mostly Ltd is considering a project which would cost $50,000 now and yield $9,000 per annum every year in perpetuity, starting a year from now. The cost of capital is 15%.

Required

Assess whether the project is viable.

Solution

Year	Cash flow $	Discount factor 15%	Present value $
0	(50,000)	1.0	(50,000)
1– ∞	9,000	1/0.15	60,000
		NPV	10,000

The project is viable because it has a positive net present value when discounted at 15%.

4.12 The timing of cash flows

Note that both annuity tables and the formulae assume that the first payment or receipt is a year from now. Always check assessment questions for when the first payment falls.

For example, if there are five equal payments starting now, and the interest rate is 8%, we should use a factor of 1 (for today's payment) + 3.312 (for the other four payments) = 4.312.

Question	Present value of a lease

Hilarious Jokes Ltd has arranged a fifteen year lease, at an annual rent of $9,000. The first rental payment is to be paid immediately, and the others are to be paid at the end of each year.

What is the present value of the lease at 9%?

A $79,074
B $72,549
C $81,549
D $70,074

Answer

The correct way to answer this question is to use the cumulative present value tables for r = 9% and n = 14 because the first payment is to be paid immediately (and not in one year's time). A common trap in a question like this would be to look up r = 9% and n = 15 in the tables. If you did this, get out of the habit now, before you take your assessment!

From the cumulative present value tables, when r = 9% and n = 14, the annuity factor is 7.786.

The first payment is made now, and so has a PV of $9,000 ($9,000 × 1.00). Payments 2-15 have a PV of $9,000 × 7.786 = $70,074.

∴ The total PV = $9,000 (1st payment) + $70,074 (Payments 2-15)

         = $79,074.

The correct answer is A.

(Alternatively, the annuity factor can be increased by 1 to take account of the fact that the first payment is *now*.

∴ annuity factor = 7.786 + 1 = 8.786

∴ PV = annuity × annuity factor

     = $9,000 × 8.786 = $79,074)

Question	Perpetuities

How much should be invested now (to the nearest $) to receive $20,000 per annum in perpetuity if the annual rate of interest is 20%?

A $4,000
B $24,000
C $93,500
D $100,000

Answer

$$PV = \frac{a}{r}$$

Where   a = annuity = $20,000

r = cost of capital as a proportion = 0.2

$$PV = \frac{\$20,000}{0.2}$$

= $100,000

The correct answer is therefore D.

5 Linking compounding and discounting

FAST FORWARD

Compounding and discounting are directly linked to each other. Make sure that you understand clearly the relationship between them.

5.1 Sinking funds

In the previous chapter we introduced you to **sinking funds**. You will remember that a sinking fund is an investment into which equal annual instalments (an **annuity**) are paid in order to earn interest, so that by the end of a given period, the investment is large enough to pay off a known commitment at that time (**final value**).

5.2 Example: A sinking fund (1)

Jamie wants to buy a Porsche 911. This will cost him $45,000 in two years' time. He has decided to set aside an equal amount each quarter until he has the amount he needs. Assuming he can earn interest in his building society account at 5% pa how much does he need to set aside each year? Assume the first amount is set aside one period from now.

(a)   Calculate the amounts using the annuity formula.
(b)   Calculate the amounts using annuity tables.

Solution

If Jamie needs $45,000 in two years' time, the present value that he needs is

$$PV = \frac{£45,000}{(1+0.05)^2}$$

= $40,816

(a) **Using the annuity formula**

The annuity factor = $\frac{1}{r}\left(1 - \frac{1}{(1+r)^n}\right)$

Where r = 0.05
n = 2

Annuity factor = $\frac{1}{0.05}\left(1 - \frac{1}{(1+0.05)^2}\right)$

= 1.8594

The amount to save each quarter is an annuity. We can therefore use the formula

Annuity = $\frac{PV}{Annuity\ factor}$

= $\frac{\$40,816}{1.8594}$

= \$21,951

Therefore Jamie must set aside \$21,951 per annum.

(b) **Using annuity tables**

When n = 2 and r = 5%, the annuity factor (from cumulative present value tables) is 1.859.

Annuity = $\frac{PV}{Annuity\ factor}$

= $\frac{\$40,816}{1.859}$

= \$21,956

The difference of \$5 (\$21,956 − \$21,951) is due to rounding.

5.3 Example: A sinking fund (2)

At this point it is worth considering the value of the fund that would have built up if we had saved \$21,956 pa for two years at an interest rate of 5%, with the first payment at the end of year 1.

Solution

The situation we are looking at here can be shown on the following time line.

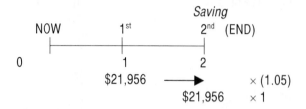

The value of the fund at the end of year 2 is:

$$21,956 + 21,956(1.05)$$

This is a geometric progression with:

A = $21,956
R = 1.05
n = 2

If S = $\dfrac{A(R^n - 1)}{R - 1}$

= $\dfrac{21,956(1.05^2 - 1)}{1.05 - 1}$

= $45,000 (to the nearest $100)

Therefore, if we were to save $21,956 for two years at 5% per annum we would achieve a final value of $45,000. Can you see how compounding and discounting really are the reverse of each other? In our first example, we calculated that Jamie needed to save $21,956 pa for two years at a cost of capital of 5%. In the second example, we demonstrated that using the equation for the sum of a geometric progression, saving $21,956 pa for two years would result in a sinking fund of $45,000.

Important!

> Work through these two examples again if you are not totally clear: it is vitally important that you understand how compounding and discounting are linked.

5.4 Mortgages

We also considered mortgages in Chapter 12. You will remember that the final value of a mortgage must be equal to the sum of the repayments. If the repayments are regular, they can be treated as an annuity, in which case the annuity formula may be used in mortgage calculations.

When an individual takes out a mortgage, the present value of the mortgage is the amount of the loan taken out. Most mortgages will be taken out at a given rate of interest for a fixed term.

Annuity = $\dfrac{\text{Present value of annuity (original vaue of mortgage)}}{\text{Annuity factor (from formula or tables)}}$

The annuity is the regular repayment value.

Let's have a look at an example.

5.5 Example: Mortgages

Tim has taken out a $30,000 mortgage over 25 years. Interest is to be charged at 12%. Calculate the monthly repayment.

Solution

Present value of mortgage = $30,000

$$\text{Annuity factor} = \frac{1}{0.12}\left(1 - \frac{1}{(1+0.12)^{25}}\right)$$

$$= 7.843$$

$$\text{Annuity (annual repayments)} = \frac{PV}{\text{annuity factor}}$$

$$= \frac{\$30,000}{7.843}$$

$$= \$3,825$$

Monthly repayment = $3,825 ÷ 12 = $318.75

Did you recognise any of these figures? Look back at Paragraph 4.7 in the previous chapter. We have used the same information but used the annuity formula method rather than the sum of a geometric progression.

5.6 Example: Interest rate changes

After nine years, the interest rate on Tim's mortgage changes to 10%. What is the new monthly repayment?

Solution

In the solution in Paragraph 4.7 in Chapter 12, it was established that the value of the mortgage after 9 years was $26,675.

After 9 years, our annuity factor changes to:

$$\text{Annuity factor} = \frac{1}{0.1}\left(1 - \frac{1}{(1+0.1)^{16}}\right)$$

$$= 7.8237$$

$$\text{Annuity (annual repayments)} = \frac{PV}{\text{annuity factor}}$$

$$= \frac{\$26,675}{7.8237}$$

$$= \$3,410$$

∴ The monthly repayments = $3,410 ÷ 12 = $284

This is the same as the answer that we calculated in Chapter 12, Paragraph 4.7 when we used the sum of a geometric progression formula.

Sinking funds are an example of **saving** whilst mortgages are an example of **borrowing**.

5.7 Borrowing versus saving

(a)   **Borrowing**

The chief advantage of borrowing money via a loan or mortgage is that the asset the money is used to purchase can be **owned now** (and therefore be put to use to earn money) rather than waiting. On the other hand, borrowing money **takes some control away from the business's managers** and **makes a business venture more risky**. Because an obligation is owed to the lender the managers may have **less freedom** to do what they like with their assets. If the business is not successful the debt will still be owed, and if the lender demands that it is repaid immediately the business might collapse.

(b)   **Saving**

The advantages of saving up are that **no interest has to be paid** and the business **does not have to surrender any control to a third party**. The savings will **earn** interest. However the money will not be available for other, potentially more profitable, uses. Also, the business cannot be **sure** in advance that it will be able to generate the cash needed over the timescale envisaged.

Assessment focus point	Note that both annuity tables and the formulae used in this chapter assume that the first payment or receipt is **a year from now**. Always check assessment questions for when the first payment falls. For example, if there are five equal payments starting **now**, and the interest rate is 8% we should use a factor of 1 (for today's payment) + 3.312 (for the other four payments) = 4.312.

Chapter Roundup

- The concept of **present value** can be thought of in two ways.

    - It is the value today of an amount to be received some time in the future

    - It is the amount which would have to be invested today to produce a given amount at some future date

- **Discounting** is the reverse of compounding. The discounting formula is $X = S \times 1/(1+r)^n$ which is a rearrangement of the compounding formula.

- **Discounted cash flow techniques** can be used to evaluate capital expenditure projects. There are two methods: the **NPV method** and the **IRR method**.

- The **Net Present Value (NPV) method** works out the present values of all items of income and expenditure related to an investment at a given rate of return, and then works out a net total. If it is **positive**, the investment is considered to be **acceptable**. If it is **negative**, the investment is considered to be **unacceptable**.

- The **IRR method** determines the rate of interest (the IRR) at which the NPV is 0. Interpolation, using the following formula, is often necessary. **The project is viable if the IRR exceeds the minimum acceptable return**.

$$IRR = a\% + \left[\frac{A}{A-B} \times (b-a) \right]\%$$

- An **annuity** is a constant sum of money received or paid each year for a given number of years.

- The **present value of an annuity** of $1 per annum receivable or payable for n years commencing in one year, discounted at r% per annum, can be calculated using the following formula.

$$PV = \frac{1}{r}\left(1 - \frac{1}{(1+r)^n} \right)$$

Note that it is the PV of an annuity of $1 and so you need to multiply it by the actual value of the annuity.

- The present value of an annuity can also be calculated by using annuity factors found in annuity tables.

$$\text{Annuity} = \frac{\text{Present value of an annuity}}{\text{Annuity factor}}$$

- A **perpetuity** is an annuity which lasts forever, instead of stopping after n years. **The present value of a perpetuity** is PV = a/r where r is the cost of capital, as a proportion.

- **Compounding and discounting are directly linked to each other**. Make sure that you understand clearly the relationship between them.

Quick Quiz

1   What does the term present value mean?

2   The discounting formula is $X = S \times \dfrac{1}{(1+r)^n}$

    Where S =
             X =
             r =
             n =

    (a)   the rate of return (as a proportion)
    (b)   the sum to be received after n time periods
    (c)   the PV of that sum
    (d)   the number of time periods

3   What are the two usual methods of capital expenditure appraisal using DCF techniques?

4   What is the formula used to calculate the IRR and what do the symbols used represent?

5   An annuity is a sum of money received every year.

    True   ☐

    False   ☐

6   What is a perpetuity?

7   What is the formula for the present value of a perpetuity?

8   If Fred were to save $7,000 per annum, and we used the formula for the sum of a geometric progression to calculate the value of the fund that would have built up over ten years at an interest rate of 20%, what is the value of A to be used in the formula if:

    (a)   the first payment is now
    (b)   the first payment is in one year's time

9   What is the main advantage of borrowing as opposed to saving?

Answers to Quick Quiz

1   The amount of money which must be invested now for n years at an interest rate of r% to give a future sum of money at the time it will be due.

2   S = (b)
     X = (c)
     r = (a)
     n = (d)

3   The Net Present Value (NPV) method
     The Internal Rate of Return (IRR) method

4    $IRR = a\% + \left[\dfrac{A}{A\text{-}B} \times (b-a) \right]\%$

     Where a = one interest rate
            b = another interest rate
            A = the NPV at rate a
            B = the NPV at rate b

5   False. It is a **constant** sum of money **received** or **paid** each year for a **given number** of years.

6   An annuity which lasts forever.

7   PV = a/r

8   (a)   A = $7,000 \times 1.2$
     (b)   A = $7,000

9   The money is available **now** to buy the required asset as opposed to at the end of the savings period.

Now try the questions below from the Exam Question Bank

Question numbers	Pages
81-88	354-357

Part G
Spreadsheets

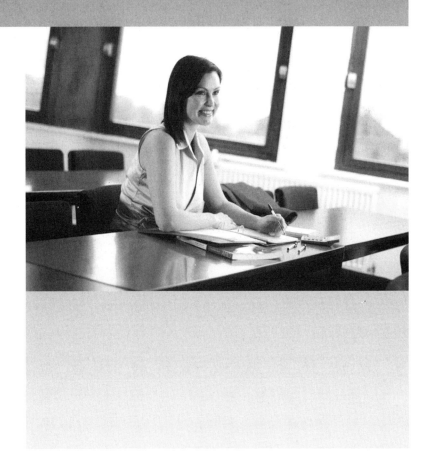

14

Spreadsheets

Introduction

Spreadsheet skills are essential for people working in a management accounting environment as much of the information produced is analysed or presented using spreadsheet software.

This chapter will look at features and functions of commonly used spreadsheet software, its advantages and disadvantages and how it is used in the day-to-day work of the Chartered Management Accountant.

Topic list	Syllabus references
1 Features and functions of spreadsheets	G, (i),(1)
2 Examples of spreadsheet formulae	G, (i),(1)
3 Basic skills	G, (i),(1)
4 Spreadsheet construction	G, (i),(1)
5 Formulae with conditions	G, (i),(1)
6 Charts and graphs	G, (i),(1)
7 Spreadsheet format and appearance	G, (i),(1)
8 Other issues	G, (i),(1)
9 Three dimensional (multi-sheet) spreadsheets	G, (i),(1)
10 Macros	G, (i),(1)
11 Advantages and disadvantages of spreadsheet software	G, (ii), (2)
12 Use of spreadsheet software	G, (iii), (3)

1 Features and functions of spreadsheets

FAST FORWARD

Use of spreadsheets is an essential part of the day-to-day work of the Chartered Management Accountant.

1.1 What is a spreadsheet?

FAST FORWARD

A spreadsheet is an electronic piece of paper divided into **rows** and **columns**. The intersection of a row and a column is known as a **cell**.

A spreadsheet is divided into **rows** (horizontal) and **columns** (vertical). The rows are numbered 1, 2, 3 . . . etc and the columns lettered A, B C . . . etc. Each individual area representing the intersection of a row and a column is called a 'cell'. A cell address consists of its row and column reference. For example, in the spreadsheet below the word '*Jan*' is in cell B2. The cell that the cursor is currently in or over is known as the 'active cell'.

The main examples of spreadsheet packages are Lotus 1 2 3 and Microsoft Excel. We will be referring to **Microsoft Excel**, as this is the most widely-used spreadsheet. A simple Microsoft Excel spreadsheet, containing budgeted sales figures for three geographical areas for the first quarter of the year, is shown below.

	A	B	C	D	E	F
1	**BUDGETED SALES FIGURES**					
2		Jan	Feb	Mar	Total	
3		$'000	$'000	$'000	$'000	
4	North	2,431	3,001	2,189	7,621	
5	South	6,532	5,826	6,124	18,482	
6	West	895	432	596	1,923	
7	Total	9,858	9,259	8,909	28,026	
8						

1.2 Why use spreadsheets?

Spreadsheets provide a tool for calculating, analysing and manipulating numerical data. Spreadsheets make the calculation and manipulation of data easier and quicker. For example, the spreadsheet above has been set up to calculate the totals **automatically.** If you changed your estimate of sales in February for the North region to $3,296, when you input this figure in cell C4 the totals (in E4 and C7) would change accordingly.

1.2.1 Uses of spreadsheets

Spreadsheets can be used for a wide range of tasks. Some common applications of spreadsheets are:

- Management accounts
- Cash flow analysis and forecasting
- Reconciliations
- Revenue analysis and comparison
- Cost analysis and comparison
- Budgets and forecasts

1.2.2 Cell contents

The contents of any cell can be one of the following.

(a) **Text**. A text cell usually contains **words**. Numbers that do not represent numeric values for calculation purposes (eg a Part Number) may be entered in a way that tells Excel to treat the cell contents as text. To do this, enter an apostrophe before the number eg '451.

(b) **Values**. A value is a **number** that can be used in a calculation.

(c) **Formulae**. A formula **refers to other cells** in the spreadsheet, and performs some sort of computation with them. For example, if cell C1 contains the formula =A1-B1, cell C1 will display the result of the calculation subtracting the contents of cell B1 from the contents of cell A1. In Excel, a formula always begins with an equals sign: = . There are a wide range of formulae and functions available.

1.2.3 Formula bar

The following illustration shows the formula bar. (If the formula bar is not visible, choose **View**, **Formula bar** from Excel's main menu.)

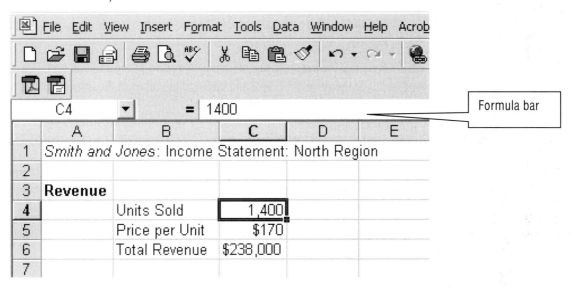

The formula bar allows you to see and edit the contents of the active cell. The bar also shows the cell address of the active cell (C3 in the example above).

2 Examples of spreadsheet formulae

FAST FORWARD

Formulas in Microsoft Excel follow a specific syntax.

All Excel formulae start with the equals sign =, followed by the elements to be calculated (the operands) and the calculation operators. Each operand can be a value that does not change (a constant value), a cell or range reference, a label, a name, or a worksheet function.

Formulae can be used to perform a variety of calculations. Here are some examples.

(a)   =C4*5. This formula **multiplies** the value in C4 by 5. The result will appear in the cell holding the formula.

(b)   =C4*B10. This **multiplies** the value in C4 by the value in B10.

(c)   =C4/E5. This **divides** the value in C4 by the value in E5. (* means multiply and / means divide by.)

(d)   =C4*B10-D1. This **multiplies** the value in C4 by that in B10 and then subtracts the value in D1 from the result. Note that generally Excel will perform multiplication and division before addition or subtraction. If in any doubt, use brackets (parentheses): =(C4*B10)–D1.

(e)   =C4*117.5%. This **adds** 17.5% to the value in C4. It could be used to calculate a price including 17.5% VAT.

(f)   =(C4+C5+C6)/3. Note that the **brackets** mean Excel would perform the addition first. Without the brackets, Excel would first divide the value in C6 by 3 and then add the result to the total of the values in C4 and C5.

(g)   = 2^2 gives you 2 **to the power** of 2, in other words 2^2. Likewise = 2^3 gives you 2 cubed and so on.

(h)   = 4^ (1/2) gives you the **square root** of 4. Likewise 27^(1/3) gives you the cube root of 27 and so on.

Without brackets, Excel calculates a formula from left to right. You can control how calculation is performed by changing the syntax of the formula. For example, the formula =5+2*3 gives a result of 11 because Excel calculates multiplication before addition. Excel would multiply 2 by 3 (resulting in 6) and would then add 5.

You may use parentheses to change the order of operations. For example =(5+2)*3 would result in Excel firstly adding the 5 and 2 together, then multiplying that result by 3 to give 21.

2.1 Displaying the formulae held in your spreadsheet

It is sometimes useful to see all formulae held in your spreadsheet to enable you to see how the spreadsheet works. There are two ways of making Excel **display the formulae** held in a spreadsheet.

(a)   You can 'toggle' between the two types of display by pressing **Ctrl** + ` (the latter is the key above the Tab key). Press Ctrl + ` again to get the previous display back.

(b)   You can also click on Tools, then on Options, then on View and tick the box next to 'Formulas'.

In the following paragraphs we provide examples of how spreadsheets and formulae may be used in an accounting context.

2.1.1 Example: formulae

	A	B	C	D	E	F
1	**BUDGETED SALES FIGURES**					
2		Jan	Feb	Mar	Total	
3		$'000	$'000	$'000	$'000	
4	North	2,431	3,001	2,189	7,621	
5	South	6,532	5,826	6,124	18,482	
6	West	895	432	596	1,923	
7	Total	9,858	9,259	8,909	28,026	
8						

(a) In the spreadsheet shown above, which of the cells have had a number typed in, and which cells display the result of calculations (ie which cells contain a formula)?

(b) What formula would you put in each of the following cells?

    (i)   Cell B7
    (ii)   Cell E6
    (iii) Cell E7

(c) If the February sales figure for the South changed from $5,826 to $5,731, what other figures would change as a result? Give cell references.

Solution

(a) Cells into which you would need to enter a value are: B4, B5, B6, C4, C5, C6, D4, D5 and D6. Cells which would perform calculations are B7, C7, D7, E4, E5, E6 and E7.

(b) (i) =B4+B5+B6 *or better* =SUM(B4:B6)

    (ii) =B6+C6+D6 *or better* =SUM(B6:D6)

    (iii) =E4+E5+E6 *or better* =SUM(E4:E6) Alternatively, the three monthly totals could be added across the spreadsheet: = SUM (B7: D7)

(c) The figures which would change, besides the amount in cell C5, would be those in cells C7, E5 and E7. (The contents of E7 would change if any of the sales figures changed.)

Question   **Sum formulae**

The following spreadsheet shows sales of two products, the Ego and the Id, for the period July to September.

	A	B	C	D	E
1	**Sigmund Ltd**				
2	*Sales analysis - Q3 20X7*				
3		M7	M8	M9	Total
4		$	$	$	$
5	Ego	3,000	4,000	2,000	9,000
6	Id	2,000	1,500	4,000	7,500
7	Total	5,000	5,500	6,000	16,500
8					

Devise a suitable formula for each of the following cells.

    (a)   Cell B7
    (b)   Cell E6
    (c)   Cell E7

Answer

(a) =SUM(B5:B6)

(b) =SUM(B6:D6)

(c) =SUM (E5:E6) *or* =SUM(B7:D7)

or (best of all) =IF(SUM(E5:E6) =SUM(B7:D7),SUM(B7:D7),"ERROR") Don't worry if you don't understand this formula when first attempting this question – we cover IF statements later in this Chapter.

Question

Formulae

The following spreadsheet shows sales, exclusive of VAT, in row 6.

	A	B	C	D	E	F	G	H
1	**Taxable Supplies plc**							
2	*Sales analysis - Branch C*							
3	*Six months ended 30 June 200X*							
4		Jan	Feb	Mar	Apr	May	Jun	Total
5		$	$	$	$	$	$	$
6	Net sales	2,491.54	5,876.75	3,485.01	5,927.7	6,744.52	3,021.28	27,546.80
7	VAT							
8	Total							
9								

Your manager has asked you to insert formulae to calculate sales tax at 17½% in row 7 and also to produce totals.

(a) Devise a suitable formula for cell B7 and cell E8.

(b) How could the spreadsheet be better designed?

Answer

(a) For cell B7 =B6*0.175   For cell E8 =SUM(E6:E7)

(b) By using a separate 'variables' holding the VAT rate and possibly the Sales figures. The formulae could then refer to these cells as shown below.

	A	B	C	D	E	F	G	H
1	**Taxable Supplies plc**							
2	*Sales analysis - Branch C*							
3	*Six months ended 30 June 200X*							
4		Jan	Feb	Mar	Apr	May	Jun	Total
5		$	$	$	$	$	$	$
6	Net sales	=B12	=C12	=D12	=E12	=F12	=G12	=SUM(B6:G6)
7	VAT	=B6*$B$13	=C6*$B$13	=D6*$B$13	=E6*$B$13	=F6*$B$13	=G6*$B$13	=SUM(B7:G7)
8	Total	=SUM(B6:B7)	=SUM(C6:C7)	=SUM(D6:D7)	=SUM(E6:E7)	=SUM(F6:F7)	=SUM(G6:G7)	=SUM(H6:H7)
9								
10								
11	*Variables*							
12	Sales	2491.54	5876.75	3485.01	5927.7	6744.52	3021.28	
13	VAT rate	0.175						
14								

3 Basic skills

Essential basic skills include how to **move around** within a spreadsheet, how to **enter** and **edit** data, how to **fill** cells, how to **insert** and **delete** columns and rows and how to improve the basic **layout** and **appearance** of a spreadsheet.

In this section we explain some **basic spreadsheeting skills**. We give instructions for Microsoft Excel, the most widely used package. Our examples should be valid with all versions of Excel released since 1997.

You should read this section while sitting at a computer and trying out the skills we describe **'hands-on'**.

3.1 Moving about

The F5 key is useful for moving around within large spreadsheets. If you press the function key **F5,** a **Go To** dialogue box will allow you to specify the cell address you would like to move to. Try this out.

Also experiment by holding down Ctrl and pressing each of the direction arrow keys in turn to see where you end up. Try using the **Page Up** and **Page Down** keys and also try **Home** and **End** and Ctrl + these keys. Try **Tab** and **Shift + Tab**, too. These are all useful shortcuts for moving quickly from one place to another in a large spreadsheet.

3.2 Editing cell contents

Suppose cell A2 currently contains the value 456. If you wish to **change the entry** in cell A2 from 456 to 123456 there are four options – as shown below.

(a)   Activate cell A2, **type** 123456 and press **Enter**.

To undo this and try the next option press **Ctrl + Z**: this will always undo what you have just done.

(b)   **Double-click** in cell A2. The cell will keep its thick outline but you will now be able to see a vertical line flashing in the cell. You can move this line by using the direction arrow keys or the Home and the End keys. Move it to before the 4 and type 123. Then press Enter.

When you have tried this press Ctrl + Z to undo it.

(c)   **Click once** before the number 456 in the formula bar. Again you will get the vertical line and you can type in 123 before the 4. Then press Enter. Undo this before moving onto (d).

(d)   Press the **function key F2**. The vertical line cursor will be flashing in cell A2 at the *end* of the figures entered there (after the 6). Press Home to get to a position before the 4 and then type in 123 and press Enter, as before.

3.3 Deleting cell contents

You may delete the contents of a cell simply by making the cell the active cell and then pressing **Delete**. The contents of the cell will disappear. You may also highlight a range of cells to delete and then delete the contents of all cells within the range.

For example, enter any value in cell A1 and any value in cell A2. Move the cursor to cell A2. Now hold down the **Shift** key (the one above the Ctrl key) and keeping it held down press the ↑ arrow. Cell A2 will stay white but cell A1 will go black. What you have done here is **selected** the range A1 and A2. Now press the Delete key. The contents of cells A1 and A2 will be deleted.

3.4 Filling a range of cells

Start with a blank spreadsheet. Type the number 1 in cell A1 and the number 2 in cell A2. Now select cells A1: A2, this time by positioning the mouse pointer over cell A1, holding down the left mouse button and moving the pointer down to cell A2. When cell A2 is highlighted release the mouse button.

Now position the mouse pointer at the **bottom right hand corner** of cell A2. When you have the mouse pointer in the right place it will turn into a **black cross**.

Then, hold down the left mouse button again and move the pointer down to cell A10. You will see an outline surrounding the cells you are trying to 'fill'.

Release the mouse button when you have the pointer over cell A10. You will find that the software **automatically** fills in the numbers 3 to 10 below 1 and 2.

Try the following variations of this technique.

(a)   Delete what you have just done and type in **Jan** in cell A1. See what happens if you select cell A1 and fill down to cell A12: you get the months **Feb, Mar, Apr** and so on.

(b)   Type the number 2 in cell A1. Select A1 and fill down to cell A10. What happens? The cells should fill up with 2's.

(c)   Type the number 2 in cell A1 and 4 in cell A2. Then select A1: A2 and fill down to cell A10. What happens? You should get 2, 4, 6, 8, and so on.

(d)   Try **filling across** as well as down.

(e)   If you click on the bottom right hand corner of the cell using the **right mouse button**, drag down to a lower cell and then release the button you should see a menu providing a variety of options for filling the cells.

3.5 The SUM button Σ

We will explain how to use the SUM button by way of a simple example. Start with a blank spreadsheet, then enter the following figures in cells A1:B5.

	A	B
1	400	582
2	250	478
3	359	264
4	476	16
5	97	125

Make cell B6 the active cell and click once on the SUM button (the button with a Σ symbol on the Excel toolbar - the Σ symbol is the mathematical sign for 'the sum of'). A formula will appear in the cell saying =SUM(B1:B5). Above cell B6 you will see a flashing dotted line encircling cells B1:B5. Accept the suggested formula by hitting the Enter key.

The formula =SUM(B1:B5) will be entered, and the number 1465 will appear in cell B6.

Next, make cell A6 the active cell and **double-click** on the SUM button. The number 1582 should appear in cell A6.

3.6 Multiplication

Continuing on with our example, next select cell C1. Type in an = sign then click on cell A1. Now type in an **asterisk** * (which serves as a **multiplication sign**) and click on cell B1. Watch how the formula in cell C1 changes as you do this. (Alternatively you can enter the cell references by moving the direction arrow keys.) Finally press Enter. Cell C1 will show the result (232,800) of multiplying the figure in Cell A1 by the one in cell B1.

Your next task is to select cell C1 and **fill in** cells C2 to C5 automatically using the **dragging technique** described above. If you then click on each cell in column C and look above at the line showing what the cell contains you will find that the software has automatically filled in the correct cell references for you: A2*B2 in cell C2, A3*B3 in cell C3 and so on.

(**Note**: The forward slash / is used to represent division in spreadsheet formulae.)

3.7 Inserting columns and rows

Suppose we also want to add each row, for example cells A1 and B1. The logical place to do this would be cell C1, but column C already contains data. We have three options that would enable us to place this total in column C.

(a)　Highlight cells C1 to C5 and position the mouse pointer on one of the **edges**. (It will change to an arrow shape.) Hold down the **left** mouse button and drag cells C1 to C5 into column D. There is now space in column C for our next set of sums. Any **formulae** that need to be changed as a result of moving cells using this method should be changed **automatically** – but always check them.

(b)　The second option is to highlight cells C1 to C5 as before, position the mouse pointer anywhere **within** column C and click on the **right** mouse button. A menu will appear offering you an option **Insert...** . If you click on this you will be asked where you want to shift the cells that are being moved. In this case you want to move them to the right so choose this option and click on OK.

(c)　The third option is to **insert a whole new column**. You do this by clicking on the letter at the top of the column (here C) to highlight the whole of it then proceeding as in (b). The new column will always be inserted to the **left** of the one you highlight.

You can now display the sum of each of the rows in column C.

You can also insert a new row in a similar way (or stretch rows).

(a)　To **insert** one row, perhaps for headings, click on the row number to highlight it, click with the right mouse button and choose insert. One row will be inserted **above** the one you highlighted. Try putting some headings above the figures in columns A to C.

(b)　To insert **several** rows click on the row number immediately **below** the point where you want the new rows to appear and, holding down the left mouse button highlight the number of rows you wish to insert. Click on the highlighted area with the right mouse button and choose Insert (or if you prefer, choose **Insert**, **Rows** from the main menu).

3.8 Changing column width

You may occasionally find that a cell is not wide enough to display its contents. When this occurs, the cell displays a series of hashes ######. There are two options available to solve this problem.

(a)   One is to **decide for yourself** how wide you want the columns to be. Position the mouse pointer at the head of column A directly over the little line dividing the letter A from the letter B. The mouse **pointer** will change to a sort of **cross**. Hold down the left mouse button and, by moving your mouse, stretch Column A to the right, to about the middle of column D, until the words you typed fit. You can do the same for column B. Then make your columns too narrow again so you can try option (b).

(b)   Often it is easier to **let the software decide for you**. Position the mouse pointer over the little dividing line as before and get the cross symbol. Then double-click with the left mouse button. The column automatically adjusts to an appropriate width to fit the widest cell in that column.

You can either adjust the width of each column individually or you can do them all in one go. To do the latter click on the button in the top left hand corner to **select the whole sheet** and then **double-click** on just one of the dividing lines: all the columns will adjust to the **'best fit'** width.

3.9 Keyboard shortcuts and toolbar buttons

Here are a few tips to improve the **appearance** of your spreadsheets and speed up your work. To do any of the following to a cell or range of cells, first **select** the cell or cells and then:

(a)   Press Ctrl + B to make the cell contents **bold.**

(b)   Press Ctrl + I to make the cell contents *italic.*

(c)   Press **Ctrl + C** to **copy** the contents of the cells.

(d)   Move the cursor and press **Ctrl + V** to **paste** the cell you just copied into the new active cell or cells.

There are also **buttons** in the Excel toolbar (shown below) that may be used to carry out these and other functions. The best way to learn about these features is to use them - enter some numbers and text into a spreadsheet and experiment with keyboard shortcuts and toolbar buttons.

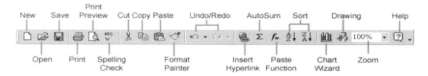

4 Spreadsheet construction

FAST FORWARD

A wide range of **formulae** and functions are available within Excel.

Spreadsheet models that will be used mainly as a calculation tool for various scenarios should ideally be constructed in **three sections**, as follows.

1   An inputs section containing the variables (eg the amount of a loan and the interest rate).
2   A calculations section containing formulae (eg the loan term and interest rate).
3   The results section, showing the outcome of the calculations.

4.1 Example: spreadsheet construction

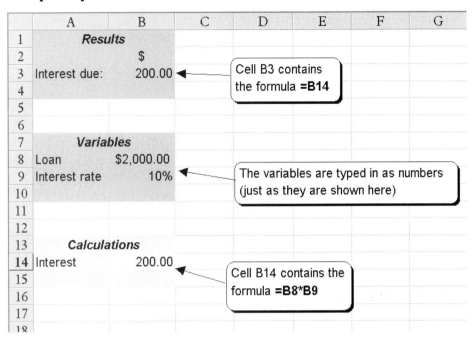

In practice, in many situations it is often **more convenient** to combine the results and calculations areas as follows.

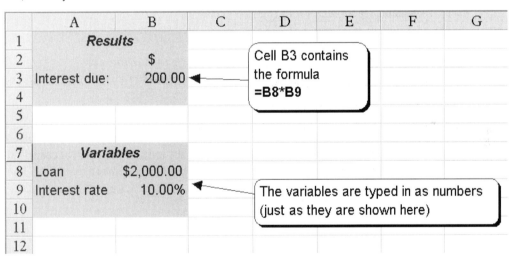

If we took out another loan of $4,789 at an interest rate of 7.25% we would simply need to **overwrite the figures in the variable section** of the spreadsheet with the new figures to calculate the interest.

Question

Answer questions (a) and (b) below, which relate to the following spreadsheet.

	A	B	C	D
1	**Boilermakers Ltd**			
2	*Department B*			
3				
4	*Production data*	Machine A	Machine B	Machine C
5	Shift 1	245.84	237.49	231.79
6	Shift 2	241.14	237.62	261.31
7	Shift 3	244.77	201.64	242.71
8	Shift 4	240.96	238.18	234.50
9				
10	*Usage data*	Machine A	Machine B	Machine C
11	Maintenance	35	71	6
12	Operational	8.47	7.98	9.31
13	Idle	1.42	2.40	0.87
14	Recovery	0	15	4
15				

(a) Cell B9 needs to contain an average of all the preceding numbers in column B. Suggest a formula which would achieve this.

(b) Cell C16 contains the formula

=C12+C13/C14-C15

What would the result be, displayed in cell C16?

Answer

This question tests whether you can evaluate formulae in the correct order. In part (a) you must remember to put brackets around the numbers required to be added, otherwise the formula will automatically divide cell B8 by 4 first and add the result to the other numbers. Similarly, in part (b), the formula performs the multiplication before the addition and subtraction.

(a)   =SUM(B5:B8)/4   An alternative is = AVERAGE(B5:B8).

(b)   59.325

4.2 Example: Constructing a cash flow projection

Suppose you wanted to set up a simple six-month cash flow projection, in such a way that you could use it to estimate how the **projected cash balance** figures will **change** in total when any **individual item** in the projection is **altered**. You have the following information.

(a) Sales were $45,000 per month in 20X5, falling to $42,000 in January 20X6. Thereafter they are expected to increase by 3% per month (ie February will be 3% higher than January, and so on).

(b) Debts are collected as follows.

  (i)   60% in month following sale.
  (ii)   30% in second month after sale.
  (iii) 7% in third month after sale.
  (iv) 3% remains uncollected.

(c) Purchases are equal to cost of sales, set at 65% of sales.

(d) Overheads were $6,000 per month in 20X5, rising by 5% in 20X6.

(e) Opening cash is an overdraft of $7,500.

(f) Dividends: $10,000 final dividend on 20X5 profits payable in May.

(g) Capital purchases: plant costing $18,000 will be ordered in January. 20% is payable with order, 70% on delivery in February and the final 10% in May.

4.2.1 Headings and layout

The first step is to put in the various **headings** required for the cash flow projection. At this stage, your spreadsheet might look as follows.

	A	B	C	D	E	F	G
1	**EXCELLENT PLC**						
2	*Cash flow projection - six months ending 30 June 20X6*						
3		*Jan*	*Feb*	*Mar*	*Apr*	*May*	*Jun*
4		$	$	$	$	$	$
5	Sales						
6	*Cash receipts*						
7	1 month in arrears						
8	2 months in arrears						
9	3 months in arrears						
10	Total operating receipts						
11							
12	Cash payments						
13	Purchases						
14	Overheads						
15	Total operating payments						
16							
17	Dividends						
18	Capital purchases						
19	Total other payments						
20							
21	Net cash flow						
22	Cash balance b/f						
23	Cash balance c/f						
24							

Note the following points.

(a) We have **increased the width** of column A to allow longer pieces of text to be inserted. Had we not done so, only the first part of each caption would have been displayed (and printed).

(b) We have developed a **simple style for headings**. Headings are essential, so that users can identify what a spreadsheet does. We have **emboldened** the company name and *italicised* other headings.

(c) When **text** is entered into a cell it is usually **left-aligned** (as for example in column A). We have **centred** the headings above each column by highlighting the cells and using the relevant buttons at the top of the screen.

(d) **Numbers** should be **right-aligned** in cells.

(e) We have left **spaces** in certain rows (after blocks of related items) to make the spreadsheet **easier to use and read**.

4.2.2 Inserting formulae

The next step is to enter the **formulae** required. For example, in cell B10 you want total operating receipts, =SUM(B7:B9).

Look for a moment at cell C7. We are told that sales in January were $42,000 and that 60% of customers settle their accounts one month in arrears. We could insert the formula =B5*0.6 in the cell and fill in the other cells along the row so that it is replicated in each month. However, consider the effect of a change in payment patterns to a situation where, say, 55% of customer debts are settled after one month. This would necessitate a **change to each and every cell** in which the 0.6 ratio appears.

An alternative approach, which makes **future changes much simpler** to execute, is to put the relevant ratio (here, 60% or 0.6) in a cell **outside** the main table and cross-refer each cell in the main table to that cell. This means that, if the percentage changes, the change need only be reflected in **one cell**, following which all cells which are dependent on that cell will **automatically use the new percentage**. We will therefore input such values in separate parts of the spreadsheet, as follows. Look at the other assumptions which we have inserted into this part of the spreadsheet.

	A	B	C	D	E
25					
26	This table contains the key variables for the 20X6 cash flow projections				
27					
28	Sales growth factor per month		1.03		
29	Purchases as % of sales		-0.65		
30					
31	Debts paid within 1 month		0.6		
32	Debts paid within 2 months		0.3		
33	Debts paid within 3 months		0.07		
34	Bad debts		0.03		
35					
36	Increase in overheads		1.05		
37					
38	Dividends (May)		-10000		
39					
40	Capital purchases		-18000		
41	January		0.2		
42	February		0.7		
43	May		0.1		
44					
45					
46	This table contains relevant opening balance data as at Jan 20X6				
47					
48	Monthly sales 20X5		45000		
49	January 20X6 sales		42000		
50	Monthly overheads 20X5		-6000		
51	Opening cash		-7500		
52					

Now we can go back to cell C7 and input =B5*C31 and then fill this in across the '1 month in arrears' row. (Note that, as we have no December sales figure, we will have to deal with cell B7 separately.) If we assume for the moment that we are copying to cells D7 through to G7 and follow this procedure, the contents of cell D7 would be shown as =C5*D31, and so on, as shown below.

	A	B	C	D	E	F	G
3		Jan	Feb	Mar	Apr	May	Jun
4		$	$	$	$	$	$
5	Sales						
6	Cash receipts						
7	1 month in arrears		=B5*C31	=C5*D31	=D5*E31	=E5*F31	=F5*G31
8	2 months in arrears						
9	3 months in arrears						
10	Total operating receipts						
11							

You may have noticed a problem. While the formula in cell C7 is fine - it multiplies January sales by 0.6 (the 1 month ratio stored in cell C31) - the remaining formulae are useless, as they **refer to empty cells** in row 31. This is what the spreadsheet would look like (assuming, for now, constant sales of $42,000 per month).

	A	B	C	D	E	F	G	
3		Jan	Feb	Mar	Apr	May	Jun	
4		$	$	$	$	$	$	
5	Sales	42000	42000	42000	42000	42000	42000	
6	Cash receipts							
7	1 month in arrears		25200	0	0	0	0	
8	2 months in arrears							
9	3 months in arrears							
10	Total operating receipts							
11								

This problem highlights the important distinction between **relative** cell references and **absolute** cell references. Usually, cell references are **relative**. A formula of =SUM(B7:B9) in cell B10 is relative. It does not really mean 'add up the numbers in cells B7 to B9'; it actually means '**add up the numbers in the three cells above this one**'. If this formula was copied to cell C10 (as we will do later), it would become =SUM(C7:C9).

This is what is causing the problem encountered above. The spreadsheet thinks we are asking it to 'multiply the number two up and one to the left by the number twenty-four cells down', and that is indeed the effect of the instruction we have given. But we are actually intending to ask it to 'multiply the number two up and one to the left by the number in cell C31'. This means that we need to create an **absolute** (unchanging) **reference** to cell C31.

Absolute cell references use **dollar signs** ($). A dollar sign before the column letter makes the column reference absolute, and one before the row number makes the row number absolute. You do not need to type the dollar signs - add them as follows.

(a) Make cell C7 the active cell and press F2 to edit it.

(b) Note where the cursor is flashing: it should be after the 1. If it is not move it with the direction arrow keys so that it is positioned somewhere next to or within the cell reference C31.

(c) Press F4.

The **function key F4** adds dollar signs to the cell reference: it becomes $C$31. Press F4 again: the reference becomes C$31. Press it again: the reference becomes $C31. Press it once more, and the simple relative reference is restored: C31.

(a) A dollar sign **before a letter** means that the **column** reference stays the same when you copy the formula to another cell.

(b) A dollar sign **before a number** means that the **row** reference stays the same when you copy the formula to another cell.

In our example we have now altered the reference in cell C7 and filled in across to cell G7, overwriting what was there previously. This is the result.

(a) Formulae

	A	B	C	D	E	F	G
3		Jan	Feb	Mar	Apr	May	Jun
4		$	$	$	$	$	$
5	Sales	42000	42000	42000	42000	42000	42000
6	Cash receipts						
7	1 month in arrears		=B5*$C$31	=C5*$C$31	=D5*$C$31	=E5*$C$31	=F5*$C$31
8	2 months in arrears						
9	3 months in arrears						
10	Total operating receipts						
11							

BPP
PROFESSIONAL EDUCATION

(b)   Numbers

	A	B	C	D	E	F	G
1		Jan	Feb	Mar	Apr	May	Jun
2		$	$	$	$	$	$
3	Sales	42000	42000	42000	42000	42000	42000
4	Cash receipts						
5	1 month in arrears		25200	25200	25200	25200	25200
6	2 months in arrears						
7	3 months in arrears						
8	Total operating receipts						
9							

Other formulae required for this projection are as follows.

(a)   **Cell B5** refers directly to the information we are given - **sales of $42,000** in January. We have input this variable in cell C49. The other formulae in row 5 (sales) reflect the predicted sales growth of 3% per month, as entered in cell C28.

(b)   Similar formulae to the one already described for row 7 are required in rows 8 and 9.

(c)   **Row 10** (total operating receipts) will display simple **subtotals**, in the form =SUM(B7:B9).

(d)   **Row 13 (purchases)** requires a formula based on the data in row 5 **(sales)** and the value in cell C29 **(purchases** as a % of sales). This model assumes no changes in stock levels from month to month, and that stocks are sufficiently high to enable this. The formula is B5 * $C$29. Note that C29 is negative.

(e)   **Row 15** (total operating payments), like row 10, requires **formulae** to create **subtotals**.

(f)   **Rows 17 and 18** refer to the **dividends and capital purchase data** input in cells C38 and C40 to 43.

(g)   **Row 21** (net cash flow) requires a **total** in the form =B10 + B15 + B21.

(h)   **Row 22** (balance b/f) requires the contents of the **previous month's closing cash** figure.

(i)   **Row 23** (balance b/f) requires the **total** of the **opening cash** figure and the **net cash flow** for the month.

The following image shows the formulae that should now be present in the spreadsheet.

	A	B	C	D	E	F	G
1	EXCELLENT PLC						
2	Cash flow projection - six months						
3		Jan	Feb	Mar	Apr	May	Jun
4		$	$	$	$	$	$
5	Sales	=C49	=B5*$C$28	=C5*$C$28	=D5*$C$28	=E5*$C$28	=F5*$C$28
6	Cash receipts						
7	1 month in arrears	=$C$48*$C$31	=B5*$C$31	=C5*$C$31	=D5*$C$31	=E5*$C$31	=F5*$C$31
8	2 months in arrears	=$C$48*$C$32	=$C$48*$C$32	=B5*$C$32	=C5*$C$32	=D5*$C$32	=E5*$C$32
9	3 months in arrears	=$C$48*$C$33	=$C$48*$C$33	=$C$48*$C$33	=B5*$C$33	=C5*$C$33	=D5*$C$33
10	Total operating receipts	=SUM(B7:B9)	=SUM(C7:C9)	=SUM(D7:D9)	=SUM(E7:E9)	=SUM(F7:F9)	=SUM(G7:G9)
11							
12	Cash payments						
13	Purchases	=B5*$C$29	=C5*$C$29	=D5*$C$29	=E5*$C$29	=F5*$C$29	=G5*$C$29
14	Overheads	=$C$50*$C$36	=$C$50*$C$36	=$C$50*$C$36	=$C$50*$C$36	=$C$50*$C$36	=$C$50*$C$36
15	Total operating payments	=SUM(B13:B14)	=SUM(C13:C14)	=SUM(D13:D14)	=SUM(E13:E14)	=SUM(F13:F14)	=SUM(G13:G14)
16							
17	Dividends	0	0	0	0	=C38	0
18	Capital purchases	=C40*C41	=C40*C42	0	0	=C40*C43	0
19	Total other payments	=SUM(B17:B18)	=SUM(C17:C18)	=SUM(D17:D18)	=SUM(E17:E18)	=SUM(F17:F18)	=SUM(G17:G18)
20							
21	Net cash flow	=B10+B15+B19	=C10+C15+C19	=D10+D15+D19	=E10+E15+E19	=F10+F15+F19	=G10+G15+G19
22	Cash balance b/f	=C51	=B23	=C23	=D23	=E23	=F23
23	Cash balance c/f	=SUM(B21:B22)	=SUM(C21:C22)	=SUM(D21:D22)	=SUM(E21:E22)	=SUM(F21:F22)	=SUM(G21:G22)
24							

Be careful to ensure you use the correct sign (negative or positive) when manipulating numbers. For example, if total operating payments in row 15 are shown as **positive**, you would need to **subtract** them from total operating receipts in the formulae in row 23. However if you have chosen to make them **negative**, to represent outflows, then you will need to **add** them to total operating receipts.

Here is the spreadsheet in its normal 'numbers' form.

	A	B	C	D	E	F	G
1	**EXCELLENT PLC**						
2	*Cash flow projection - six months ending 30 June 20X6*						
3		*Jan*	*Feb*	*Mar*	*Apr*	*May*	*Jun*
4		$	$	$	$	$	$
5	Sales	42,000	43,260	44,558	45,895	47,271	48,690
6	*Cash receipts*						
7	1 month in arrears	27,000	25,200	25,956	26,735	27,537	28,363
8	2 months in arrears	13,500	13,500	12,600	12,978	13,367	13,768
9	3 months in arrears	3,150	3,150	3,150	2,940	3,028	3,119
10	Total operating receipts	43,650	41,850	41,706	42,653	43,932	45,250
11							
12	*Cash payments*						
13	Purchases	-27,300	-28,119	-28,963	-29,831	-30,726	-31,648
14	Overheads	-6,000	-6,300	-6,300	-6,300	-6,300	-6,300
15	Total operating payments	-33,300	-34,419	-35,263	-36,131	-37,026	-37,948
16							
17	Dividends	0	0	0	0	-10,000	0
18	Capital purchases	-3,600	-12,600	0	0	-1,800	0
19	Total other payments	-3,600	-12,600	0	0	-11,800	0
20							
21	Net cash flow	6,450	-5,169	6,443	6,521	-4,894	7,302
22	Cash balance b/f	-7,500	-1,050	-6,219	224	6,746	1,852
23	Cash balance c/f	-1,050	-6,219	224	6,746	1,852	9,154
24							

4.2.3 Tidy the spreadsheet up

Our spreadsheet needs a little **tidying up**. We will do the following.

(a)   Add in **commas** to denote thousands of dollars.

(b)   Put **zeros** in the cells with no entry in them.

(c)   Change **negative numbers** from being displayed with a **minus sign** to being displayed in **brackets**.

	A	B	C	D	E	F	G
1	EXCELLENT PLC						
2	Cash flow projection - six months ending 30 June 20X6						
3		Jan	Feb	Mar	Apr	May	Jun
4		$	$	$	$	$	£
5	Sales	42,000	43,260	44,558	45,895	47,271	48,690
6	Cash receipts						
7	1 month in arrears	27,000	25,200	25,956	26,735	27,537	28,363
8	2 months in arrears	13,500	13,500	12,600	12,978	13,367	13,768
9	3 months in arrears	3,150	3,150	3,150	2,940	3,028	3,119
10	Total operating receipts	43,650	41,850	41,706	42,653	43,932	45,250
11							
12	Cash payments						
13	Purchases	(27,300)	(28,119)	(28,963)	(29,831)	(30,726)	(31,648)
14	Overheads	(6,300)	(6,300)	(6,300)	(6,300)	(6,300)	(6,300)
15	Total operating payments	(33,600)	(34,419)	(35,263)	(36,131)	(37,026)	(37,948)
16							
17	Dividends	0	0	0	0	(10,000)	0
18	Capital purchases	(3,600)	(12,600)	0	0	(1,800)	0
19	Total other payments	(3,600)	(12,600)	0	0	(11,800)	0
20							
21	Net cash flow	6,450	(5,169)	6,443	6,521	(4,894)	7,302
22	Cash balance b/f	(7,500)	(1,050)	(6,219)	224	6,746	1,852
23	Cash balance c/f	(1,050)	(6,219)	224	6,746	1,852	9,154
24							

4.2.4 Changes in assumptions (what if? analysis)

We referred to earlier to the need to design a spreadsheet so that **changes in assumptions** do **not** require **major changes** to the spreadsheet. This is why we set up two separate areas of the spreadsheet, one for 20X6 assumptions and one for opening balances. Consider each of the following.

(a) Negotiations with suppliers and gains in productivity have resulted in cost of sales being reduced to 62% of sales.

(b) The effects of a recession have changed the cash collection profile so that receipts in any month are 50% of prior month sales, 35% of the previous month and 10% of the month before that, with bad debt experience rising to 5%.

(c) An insurance claim made in 20X5 and successfully settled in December has resulted in the opening cash balance being an overdraft of $3,500.

(d) Sales growth will only be 2% per month.

All of these changes can be made quickly and easily. The two tables are revised as follows.

	A	B	C	D	E
25					
26	This table contains the key variables for the 20X6 cash flow projections				
27					
28	Sales growth factor per month		1.02		
29	Purchases as % of sales		-0.62		
30					
31	Debts paid within 1 month		0.5		
32	Debts paid within 2 months		0.35		
33	Debts paid within 3 months		0.1		
34	Bad debts		0.05		
35					
36	Increase in overheads		1.05		
37					
38	Dividends (May)		-10000		
39					
40	Capital purchases		-18000		
41	January		0.2		
42	February		0.7		
43	May		0.1		
44					
45					
46	This table contains relevant opening balance data as at Jan 20X6				
47					
48	Monthly sales 19X5		45000		
49	January 1996 sales		42000		
50	Monthly overheads 19X5		-6000		
51	Opening cash		-3500		
52					

The resulting (recalculated) spreadsheet would look like this.

	A	B	C	D	E	F	G
1	EXCELLENT PLC						
2	Cash flow projection - six months ending 30 June 20X6						
3		Jan	Feb	Mar	Apr	May	Jun
4		$	$	$	$	$	$
5	Sales	42,000	42,840	43,697	44,571	45,462	46,371
6	Cash receipts						
7	1 month in arrears	22,500	21,000	21,420	21,848	22,285	22,731
8	2 months in arrears	15,750	15,750	14,700	14,994	15,294	15,600
9	3 months in arrears	4,500	4,500	4,500	4,200	4,284	4,370
10	Total operating receipts	42,750	41,250	40,620	41,042	41,863	42,701
11							
12	Cash payments						
13	Purchases	-26,040	-26,561	-27,092	-27,634	-28,187	-28,750
14	Overheads	-6,300	-6,300	-6,300	-6,300	-6,300	-6,300
15	Total operating payments	-32,340	-32,861	-33,392	-33,934	-34,487	-35,050
16							
17	Dividends	0	0	0	0	-10,000	0
18	Capital purchases	-3,600	-12,600	0	0	-1,800	0
19	Total other payments	-3,600	-12,600	0	0	-11,800	0
20							
21	Net cash flow	6,810	-4,211	7,228	7,109	-4,423	7,650
22	Cash balance b/f	-3,500	3,310	-901	6,327	13,436	9,012
23	Cash balance c/f	3,310	-901	6,327	13,436	9,012	16,663
24							

Commission calculations

The following four insurance salesmen each earn a basic salary of $14,000 pa. They also earn a commission of 2% of sales. The following spreadsheet has been created to process their commission and total earnings. Give an appropriate formula for each of the following cells.

(a) Cell D4

(b) Cell E6

(c) Cell D9

(d) Cell E9

	A	B	C	D	E	
1	*Sales team salaries and commissions - 200X*					
2	Name	Sales	Salary	Commission	Total earnings	
3		$	$	$	$	
4	Northington	284,000	14,000	5,680	19,680	
5	Souther	193,000	14,000	3,860	17,860	
6	Weston	12,000	14,000	240	14,240	
7	Easterman	152,000	14,000	3,040	17,040	
8						
9	Total	641,000	56,000	12,820	68,820	
10						
11						
12	*Variables*					
13	Basic Salary	14,000				
14	Commission rate	0.02				
15						

Answer

Possible formulae are as follows.

(a) =B4*$B$14

(b) =C6+D6

(c) =SUM(D4:D7)

(d) There are a number of possibilities here, depending on whether you set the cell as the total of the earnings of each salesman (cells E4 to E7) or as the total of the different elements of remuneration (cells C9 and D9). Even better, would be a formula that checked that both calculations gave the same answer. A suitable formula for this purpose would be:

=IF(SUM(E4:E7)=SUM(C9:D9),SUM(E4:E7),"ERROR")

We will explain this formula in more detail in the next section.

5 Formulae with conditions

FAST FORWARD

If statements are used in conditional formulae.

Suppose the company employing the salesmen in the above question awards a bonus to those salesmen who exceed their target by more than $1,000. The spreadsheet could work out who is entitled to the bonus.

To do this we would enter the appropriate formula in cells F4 to F7. For salesperson Easterman, we would enter the following in cell F7:

=IF(D4>1000,"BONUS"," ")

We will now explain this formula.

IF statements follow the following structure (or syntax).

=IF(logical_test,value_if_true,value_if_false)

The logical_test is any value or expression that can be evaluated to Yes or No. For example, D4>1000 is a logical expression; if the value in cell D4 is over 1000, the expression evaluates to Yes. Otherwise, the expression evaluates to No.

Value_if_true is the value that is returned if the answer to the logical_test is Yes. For example, if the answer to D4>1000 is Yes, and the value_if_true is the text string "BONUS", then the cell containing the IF function will display the text "BONUS".

Value_if_false   is the value that is returned if the answer to the logical_test is No. For example, if the value_if_false is two sets of quote marks "" this means display a blank cell if the answer to the logical test is No. So in our example, if D4 is not over 1000, then the cell containing the IF function will display a blank cell.

Note the following symbols which can be used in formulae with conditions:

<	less than (like L (for 'less') on its side)
<=	less than or equal to
=	equal to
>=	greater than or equal to
>	greater than
<>	not equal to

Care is required to ensure **brackets** and **commas** are entered in the right places. If, when you try out this kind of formula, you get an error message, it may well be a simple mistake, such as leaving a comma out.

5.1 Examples of formulae with conditions

A company offers a discount of 5% to customers who order more than $1,000 worth of goods. A spreadsheet showing what customers will pay might look like this.

	A	B	C	D
1	**Discount Traders Ltd**			
2	*Sales analysis - April 200X*			
3	Customer	Sales	5% discount	Sales (net)
4		$	$	$
5	Arthur	956.00	0.00	956.00
6	Dent	1423.00	71.15	1351.85
7	Ford	2894.00	144.70	2749.30
8	Prefect	842.00	0.00	842.00
9				

The formula in cell C5 is: =IF(B5>1,000,(0.05*B5),0). This means, if the value in B5 is greater than $1,000 multiply it by 0.05, otherwise the discount will be zero. Cell D5 will calculate the amount net of discount, using the formula: =B5-C5. The same conditional formula with the cell references changed will be found in cells C6, C7 and C8. **Strictly**, the variables $1,000 and 5% should be entered in a **different part** of the spreadsheet.

Here is another example.   Suppose the pass mark for an examination is 50%. You have a spreadsheet containing candidate's scores in column B. If a score is held in cell B10, an appropriate formula for cell C10 would be:

=IF(B10<50,"FAILED","PASSED").

6 Charts and graphs

Excel includes the facility to produce a range of charts and graphs. The **chart wizard** provides a tool to simplify the process of chart construction.

Using Microsoft Excel, It is possible to display data held in a range of spreadsheet cells in a variety of charts or graphs. We will use the Discount Traders Ltd spreadsheet shown below to generate a chart.

	A	B	C	D
1	**Discount Traders Ltd**			
2	*Sales analysis - April 200X*			
3	Customer	Sales	5% discount	Sales (net)
4		$	$	$
5	Arthur	956.00	0.00	956.00
6	Dent	1423.00	71.15	1351.85
7	Ford	2894.00	144.70	2749.30
8	Prefect	842.00	0.00	842.00
9				

The data in the spreadsheet could be used to generate a chart, such as those shown below. We explain how later in this section.

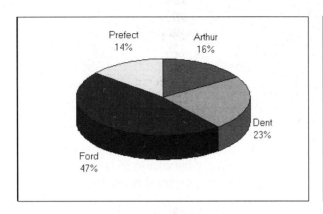
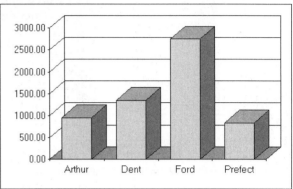

The Chart Wizard, which we explain in a moment, may also be used to generate a line graph. A line graph would normally be used to track a trend over time. For example, the chart below graphs the Total Revenue figures shown in Row 7 of the following spreadsheet.

	A	B	C	D	E	F	G	H	I
1									
2	**Revenue 2003-2006**								
3									
4	**Net revenue:**	2003	2004	2005	2006				
5	Products	24,001	27,552	34,823	39,205				
6	Services	5,306	5,720	6,104	6,820				
7	Total Revenue	29,307	33,272	40,927	46,025				
8									
9									

Total Revenue 2003-2006

6.1 The Chart Wizard

Charts and graphs may be generated simply by **selecting the range** of figures to be included, then using Excel's Chart Wizard. The Discount Traders spreadsheet referred to earlier is shown again below.

	A	B	C	D
1	**Discount Traders Ltd**			
2	*Sales analysis - April 200X*			
3	Customer	Sales	5% discount	Sales (net)
4		$	$	$
5	Arthur	956.00	0.00	956.00
6	Dent	1423.00	71.15	1351.85
7	Ford	2894.00	144.70	2749.30
8	Prefect	842.00	0.00	842.00
9				

To chart the **net sales** of the different **customers**, follow the following steps.

Step 1   Highlight cells A5:A8, then move your pointer to cell D5, hold down **Ctrl** and drag to also select cells D5:D8.

Step 2   Look at the **toolbar** at the top of your spreadsheet. You should see an **icon** that looks like a small bar chart. Click on this icon to start the 'Chart Wizard'.

The following steps are taken from the Excel 2000 Chart Wizard. Other versions may differ slightly.

Step 3   Pick the type of chart you want. We will choose chart type **Column** and then select the sub-type we think will be most effective. (To produce a graph, select a type such as **Line**.)

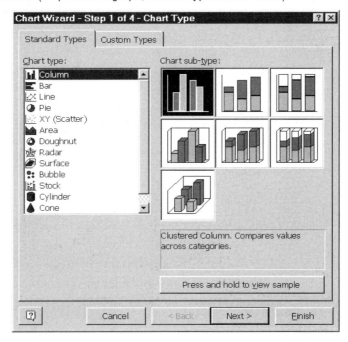

Step 4 This step gives us the opportunity to confirm that the data we selected earlier was correct and to decide whether the chart should be based on **columns** (eg Customer, Sales, Discount etc) or **rows** (Arthur, Dent etc). We can accept the default values and click Next.

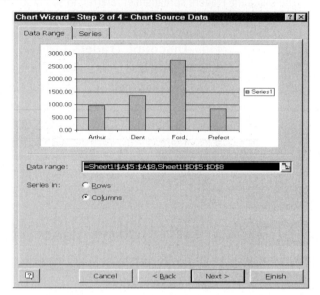

Step 5 Next, specify your chart **title** and axis **labels**. Incidentally, one way of remembering which is the **X axis** and which is the **Y axis** is to look at the letter Y: it is the only letter that has a vertical part pointing straight up, so it must be the vertical axis! Click Next to move on.

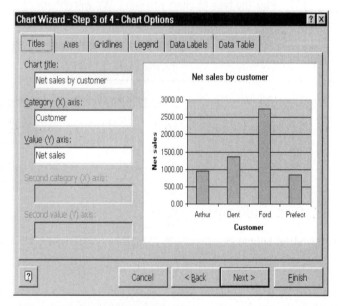

As you can see, there are other index tabs available. You can see the effect of selecting or deselecting each one in **preview** - experiment with these options as you like then click Next.

Step 6 The final step is to choose whether you want the chart to appear on the same worksheet as the data or on a separate sheet of its own. This is a matter of personal preference – for this example choose to place the chart as an object within the existing spreadsheet.

6.2 Changing existing charts

Even after your chart is 'finished' you may change it in a variety of ways.

(a)   You can **resize it** simply by selecting it and dragging out its borders.

(b)   You can change **each element** by **double clicking** on it then selecting from the options available.

(c)   You could also select any item of **text** and alter the wording, size or font, or change the **colours** used.

(d)   In the following illustration, the user has double-clicked on the Y axis to enable them to **change the scale**.

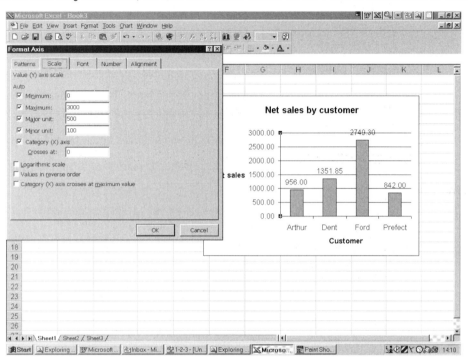

7 Spreadsheet format and appearance

Good presentation can help people understand the contents of a spreadsheet.

7.1 Titles and labels

A spreadsheet should be headed up with a title which **clearly defines its purpose**. Examples of titles are follows.

(a)   Income statement for the year ended 30 June 200X.

(b)   (i)   Area A: Sales forecast for the three months to 31 March 200X.
         (ii)   Area B: Sales forecast for the three months to 31 March 200X.
         (iii)   Combined sales forecast for the three months to 31 March 200X.

(c)   Salesmen: Analysis of earnings and commission for the six months ended 30 June 200X.

Row and **column** headings (or labels) should clearly identify the contents of the row/column. Any assumptions made that have influenced the spreadsheet contents should be clearly stated.

7.2 Formatting

There are a wide range of options available under the **Format** menu. Some of these functions may also be accessed through toolbar **buttons**. Formatting options include the ability to:

(a) Add **shading** or **borders** to cells.

(b) Use **different sizes of text** and different **fonts**.

(c) Choose from a range of options for presenting values, for example to present a number as a **percentage** (eg 0.05 as 5%), or with commas every third digit, or to a specified number of **decimal places** etc.

Experiment with the various formatting options yourself.

7.2.1 Formatting numbers

Most spreadsheet programs contain facilities for presenting numbers in a particular way. In Excel you simply click on **Format** and then **Cells ...**to reach these options.

(a) **Fixed format** displays the number in the cell rounded off to the number of decimal places you select.

(b) **Currency format** displays the number with a '$' in front, with commas and not more than two decimal places, eg $10,540.23.

(c) **Comma format** is the same as currency format except that the numbers are displayed without the '$'.

(d) **General format** is the format assumed unless another format is specified. In general format the number is displayed with no commas and with as many decimal places as entered or calculated that fit in the cell.

(e) **Percent format** multiplies the number in the display by 100 and follows it with a percentage sign. For example the number 0.548 in a cell would be displayed as 54.8%.

(f) **Hidden format** is a facility by which values can be entered into cells and used in calculations but are not actually displayed on the spreadsheet. The format is useful for hiding sensitive information.

7.3 Gridlines

One of the options available under the **Tools**, **Options** menu, on the **View** tab, is an option to remove the gridlines from your spreadsheet.

Compare the following two versions of the same spreadsheet. Note how the formatting applied to the second version has improved the spreadsheet presentation.

	A	B	C	D	E
1	Sales team salaries and commissions - 200X				
2	Name	Sales	Salary	Commis	Total earnings
3		$	$	$	$
4	Northington	284,000	14,000	5,680	19,680
5	Souther	193,000	14,000	3,860	17,860
6	Weston	12,000	14,000	240	14,240
7	Easterman	152,000	14,000	3,040	17,040
8					
9	Total	641,000	56,000	12,820	68,820
10					

	A	B	C	D	E
1	Sales team salaries and commissions - 200X				
2	*Name*	*Sales*	*Salary*	*Commission*	*Total earnings*
3		$	$	$	$
4	Northington	284,000	14,000	5,680	19,680
5	Souther	193,000	14,000	3,860	17,860
6	Weston	12,000	14,000	240	14,240
7	Easterman	152,000	14,000	3,040	17,040
8					
9	Total	641,000	56,000	12,820	68,820
10					

8 Other issues: printing; controls; using spreadsheets with word processing software

FAST FORWARD

Backing up is a key security measure. **Cell protection** and **passwords** can also be used to prevent unauthorised access.

8.1 Printing spreadsheets

The print options for your spreadsheet may be accessed by selecting **File** and then **Page Setup**. The various Tabs contain a range of options. You specify the area of the spreadsheet to be printed in the Print area box on the Sheet tab. Other options include the ability to repeat headings on all pages and the option to print gridlines if required (normally they wouldn't be!)

Experiment with these options including the options available under Header/Footer.

Page Setup [?] [X]

| Page | Margins | Header/Footer | Sheet |

Print area: A1:E10   Print...

Print titles   Print Preview

Rows to repeat at top:

Columns to repeat at left: Options...

Print

☑ Gridlines   ☑ Row and column headings

☐ Black and white   Comments: (None)

☐ Draft quality

Page order

⦿ Down, then over

○ Over, then down

OK   Cancel

8.2 Controls

There are facilities available in spreadsheet packages which can be used as controls – to prevent unauthorised or accidental amendment or deletion of all or part of a spreadsheet.

(a) **Saving** and **back-up**. When working on a spreadsheet, save your file regularly, as often as every ten minutes. This will prevent too much work being lost in the advent of a system crash. Spreadsheet files should be included in standard back-up procedures.

(b) **Cell protection**. This prevents the user from inadvertently changing or erasing cells that should not be changed. Look up how to protect cells using Excel's Help facility. (Select Help from the main menu within Excel, then select Contents and Index, click on the Find tab and enter the words 'cell protection'.)

(c) **Passwords.** You can set a password for any spreadsheet that you create. In Excel, simply click on **Tools,** then on **Protection,** then on **Protect Sheet** or **Protect Workbook**, as appropriate.

8.3 Using spreadsheets with word processing software

There may be a situation where you wish to incorporate the contents of all or part of a spreadsheet into a **word processed report**. There are a number of options available to achieve this.

(a) The simplest, but least professional option, is to **print out** the spreadsheet and interleave the page or pages at the appropriate point in your word processed document.

(b) A neater option if you are just including a small table is to select and **copy** the relevant cells from the spreadsheet to the computer's clipboard by selecting the cells and choosing Edit, Copy. Then switch to the word processing document, and **paste** them in at the appropriate point.

(c) Office packages, such as Microsoft Office allow you to easily use spreadsheets and word processing files together.

For example, a new, blank spreadsheet can be '**embedded**' in a document by selecting Insert, Object then, from within the Create New tab, selecting Microsoft Excel worksheet. The spreadsheet is then available to be worked upon, allowing the easy manipulation of numbers using all the facilities of the spreadsheet package. Clicking outside the spreadsheet will result in the spreadsheet being inserted in the document.

The contents of an existing spreadsheet may be inserted into a Word document by choosing Insert, Object and then activating the Create from File tab. Then click the Browse button and locate the spreadsheet file. Highlight the file, then click Insert, and then OK. You may then need to move and resize the object, by dragging its borders, to fit your document.

9 Three dimensional (multi-sheet) spreadsheets

`AST FORWARD` Spreadsheet packages permit the user to work with **multiple sheets** that refer to each other.

9.1 Background

In early spreadsheet packages, a spreadsheet file consisted of a single worksheet. Excel provides the option of multi-sheet spreadsheets, consisting of a series of related sheets. Excel files which contain more than one worksheet are often called **workbooks**.

For example, suppose you were producing a profit forecast for two regions, and a combined forecast for the total of the regions. This situation would be suited to using separate worksheets for each region and another for the total. This approach is sometimes referred to as working in **three dimensions**, as you are able to flip between different sheets stacked in front or behind each other. Cells in one sheet may **refer** to cells in another sheet. So, in our example, the formulae in the cells in the total sheet would refer to the cells in the other sheets.

Excel has a series of 'tabs', one for each worksheet at the foot of the spreadsheet.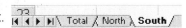

9.2 How many sheets?

Excel can be set up so that it always opens a fresh file with a certain number of worksheets ready and waiting for you. Click on **Tools ... Options** ... and then the **General** tab and set the number *Sheets in new workbook* option to the number you would like each new spreadsheet file to contain (sheets may be added or deleted later).

If you subsequently want to insert more sheets you just **right click** on the index tab after which you want the new sheet to be inserted and choose **Insert** ... and then **Worksheet**. By default sheets are called **Sheet 1, Sheet 2** etc. However, these may be changed. To **rename** a sheet in **Excel, right click** on its index tab and choose the rename option.

9.3 Pasting from one sheet to another

When building a spreadsheet that will contain a number of worksheets with identical structure, users often set up one sheet, then copy that sheet and amend the sheet contents. [To copy a worksheet in Excel, from within the worksheet you wish to copy, select Edit, Move or Copy sheet, and tick the Create a copy box.] A 'Total' sheet would use the same structure, but would contain formulae totalling the individual sheets.

9.4 Linking sheets with formulae

Formulae on one sheet may refer to data held on another sheet. The links within such a formula may be established using the following steps.

Step 1   In the cell that you want to refer to a cell from another sheet, type =.

Step 2   Click on the index tab for the sheet containing the cell you want to refer to and select the cell in question.

Step 3   Press Enter or Return.

9.5 Uses for multi-sheet spreadsheets

There are a wide range of situations suited to the multi-sheet approach. A variety of possible uses follow.

(a) A model could use one sheet for variables, a second for calculations, and a third for outputs.

(b) To enable quick and easy **consolidation** of similar sets of data, for example the financial results of two subsidiaries or the budgets of two departments.

(c) To provide **different views** of the same data. For instance you could have one sheet of data sorted in product code order and another sorted in product name order.

10 Macros

FAST FORWARD

A **macro** is an automated process that may be written by recording key-strokes and mouse clicks.

A macro is a sort of mini-program that automates keystrokes or actions. Macros are often used within spreadsheets. Macros may be written using a type of code – like a programming language. However, most spreadsheet users produce macros by asking the spreadsheet to record their actions – this automatically generates the macro 'code' required.

Macros can get **very complex** indeed – in fact you **can** build whole applications using them. (Doing so is a very good introduction to programming proper.)

We are **not** going to be demonstrating anything very elaborate, here. We are just going to show you how macros can be used to **eliminate a few key-strokes and mouse clicks** for tasks that you have to **perform frequently** enough to warrant writing a macro in the first place.

We are going to explain the basic principles of macros by reference to Microsoft **Excel.**

10.1 A simple macro

Suppose you decided that **every spreadsheet you created** should have your **first name and surname** in the bottom right corner of the footer in **Arial 8pt font**. You could write a macro and do all of this just by pressing two keys.

To write this macro you would proceed as follows. Follow this example through **hands-on** if possible.

Step 1 **Excel:** Open a fresh file. Click on the **Tools** menu and then on the option **Macro**

Step 2 This gives a sub-menu including the option **Record New Macro**. Select this.

Step 3 A dialogue box like the following will appear.

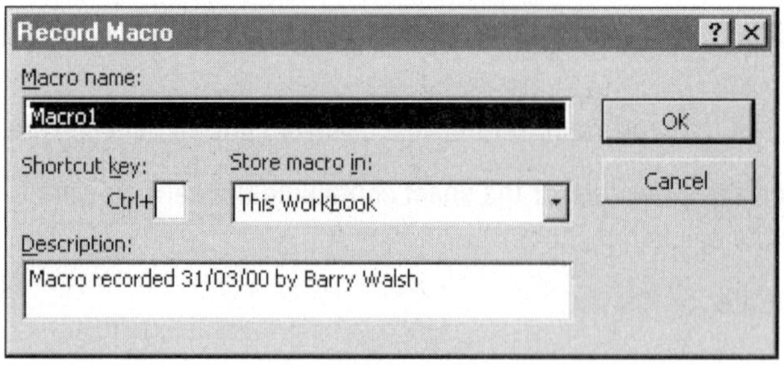

Step 4   Give the macro a name such as InsertName and press **Tab**. Excel will not allow spaces within macro names.

Step 5   Choose a shortcut key. This must be a **letter**, and it should be one that you don't frequently use for other purposes such as Ctrl + C or Ctrl + B. We will choose **Ctrl + m**

(Note that we use lower case **m;** if we had used **M** we would subsequently have to type Ctrl +**Shift** +m to start the macro).

Step 6   Accept the option to store the macro in **This Workbook** and **click on OK**

Step 7   Everything you do is now being **recorded**.

Step 8   From the menu select **View, Header and Footer.**

Step 9   Click on **Custom Footer** and click into the **Right section**.

Step 10   Type your name and highlight the text by clicking and dragging the cursor over it.

Step 11   Click on the **A** button to activate the font menu, and select Arial 8pt.

Step 12   Close the menus by clicking on **OK**. (Three **OK** boxes require clicking.)

Step 13   Click on the stop recording button.

Always start a macro by **returning the cursor to cell A1** (by pressing Ctrl + Home), even if it is already there. You may well not want to make your first entry in cell A1, but if you select your first real cell (B4 say) **before** you start recording, the macro will always begin at the currently active cell, whether it is B4 or Z256.

Always finish a macro by **selecting the cell** where the **next entry** is required.

That's all there is to it. Test your macro now by **selecting a fresh sheet** and then pressing Ctrl + m together. Then type 'Test' in cell A1 (as Excel will not Print Preview a blank sheet), and select **File, Print Preview.** You will see your name has been inserted into the footer.

Save your file with a suitable name and **close down** your spreadsheet package completely. Then open it up again and open a completely **new file**. Press Ctrl + m. Regrettably, nothing will happen. This does not mean that your macro is lost forever, just that it is not currently in the computer's memory (because you closed down the package).

However, if you **open up the file you just saved**, your macro will work again, because it is actually **stored** in that file. If you want your macro to be **available to you whenever** you want it you have the following choices.

(a)   Keep this file, with no contents other than your 'name' macro (and any others you may write) and always use it as the basis for any new spreadsheets you create, which will subsequently be saved with new file names.

(b)   You can add the macro to your **Personal Macro Workbook.** You do this at the point when you are naming your workbook and choosing a shortcut key, by changing the option in the **Store macro in:** box from This Workbook to Personal Macro Workbook. The macro will then be loaded into memory whenever you start up Excel and be available in any spreadsheet you create.

If you forget to assign a keyboard shortcut to a macro (or do not want to do so), you can still run your macros by clicking on Tools ...Macro ... Macros. This gives you a list of all the macros currently available. Select the one you want then click on Run.

Do not accept the default names offered by Excel of Macro1, Macro2 etc. You will soon forget what these macros do, unless you give them a meaningful name.

11 Advantages and disadvantages of spreadsheet software

11.1 Advantages of spreadsheets

- Excel is easy to learn and to use
- Spreadsheets make the calculation and manipulation of data easier and quicker
- They enable the analysis, reporting and sharing of financial information
- They enable 'what-if' analysis to be performed very quickly

11.2 Disadvantages of spreadsheets

- A spreadsheet is only as good as its original design, garbage in = garbage out!
- Formulae are hidden from sight so the underlying logic of a set of calculations may not be obvious
- A spreadsheet presentation may make reports appear infallible
- Research shows that a high proportion of large models contain critical errors
- A database may be more suitable to use with large volumes of data

Question   Spreadsheet advantages

An advantage of a spreadsheet program is that it

A   Can answer 'what if?' questions
B   Checks for incorrect entries
C   Automatically writes formulae
D   Can answer 'when is?' questions

Answer

The correct answer is A.

12 Uses of spreadsheet software

FAST FORWARD

Spreadsheets can be used in a variety of accounting contexts. You should practise using spreadsheets, **hands-on experience** is the key to spreadsheet proficiency.

Chartered management accountants will use spreadsheet software in activities such as budgeting, forecasting, reporting performance, variance analysis and discounted cashflow calculations.

12.1 Budgeting

Spreadsheet packages for budgeting have a number of advantages.

(a)   Spreadsheet packages have a facility to perform **'what if' calculations** at great speed. For example, the consequences throughout the organisation of sales growth per month of nil, $1/2$%, 1%, $1^1/2$% and so on can be calculated very quickly.

(b)   Preparing budgets may be complex; budgets may need to go through several drafts. If one or two figures are changed, the **computer will automatically make all the computational changes to the other figures**.

(c)   A spreadsheet model will **ensure that the preparation of the individual budgets is co-ordinated**. Data and information from the production budget, for example, will be automatically fed through to the material usage budget (as material usage will depend on production levels).

These advantages of spreadsheets make them ideal for taking over the **manipulation of numbers**, leaving staff to get involved in the real planning process.

12.2 Forecasting

The complicated calculations that we looked at in Chapters 10 and 11 are considerably easier to do using spreadsheets. For example, the '**insert function**' menu option can be used to calculate the intercept and slope of a regression line. Pre-programmed formulae are beyond the scope of your assessment but you may want to spend some time investigating this very useful part of Excel.

Question   **Forecasting**

George makes a product called the Omega for which quarterly sales forecasts are developed. Quarter 1 represents the three months ending 31 March; quarter 2, the three months ending 30 June; quarter 3, the three months ending 30 September; and quarter 4, the three months ending 31 December.

George uses the linear regression formula $y = a + bx$ to forecast Omega sales volumes in each quarter. In the formula, y represents the trend, a is a constant and b is the slope of the regression line. The regression formula is based on data for the last nine years and so the value of x for the fourth quarter of 20X4, the three months ending 31 December 20X4, is 36.

The values used for forecasting Omega sales volumes are:

$a = 10,000$
$b = 400$
x = the quarter number

The seasonal variation for the first quarter of 20X5, the three months ending 31 March 20X5, is +500 and the seasonal variation for the second quarter, the three months ending 30 June 20X5, is –1000.

Required

Enter the formulae for the trend and sales volume forecasts for the first two quarters of 20X5 in cells B7 to C8 in the spreadsheet template below.

	A	B	C
1	a	10,000	
2	b	400	
3	x at 31 December 20X4	36	
4	Period	3 months to 31 March 20X5	3 months to 30 June 20X5
5	Quarter	1	2
6	Seasonal variation	+500	−1,000
7	Trend = y		
8	Forecast		

Answer

	A	B	C
1	a	10,000	
2	b	400	
3	x at December 20X4	36	
4	Period	3 months to 31 March 20X5	3 months to 30 June 20X5
5	Quarter	1	2
6	Seasonal variation	+500	−1,000
7	Trend = y	=B1+B2*(B3+B5)	=B1+B2*(B3+C5)
8	Forecast	=B7+B6	=C7+C6

You are given the formula for the trend (the linear regression formula) and so you simply need to substitute the appropriate spreadsheet cell references for the *a, b* and *x* for the quarters in question. For example, the value of *a* is found in cell B1 whatever the quarter, and so *a* in the spreadsheet formula is B1. Likewise the value of *b* does not change with time. But the value of *x* does change and so you cannot simply use B3 but must amend the value in B3 to reflect the quarter you are dealing with. For example, the three months to 30 June 20X5 would have an *x* value of 38 and so you need to add 2 (the value in cell C5) to the value in B3 to get the appropriate value for *x*. The forecasts are simply your trend values (so the value in cell B7 or C7) adjusted by the seasonal variation (the value in cell B6 or C6).

12.3 Reporting performance

Reporting performance may involve **calculations** performed using spreadsheets and/or the **production of graphs and charts**, covered in Section 6 of this chapter. This information can then be **inserted into a word processed report** (see paragraph 8.3)

12.4 Variance analysis

Variances measure the difference between **actual results** and **expected results**. A wise manager will use variance analysis as a method of **controlling** the business. This will only work if reports are produced on a **timely** basis and spreadsheets will help with this process.

 Question   **Actual sales compared with budget sales**

	A	B	C	D	E
1	Sales team comparison of actual against budget sales				
2	Name	Sales (Budget)	Sales (Actual)	Difference	% of budget
3		$	$	$	$
4	Northington	275,000	284,000	9,000	3.27
5	Souther	200,000	193,000	(7,000)	(3.50)
6	Weston	10,000	12,000	2,000	20.00
7	Easterman	153,000	152,000	(1,000)	(0.65)
8					
9	Total	638,000	641,000	3,000	0.47
10					

Give a suitable formula for each of the following cells.

    (a)   Cell D4

    (b)   Cell E6

    (c)   Cell E9

Answer

(a)   =C4-B4.

(b)   =(D6/B6)*100.

(c)   =(D9/B9)*100. Note that in (c) you **cannot simply add up the individual percentage differences**, as the percentages are based on different quantities.

12.5 Discounted cashflow calculations

NPV and IRR (see Chapter 13) can be calculated using spreadsheet functions.

The NPV and IRR functions are best explained through a worked example. Suppose an organisation is considering undertaking a project, the financial details of which are shown below.

Project: new network system for administration department

Development and hardware purchase costs (all incurred now)		$150,000
Operating costs of new system (cash outflows per annum)	$55,000	
Annual savings from new system (cash inflow)	$115,000	
Annual net savings (net cash inflows)		$60,000
Expected system life	4 years	
Required return on investment	15% pa	

An **NPV calculation** for this project could be performed in Excel as follows.

	A	B	C	D
1	**NPV calculation**			
2			$	
3	Costs incurred now		(150,000)	
4	Benefits in year 1	60,000		
5	Benefits in year 2	60,000		
6	Benefits in year 3	60,000		
7	Benefits in year 4	60,000		
8	Discounted value		171,299	
9	**Net present value**		21,299	
10				
11	**Variables**			
12				
13	Discount rate	15%		
14				

The underlying formula are shown below, together with the 'function wizard' entries used (click on the *fx* symbol in the toolbar, or select Insert, Function, to start the function wizard – NPV and IRR are **Financial** functions).

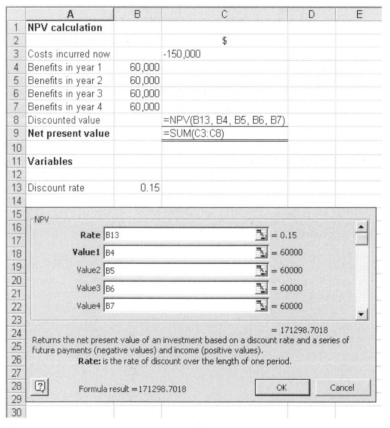

In this example, the present value of the expected **benefits** of the project **exceed** the present value of its **costs**, all discounted at 15% pa, and so the project is financially **justifiable** because it would be expected to earn a yield greater than the minimum target return of 15%. Payback of the development costs and hardware costs of $150,000 would occur after 2½ years.

An internal rate of return (**IRR**) calculation requires you to calculate the **rate of return** on a project or investment and then **compare** this rate of return with the **cost of capital**.

If a project earns a higher rate of return than the cost of capital, it will have a positive NPV and should therefore go ahead (from a financial point of view).

If the rate of return is lower than the cost of capital, the NPV will be negative - the project is not financially worthwhile.

If a project earns a return which is exactly equal to the cost of capital, the NPV will be 0, meaning the project will break-even financially.

In our example the IRR is 22%, easily exceeding the cost of capital of 15%. The IRR calculation may be set up using the function wizard (click on the *fx* symbol in the toolbar, or select **Insert**, **Function**, to start the function wizard – NPV and IRR are **Financial** functions).

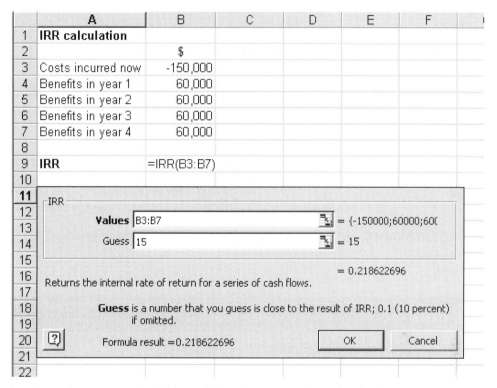

	A	B
1	**IRR calculation**	
2		$
3	Costs incurred now	(150,000)
4	Benefits in year 1	60,000
5	Benefits in year 2	60,000
6	Benefits in year 3	60,000
7	Benefits in year 4	60,000
8		
9	**IRR**	22%
10		

Chapter Roundup

- Use of spreadsheets is an essential part of the day-to-day work of the Chartered Management Accountant.

- A spreadsheet is an electronic piece of paper divided into **rows** and **columns**. The intersection of a row and a column is known as a **cell**.

- Formulas in Microsoft Excel follow a specific syntax.

- Essential basic skills include how to **move around** within a spreadsheet, how to **enter** and **edit** data, how to **fill** cells, how to **insert** and **delete** columns and rows and how to improve the basic **layout** and **appearance** of a spreadsheet.

- A wide range of **formulae** and functions are available within Excel.

- **If statements** are used in conditional formulae.

- Excel includes the facility to produce a range of charts and graphs. The **chart wizard** provides a tool to simplify the process of chart construction.

- Good presentation can help people understand the contents of a spreadsheet.

- **Backing up** is a key security measure. **Cell protection** and **passwords** can also be used to prevent unauthorised access.

- Spreadsheet packages permit the user to work with **multiple sheets** that refer to each other.

- A **macro** is an automated process that may be written by recording key-strokes and mouse clicks.

- Spreadsheets can be used in a variety of accounting contexts. You should practise using spreadsheets, **hands-on experience** is the key to spreadsheet proficiency.

Quick quiz

1   List three types of cell contents.

2   What do the F5 and F2 keys do in Excel?

3   What technique can you use to insert a logical series of data such as 1, 2 …. 10, or Jan, Feb, March etc?

4   How do you display formulae instead of the results of formulae in a spreadsheet?

5   Which function key may be used to change cell references within a selected formula from absolute to relative – and vice-versa?

6   List five possible changes that may improve the appearance of a spreadsheet.

7   List three possible uses for a multi-sheet (3D) spreadsheet.

8   You are about to key an exam mark into cell B4 of a spreadsheet. Write an IF statement, to be placed in cell C4, that will display PASS in C4 if the student mark is 50 or above - and or will display FAIL if the mark is below 50 (all student marks are whole numbers).

9   Give two ways of starting Excel's function wizard.

10   List five activities for which a Chartered Management Accountant could use spreadsheets.

Answers to quick quiz

1   Text, values or formulae.

2   F5 opens a GoTo dialogue box which is useful for navigating around large spreadsheets. F2 puts the active cell into edit mode.

3   You can use the technique of 'filling' - selecting the first few items of a series and dragging the lower right corner of the selection in the appropriate direction.

4   Select Tools, Options, ensure the View tab is active then tick the Formulas box within the window options area.

5   The F4 key.

6   Removing gridlines, adding shading, adding borders, using different fonts and font sizes, presenting numbers as percentages or currency or to a certain number of decimal places.

7   The construction of a spreadsheet model with separate Input, Calculation and Output sheets. They can help consolidate data from different sources. They can offer different views of the same data.

8   =IF(A4>49,"PASS","FAIL ")

9   You could click on the *fx* symbol in the toolbar, or use the menu item Insert, Function, to start the function wizard.

10 Budgeting, forecasting, reporting performance, variance analysis, discounted cashflow calculations

Now try the questions below from the Exam Question Bank

Question numbers	Pages
89-98	357-360

Appendix
Mathematical tables

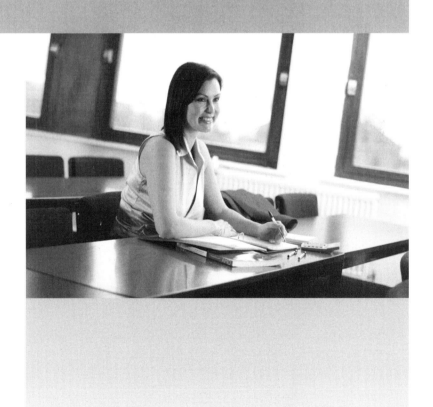

Logarithms

	0	1	2	3	4	5	6	7	8	9	1	2	3	4	5	6	7	8	9
10	0000	0043	0086	0128	0170	0212	0253	0294	0334	0374	4	9	13	17	21	26	30	34	38
											4	8	12	16	20	24	28	32	37
11	0414	0453	0492	0531	0569	0607	0645	0682	0719	0755	4	8	12	15	19	23	27	31	35
											4	7	11	15	19	22	26	30	33
12	0792	0828	0864	0899	0934	0969	1004	1038	1072	1106	3	7	11	14	18	21	25	28	32
											3	7	10	14	17	20	24	27	31
13	1139	1173	1206	1239	1271	1303	1335	1367	1399	1430	3	7	10	13	16	20	23	26	30
											3	7	10	12	16	19	22	25	29
14	1461	1492	1523	1553	1584	1614	1644	1673	1703	1732	3	6	9	12	15	18	21	24	28
											3	6	9	12	15	17	20	23	26
15	1761	1790	1818	1847	1875	1903	1931	1959	1987	2014	3	6	9	11	14	17	20	23	26
											3	5	8	11	14	16	19	22	25
16	2041	2068	2095	2122	2148	2175	2201	2227	2253	2279	3	5	8	11	14	16	19	22	24
											3	5	8	10	13	15	18	21	23
17	2304	2330	2355	2380	2405	2430	2455	2480	2504	2529	3	5	8	10	13	15	18	20	23
											2	5	7	10	12	15	17	19	22
18	2553	2577	2601	2625	2648	2672	2695	2718	2742	2765	2	5	7	9	12	14	16	19	21
											2	5	7	9	11	14	16	18	21
19	2788	2810	2833	2856	2878	2900	2923	2945	2967	2989	2	4	7	9	11	13	16	18	20
											2	4	6	8	11	13	15	17	19
20	3010	3032	3054	3075	3096	3118	3139	3160	3181	3201	2	4	6	8	11	13	15	17	19
21	3222	3243	3263	3284	3304	3324	3345	3365	3385	3404	2	4	6	8	10	12	14	16	18
22	3424	3444	3464	3483	3502	3522	3541	3560	3579	3598	2	4	6	8	10	12	14	15	17
23	3617	3636	3655	3674	3692	3711	3729	3747	3766	3784	2	4	6	7	9	11	13	15	17
24	3802	3820	3838	3856	3874	3892	3909	3927	3945	3962	2	4	5	7	9	11	12	14	16
25	3979	3997	4014	4031	4048	4065	4082	4099	4116	4133	2	3	5	7	9	10	12	14	15
26	4150	4166	4183	4200	4216	4232	4249	4265	4281	4298	2	3	5	7	8	10	11	13	15
27	4314	4330	4346	4362	4378	4393	4409	4425	4440	4456	2	3	5	6	8	9	11	13	14
28	4472	4487	4502	4518	4533	4548	4564	4579	4594	4609	2	3	5	6	8	9	11	12	14
29	4624	4639	4654	4669	4683	4698	4713	4728	4742	4757	1	3	4	6	7	9	10	12	13
30	4771	4786	4800	4814	4829	4843	4857	4871	4886	4900	1	3	4	6	7	9	10	11	13
31	4914	4928	4942	4955	4969	4983	4997	5011	5024	5038	1	3	4	6	7	8	10	11	12
32	5051	5065	5079	5092	5105	5119	5132	5145	5159	5172	1	3	4	5	7	8	9	11	12
33	5185	5198	5211	5224	5237	5250	5263	5276	5289	5302	1	3	4	5	6	8	9	10	12
34	5315	5328	5340	5353	5366	5378	5391	5403	5416	5428	1	3	4	5	6	8	9	10	11
35	5441	5453	5465	5478	5490	5502	5514	5527	5539	5551	1	2	4	5	6	7	9	10	11
36	5563	5575	5587	5599	5611	5623	5635	5647	5658	5670	1	2	4	5	6	7	8	10	11
37	5682	5694	5705	5717	5729	5740	5752	5763	5775	5786	1	2	3	5	6	7	8	9	10
38	5798	5809	5821	5832	5843	5855	5866	5877	5888	5899	1	2	3	5	6	7	8	9	10
39	5911	5922	5933	5944	5955	5966	5977	5988	5999	6010	1	2	3	4	5	7	8	9	10
40	6021	6031	6042	6053	6064	6075	6085	6096	6107	6117	1	2	3	4	5	6	8	9	10
41	6128	6138	6149	6160	6170	6180	6191	6201	6212	6222	1	2	3	4	5	6	7	8	9
42	6232	6243	6253	6263	6274	6284	6294	6304	6314	6325	1	2	3	4	5	6	7	8	9
43	6335	6345	6355	6365	6375	6385	6395	6405	6415	6425	1	2	3	4	5	6	7	8	9
44	6435	6444	6454	6464	6474	6484	6493	6503	6513	6522	1	2	3	4	5	6	7	8	9
45	6532	6542	6551	6561	6571	6580	6590	6599	6609	6618	1	2	3	4	5	6	7	8	9
46	6628	6637	6646	6656	6665	6675	6684	6693	6702	6712	1	2	3	4	5	6	7	7	8
47	6721	6730	6739	6749	6758	6767	6776	6785	6794	6803	1	2	3	4	5	5	6	7	8
48	6812	6821	6830	6839	6848	6857	6866	6875	6884	6893	1	2	3	4	4	5	6	7	8
49	6902	6911	6920	6928	6937	6946	6955	6964	6972	6981	1	2	3	4	4	5	6	7	8

Logarithms

	0	1	2	3	4	5	6	7	8	9	1	2	3	4	5	6	7	8	9
50	6990	6998	7007	7016	7024	7033	7042	7050	7059	7067	1	2	3	3	4	5	6	7	8
51	7076	7084	7093	7101	7110	7118	7126	7135	7143	7152	1	2	3	3	4	5	6	7	8
52	7160	7168	7177	7185	7193	7202	7210	7218	7226	7235	1	2	2	3	4	5	6	7	7
53	7243	7251	7259	7267	7275	7284	7292	7300	7308	7316	1	2	2	3	4	5	6	6	7
54	7324	7332	7340	7348	7356	7364	7372	7380	7388	7396	1	2	2	3	4	5	6	6	7
55	7404	7412	7419	7427	7435	7443	7451	7459	7466	7474	1	2	2	3	4	5	5	6	7
56	7482	7490	7497	7505	7513	7520	7528	7536	7543	7551	1	2	2	3	4	5	5	6	7
57	7559	7566	7574	7582	7589	7597	7604	7612	7619	7627	1	2	2	3	4	5	5	6	7
58	7634	7642	7649	7657	7664	7672	7679	7686	7694	7701	1	1	2	3	4	4	5	6	7
59	7709	7716	7723	7731	7738	7745	7752	7760	7767	7774	1	1	2	3	4	4	5	6	7
60	7782	7789	7796	7803	7810	7818	7825	7832	7839	7846	1	1	2	3	4	4	5	6	6
61	7853	7860	7868	7875	7882	7889	7896	7903	7910	7917	1	1	2	3	4	4	5	6	6
62	7924	7931	7938	7945	7952	7959	7966	7973	7980	7987	1	1	2	3	3	4	5	6	6
63	7993	8000	8007	8014	8021	8028	8035	8041	8048	8055	1	1	2	3	3	4	5	5	6
64	8062	8069	8075	8082	8089	8096	8102	8109	8116	8122	1	1	2	3	3	4	5	5	6
65	8129	8136	8142	8149	8156	8162	8169	8176	8182	8189	1	1	2	3	3	4	5	5	6
66	8195	8202	8209	8215	8222	8228	8235	8241	8248	8254	1	1	2	3	3	4	5	5	6
67	8261	8267	8274	8280	8287	8293	8299	8306	8312	8319	1	1	2	3	3	4	5	5	6
68	8325	8331	8338	8344	8351	8357	8363	8370	8376	8382	1	1	2	3	3	4	4	5	6
69	8388	8395	8401	8407	8414	8420	8426	8432	8439	8445	1	1	2	2	3	4	4	5	6
70	8451	8457	8463	8470	8476	8482	8488	8494	8500	8506	1	1	2	2	3	4	4	5	6
71	8513	8519	8525	8531	8537	8543	8549	8555	8561	8567	1	1	2	2	3	4	4	5	5
72	8573	8579	8585	8591	8597	8603	8609	8615	8621	8627	1	1	2	2	3	4	4	5	5
73	8633	8639	8645	8651	8657	8663	8669	8675	8681	8686	1	1	2	2	3	4	4	5	5
74	8692	8698	8704	8710	8716	8722	8727	8733	8739	8745	1	1	2	2	3	4	4	5	5
75	8751	8756	8762	8768	8774	8779	8785	8791	8797	8802	1	1	2	2	3	3	4	5	5
76	8808	8814	8820	8825	8831	8837	8842	8848	8854	8859	1	1	2	2	3	3	4	5	5
77	8865	8871	8876	8882	8887	8893	8899	8904	8910	8915	1	1	2	2	3	3	4	4	5
78	8921	8927	8932	8938	8943	8949	8954	8960	8965	8971	1	1	2	2	3	3	4	4	5
79	8976	8982	8987	8993	8998	9004	9009	9015	9020	9025	1	1	2	2	3	3	4	4	5
80	9031	9036	9042	9047	9053	9058	9063	9069	9074	9079	1	1	2	2	3	3	4	4	5
81	9085	9090	9096	9101	9106	9112	9117	9122	9128	9133	1	1	2	2	3	3	4	4	5
82	9138	9143	9149	9154	9159	9165	9170	9175	9180	9186	1	1	2	2	3	3	4	4	5
83	9191	9196	9201	9206	9212	9217	9222	9227	9232	9238	1	1	2	2	3	3	4	4	5
84	9243	9248	9253	9258	9263	9269	9274	9279	9284	9289	1	1	2	2	3	3	4	4	5
85	9294	9299	9304	9309	9315	9320	9325	9330	9335	9340	1	1	2	2	3	3	4	4	5
86	9345	9350	9355	9360	9365	9370	9375	9380	9385	9390	1	1	2	2	3	3	4	4	5
87	9395	9400	9405	9410	9415	9420	9425	9430	9435	9440	0	1	1	2	2	3	3	4	4
88	9445	9450	9455	9460	9465	9469	9474	9479	9484	9489	0	1	1	2	2	3	3	4	4
89	9494	9499	9504	9509	9513	9518	9523	9528	9533	9538	0	1	1	2	2	3	3	4	4
90	9542	9547	9552	9557	9562	9566	9571	9576	9581	9586	0	1	1	2	2	3	3	4	4
91	9590	9595	9600	9605	9609	9614	9619	9624	9628	9633	0	1	1	2	2	3	3	4	4
92	9638	9643	9647	9652	9657	9661	9666	9671	9675	9680	0	1	1	2	2	3	3	4	4
93	9685	9689	9694	9699	9703	9708	9713	9717	9722	9727	0	1	1	2	2	3	3	4	4
94	9731	9736	9741	9745	9750	9754	9759	9763	9768	9773	0	1	1	2	2	3	3	4	4
95	9777	9782	9786	9791	9795	9800	9805	9809	9814	9818	0	1	1	2	2	3	3	4	4
96	9823	9827	9832	9836	9841	9845	9850	9854	9859	9863	0	1	1	2	2	3	3	4	4
97	9868	9872	9877	9881	9886	9890	9894	9899	9903	9908	0	1	1	2	2	3	3	4	4
98	9912	9917	9921	9926	9930	9934	9939	9943	9948	9952	0	1	1	2	2	3	3	4	4
99	9956	9961	9965	9969	9974	9978	9983	9987	9991	9996	0	1	1	2	2	3	3	3	4

Tables

Area under the normal curve

This table gives the area under the normal curve between the mean and the point Z standard deviations above the mean. The corresponding area for deviations below the mean can be found by symmetry.

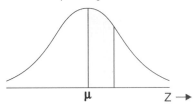

$Z = \dfrac{(x-\mu)}{\sigma}$	0.00	0.01	0.02	0.03	0.04	0.05	0.06	0.07	0.08	0.09
0.0	.0000	.0040	.0080	.0120	.0160	.0199	.0239	.0279	.0319	.0359
0.1	.0398	.0438	.0478	.0517	.0557	.0596	.0636	.0675	.0714	.0753
0.2	.0793	.0832	.0871	.0910	.0948	.0987	.1026	.1064	.1103	.1141
0.3	.1179	.1217	.1255	.1293	.1331	.1368	.1406	.1443	.1480	.1517
0.4	.1554	.1591	.1628	.1664	.1700	.1736	.1772	.1808	.1844	.1879
0.5	.1915	.1950	.1985	.2019	.2054	.2088	.2123	.2157	.2190	.2224
0.6	.2257	.2291	.2324	.2357	.2389	.2422	.2454	.2486	.2517	.2549
0.7	.2580	.2611	.2642	.2673	.2704	.2734	.2764	.2794	.2823	.2852
0.8	.2881	.2910	.2939	.2967	.2995	.3023	.3051	.3078	.3106	.3133
0.9	.3159	.3186	.3212	.3238	.3264	.3289	.3315	.3340	.3365	.3389
1.0	.3413	.3438	.3461	.3485	.3508	.3531	.3554	.3577	.3599	.3621
1.1	.3643	.3665	.3686	.3708	.3729	.3749	.3770	.3790	.3810	.3830
1.2	.3849	.3869	.3888	.3907	.3925	.3944	.3962	.3980	.3997	.4015
1.3	.4032	.4049	.4066	.4082	.4099	.4115	.4131	.4147	.4162	.4177
1.4	.4192	.4207	.4222	.4236	.4251	.4265	.4279	.4292	.4306	.4319
1.5	.4332	.4345	.4357	.4370	.4382	.4394	.4406	.4418	.4429	.4441
1.6	.4452	.4463	.4474	.4484	.4495	.4505	.4515	.4525	.4535	.4545
1.7	.4554	.4564	.4573	.4582	.4591	.4599	.4608	.4616	.4625	.4633
1.8	.4641	.4649	.4656	.4664	.4671	.4678	.4686	.4693	.4699	.4706
1.9	.4713	.4719	.4726	.4732	.4738	.4744	.4750	.4756	.4761	.4767
2.0	.4772	.4778	.4783	.4788	.4793	.4798	.4803	.4808	.4812	.4817
2.1	.4821	.4826	.4830	.4834	.4838	.4842	.4846	.4850	.4854	.4857
2.2	.4861	.4864	.4868	.4871	.4875	.4878	.4881	.4884	.4887	.4890
2.3	.4893	.4896	.4898	.4901	.4904	.4906	.4909	.4911	.4913	.4916
2.4	.4918	.4920	.4922	.4925	.4927	.4929	.4931	.4932	.4934	.4936
2.5	.4938	.4940	.4941	.4943	.4945	.4946	.4948	.4949	.4951	.4952
2.6	.4953	.4955	.4956	.4957	.4959	.4960	.4961	.4962	.4963	.4964
2.7	.4965	.4966	.4967	.4968	.4969	.4970	.4971	.4972	.4973	.4974
2.8	.4974	.4975	.4976	.4977	.4977	.4978	.4979	.4979	.4980	.4981
2.9	.4981	.4982	.4982	.4983	.4984	.4984	.4985	.4985	.4986	.4986
3.0	.49865	.4987	.4987	.4988	.4988	.4989	.4989	.4989	.4990	.4990
3.1	.49903	.4991	.4991	.4991	.4992	.4992	.4992	.4992	.4993	.4993
3.2	.49931	.4993	.4994	.4994	.4994	.4994	.4994	.4995	.4995	.4995
3.3	.49952	.4995	.4995	.4996	.4996	.4996	.4996	.4996	.4996	.4997
3.4	.49966	.4997	.4997	.4997	.4997	.4997	.4997	.4997	.4997	.4998
3.5	.49977									

Present value table

Present value of $1 ie $(1+r)-n$ where r = interest rate, n = number of periods until payment or receipt.

Periods	Interest rates (r)									
(n)	1%	2%	3%	4%	5%	6%	7%	8%	9%	10%
1	0.990	0.980	0.971	0.962	0.952	0.943	0.935	0.926	0.917	0.909
2	0.980	0.961	0.943	0.925	0.907	0.890	0.873	0.857	0.842	0.826
3	0.971	0.942	0.915	0.889	0.864	0.840	0.816	0.794	0.772	0.751
4	0.961	0.924	0.888	0.855	0.823	0.792	0.763	0.735	0.708	0.683
5	0.951	0.906	0.863	0.822	0.784	0.747	0.713	0.681	0.650	0.621
6	0.942	0.888	0.837	0.790	0.746	0.705	0.666	0.630	0.596	0.564
7	0.933	0.871	0.813	0.760	0.711	0.665	0.623	0.583	0.547	0.513
8	0.923	0.853	0.789	0.731	0.677	0.627	0.582	0.540	0.502	0.467
9	0.914	0.837	0.766	0.703	0.645	0.592	0.544	0.500	0.460	0.424
10	0.905	0.820	0.744	0.676	0.614	0.558	0.508	0.463	0.422	0.386
11	0.896	0.804	0.722	0.650	0.585	0.527	0.475	0.429	0.388	0.350
12	0.887	0.788	0.701	0.625	0.557	0.497	0.444	0.397	0.356	0.319
13	0.879	0.773	0.681	0.601	0.530	0.469	0.415	0.368	0.326	0.290
14	0.870	0.758	0.661	0.577	0.505	0.442	0.388	0.340	0.299	0.263
15	0.861	0.743	0.642	0.555	0.481	0.417	0.362	0.315	0.275	0.239
16	0.853	0.728	0.623	0.534	0.458	0.394	0.339	0.292	0.252	0.218
17	0.844	0.714	0.605	0.513	0.436	0.371	0.317	0.270	0.231	0.198
18	0.836	0.700	0.587	0.494	0.416	0.350	0.296	0.250	0.212	0.180
19	0.828	0.686	0.570	0.475	0.396	0.331	0.277	0.232	0.194	0.164
20	0.820	0.673	0.554	0.456	0.377	0.312	0.258	0.215	0.178	0.149

Periods	Interest rates (r)									
(n)	11%	12%	13%	14%	15%	16%	17%	18%	19%	20%
1	0.901	0.893	0.885	0.877	0.870	0.862	0.855	0.847	0.840	0.833
2	0.812	0.797	0.783	0.769	0.756	0.743	0.731	0.718	0.706	0.694
3	0.731	0.712	0.693	0.675	0.658	0.641	0.624	0.609	0.593	0.579
4	0.659	0.636	0.613	0.592	0.572	0.552	0.534	0.516	0.499	0.482
5	0.593	0.567	0.543	0.519	0.497	0.476	0.456	0.437	0.419	0.402
6	0.535	0.507	0.480	0.456	0.432	0.410	0.390	0.370	0.352	0.335
7	0.482	0.452	0.425	0.400	0.376	0.354	0.333	0.314	0.296	0.279
8	0.434	0.404	0.376	0.351	0.327	0.305	0.285	0.266	0.249	0.233
9	0.391	0.361	0.333	0.308	0.284	0.263	0.243	0.225	0.209	0.194
10	0.352	0.322	0.295	0.270	0.247	0.227	0.208	0.191	0.176	0.162
11	0.317	0.287	0.261	0.237	0.215	0.195	0.178	0.162	0.148	0.135
12	0.286	0.257	0.231	0.208	0.187	0.168	0.152	0.137	0.124	0.112
13	0.258	0.229	0.204	0.182	0.163	0.145	0.130	0.116	0.104	0.093
14	0.232	0.205	0.181	0.160	0.141	0.125	0.111	0.099	0.088	0.078
15	0.209	0.183	0.160	0.140	0.123	0.108	0.095	0.084	0.074	0.065
16	0.188	0.163	0.141	0.123	0.107	0.093	0.081	0.071	0.062	0.054
17	0.170	0.146	0.125	0.108	0.093	0.080	0.069	0.060	0.052	0.045
18	0.153	0.130	0.111	0.095	0.081	0.069	0.059	0.051	0.044	0.038
19	0.138	0.116	0.098	0.083	0.070	0.060	0.051	0.043	0.037	0.031
20	0.124	0.104	0.087	0.073	0.061	0.051	0.043	0.037	0.031	0.026

Cumulative present value table

This table shows the present value of $1 per annum, receivable or payable at the end of each year for n years

$$\frac{1-(1+r)^{-n}}{r}.$$

Periods					Interest rates (r)					
(n)	1%	2%	3%	4%	5%	6%	7%	8%	9%	10%
1	0.990	0.980	0.971	0.962	0.952	0.943	0.935	0.926	0.917	0.909
2	1.970	1.942	1.913	1.886	1.859	1.833	1.808	1.783	1.759	1.736
3	2.941	2.884	2.829	2.775	2.723	2.673	2.624	2.577	2.531	2.487
4	3.902	3.808	3.717	3.630	3.546	3.465	3.387	3.312	3.240	3.170
5	4.853	4.713	4.580	4.452	4.329	4.212	4.100	3.993	3.890	3.791
6	5.795	5.601	5.417	5.242	5.076	4.917	4.767	4.623	4.486	4.355
7	6.728	6.472	6.230	6.002	5.786	5.582	5.389	5.206	5.033	4.868
8	7.652	7.325	7.020	6.733	6.463	6.210	5.971	5.747	5.535	5.335
9	8.566	8.162	7.786	7.435	7.108	6.802	6.515	6.247	5.995	5.759
10	9.471	8.983	8.530	8.111	7.722	7.360	7.024	6.710	6.418	6.145
11	10.368	9.787	9.253	8.760	8.306	7.887	7.499	7.139	6.805	6.495
12	11.255	10.575	9.954	9.385	8.863	8.384	7.943	7.536	7.161	6.814
13	12.134	11.348	10.635	9.986	9.394	8.853	8.358	7.904	7.487	7.103
14	13.004	12.106	11.296	10.563	9.899	9.295	8.745	8.244	7.786	7.367
15	13.865	12.849	11.938	11.118	10.380	9.712	9.108	8.559	8.061	7.606
16	14.718	13.578	12.561	11.652	10.838	10.106	9.447	8.851	8.313	7.824
17	15.562	14.292	13.166	12.166	11.274	10.477	9.763	9.122	8.544	8.022
18	16.398	14.992	13.754	12.659	11.690	10.828	10.059	9.372	8.756	8.201
19	17.226	15.679	14.324	13.134	12.085	11.158	10.336	9.604	8.950	8.365
20	18.046	16.351	14.878	13.590	12.462	11.470	10.594	9.818	9.129	8.514

Periods					Interest rates (r)					
(n)	11%	12%	13%	14%	15%	16%	17%	18%	19%	20%
1	0.901	0.893	0.885	0.877	0.870	0.862	0.855	0.847	0.840	0.833
2	1.713	1.690	1.668	1.647	1.626	1.605	1.585	1.566	1.547	1.528
3	2.444	2.402	2.361	2.322	2.283	2.246	2.210	2.174	2.140	2.106
4	3.102	3.037	2.974	2.914	2.855	2.798	2.743	2.690	2.639	2.589
5	3.696	3.605	3.517	3.433	3.352	3.274	3.199	3.127	3.058	2.991
6	4.231	4.111	3.998	3.889	3.784	3.685	3.589	3.498	3.410	3.326
7	4.712	4.564	4.423	4.288	4.160	4.039	3.922	3.812	3.706	3.605
8	5.146	4.968	4.799	4.639	4.487	4.344	4.207	4.078	3.954	3.837
9	5.537	5.328	5.132	4.946	4.772	4.607	4.451	4.303	4.163	4.031
10	5.889	5.650	5.426	5.216	5.019	4.833	4.659	4.494	4.339	4.192
11	6.207	5.938	5.687	5.453	5.234	5.029	4.836	4.656	4.486	4.327
12	6.492	6.194	5.918	5.660	5.421	5.197	4.988	4.793	4.611	4.439
13	6.750	6.424	6.122	5.842	5.583	5.342	5.118	4.910	4.715	4.533
14	6.982	6.628	6.302	6.002	5.724	5.468	5.229	5.008	4.802	4.611
15	7.191	6.811	6.462	6.142	5.847	5.575	5.324	5.092	4.876	4.675
16	7.379	6.974	6.604	6.265	5.954	5.668	5.405	5.162	4.938	4.730
17	7.549	7.120	6.729	6.373	6.047	5.749	5.475	5.222	4.990	4.775
18	7.702	7.250	6.840	6.467	6.128	5.818	5.534	5.273	5.033	4.812
19	7.839	7.366	6.938	6.550	6.198	5.877	5.584	5.316	5.070	4.843
20	7.963	7.469	7.025	6.623	6.259	5.929	5.628	5.353	5.101	4.870

Probability

A∪B = A **or** B. A∩B = A **and** B (overlap). P(B/A) = probability of B, **given** A.

Rules of addition

If A and B are *mutually exclusive*: $P(A∪B) = P(A) + P(B)$
If A and B are **not** mutually exclusive: $P(A∪B) = P(A) + P(B) - P(A∩B)$

Rules of multiplication

If A and B are *independent*: $P(A∩B) = P(A) * P(B)$
If A and B are **not** independent: $P(A∩B) = P(A) * P(B/A)$

E(X) = expected value = probability * payoff

Quadratic equations

If $aX^2 + bX + c = 0$ is the general quadratic equation, then the two solutions (roots) are given by

$$X = \frac{-b \pm \sqrt{b^2 - 4ac}}{2a}$$

Descriptive statistics

Arithmetic mean

$$\bar{x} = \frac{\sum x}{n} \text{ or } \bar{x} = \frac{\sum fx}{\sum f}$$

Standard deviation

$$\sqrt{\frac{\sum (x - \bar{x})^2}{n}}$$

$$SD = \sqrt{\frac{\sum fx^2}{\sum f} - \bar{x}^2} \text{ (frequencydistribution)}$$

Index numbers

Price relative = 100 * P_1 / P_0

Quantity relative = 100 * Q_1 / Q_0

Price: $\dfrac{\sum W \times P_1 / P_0}{\sum W} \times 100$ where W denotes weights

Quantity: $\dfrac{\sum W \times Q_1 / Q_0}{\sum W} \times 100$ where W denotes weights

Time series

Additive model: Series = Trend + Seasonal + Random

Multiplicative model: Series = Trend * Seasonal * Random

Linear regression and correlation

The linear regression equation of Y on X is given by:

Y $= a + bX$ *or*

$Y - \overline{Y} = b(X - \overline{X})$, where

b $= \dfrac{\text{Covariance}(XY)}{\text{Variance}(X)} = \dfrac{n \sum XY - (\sum X)(\sum Y)}{n \sum X^2 - (\sum X)^2}$

and a = $\overline{Y} - b\overline{X}$,

or solve $\sum Y = na + b \sum X$

$\sum XY = a \sum X + b \sum X^2$

Coefficient of correlation (r)

r $= \dfrac{\text{Covariance}(XY)}{\sqrt{VAR(X).VAR(Y)}}$

$= \dfrac{n \sum XY - (\sum X)(\sum Y)}{\sqrt{[n \sum X^2 - (\sum X)^2][n \sum Y^2 - (\sum Y)^2]}}$

R(rank) = $1 - \left[\dfrac{6 \sum d^2}{n(n^2 - 1)} \right]$

Financial mathematics

Compound Interest (Values and Sums)

Future Value of S_1 of a sum X, invested for n periods, compounded at r% interest:

$$S = X[1+r]^n$$

Annuity

Present value of an annuity of $1 per annum receivable or payable, for n years, commencing in one year, discounted at r% per annum:

$$PV = \frac{1}{r}\left[1 - \frac{1}{[1+r]^n}\right]$$

Perpetuity

Present value of $1 per annum, payable or receivable in perpetuity, commencing in one year discounted at r% per annum

$$PV = \frac{1}{r}$$

Question bank

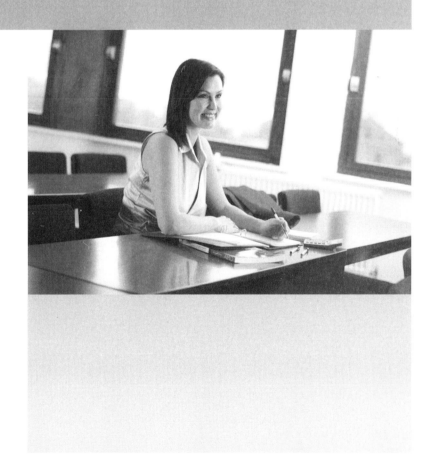

1   The expression $\dfrac{(x^2)^3}{x^6}$ equals

   A   0
   B   1
   C   x
   D x^2

2   The term $\dfrac{1}{x}$ can also be written as

   A $-x$

   B x^{-1}

   C x^2

   D $x-1$

3   Lynn and Laura share out a certain sum of money in the ratio 4 : 5, and Laura ends up with $6.

   (a)   How much was shared out in the first place?

   (b)   How much would have been shared out if Laura had got $6 and the ratio had been 5 : 4 instead of 4 : 5?

4   What is 23% of $5,000?

5   What is $18 as a percentage of $45?

6   Deirdre Fowler now earns $25,000 per annum after an annual increase of 2.5%. What was her annual salary to the nearest $ before the increase?

7   If purchases at Watkins Ltd are $200,000 in 20X0 and there was a percentage decrease of 5% in 20X1, what are purchases in 20X1?

8   An accountant charges $X per hour to which sales tax of 17.5% is added. If her final hourly charge is $235, what is the value of X?

9   In the formula $Q = \sqrt{\dfrac{2C_oD}{C_h}}$, if $C_o = \$40$, $D = 48,000$ and $Q = 200$, then C_h is closest in value to

   A $3.43
   B $11.77
   C $96.00
   D $138.56

10   If demand $D = 30 - 3P$, how is price (P) expressed in terms of D?

   A $P = 10 - D$
   B $P = D/27$
   C $P = 10 + D/3$
   D $P = 10 - D/3$

11 If $x^3 = 4.913$, then x =

12 If $34x - 7.6 = (17x - 3.8) \times (x + 12.5)$, then x =

13 If $y = aX^b$ and a = 9 minutes, X = 7 and b = −0.24. What is the value of Y to two decimal places?

14 Solve the inequality $3(X + 4) < 2X + 1$

15 Solve the following simultaneous equations.

$x - y = -9$

$9x - 13y = -97$

X =   y =

16 The sum of the squares of two positive numbers (x and y) is 890, and the difference between the two numbers is 4. Find a quadratic equation in terms of either x or y.

17 A rectangle has a perimeter of 44 metres and an area of 112 square metres. Find a quadratic equation in terms of either length 'a' or breadth 'b'.

18 Solve the following quadratic equation.

$-3x^2 + 6x + 24 = 0$

X =   or

19 A survey is being carried out to find out the number of goals scored by the ten most popular football clubs in Britain in their past ten matches to see if there is much variation between the teams. What sort of data is being collected in such a survey?

A   Quantitative   Continuous
B   Quantitative   Discrete
C   Qualitative   Continuous
D   Qualitative   Discrete

20   A distributor has recorded the following demand for a stock item over the last 200 days.

Daily demand	Number of days
Units	
50	27
51	35
52	38
53	42
54	57

If these data are representative of the normal pattern of sales, what is the probability of a daily demand of 53 units?

A   17.5%
B   19.5%
C   21.0%
D   28.5%

21   Next year, sales may rise, fall or remain the same as this year, with the following respective probabilities: 0.61, 0.17 and 0.22.

The probability of sales remaining the same or rising is

A   0.13
B   0.17
C   0.70
D   0.83

22   A salesman has three small areas to cover, areas x, y and z. He never sells more than one item per day and the probabilities of making a sale when he visits each area are as follows.

Area	Probability
x	0.40
y	0.35
z	0.25

He visits only one area each day. He visits area x twice as often as he visits areas y and z.

Calculate the EV of probability of a sale in each of the areas x, y and z and the probabilities of visiting each of the areas.

Probability of visiting area x =

Probability of visiting area y =

Probability of visiting area z =

EV of probability of a sale in area x =

EV of probability of a sale in area y =

EV of probability of a sale in area z =

Select your answers from the list below.

0.0625

0.0825

0.20

0.25

0.25

0.50

23 Calculate the following probabilities, giving all answers correct to 3 significant figures.

(a) Drawing two aces from a pack of 52 playing cards in two successive draws (with and without replacement).

With replacement ☐

Without replacement ☐

(b) Drawing the ace of hearts and the ace of spades in that order (assuming replacement).

☐

(c) It is assumed that home, car and television ownership are independent. Selecting from a list of respondents to a questionnaire used in a sample survey it was found that 50% owned their own homes, 60% owned a car and 90% had a television set. The probability that a respondent who owned:

(i) his home and a car = ☐

(ii) all three of the above assets = ☐

(iii) none of the above assets = ☐

(d) Suppose that 50% of respondents owned their own homes and 60% owned a car. In addition, it was found that the percentage of home owners who owned a car was 80%.

(i) Find the percentage of car owners amongst those respondents who do not own their own home.

☐

(ii) If a car owner is selected at random, find the probability that he/she is also a home owner.

☐

24 A business is deciding whether to buy a new machine. The machine may contribute extra profits of $15,000 or $19,000 or a loss of $1,000, with associated probabilities of 0.2, 0.6 and 0.1 respectively.

What is the expected profit?

A $35,000

B $14,500

C $19,000

D $11,667

25   What is illustrated in this diagram?

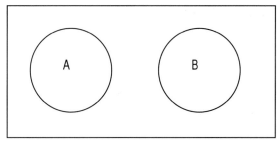

A   A pie chart
B   A Venn diagram illustrating two mutually exclusive outcomes
C   An ogive
D   A Venn diagram illustrating complementary outcomes

26   Which of the following rules of probability is used when we wish to determine the probability of one event or another occurring and the two events are not mutually exclusive?

A $P(A) + P(B)$
B $P(A) \times P(B)$
C $P(A)/P(B)$
D $P(A) + P(B) - P(A \text{ and } B)$

27   Which of the following is/are limitations of using expected values when evaluating decisions?

I   Expected values do not consider attitudes to risk
II   All the profits and probabilities need to be estimated
III   The time value of money may not be taken into account
IV   They do not allow for changes in circumstances

A   I and IV
B   II and IV
C   I, II and III
D   II, III and IV

28   A quality inspector examines 25, 50 and 75 items from three production lines, red, yellow and green respectively. Records of previous inspections show that the rate of faulty items on each production line is

Red	Yellow	Green
4%	12%	20%

Complete the following table by filling in the values represented by letters.

	Red	Yellow	Green	Total
Good				C
Faulty	A	B		
Total	25	50	75	150

A = [   ]

B = [   ]

C = [   ]

29　In a histogram, one class is two thirds the width of the other classes.

　　If the score in that class is 20, the correct height to plot on the histogram is

　　A　13.33
　　B　21.00
　　C　30.00
　　D　33.33

30　A histogram uses a set of bars to represent a grouped frequency table. To be correctly presented, the histogram must show the relationship of the rectangles to the frequencies by reference to the

　　A　Diagonal of each bar
　　B　Area of each bar
　　C　Width of each bar
　　D　Height of each bar

31　The graph below is an ogive showing the value of invoices selected in a sample.

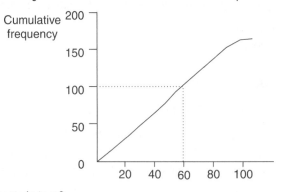

　　Which of the following statements is true?

　　A　There are 100 sales with values of $60

　　B　There are more than 100 sales with values of $60 or more

　　C　There are 100 sales with values of less than $60

　　D　There are more than 100 sales with values of $60 or more and there are 100 sales with values of less than $60

The following data relate to questions 32-34

The distribution of average weekly wages paid to direct labour employees at the factory of Parrots Ltd is as follows.

Weekly average wage $	Number of employees	Frequency density	Cumulative frequency
51 and < 61	13	A	
61 and < 66	12	B	
66 and < 71	16	C	
71 and < 76	21		E
76 and < 81	25		F
81 and < 86	20		
86 and < 91	14		
91 and < 101	9	D	G

32   Using a standard interval size of $5, calculate the frequency densities corresponding to the letters A, B, C and D.

A = [   ]

B = [   ]

C = [   ]

D = [   ]

33   Illustrate the data given above by means of a histogram.

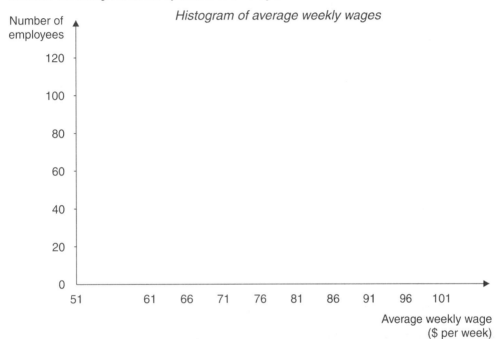

Histogram of average weekly wages

34   Calculate cumulative frequencies corresponding to the letters E, F and G as shown in the table above.

E = [   ]

F = [   ]

G = [   ]

35   Illustrate the data given above by means of an ogive.

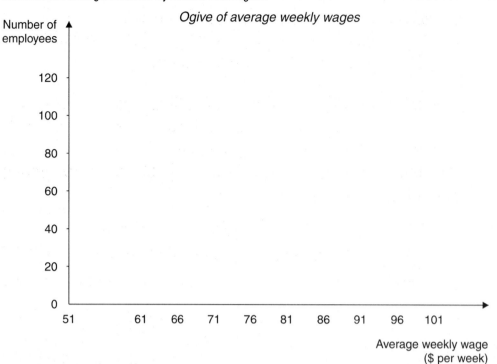

36   Over a period, a firm made purchases of $800, $1,000, $1,100 and $1,200 on items, the unit cost of which were $5.00, $6.25, $5.50 and $6.00 respectively.

To the nearest penny, the mean price paid per item was

A $5.69
B $5.70
C $5.71
D $5.72

37   The following scores are observed for the times taken to complete a task, in minutes.

24, 68, 28, 30, 42, 48, 18, 34, 22, 16

The median score is

A   26
B   28
C   29
D   32

38   The arithmetic mean of nineteen numbers is 10. When a twentieth number, x, is added the overall mean becomes 11. What is the value of x?

A   15
B   20
C   25
D   30

39   The sales of colour televisions on each of 40 days was as follows.

Daily sales	Frequency f	Midpoint x	fx
$> 0 \leq 3$	8		
$> 3 \leq 6$	16		
$> 6 \leq 9$	12		
$> 9 \leq 12$	4		
	40		

Fill in the gaps in the table above.

The variables in the table are discrete/continuous.

The arithmetic mean of the data = ...

40   Journey times to work of employees of a company were as follows.

Time Minutes	No of employees
less than 10	14
10 but " " 20	26
20 " " " 30	64
30 " " " 40	46
40 " " " 50	28
50 " " " 60	16
60 " " " 80	8
80 " " " 100	4

Required:

Calculate the mean journey time, giving your answer correct to two correct decimal places.

        [   ] minutes

41   Given that $\Sigma\ fx = 23$, $\Sigma\ fx = 79$ and $\Sigma\ fx^2 = 1{,}161$, calculate the standard deviation (to two decimal places)

        [   ]

42   A statistician wishes to compare the dispersion of four frequency distributions. Data for the distributions are as follows:

Distribution	Mean	Standard deviation
1	$140	$33
2	$25,104	$6,290
3	77 kg	27 kg
4	154 miles	32 miles

The relative dispersion of the distributions is to be measured using the coefficient of variation. Which frequency distribution has the largest coefficient of variation?

A   Distribution 1
B   Distribution 2
C   Distribution 3
D   Distribution 4

43   What is the variance of the five numbers, 4, 6, 8, 12, 15?

A   8.9
B   9.0
C   16
D   80

44   The weights of elephants are normally distributed. The mean weight is 5,200 kg and the probability of an elephant weighing over 6,000 kg is 0.0314. What is the standard deviation of the weights of elephants?

A   186 kg
B   215 kg
C   372 kg
D   430 kg

45   A normal distribution has a mean of 60 and a standard deviation of 3.8.

The probability of a score of 56 or less is

A   85%
B   50%
C   35%
D   15%

46   In a normal distribution with a standard deviation of 90, 28.23% of the population lies between the mean and 900. The mean is

A   860
B   850
C   840
D   830

47   A normal distribution has a mean of 200 and a variance of 1,600.

Approximately 20% of the population is above which of the following values?

A   234
B   240
C   251
D   278

48   Consider the following normal distribution.

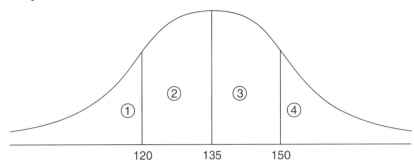

120   135   150

Which area represents the probability that:

(a) $x < 120$
(b)   x is between 120 and 150
(c) $x > 150$
(d) $x > 120$

49   A company produces batteries whose lifetimes are normally distributed with a mean of 100 hours. It is known that 96% of the batteries last at least 40 hours. Throughout this question all answers should be given correct to one decimal place.

(a)   If P(z > a) = 0.96, use normal distribution tables to find the value of 'a'.

       a = [   ]

(b)   Estimate the standard deviation lifetime.

       [   ]

(c)   Calculate the percentage of batteries that will last less than 57 hours.

       [   ]

(d)   The company is liable to replace any battery which lasts for less than 40 hours. The company wishes to reduce the percentage of defective batteries from the current level of 4% to 2%.

       (i)   Use normal tables to find the value 'b' such that P(z < b) = 2%.

               [   ]

       (ii)   The company can use a chemical procedure which changes the values of the mean and standard deviation. If the standard deviation is set at 35 hours, find the mean lifetime which will reduce the percentage of defectives to 2%.

               [   ]

50   An index of machine prices has year 1 as the base year, with an index number of 100. By the end of year 9 the index had risen to 180 and by the end of year 14 it had risen by another 18 points.

What was the percentage increase in machine prices between years 9 and 14?

A   2%

B   9%

C   10%

D   18%

51   The mean weekly take-home pay of the employees of Staples and a price index for the 11 years from 20X0 to 20Y0 are as follows.

Year	Weekly wage $	Price index (20X0 = 100)
20X0	150	100
20X1	161	103
20X2	168	106
20X3	179	108
20X4	185	109
20X5	191	112
20X6	197	114
20X7	203	116
20X8	207	118
20X9	213	121
20Y0	231	123

Complete the following table in order to construct a time series of real wages for 20X0 to 20Y0 using a price index with 20X6 as the base year.

Year	Index	Real wage $
20X0		
20X1		
20X2		
20X3		
20X4		
20X5		
20X6		
20X7		
20X8		
20X9		
20Y0		

52   Stuart Ltd wishes to construct a price index for three commodities, A, B and C.

	20X0 Quantities	Prices relative to 20X0 (%) 20X1	Prices relative to 20X0 (%) 20X2
A	5,000	100	110
B	6,000	108	115
C	3,000	90	100

Required:

(a)   Calculate the weighted average of price relative index for 20X1 with base 20X0 using 20X0 quantities as weights. Give your answer to one decimal place.

[   ]

(b)   Calculate the weighted average of price relative index for 20X2 with base 20X0 using 20X0 quantities as weights. Give your answer to one decimal place.

[   ]

53   The correlation between x and y is 0.95. This means that:

A   There is a weak relationship between x and y
B   There is a strong relationship between x and y
C   y is 95% of x
D   x is 95% of y

54   The following scatter diagrams can be associated with which correlation coefficients?

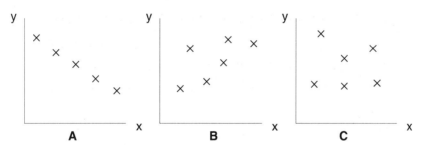

I   0
II   − 1
III   + 0.8

A = [   ]

B = [   ]

C = [   ]

55   What is the Pearsonian correlation coefficient, r, for the following data?

X	Y
1	6
2	5
3	3
4	8

A   − 0.25
B   − 0.06
C   + 0.06
D   + 0.25

56   If $n = 4$
$\sum X = 10$
$\sum Y = 22$
$\sum X^2 = 30$
$\sum XY = 57$
$\sum Y^2 = 134$

The Pearson correlation coefficient is

A   −0.25
B   −0.06
C   +0.06
D   +0.25

57   Seven novels were reviewed by two different book critics, and the novels were ranked as follows.

	Critic 1 Rank	Critic 2 Rank
Captain Corelli's guitar	2	1
Debbie Jones's diary	1	3
The songs of a bird	4	7
Cold love in a warm climate	6	5
Raging wars and peacefulness	5	6
Charlotte Black	3	2
The name of the tulip	7	4

The rank correlation coefficient is

A   −0.464
B   −0.536
C   +0.464
D   +0.536

58   In calculating the regression equation linking two variables, the standard formulae for the regression coefficients are given in terms of X and Y. Which of the following is not true?

      I   X must be the variable which will be forecast

      II   It does not matter which variable is which

      III   Y must be the dependent variable

      IV   Y must be the variable shown on the vertical axis of a scattergram

      A   I and II

      B   I, II and III

      C   I, II and IV

      D   I, III and IV

59   If ΣX = 21

         ΣY = 184

         ΣX^2 = 91

         ΣXY = 587

         n   = 7

    Which of the following values for a and b are correct in the formula Y = a + bx?

	a	b
A	−22.5	−1.25
B	−22.5	+1.25
C	+22.5	−1.25
D	+22.5	+1.25

60   The regression equation Y = 5 + 4X has been calculated from 6 pairs of values, with X ranging from 1 to 10. The correlation coefficient is 0.9. It is estimated that Y = 85 when X = 20. Which of the following are true?

      I   The estimate is not reliable because the sample is small

      II   The estimate is reliable

      III   The estimate is not reliable because the correlation is low

      IV   The estimate is not reliable because X is outside the range of the data

      A   I and II only

      B   I and III only

      C   I and IV only

      D   II and IV only

61   When the value of one variable is related to the value of another, they are said to be correlated. Correlation therefore means an inter-relationship or correspondence.

    If the following points were plotted on a graph, what sort of correlation would they display? (Tick as appropriate)

(a)	(2, 3)		Perfect positive correlation
	(3, 4.5)	?	Perfect negative correlation
	(4, 6)		Uncorrelated
(b)	(2, 3)		Perfect positive correlation
	(3, 1.5)	?	Perfect negative correlation
	(4, 0)		Uncorrelated
(c)	(2, 3)		Perfect positive correlation
	(4, 0)	?	Perfect negative correlation
	(4, 6)		Uncorrelated

62　A small company has recorded the following data on volumes and costs of production for the last ten months.

X = Production ('000 units)	4	6	9	10	8	5	7	11	12
Y = Costs ($'000)	11	12	19	22	20	16	13	24	20

	Production	Costs	
Sums	$\sum X$ = 82	$\sum Y$ = 172	$\sum XY$ = 1,492
Sums of squares	$\sum X^2$ = 736	$\sum Y^2$ = 3,136	

Required:

(a)　If the regression equation of costs (Y) on production (X) = Y = a + bX, calculate the following.

　　(i)　Calculate the value of b to 4 decimal places.

　　　　

　　(ii)　Calculate the value of a to 2 decimal places.

　　　　

(b)　If the regression equation based on the data given above was calculated to be Y = 7 + 1.5X with a Pearson correlation coefficient of 0.8, answer the following questions.

　　(i)　What would the fixed costs of the factory be?

　　　　

　　(ii)　Plot the regression line Y = 7 + 1.5X on the axes provided.

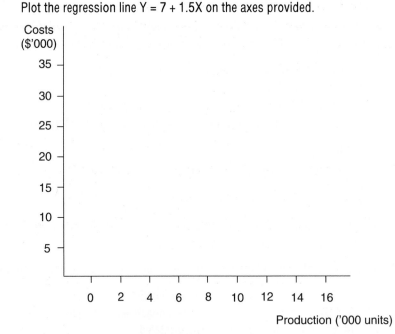

Costs ($'000)

Production ('000 units)

　　(iii)　Predict the total production costs for next month if an output volume of 10,000 units is forecast.

63   A company is building a model in order to forecast total costs based on the level of output. The following data is available for last year.

Month	Output '000 units (X)	Costs $'000 (Y)
January	16	170
February	20	240
March	23	260
April	25	300
May	25	280
June	19	230
July	16	200
August	12	160
September	19	240
October	25	290
November	28	350
December	12	200

Required:

(a)   Plot a scattergraph of costs on output using the axes provided below.

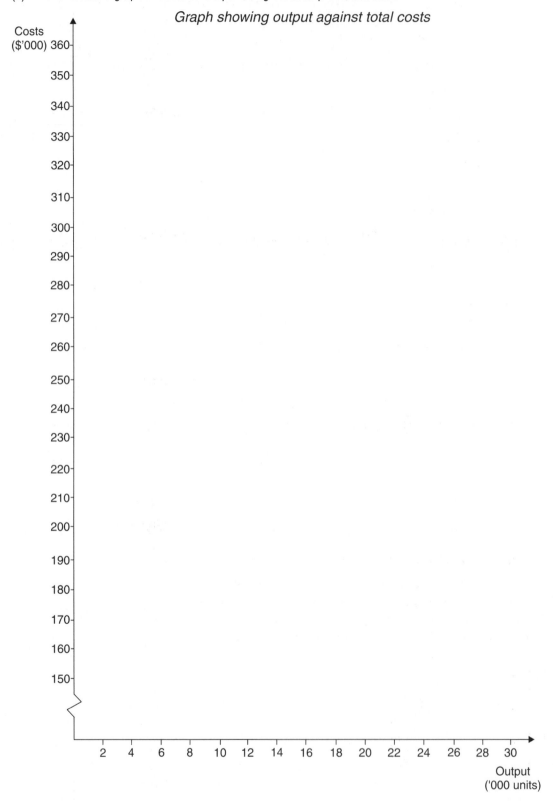

Graph showing output against total costs

(b) If $\sum X$ = 240

$\sum Y$ = 2,920

$\sum X^2$ = 5,110

$\sum Y^2$ = 745,200

$\sum XY$ = 61,500

Calculate the correlation coefficient between output and costs, stating your answer correct to 3 decimal places ☐

64   Based on the last 7 periods, the underlying trend of sales is y = 690.24 − 2.75x. If the 8th period has a seasonal factor of −25.25, assuming an additive forecasting model, then the forecast for that period, in whole units is

A   643

B   646

C   668

D   671

65   Which of the following are necessary if forecasts obtained from a time series analysis are to be reliable?

I   There must be no seasonal variation

II   The trend must be increasing

III   The model used must fit the past data

IV   There must be no unforeseen events

A   I and III only

B   I and IV only

C   II and III only

D   III and IV only

66   The results of an additive time series model analysing production are shown below.

	Weekly production '000 units
Week 1	−4
Week 2	+5
Week 3	+9
Week 4	−6

Which of the following statements is/are true in relation to the data shown in the table above?

I   Production is on average 9,000 units above the trend in week 3.

II   Production is on average 4% below the trend in week 1.

III   Production is on average 5% above the trend in week 2.

IV   Production in week 4 is typically 6% below the trend.

A   I only

B   I and II only

C   I and III only

D   II and IV only

67   A time series was analysed using a multiplicative model. The seasonal variations given by actual value ÷ trend, are adjusted so that they total 4.

	Quarter			
	1	2	3	4
Unadjusted average	1.09	0.93	1.17	0.78

The correct adjusted average is

A   Quarter 1 adjusted average = 1.0975
B   Quarter 2 adjusted average = 0.96
C   Quarter 3 adjusted average = 1.1400
D   Quarter 4 adjusted average = 0.7725

68   In a time series analysis, the multiplicative model is used to forecast sales and the following seasonal variations apply.

Quarter	1	2	3	4
Seasonal variation	0.45	1.22	1.31	?

The seasonal variation for quarter 4 is

A   0.02
B   1.02
C   1.98
D   2.98

69   In 20X8, seasonal variations and trend values in quarters 1-4 are as follows.

Quarter	Seasonal variation	Trend
1	0.6	4,500
2	0.4	4,800
3	1.2	5,200
4	1.0	5,300

Match the sales values forecast with the correct quarters shown below.

Quarter	Sales forecast
1	6,591
2	7,489
3	2,364
4	3,358

70   The accountant at Hopwood Trends Ltd has carried out a time series analysis of quarterly sales, calculating the moving average trend and average seasonal variations using the additive method. She has only partially completed this analysis. The calculations carried out so far are shown in the following table.

Year	Quarter	Sales	Moving total of 4 quarters' sales	Moving average of 4 quarters' sales	Trend	Seasonal variation
20X2	1	200				
	2	110				
			870	217.5		
	3	320			219	+101
			884	221.0		
	4	240			222	+18
			892	223.0		
20X3	1	214			225	-11
			906	226.5		
	2	118			229	-111
			926	231.5		
	3	334			232	+102
			932	233.0		
	4	260			234	+26
			938	234.5		
20X4	1	220			235	-15
			A	C		
	2	124			E	F
			B	D		
	3	340				
	4	278				

(a)   Complete the table by finding the missing values indicated by the letters. All answers should be correct to the nearest whole number except for C and D which should be correct to one decimal place.

A = ☐

B = ☐

C = ☐

D = ☐

E = ☐

F = ☐

(b) Complete the following table to calculate the seasonal components. Find the values represented by letters, giving your answers to one decimal place throughout.

Year	Quarter 1	2	3	4	Total
20X2			..	..	
20X3	..	..	..	..	
20X4	..	..			
Average seasonal variation	..	..	..	..	G
Adjustment	H	..	..	..	..
Adjusted seasonal variation	I	J	K	L	

G = [ ]

H = [ ]

I = [ ]

J = [ ]

K = [ ]

L = [ ]

(c) Seasonally adjust the sales for the fourth quarter of 20X4.

[ ]

(d) If the predicted trend for the first quarter in 20X5 is 245, forecast the actual sales. [ ]

71 The regression equation of a linear trend is given by T = 52 + 6.3t where time t = 1 in the first quarter of 2006. What is the trend for the third quarter of 2010 giving your answer to three significant figures?

[ ]

72 A time series for weeks 1 to 12 has been analysed into a trend and seasonal variations, using the additive model. The trend value is 84 + 0.7w, where w is the week number. The actual value for week 9 is 88.7. What is the seasonal variation for week 9?

A   - 1.6
B   - 0.9
C   + 0.9
D   + 1.6

73   A time series analysis has been performed on data for weeks 1 to 20. The trend line is given by 3,150 + 72X, where X is the week number. The average seasonal variation (using the additive model) for weeks whose numbers are divisible by 4 (ie weeks 4,8,12 etc) is – 47. The actual figure for week 12 was 4,000. What was the residual for that week?

A   - 61
B   - 14
C   + 19
D   + 33

74   How much will an investor have after eight years if he invests $2,000 at 12% per annum simple interest?

A $1,920
B $3,680
C $3,920
D $4,952

75   In four years, an investment of $900 has grown to $1,548. What has been the monthly rate of simple interest?

A   1.1%
B   1.5%
C   15%
D   18%

76   A one-year investment yields a return of 20%. The cash returned from the investment, including principal and interest is $3,000. The interest is

A $300
B $400
C $500
D $600

77   It is estimated that a particular cost will decline by 8% per annum on a compound basis.

If the cost is now $12,000, by the end of year 3 the cost will be approximately

A $8,597
B $9,120
C $9,344
D $10,157

78   House prices rise at 3% per calendar month. The annual rate of increase correct to one decimal place is

A   42.6%
B   36.0%
C   14.26%
D   12.36%

79   (a)   The effective annual rate of interest of 15% nominal per annum compounded quarterly is [ ] %

(b)   The effective annual rate of interest of 24% nominal per annum compounded monthly is [ ] %

80   The treasurer of Hound Camping Ltd needed to invest some surplus cash. He decided to make the following investments. Calculate the interest earned on each of the following investments (correct to the nearest $).

(a) $8,000 was placed in a bank deposit account for three years. The expected annual rate of interest is 11%, calculated yearly.

[   ]

(b) $15,000 was placed in a savings account for five years, with interest added yearly at 14%.

[   ]

(c) $6,000 was placed in an account for four years where the annual interest rate is expected to be 10% for the first two years and 15% in years 3 and 4, with interest added at the end of each year.

[   ]

The treasurer is also considering three further investments A, B and C. In each case calculate the effective annual rate of interest to 2 decimal places.

(d)   Investment A would last for three years, and pay interest at a nominal rate of 10.5%. Compound interest would be added every half year.

[   ]

(e)   Investment B would last for five years, with a nominal interest rate of 12%, payable monthly.

[   ]

(f)   Investment C would last for four years, with a nominal interest rate of 12%, payable quarterly.

[   ]

81   A firm has arranged a ten-year lease, at an annual rent of $12,000. The first rental payment has to be paid immediately, and the others are to be paid at the end of each year.

What is the present value of the lease at 12%?

A $63,936
B $67,800
C $75,936
D $79,800

82   A mortgage of $60,000 is to be repaid by 15 equal year-end payments. If interest is charged at 9% the value of the annual payment (using tables) correct to the nearest $10 is

A $2,050
B $4,000
C $6,830
D $7,440

83 The NPV of an investment is $460 when the discount rate is 10% and $320 when it is 24%. Estimate the internal rate of return to two decimal places.

    A   17.00%

    B   18.20%

    C   56.00%

    D   It is not possible to estimate the IRR unless one of the NPVs is negative

84 Over a period of 12 months, the present value of the payments made on a credit card is $21,000 at a discount rate of 3% per month. What is the equivalent constant monthly amount, to the nearest $?

    A $1,750

    B $2,110

    C $8,743

    D $14,721

85 Which of the following mutually exclusive projects would you advise your client to undertake if only one could be undertaken, given *only* the following information.

	IRR	NPV
	%	$
Project A	15.6	1,600
Project B	16.7	1,400
Project C	17.6	1,200
Project D	18.5	1,000

    A   Project A

    B   Project B

    C   Project C

    D   Project D

86 Daisy Ltd is considering whether to make an investment costing $28,000 which would earn $8,000 cash per annum for five years. The company expects to make a return of at least 11% per annum.

Complete the following table and state whether the project is viable or not.

Year	Cash flow	Discount factor	Present value
	$	11%	$
0			
1			
2			
3			
4			
5			
		NPV	

Project viable   Yes   [   ]

                 No   [   ]

87   Daisy Hoof Ltd is considering a project to purchase some equipment which would generate the following cash flows.

Year	Cash flow $
0	(50,000)
1	18,000
2	25,000
3	15,000
4	10,000

The estimated trade-in value of the equipment, which is $2,000, has not been included in the cash flows above.

The company has a cost of capital of 16%.

Required:

(a)   Complete the following table by filling in the values represented by letters. Calculate present values to the nearest $.

Year	Net cash flow $	Discount factor 16%	Present value $
0	..	B	
1	..	..	D
2	..	..	E
3	..	C	
4	A	..	
		Net Present Value =	F

A = [ ]

B = [ ]

C = [ ]

D = [ ]

E = [ ]

F = [ ]

(b)   The company wishes to calculate the internal rate of return of the project and in order to do this the net present value at a different rates of interest must be calculated. Estimate the net present value to the nearest $ using a discount rate of 18%.

Net present value = [ ]

(c)   Estimate the internal rate of return to one decimal place using the formula

$$IRR = R_1 + \left[\frac{NPV_1}{NPV_1 - NPV_2} \times (R_2 - R_1) \right]\%$$

IRR = [ ]

88   A retailer is facing increasing competition from new shops that are opening in his area. He thinks that if he does not modernise his premises, he will lose sales. A local builder has estimated that the cost of modernising the shop will be $40,000 if the work is started now. The retailer is not sure whether to borrow the money and modernise the premises now, or to save up and have the work carried out when he has sufficient funds in the future. Current forecasts show that if he delays the work for three years, the cost of the modernisation is likely to rise by 4% per annum.

Investigations have revealed that, if he borrows, he will have to pay interest at the rate of 3% per quarter, but if he saves the money himself he will only earn 2% per quarter.

Required:

(a)   The retailer borrows $40,000 at 3% per quarter, and repays $X at the end of each quarter for three years.

   (i)   Use tables to find the present value of the repayments as a function of X.

   | |

   (ii)   Find the value of X to the nearest $.

   | |

(b)   If the retailer decides to save money at 2% per quarter so that he has sufficient funds to carry out the work in three years' time, complete the following shaded boxes.

   (i)   The cost of modernisation in three years' time correct to 2 decimal places.

   | |

   (ii)   If twelve instalments of $Y are invested, the first being paid immediately, use tables to find the present value of the instalments as a function of Y.

   | |

   (iii)   Use tables to find the value of Y to the nearest $10.

   | |

(c)   On the basis of the results that you have calculated above, what would you advise the retailer to do? (Tick as appropriate).

   Modernise now | |

   Save and modernise later | |

89   Which **one** of the following tasks is a spreadsheet **not** able to perform?

   A   The presentation of numerical data in the form of graphs and charts
   B   The application of logical tests to data
   C   The application of 'What If' scenarios
   D   Automatic correction of all data entered by the operator into the spreadsheet

90 Spreadsheets are a well-known type of software application. All the following statements about spreadsheets are true expect one. Which **one** of the statements is **untrue**?

A   Spreadsheets can import information from documents created in other applications
B   Microsoft Access is a more advanced spreadsheet package than Microsoft Excel
C   It is possible to use a spreadsheet to sort data in a variety of ways
D   Spreadsheet packages usually include a facility to graph numeric data

Questions 91 to 93 refer to the spreadsheet shown below.

	A	B	C	D	E	F	G	H	I
1				Income and Costs forecast for Smith and Peters					
2									
3				Month 1	Month 2	Month 3	Month 4	Month 5	Month 6
4				$	$	$	$	$	$
5	Opening position								
6									
7	Income			15,000	15,000	15,000	15,000	15,000	15,000
8									
9	Costs								
10	Staff costs								
11	Project Manager			2,500	2,500	2,500	2,500	2,500	2,500
12	Senior Developer			1,900	1,900	1,900	1,900	1,900	1,900
13	Developer 1			1,600	1,600	1,600	1,600	1,600	1,600
14	Developer 2			1,500	1,500	1,500	1,500	1,500	1,500
15	Developer 3			1,500	1,500	1,500	1,500	1,500	1,500
16	Support Staff			1,200	1,200	1,200	1,200	1,200	1,200
17	National insurance @ 10%			1,020	1,020	1,020	1,020	1,020	1,020
18	Total staff costs			11,220	11,220	11,220	11,220	11,220	11,220
19									
20	Insurances			50	50	50	50	50	50
21	Telephone, Telecom			250	250	250	250	250	250
22	Hardware/Software			500	500	500	500	500	500
23	Rent			800	800	800	800	800	800
24	Stationery			100	100	100	100	100	100
25	Accounting			300	300	300	300	300	300
26	Marketing			100	100	100	100	100	100
27	Other costs			250	250	250	250	250	250
28	Total other costs			2,350	2,350	2,350	2,350	2,350	2,350
29									
30	Total costs			13,570	13,570	13,570	13,570	13,570	13,570
31									
32	End month position			1,430	2,860	4,290	5,720	7,150	8,580
33									

91 The cell F5 (column F row 5) shows the opening position for month 3. The value in this cell is a formula.

Which of the following would not be a correct entry for this cell?

A   =E7-E30+D32
B   =E5+E7-E30
C   =E32
D   =2860

92 The formula in D17 (column D row 17) adds a percentage national insurance charge to the sub total of staff costs. Which of the formulae shown below would be the **best** formula for cell D17?

A   =SUM(D11:D16)*0.1
B   =SUM(D11:D16)*$C17
C   =SUM(D11:D16)*10%
D   =SUM(D11:D16)*C17

BPP
PROFESSIONAL EDUCATION

93   The cell D30 (column D row 30) shows the total costs. Which of the following is the **correct** formula for this cell?

    A   =D28+D18
    B   =SUM(D11:D28)
    C   =SUM(D7:D28)
    D   D18+D28

94   The data that can be entered onto a spreadsheet comprises which of the following?

    A   Text and numbers
    B   Formulae, text and numbers
    C   Numbers and formulae
    D   Text and formulae

Questions 95, 96, 97 and 98 refer to the Employment targets and bonuses spreadsheet shown below. This spreadsheet shows the target sales for each employee (column C) and the amount that they actually sold (column D). The bonus value is calculated by subtracting the actual sales from the target sales. If the employee has failed to achieve their target level, then there is no bonus. The target figure for next month (column F) is calculated by multiplying the target figure by a defined growth rate (cell B15).

	A	B	C	D	E	F	G
1							
2	Employment targets and bonuses						
3							
4	Employee No		Target	Actual	Bonus	Next month	
5	345	Rianne	2,100.00	2,000.00	0.00	2,121.00	
6	567	Sian	4,300.00	4,400.00	100.00	4,343.00	
7	543	Claire	2,345.00	2,300.00	0.00	2,368.45	
8	231	Mark	5,680.00	5,600.00	0.00	5,736.80	
9	890	Danny	345.00	500.00	155.00	348.45	
10							
11			14,770.00	14,800.00		14,917.70	
12	Sales staff	5					
13	Income/staff	2,960					
14							
15	Growth rate	1.00%					

95   In the spreadsheet what is the formula in C11 (column C row 11)?

    A   =SUM(C5:C9)
    B   =TOTAL(C5:C9)
    C   =SUM(C5:C11)
    D   =TOTAL (C5:C9)

96   In the spreadsheet the figure in E5 (column E row 5) is calculated by subtracting the value in D5 (column D row 5) from the value in C5 (column C row 5). However, if the calculated value is negative, then the value returned in E5 is zero.

In the spreadsheet what is the formula in E5?

A   =IF(D5-C5>0,D5-C5,0)
B   =IF(C5-D5>0,C5-D5,0)
C   =IF(C5-D5>0,0,C5-D5)
D   =IF(D5-C5>0,0,D5-C5)

97   The value in cell B12 (column C row 12) is a formula. It shows how many sales people are in the spreadsheet.

In the spreadsheet what is the formula in B12?

A   =SUM(A5:A9)
B   =TOTAL(A5:A9)
C   =COUNT(A5:A9)
D   =CALCULATE(A5:A9)

98   The value in F5 (column F row 5) is calculated by C5 (column C row 5) by the growth value in B15 (column B row 15). the formula in F5 is then copied down to rows 6, 7, 8 and 9

What should the formula be in F5 to allow this to be done accurately and quickly?

A   =$C5+($C5*$B$15)
B   =$C$5+($C5*$B$15)
C   =$C5+($C$5*$B$15)
D   =$C5+($C5*$B15)

Answer bank

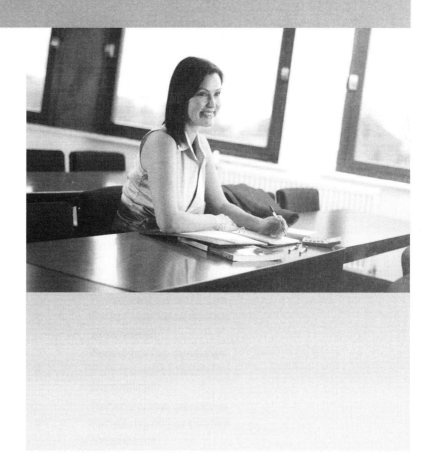

BPP
PROFESSIONAL EDUCATION

1   B $\dfrac{(x^2)^3}{x^6} = x^{(2 \times 3) - 6} = x^{6-6} = x^0 = 1$ (always)

You should have been able to eliminate option A straightaway since you should have been able to see that the correct answer is x or x to the power of something. Remember, x^0 **always** equals 1.

Options C and D are incorrect because $\dfrac{x^6}{x^6}$ **does not** equal x or x^2.

2   B   The term x^{-1} equals $\dfrac{1}{x}$ by definition.

3   (a) $10.80

Workings

Laura's share = $6 = 5 parts
Therefore one part is worth $6 ÷ 5 = $1.20
Total of 9 parts shared out originally
Therefore total was 9 × $1.20 = $10.80

(b) $13.50

Workings

Laura's share = $6 = 4 parts
Therefore one part is worth $6 ÷ 4 = $1.50
Therefore original total was 9 × $1.50 = $13.50

4   $1,150

Workings

23% of $5,000 = 0.23 × $5,000 = $1,150

5   40%

Workings

$18 as a percentage of $45 = $\dfrac{18}{45} \times 100\% = \dfrac{1}{2.5} \times 100\% = 40\%$

6    $24,390

Workings

	%
Deirdre's salary *before* increase (original)	100.0
Salary increase	2.5
Deirdre's salary after increase (final)	102.5

102.5% = $25,000 (final salary)

$1\% = \dfrac{\$25,000}{102.5}$

= $243.90 (to 2 dp)

∴ 100% (original salary *before* increase) = $243.90 × 100

= $24,390 (to nearest $)

7    $190,000

Workings

	%
Purchases – 20X0 (original)	100
Percentage decrease	–5
Purchases – 20X1 (final)	95

If   100% = $200,000
      1% = $2,000
∴   95% = $2,000 × 95
          = $190,000

8    $200

Workings

Initial fee, X = 100%

Sales tax = 17.5%

Final fee = 117.5% = $235

$1\% = \dfrac{\$235}{117.5}$

$100\% = \dfrac{\$235}{117.5} \times 100$

= $200

9   C

$$Q = \sqrt{\frac{2C_0 D}{C_h}}$$

$$200 = \sqrt{\frac{2 \times 40 \times 48,000}{C_h}}$$

Square both sides

$$200^2 = \frac{2 \times 40 \times 48,000}{C_h}$$

$$C_h = \frac{2 \times 40 \times 48,000}{200^2}$$

$$C_h = \$96$$

If you selected one of the other options, then work through the solution again remembering that if you do anything to one side of an equation, you must make sure you do the same to the other side of the equation as well.

10   D

If
$$D = 30 - 3P$$
$$D - 30 = -3P$$
$$3P = 30 - D$$
$$P = \frac{30}{3} - \frac{D}{3}$$
$$P = 10 - \frac{D}{3}$$

Option A is incorrect since you have divided the 30 by 3 but not the D.

Option B is incorrect because you have (incorrectly) calculated that $D = 30 - 3P$ is $D = 27P$. This would only be the case if there were brackets as such ($D = (30 - 3)P$).

Option C is incorrect because you have forgotten to change the sign of the D from positive to negative when you took it to the other side of the equation.

11    $x = \boxed{1.7}$

$$x^3 = 4.913$$

$x = 1.7$ (take the cube root of each side).

12    $x = \boxed{-10.5}$

$$34x - 7.6 = (17x - 3.8) \times (x + 12.5)$$

This one is easy if you realise that $17 \times 2 = 34$ and $3.8 \times 2 = 7.6$, so $2(17x - 3.8) = 34x - 7.6$

We can then divide each side by $17x - 3.8$ to get

$$2 = x + 12.5$$

$-10.5 = x$ (subtract 12.5 from each side).

13   $Y = aX^b$
     $= 9 \times 7^{-0.24}$
     $= 5.64$

14   $3(X + 4) < 2X + 1$
     $3X + 12 < 2X + 1$ (multiply out the brackets)
        $3X < 2X - 11$ (subtract 12 from both sides)
     $X < -11$ (subtract 2X from both sides)

15   $x = \boxed{-5}$ $y = \boxed{4}$

Workings

$x - y = -9$	(1)
$9x - 13y = -97$	(2)
$9x - 9y = -81$	(3) (1) $\times$ 9
$4y = 16$	(3) $-$ (2)
$y = 4$	

Substituting in (1) we get

$x - 4 = -9$
$x = -9 + 4$
$x = -5$

16   $\boxed{x^2 - 4x - 437 = 0}$ or $\boxed{y^2 + 4y - 437 = 0}$

Workings

Let the two positive numbers be x and y.

$x^2 + y^2 = 890$	(1)
$x - y = 4$	(2)
$y = x - 4$	(3) (from (2)).

Substituting in (1) we get

$x^2 + (x - 4)^2 = 890$
$x^2 + (x^2 - 8x + 16) = 890$
$2x^2 - 8x - 874 = 0$
$x^2 - 4x - 437 = 0$

Alternatively $x = y + 4$ (3)

and hence $(y + 4)^2 + y^2 = 890$

$y^2 + 8y + 16 + y^2 = 890$
$2y^2 + 8y - 874 = 0$
$y^2 + 4y - 437 = 0$

17    $-b^2 + 22b - 112 = 0$ or $-a^2 + 22a - 112 = 0$

Workings

Let the length and breadth of the rectangle be a and b.

$2a + 2b = 44$

$\quad a + b = 22$ (1)

$\quad\quad ab = 112$ (2)

From (1) we get $a = 22 - b$

Substituting in (2) we get

$\quad\quad b(22 - b) = 112$

$-b^2 + 22b - 112 = 0$

By symmetry the same equation:

$-a^2 + 22a - 112 = 0$

can be solved for 'a'.

18    $x =$ $\boxed{-2}$ or $\boxed{+4}$

Workings

$-3x^2 + 6x + 24 = 0$

This can be solved using:

$$x = \frac{-b \pm \sqrt{b^2 - 4ac}}{2a}$$

Where $a = -3, b = 6, c = 24$

$$x = \frac{-6 \pm \sqrt{(6^2 + 4 \times 3 \times 24)}}{(2 \times -3)}$$

$$= \frac{-6 \pm \sqrt{324}}{(-6)}$$

$$= \frac{[-6 \pm 18]}{(-6)}$$

$$= -2 \text{ or } +4.$$

19   B   The number of goals scored is an example of **quantitative data** as they can be measured. Since the number of goals scored cannot take on any value, they can only score 1, 2, 3 or any **whole** number of goals (they cannot score 2½ goals) the data are said to be **discrete**.

You should have been able to eliminate options C and D immediately since qualitative data are data that cannot be measured but which reflect some quality of what is being observed.

20   C   A demand of 53 units occurred on 42 days out of a total of 200.

$$P(\text{demand} = 53 \text{ units}) = \frac{42}{200} \times 100\%$$

$$= 21\%$$

If you selected option A, you calculated the probability that daily demand was 51 units instead of 53.

If you selected option B, you calculated the probability that daily demand was 52 units instead of 53.

If you selected option D, you calculated the probability that daily demand was 54 units instead of 53.

21   D   Probability of A or B occurring = P(A) + P(B) provided A and B cannot both be true.

Pr(sales remain same or rise) = P(same) + P(rise)
$$= 0.61 + 0.22$$
$$= 0.83$$

You must make sure that you understand the laws of probability so that you can apply them correctly to objective test questions such as this.

22

Probability of visiting area x	=	0.50
Probability of visiting area y	=	0.25
Probability of visiting area z	=	0.25
EV of probability of a sale in area x	=	0.20
EV of probability of a sale in area y	=	0.0875
EV of probability of a sale in area z	=	0.0625

Workings

The probabilities of visiting each area are obtained from the ratios in which he visits them.

Area	Ratio	Probability
x	2	2/4 = 0.50
y	1	1/4 = 0.25
z	1	1/4 = 0.25
	4	1.00

The expected value (EV) of probability of a sale = P(sale) × P(visiting area).

Area	P(sale)	P(visiting area)	EV of probability of a sale
x	0.40	0.50	0.20
y	0.35	0.25	0.0875
z	0.25	0.25	0.0625

23   (a)   With replacement $\boxed{\dfrac{1}{169}}$

Without replacement $\boxed{\dfrac{1}{221}}$

Workings

Assuming replacement

$P(\text{Ace}) = \dfrac{4}{52} = \dfrac{1}{13}$

$P(\text{Ace on second draw}) = \dfrac{1}{13}$

$P(\text{Ace followed by Ace with replacement}) = \left(\dfrac{1}{13}\right) \times \left(\dfrac{1}{13}\right) = \dfrac{1}{169}$

Without replacement

$P(\text{Ace}) = \dfrac{1}{13}$

$P(\text{Ace on second draw}) = \dfrac{3}{51} = \dfrac{1}{17}$

$P(\text{Ace followed by Ace without replacement}) = \left(\dfrac{1}{13}\right) \times \left(\dfrac{1}{17}\right) = \dfrac{1}{221}$

(b) $\boxed{\dfrac{1}{2,704}}$

Workings

$P(\text{Drawing ace of Hearts}) = \dfrac{1}{52}$

$P(\text{Drawing ace of Spades}) = \dfrac{1}{52}$ (if replacement is assumed)

$P(\text{Ace of hearts followed by ace of Spades}) = \left(\dfrac{1}{52}\right) \times \left(\dfrac{1}{52}\right) = \dfrac{1}{2,704}$

(c)   (i) $\boxed{0.3}$

(ii) $\boxed{0.27}$

(iii) $\boxed{0.02}$

Workings

$P(\text{Own Home}) = P(H) = 0.5$

$P(\text{Own Car}) = P(C) = 0.6$

$P(\text{Own TV}) = P(TV) = 0.9$

(i)   P(Home and Car) = P(Home) × P(Car)

        = 0.5 × 0.6

        = 0.3

(ii)   P(all three owned) = P(Home) × P(car) × P(TV)

        = 0.5 × 0.6 × 0.9

        = 0.27

(iii)   P(None owned) = (1 − P(H)) (1 − P(C)) (1 − P(TV))

        = 0.5 × 0.4 × 0.1

        = 0.02

(d)   (i) | 40% |

        (ii) | 66.67% |

Workings

Out of every 100 respondents, 50 own their own homes and 50 do not. This gives the bottom row of the contingency table shown below. Similarly the total column is determined by the 60% of respondents who own cars. Of the 50 home owners, 40 people (80% × 50) also own cars. The table can now be completed as follows.

	Home owner	Not home owner	Total
Car	40	20	60
No car	10	30	40
Total	50	50	100

(i)   Of the 50 respondents who do not own homes, only 20 own cars = 20/50 × 100% = 40%

(ii)   Of the 60 who own cars, only 40 are home owners = 40/60 × 100% = 66.7%

24   B   Expected profit = (15,000 × 0.2) + (19,000 × 0.6) + (1,000 × 0.1)

        = 3,000 + 11,400 + 100

        = $14,500

If you selected option A, you have totalled all profits.

If you selected option C, you have selected the option with the highest probability.

If you selected option D, you have averaged the profits without using the probabilities.

25   B   The diagram is a Venn diagram illustrating two mutually exclusive outcomes.

26   D   The rule of addition for two events which are not mutually exclusive = P(A or B)

        = P(A) + P(B)

        − P(A and B)

If you selected option A, this is the rule of addition for two mutually exclusive events.

Option B is the simple multiplication or AND law.

27   I and III are limitations of expected values.

II and IV would be limitations regardless of which decision making tool was used.

28   A = | 1 |

      B = | 6 |

      C = | 128 |

Workings

	Red	Yellow	Green	Total
Good	25 – 1 = 24	50 – 6 = 44	75 – 15 = 60	128
Faulty	4% × 25 = 1	12% × 50 = 6	20% × 75 = 15	22
Total	25	50	75	150

29   C   Height of histogram = $\dfrac{20}{\frac{2}{3}}$ = 30

If you selected option A, you multiplied 20 by 2/3 instead of dividing it by 2/3.

Option B is incorrect because it represents the score in the class under consideration.

Option D represents the score in the class (20) plus 2/3 of 20 = 20 + 13.33 = 33.33.

30   B   A histogram is a chart that looks like a bar chart except that the bars are joined together. On a histogram, frequencies are presented by the **area** covered by the bars.

31   C   An ogive represents a cumulative frequency distribution which shows the cumulative number of items with a value less than or equal to, or alternatively greater than or equal to, a certain amount. This is a 'less than' ogive.

32   A = | 6.5 |

      B = | 12 |

      C = | 16 |

      D = | 4.5 |

Workings

The first and last intervals have widths of $10, ie twice the standard width. Their frequencies must therefore be halved in order to calculate the frequency density. In all other cases, the frequency density is the same as the frequency (or number of employees).

Weekly average wage $	Number of employees	Frequency density
51 and <61	13	6.5
61 and <66	12	12
66 and <71	16	16
71 and <76	21	21
76 and <81	25	25
81 and <86	20	20
86 and <91	14	14
91 and <101	9	4.5

33

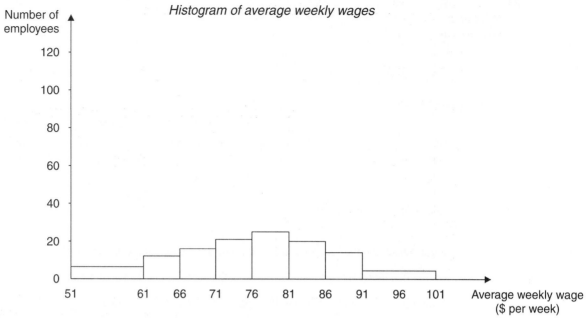

Histogram of average weekly wages

34   E = [62]

      F = [87]

      G = [130]

Workings

Average weekly wage $	Number of employees	Cumulative frequency
51 and <61	13	13
61 and <66	12	25
66 and <71	16	41
71 and <76	21	62
76 and <81	25	87
81 and <86	20	107
86 and <91	14	121
91 and <101	9	130

35

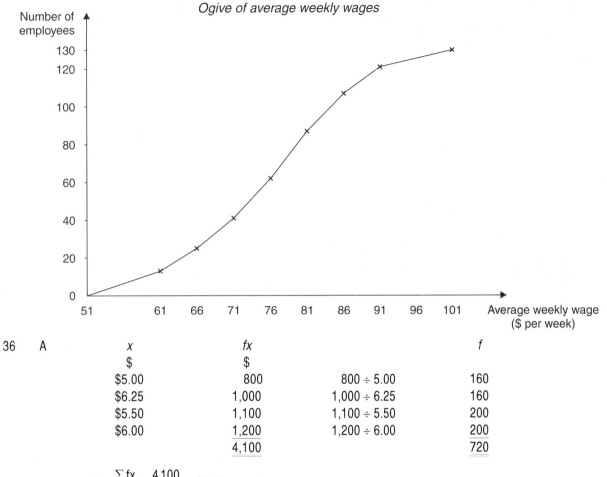

Ogive of average weekly wages

36   A

x	fx		f
$	$		
$5.00	800	800 ÷ 5.00	160
$6.25	1,000	1,000 ÷ 6.25	160
$5.50	1,100	1,100 ÷ 5.50	200
$6.00	1,200	1,200 ÷ 6.00	200
	4,100		720

$$\therefore \ \overline{x} = \frac{\sum fx}{\sum f} = \frac{4,100}{720} = \$5.69$$

37   C   In order of magnitude, scores are

16   18   22   24   28   30   34   42   48   68

Position of median is $\frac{10+1}{2} = 5\frac{1}{2}$ and therefore the median is the average of the 5th and 6th items, ie of 28 and 30. The median is therefore 29.

38   D   **Arithmetic mean** $= \dfrac{\sum x}{n}$

$$\therefore \ 10 = \frac{\sum x}{19}$$

$\sum x \quad = 10 \times 19$

$\quad\quad = 190$

Let x = twentieth number

$190 + x \ = \ 20 \times 11$

$190 + x \ = \ 220$

$$x = 220 - 190$$
$$= 30$$

39

Daily sales	Frequency f	Midpoint x	fx
> 0 ≤ 3	8	2	16
> 3 ≤ 6	16	5	80
> 6 ≤ 9	12	8	96
> 9 ≤ 12	4	11	44
	40		236

The variables in the table are **discrete**. The arithmetic mean of the data =

$$\frac{\sum fx}{\sum f} = \frac{236}{40} = 5.9 \text{ televisions per day}$$

40 ┌─────────┐
      │ 32.67 │ minutes
      └─────────┘

Workings

Times	Midpoint x	Frequency f	fx
0 – 10	5	14	70
10 – 20	15	26	390
20 – 30	25	64	1,600
30 – 40	35	46	1,610
40 – 50	45	28	1,260
50 – 60	55	16	880
60 – 80	70	8	560
80 – 100	90	4	360
		206	6,730

$$\text{Mean } \bar{x} = \frac{\sum fx}{\sum f} = \frac{6,730}{206} = 32.67 \text{ minutes}$$

41 ┌─────────┐
      │ 32.67 │
      └─────────┘

Workings

$$\bar{X} = \frac{\sum fX}{\sum f}$$

$$\sigma = \sqrt{\frac{\sum fX^2}{\sum f} - \bar{X}^2} = \sqrt{\frac{1161}{23} - \left(\frac{79}{23}\right)^2} = \sqrt{50.478 - 11.798}$$

$$= \sqrt{38.68} = 6.22$$

42　C　The formula for the coefficient of variation is $\dfrac{\text{Standard deviation}}{\text{Mean}}$

Distribution	Coefficient of variation
1	0.24
2	0.25
3	0.35 ◄──────── largest
4	0.21

Option C is therefore correct.

If you chose any of the other options you did not calculate the coefficient of variation using the correct formula.

43　C　The arithmetic mean of the five numbers, $\bar{x}$, is equal to $\dfrac{4 + 6 + 8 + 12 + 15}{5} = \dfrac{45}{5} = 9$

We can now calculate the variance:

x	$x - \bar{x}$	$(x - \bar{x})^2$
4	−5	25
6	−3	9
8	−1	1
12	3	9
15	6	36
	$\sum(x - \bar{x})^2 =$	80

$\text{Variance} = \dfrac{\sum(x - \bar{x})^2}{n} = \dfrac{80}{5} = 16$

The correct answer is therefore C.

If you selected option A, you calculated the standard deviation.
If you selected option B you calculated the arithmetic mean.
If you selected option D, you forgot to divide $\sum(x - \bar{x})^2$ by n (or 5).

44　D

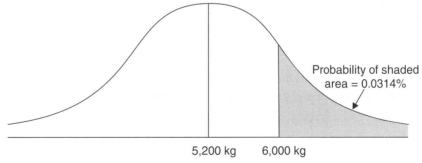

Probability of shaded area = 0.0314%

5,200 kg　　6,000 kg

Pr(elephants weigh between 5,200 kg and 6,000 kg) = 0.5 − 0.0314
= 0.4686

From normal distribution tables, 0.4686 corresponds to a z value of 1.86.

If $z = \dfrac{x - \mu}{\sigma}$

$1.86 = \dfrac{6{,}000 - 5{,}200}{\sigma}$

$\sigma = \dfrac{6{,}000 - 5{,}200}{1.86}$

$= 430 \text{ kg}$

The correct answer is therefore D.

Make sure that you draw a sketch of the area that you are interested in when answering an objective test question such as this. It will help to clarify exactly what you are trying to do.

45   D

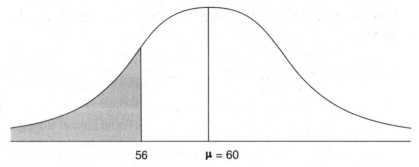

56          $\mu = 60$

We are interested in the shaded area of the graph above, which we can calculate using normal distribution tables.

$z = \dfrac{x - \mu}{\sigma}$

$= \dfrac{56 - 60}{3.8}$

$= 1.05$

A z value of 1.05 corresponds to a probability of 0.3531.

The shaded area has a corresponding probability of 0.5 − 0.3531 = 0.1469 or 0.15 or 15%.

Option A is incorrect because it represents the probability of getting a score of 56 or more.

Option B represents the probability of getting a score of 60 or less, ie 50% (the mean represents the point below which 50% of the population lie and above which 50% of the population lie).

If you selected option C, you forgot to deduct your answer from 0.5.

46   D   28.23% of the population lies between 900 and the mean. Therefore 0.2823 corresponds to a z value of 0.78 (from normal distribution tables).

If $z = \dfrac{x - \mu}{\sigma}$

$$0.78 = \dfrac{900 - \mu}{90}$$

$$0.78 \times 90 = 900 - \mu$$

$$70.2 = 900 - \mu$$

$$\mu = 900 - 70.2$$

$$= 829.8 \text{ or } 830$$

Draw a sketch of the area we are concerned with in this question if you had difficulty understanding the answer.

47   A

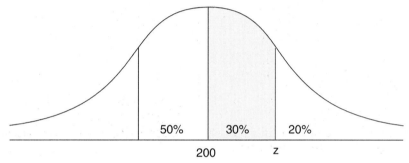

We need to find the point z standard deviations above the mean such that 20% of the frequencies are above it and 30% (50% – 20%) of the frequencies lie between the point z and the mean.

From normal distribution tables, it can be seen that 30% of frequencies lie between the mean and the point 0.84 standard deviations from the mean.

If $z = \dfrac{x - \mu}{\sigma}$

$$0.84 = \dfrac{x - 200}{\sqrt{1,600}} = \dfrac{x - 200}{40}$$

$$33.6 = x - 200$$

$$x = 200 + 33.6$$

$$= 233.6 \text{ or } 234 \text{ (to the nearest whole number)}$$

If you selected option B, you incorrectly added one standard deviation to the mean instead of 0.84 standard deviations.

If you selected option C you have added 1.28 standard deviations to the mean instead of 0.84 standard deviations.

If you selected option D, you have found 200 + (1.96 × 40) which accounts for 47.5% of the area from 200 to point z.

48   (a)   ①

       (b)   ② + ③

       (c)   ④

       (d)   ② + ③ + ④ = ② + 0.5

49   (a) | −1.75 |

         Working

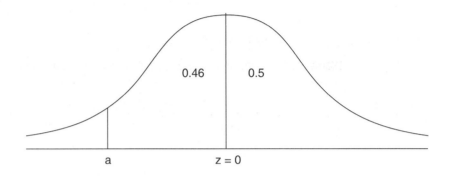

The normal distribution graph above shows the point a above which 96% of the population lies.

Normal distribution tables show that, a z value of 1.75 corresponds to a probability of 0.46. Since a is less than 0, its value is −1.75.

       (b) | 34.3 hours |

         Working

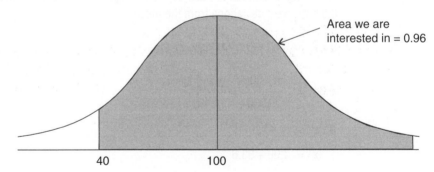

Using $z = \dfrac{x - \mu}{\sigma}$

where $\quad z = 1.75$

$\qquad\quad x = 40$

$\qquad\quad \mu = 100$

$$1.75 = \frac{40 - 100}{\sigma}$$

$$\sigma = \frac{40 - 100}{1.75}$$

$$= 34.3 \text{ hours (to 1 decimal place)}$$

(c) $\boxed{10.6\%}$

Working

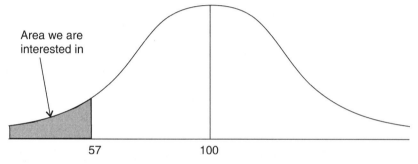

Using $z = \dfrac{x - \mu}{\sigma}$

$$z = \frac{57 - 100}{34.3}$$

$$z = 1.25$$

When z = 1.25, the proportion of batteries lasting between 57 and 100 hours is 0.3944 (from normal distribution tables). The area that we are interested in is the area to the left of 57 hours (shaded area on the graph) = 0.5 − 0.3944 = 0.1056 = 10.6% (to 1 decimal place).

(d) (i)   −2.05

(ii) 111.8

Workings

(1)

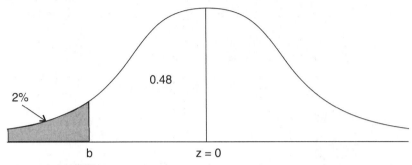

0.48

2%

b   z = 0

The area between b and 0 = 48% (0.48), and so from normal distribution tables, the value of b shown in the graph above is −2.05.

(2)

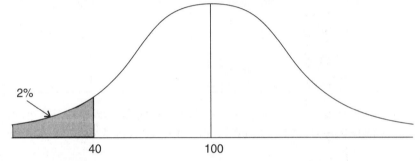

2%

40   100

We want 2% of batteries to last for less than 40 hours. From normal distribution tables, this corresponds to a z value of −2.05.

If $z = \dfrac{X - \mu}{\sigma}$

$$-2.05 = \frac{40 - \mu}{35}$$

$$(-2.05 \times 35) = 40 - \mu$$

$$-71.75 = 40 - \mu$$

$$\mu = 40 + 71.75$$

$$= 111.75$$

$$= 111.8 \text{ (to 1 decimal place)}$$

50   C   To find the percentage increase since year 9, we must take the increase as a percentage of the year 9 value. The increase in the index of 18 points between year 9 and year 14 is therefore a percentage increase of (18/180 × 100%) = 10%.

The correct answer is therefore C.

If you selected option D you interpreted the increase of 18 points as an increase of 18% which is incorrect.

51

Year	Index	Real wage
		$
20X0	88	170
20X1	90	179
20X2	93	181
20X3	95	188
20X4	96	193
20X5	98	195
20X6	100	197
20X7	102	199
20X8	104	199
20X9	106	201
20Y0	108	214

The index number for each year with 20X6 as the base year will be the original index number divided by 1.14, and the real wages for each year will be (money wages × 100)/index number for the year.

52   (a) | 101.3 |

Workings

Weighted average of price relative index = $\dfrac{\sum W \times P_1 / P_0}{\sum W} \times 100$

where P_1 = price in 20X1
        P_0 = price in 20X0

Price relatives

	Price relative P_1/P_0
A	100/100 = 1.00
B	108/100 = 1.08
C	90/100 = 0.90

Weightings (W)

	Q_0
A	5,000
B	6,000
C	3,000
	14,000

Index

$$W \times P_1/P_0$$

A	$1.00 \times 5,000 =$	5,000
B	$1.08 \times 6,000 =$	6,480
C	$0.90 \times 3,000 =$	2,700
		14,180

$$\text{Index} = \frac{14,180}{14,000} \times 100 = 101.3 \text{ (to 1 decimal place)}$$

(b) | 110.0 |

Workings

Weighted average of price relative index $= \dfrac{\sum W \times P_1/P_0}{\sum W} \times 100$

Price relatives

	Price relative P_1/P_0
A	$110/100 = 1.1$
B	$115/100 = 1.15$
C	$100/100 = 1.0$

Weightings (W) = 14,000 (as calculated in (a))

Index

$$W \times P_1/P_0$$

A	$1.1 \times 5,000 =$	5,500
B	$1.15 \times 6,000 =$	6,900
C	$1.00 \times 3,000 =$	3,000
		15,400

$$\text{Index} = \frac{15,400}{14,000} \times 100 = 110.0$$

53   B   A correlation coefficient close to 1 indicates a strong relationship between two variables.

54   A | II |

   B | III |

   C | I |

55   D

X	Y	X²	Y²	XY
1	6	1	36	6
2	5	4	25	10
3	3	9	9	9
4	8	16	64	32
10	22	30	134	57

$n = 4$

$$r = \frac{n\sum XY - (\sum X)(\sum Y)}{\sqrt{\left(n\sum X^2 - (\sum X)^2 \left(n\sum Y^2 - \sum Y^2\right)\right)}}$$

$$= \frac{(4 \times 57) - (10 \times 22)}{\sqrt{\left[(4 \times 30) - 10^2\right] \times \left[(4 \times 134) - 22^2\right]}}$$

$$= \frac{8}{\sqrt{20 \times 52}} = \frac{8}{\sqrt{1040}} = 0.248$$

56   D   The formula for the product moment correlation coefficient is provided in your assessment. There are no excuses for getting this question wrong.

$$r = \frac{n\sum XY - \sum X\sum Y}{\sqrt{[n\sum X^2 - (\sum X)^2][n\sum Y^2 - (\sum Y)^2]}}$$

$$= \frac{(4 \times 57) - (10 \times 22)}{\sqrt{[4 \times 30 - 10^2][4 \times 134 - 22^2]}}$$

$$= \frac{8}{\sqrt{1,040}}$$

$$= +0.25$$

57   D

	Critic 1 Rank	Critic 2 Rank	d	d^2
Captain Corelli's guitar	2	1	1	1
Debbie Jones's diary	1	3	2	4
The songs of a bird	4	7	3	9
Cold love in a warm climate	6	5	1	1
Raging wars and peacefulness	5	6	1	1
Charlotte Black	3	2	1	1
The name of the tulip	7	4	3	9
			$\sum d^2 =$	26

$$R = 1 - \left[\frac{6 \sum d^2}{n(n^2 - 1)} \right]$$

$$= 1 - \left[\frac{6 \times 26}{7 \times (49 - 1)} \right]$$

$$= 1 - \frac{156}{336}$$

$$= 0.536$$

58   C   The independent variable is denoted by X and the dependent one by Y. Statement III is therefore correct. You should have been able to eliminate options B and D straightaway.

The variable to be forecast must always be Y. Statement I is therefore not true.

In calculating the correlation coefficient, it does not matter which variable is X and which is Y, and a totally different regression line equation will result if X and Y are interchanged. Statement II is therefore not true.

Scattergrams are used to show whether or not there is a relationship between X and Y and it does not matter which variable is associated with a particular axis. Statement IV is therefore not true.

All statements (except for III) are not true. The correct answer is therefore C.

59   D   Where $y = a + bx$

$$b = \frac{n \sum XY - \sum X \sum Y}{n \sum X^2 - (\sum X)^2}$$

$$= \frac{(7 \times 587) - (21 \times 184)}{(7 \times 91) - (21^2)}$$

$$= \frac{245}{196}$$

$$= 1.25$$

$$a = \overline{Y} - b\overline{X}$$

$$= \frac{184}{7} - \frac{(1.25 \times 21)}{7}$$

$$= 22.5$$

The correct answer is therefore D.

60   C   The sample of only six pairs of values is very small and is therefore likely to reduce the reliability of the estimate. Statement I is therefore true.

With such a small sample and the extrapolation required, the estimate is unlikely to be reliable. Statement II is therefore not true.

Since a correlation coefficient of 0.9 would be regarded as strong (it is a high value) the estimate would be reliable. Statement III is therefore not true.

When X = 20, we don't know anything about the relationship between X and Y since the sample data only goes up to X = 10. Statement IV is therefore true.

61   (a)

(2, 3) (3, 4.5) (4, 6)	?	Perfect positive correlation Perfect negative correlation Uncorrelated	✓

(b)

(2, 3) (3, 1.5) (4, 0)	?	Perfect positive correlation Perfect negative correlation Uncorrelated	✓

(c)

(2, 3) (4, 0) (4, 6)	?	Perfect positive correlation Perfect negative correlation Uncorrelated	✓

Workings

(a)   If these points were plotted on a scatter diagram, all the pairs of values would lie on an upward-sloping straight line with a gradient of +1.5. $\left[\text{Gradient} = \dfrac{6-3}{4-2} = \dfrac{3}{2} = 1.5\right]$. This would be indicative of PERFECT POSITIVE CORRELATION.

(b)   If these points were plotted on a scatter diagram, all the pairs of values would lie on a downward-sloping straight line with a gradient of −1.5. $\left[\text{Gradient} = \dfrac{0-3}{4-2} = \dfrac{-3}{2} = -1.5\right]$. This would be indicative of PERFECT NEGATIVE CORRELATION.

(c)   If these points were plotted on a scatter diagram there would not be evidence of any correlation existing since when x = 4, the corresponding y values are equal to 0 or 6.

62   (a)   (i)

1.2830

(ii)

6.68

Workings

The regression line is Y = a + bX

where $b = \dfrac{n\sum XY - \sum X \sum Y}{n\sum X^2 - (\sum X)^2}$

$a = \overline{Y} - b\overline{X}$

$b = \dfrac{10 \times 1{,}492 - 82 \times 172}{10 \times 736 - 82^2} = 1.2830$

$a = 17.2 - 1.283 \times 8.2 = 6.68$

Thus Y = 6.68 + 1.283X ($'000).

(b)   (i)   7,000

When production is zero, X = 0 and Y = 7.

∴ Fixed costs = $7,000

(ii)

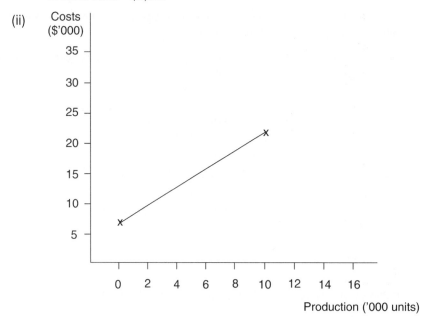

Production ('000 units)

Workings

When X = 0, Y = 7
When X = 10, Y = 7 + 15 = 22

(iii) $22,000

When production is 10,000, then X = 10 and Y = 22 and total production costs are therefore $22,000.

63   (a)

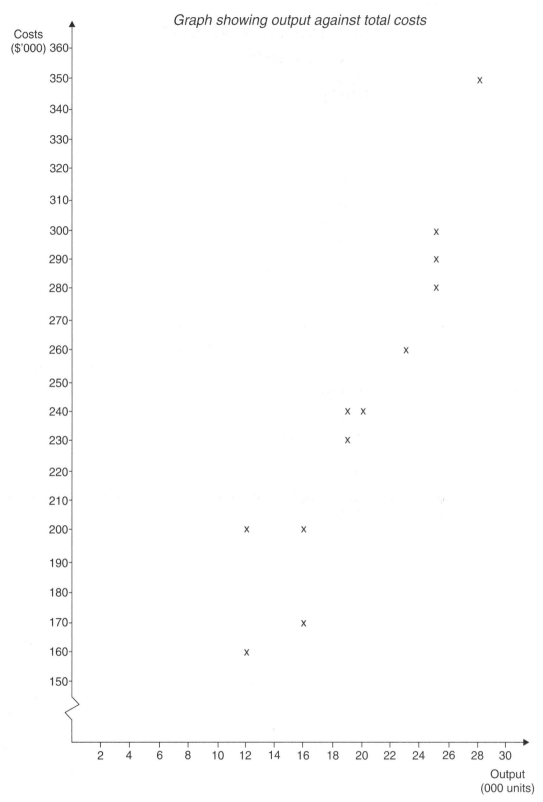

Graph showing output against total costs

(b) $\boxed{0.946}$

Workings

The correlation coefficient, r, is calculated using the following formula.

$$r = \frac{n\sum Y - \sum X \sum Y}{\sqrt{[n\sum X^2 - (\sum X)^2][n\sum Y^2 - (\sum Y)^2]}}$$

$$= \frac{37,200}{\sqrt{(12 \times 5,110 - 240^2)(12 \times 745,200 - 2,920^2)}}$$

$$= \frac{37,200}{\sqrt{3,720 \times 416,000}}$$

$$= \frac{37,200}{39,338.531}$$

$$= 0.946$$

64   A   If x = 8, y = 690.24 − (2.75 × 8) = 668.24

Forecast = trend + seasonal component = 668.24 − 25.25 = 642.99 = 643 (to the nearest unit)

If you selected option B, you calculated the forecast for the seventh period and deducted the seasonal component of the eighth period.

If you selected option C, you correctly forecast the trend for the eighth period but forgot to deduct the seasonal component.

If you selected option D, you simply calculated the trend for the seventh period instead of the eighth period.

65   D   I   Provided the seasonal variation remains the same in the future as in the past, it will not make forecasts unreliable.

           II   Provided a multiplicative model is used, the fact that the trend is increasing need not have any adverse effect on the reliability of forecasts.

           III   If the model being used is inappropriate, for example, if an additive model is used when the trend is changing sharply, forecasts will not be very reliable.

           IV   Forecasts are made on the assumption that everything continues as in the past.

III and IV are therefore necessary and hence the correct answer is D.

66   A   I   With an additive model, the weekly component represents the average value of actual production minus the trend for that week, so a component of +9 means production is 9,000 units above the trend.

This is the only correct statement.

If you selected option B, C or D, you have confused the additive variation of −4, +5 and −6 (actually −4,000 units, +5,000 units and −6,000 units respectively) with the multiplicative variation of −4%, +5% and −6% respectively.

67   A

	Quarter				
	1	2	3	4	Total
Unadjusted average	1.09	0.93	1.17	0.78	3.97
Adjustment	0.0075	0.0075	0.0075	0.0075	0.03
Adjusted average	1.0975	0.9375	1.1775	0.7875	4.000

$4 - 3.97 = 0.03$

We therefore need to add $0.03 \div 4 = 0.0075$ to each average.

From the table above, it can be seen that the first quarter adjusted average is 1.0975 as per option A.

If you selected option B, you added the entire deficit of 0.03 to the second quarter average instead of spreading it across all four averages.

If you selected option C, you subtracted the entire deficit of 0.03 from the third quarter average rather than sharing it across all four averages.

If you selected option D, you have subtracted the deficit of 0.0075 from each quarter's average, instead of adding it.

68   B   As this is a multiplicative model, the seasonal variations should sum (in this case) to 4 (an average of 1) as there are four quarters.

Let x = seasonal variation for quarter 4.

$$0.45 + 1.22 + 1.31 + x = 4$$
$$2.98 + x = 4$$
$$x = 4 - 2.98$$
$$= 1.02$$

If you selected option A you subtracted the sum of the seasonal variations from 3 instead of 4.

If you selected option D, you forgot to subtract the sum of the seasonal variations for quarters 1-3 from 4.

69

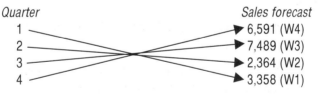

Quarter		Sales forecast
1		6,591 (W4)
2		7,489 (W3)
3		2,364 (W2)
4		3,358 (W1)

Workings

(1)   The trend changes from 4,500 to 5,300. The growth rate is $\dfrac{5,300}{4,500} = 1.178 = 17.8\%$.

Expressed per quarter (there are four quarters) this is $1.178^{1/3} = 1.056$ or 5.6% per quarter.

Therefore, in quarter 1, the forecast for actual sales $= 5,300 \times 1.056 \times 0.6 = 3,358$.

(2)   The trend changes from 4,500 to 5,300. The growth rate is $\dfrac{5,300}{4,500} = 1.178 = 17.8\%$.

Expressed per quarter (there are four quarters) this is $1.178^{1/3} = 1.056$ or 5.6% per quarter.

Therefore, in quarter 2, the forecast for actual sales $= 5,300 \times 1.056^2 \times 0.4 = 2,364$.

(3) The trend changes from 4,500 to 5,300. The growth rate is $\frac{5,300}{4,500}$ = 1.178 = 17.8%.

Expressed per quarter (there are four quarters) this is $1.178^{1/3}$ = 1.056 or 5.6% per quarter. Therefore, in quarter 3, the forecast for actual sales = $5,300 \times 1.056^3 \times 1.2$ = 7,489.

(4) The trend changes from 4,500 to 5,300. The growth rate is $\frac{5,300}{4,500}$ = 1.178 = 17.8%.

Expressed per quarter (there are four quarters) this is $1.178^{1/3}$ = 1.056 or 5.6% per quarter.

Therefore, in quarter 4, the forecast for actual sales = $5,300 \times 1.056^4 \times 1$ = 6,591.

70 (a) A = | 944 |

B = | 962 |

C = | 236.0 |

D = | 240.5 |

E = | 238 |

F = | −114 |

Workings

Year	Quarter	Sales	Moving total of 4 quarters' sales	Moving average of 4 quarters' sales	Trend	Seasonal variation
20X2	1	200				
	2	110				
			870	217.5		
	3	320			219	+101
			884	221.0		
	4	240			222	+18
			892	223.0		
20X3	1	214			225	-11
			906	226.5		
	2	118			229	-111
			926	231.5		
	3	334			232	+102
			932	233.0		
	4	260			234	+26
			938	234.5		
20X4	1	220			235	-15
			944	236.0		
	2	124			238	−114
			962	240.5		
	3	340				
	4	278				

A = 260 + 220 + 124 + 340 = 944

B = 220 + 124 + 340 + 278 = 962

C = 944 ÷ 4 = 236.0

D = 962 ÷ 4 = 240.5

E = (236.0 + 240.5) ÷ 2 = 476.5 ÷ 2 = 238.25

F = 124 − 238 = −114

(b) G = ⊡ −2

H = ⊡ +0.5

I = ⊡ −12.5

J = ⊡ −112.0

K = ⊡ +102.0

L = ⊡ +22.5

Workings

Year	1	2	3	4	Total
			Quarter		
20X2			+101	+18	
20X3	−11	−111	+102	+26	
20X4	−12.5	−114			
Average seasonal variation	−13.0	−112.5	+101.5	+22.0	−2
Adjustment	+0.5	+0.5	+0.5	+0.5	+2
Adjusted seasonal variation	−12.5	−112.0	+102.0	+22.5	0

The seasonal variations from the table in (a) are the initial entries in the table shown above. The seasonal variations are averaged by adding them together and dividing by two. The total of the averages gives the value of G, which should ideally be zero. (In this case it is −2.) We adjust the average seasonal variations by subtracting G/4 (−2/4 = −0.5) from each average which in this case means adding H = 0.5 in order to obtain the adjusted seasonal variations I to L.

(c) ⊡ 255.5

Workings

The additive model is A = T + S and we seasonally adjust the data in order to estimate the trend, T.

T = A − S
  = 278 − 22.5
  = 255.5

(d)   232.5

Workings

The additive model is A = T + S. Forecast sales are calculated by adding the adjusted seasonal variation (S) to the predicted trend (T).

Forecast sales   = 245 – 12.5

                 = 232.5

71   172

Working

In Q3 of 2010, t = 19

T = 52 + (6.3 × 19) = 171.7

   = 172 to three significant figures

72   A   For week 9, the trend value is 84 + (0.7 × 9) = 90.3

         The seasonal variation is actual – trend   = 88.7 – 90.3

                                                        = – 1.6

73   D   The residual is the difference between the actual data and the figure predicted by the time series analysis. It is the unexplained element in the actual figure.

Actual		4,000
Trend (3,150 + 72 × 12)	4,014	
Seasonal variation	(47)	
		(3,967)
		33

74   C   S = X + nrX
            = $2,000 + (8 × 0.12 × $2,000)
            = $2,000 + $1,920
            = $3,920

         If you selected option A, you calculated the interest element only and forgot to add on the original capital value.

         If you selected option B, you used n = 7 instead of n = 8.

         If you selected option D, you used the compound interest formula instead of the simple interest formula.

75   B   If S = X + nrX

$$S - X = nrX \text{ (note } S - X = \text{ interest element)}$$

$$\$1{,}548 - \$900 = nrX$$

$$4 \text{ years} = 4 \times 12 = 48 \text{ months} = n$$

$$\therefore \quad \$648 = 48\,r \times \$900$$

$$\therefore \quad r = \frac{£648}{48 \times £900}$$

$$r = 0.015 \text{ or } 1.5\%$$

If you selected option C, you misinterpreted 0.015 as 15% instead of 1.5%.

If you selected option D, you calculated the annual rate of interest instead of the monthly rate.

76   C $3,000 = 120% of the original investment

$$\therefore \text{ Original investment} = \frac{100}{120} \times \$3{,}000$$

$$= \$2{,}500$$

$$\therefore \text{ Interest} = \$3{,}000 - \$2{,}500$$
$$= \$500$$

Make sure that you always tackle this type of question by establishing what the original investment was first.

If you selected option D, you simply calculated 20% of $3,000 which is incorrect.

77   C   If a cost declines by 8% per annum on a compound basis, then at the end of the first year it will be worth 0.92 the original value.

Now = $12,000
End of year 1 = $12,000 × 0.92
End of year 2 = $12,000 × 0.92^2
End of year 3 = $12,000 × 0.92^3

∴ At the end of year 3, $12,000 will be worth

$12,000 × $(0.92)^3$ = $9,344

If you selected option A, you calculated the value after four years, not three.

If you selected option B, you have assumed that the cost will decline by 8% × 3 = 24% over 3 years therefore leaving a value of $12,000 − ($12,000 × 24%) = $12,000 − $2,880 = $9,120.

If you selected option D, you calculated the value after two years, not three.

78   A   If house prices rise at 3% per calendar month, this is equivalent to

$(1.03)^{12}$ = 1.426 or 42.6% per annum

If you selected option B, you forgot to take the effect of compounding into account, ie 3% × 12 = 36%.

If you selected option C, you incorrectly translated 1.426 into 14.26% instead of 42.6% per annum.

If you selected option D, you forget to raise 1.03 to the power of 12, instead you multiplied it by 12.

79 (a) | 15.87 | %

Working

15% per annum (nominal rate) is 3.75% per quarter. The effective annual rate of interest is

$[1.0375^4 - 1] = 0.1587 = 15.87\%$

(b) | 26.82 | %

Working

24% per annum (nominal rate) is 2% per month. The effective annual rate of interest is

$[1.02^{12} - 1] = 0.2682 = 26.82\%$

80 (a) | $2,941 |

Working

Value after 3 years = $8,000 × 1.11^3 = $10,941 (to the nearest $)

∴ Interest = $10,941 − $8,000
= $2,941

(b) | $13,881 |

Working

Value after 5 years = $15,000 × 1.14^5 = $28,881 (to the nearest $)

∴ Interest = $28,881 − $15,000
= $13,881

(c) | $3,601 |

Working

Value after 4 years = $6,000 × 1.1^2 × 1.15^2 = $9,601 (to the nearest $)

∴ Interest = $9,601 − $6,000
= $3,601

(d) | 10.78% |

Working

Rate of interest = 5.25% every six months

∴ Six monthly ratio = 1.0525

∴ Annual ratio = 1.0525^2
= 1.1078

∴ Effective annual rate = 10.78% (to 2 decimal places)

(e) ┌─────────┐
     │ 12.68% │
     └─────────┘

Working

Rate of interest = 1% every month

∴ Monthly ratio = 1.01

∴ Annual ratio = 1.01^{12}

               = 1.1268

∴ Effective annual rate = 12.68% (to 2 decimal places)

(f) ┌─────────┐
     │ 12.55% │
     └─────────┘

Working

Rate of interest = 3% per quarter

∴ Quarterly ratio = 1.03

∴ Annual ratio = 1.03^4

               = 1.1255

∴ Effective annual rate = 12.55% (to 2 decimal places)

81   C   Present value of the lease for years 1 – 9 = $12,000 × 5.328

                 Present value of the lease for years 0 – 9 = $12,000 × (1 + 5.328)

                                                = $12,000 × 6.328

                                                  = $75,936

If you selected option A, you calculated the PV of the lease for years 1-9 only. If the first payment is made now, you must remember to add 1 to the 5.328.

Option B represents the PV of the lease for years 1-10 (the first payment being made in a one year's time), ie $12,000 × 5.650 = $67,800.

Option D is incorrect because it represents the PV of the lease for years 1-10 plus an additional payment now (ie $12,000 × (1 + 5.650) = $79,800.

82   D   Let A = annual repayments

                 These repayments, A are an annuity for 15 years at 9%.

$$\text{Annuity (A)} = \frac{\text{PV of mortgage}}{\text{Annuity factor}}$$

PV of mortgage = $60,000

Annuity factor = 8.061 (9%, 15 years from CDF tables)

$$\therefore \text{Annuity} = \frac{\$60,000}{8.061}$$

                        = $7,440 (to the nearest $10)

If you selected option A you have confused mortgages with sinking funds and have calculated the PV of the mortgage as if it occurred at time 15 instead of time 0.

If you selected option B you have forgotten to take account of the interest rates (ie 9% for 15 years). You have simply divided $60,000 by 15.

If you selected option C, you have not taken into account the fact that the repayments happen at the year end and that the first repayment is in one year's time and not now.

83   C   The IRR can be calculated using the following formula.

$$IRR = a\% + \left[\frac{A}{A-B} \times (b-a) \right]\%$$

where a = 10%
         b = 24%
         A = $460
         B = $320

$$IRR = 10\% + \left[\frac{\$460}{\$460 - £320} \times (24-10) \right]\%$$

$$= 10\% + 46\%$$

$$= 56\%$$

If you selected option A, you have calculated the arithmetic mean of 10% and 24% instead of using the IRR formula.

If you selected option B you have used an NPV of –$320 instead of +$320 in your calculation.

If you selected option D, you must realise that it is possible to use either two positive or two negative NPVs as well as a positive and negative NPV. Using the former method, however, the results will be less accurate.

84   B   The payments made on a credit card are an annuity of $x per month.

From cumulative present value tables (3%, 12 periods) the annuity factor is 9.954.

$$\text{If Annuity} = \frac{\text{PV of annuity}}{\text{Annuity factor}}$$

$$\text{Annuity} = \frac{\$21,000}{9.954}$$

$$= \$2,110$$

If you selected option A, you have simply divided $21,000 by 12 without any reference to discounting.

If you selected option C, you have misread the cumulative present value tables (and used the annuity factor for 12% and 3 periods instead of 12 periods and 3%).

If you selected option D, you have calculated the present value of $21,000 in 12 time periods at a discount rate of 3% instead of finding the monthly annuity whose present value over 12 months at 3% gives $21,000.

85   A   Project A has the highest NPV. When comparing projects it is the NPV of each project which should be calculated and compared. The correct answer is therefore A.

Mutually exclusive projects should not be selected by comparing the IRRs – Option D is therefore incorrect, even though it has the highest IRR, it does not have the highest NPV.

Projects B and C do not have the highest NPVs either and so options B and C are incorrect.

86

Year	Cash flow	Discount factor	Present value
	$	11%	$
0	(28,000)	1.000	(28,000)
1	8,000	0.901	7,208
2	8,000	0.812	6,496
3	8,000	0.731	5,848
4	8,000	0.659	5,272
5	8,000	0.593	4,744
		NPV	1,568

Project viable   Yes   ✓

No   ☐

The NPV is positive, therefore the project is viable because it earns more than 11% per annum.

87   (a)   A = $12,000

B =   1

C =   0.641

D = $15,516

E = $18,575

F = $330

Workings

Year	Cash flow	Discount factor	Present value
	$	16%	$
0	(50,000)	1.000	(50,000)
1	18,000	0.862	15,516
2	25,000	0.743	18,575
3	15,000	0.641	9,615
4	12,000	0.552	6,624
		NPV	330

(b) ┌─────────┐
    │ −$1,477 │
    └─────────┘

Workings

Year	Cash flow	Discount factor	Present value
	$	18%	$
0	(50,000)	1.000	(50,000)
	18,000	0.847	15,246
2	25,000	0.718	17,950
	15,000	0.609	9,135
4	12,000	0.516	6,192
		NPV	(1,477)

(c) ┌─────────┐
    │ 16.4%   │
    └─────────┘

Workings

Estimated IRR = $16\% + \left[\dfrac{330}{330 + 1,477} \times (18 - 16) \right]\%$ = 16.4% (to 1 decimal place).

88   (a)   (i) ┌─────────┐
               │ 9.954x │
               └─────────┘

           (ii) ┌─────────┐
                │ $4,018 │
                └─────────┘

Workings

The bank pays out the loan now so the present value of the loan is $40,000.

The annuity is the amount that needs to be paid at the end of each quarter.

The annuity factor can be found in the cumulative present value tables; the cost of capital is 3%, and the number of time periods we are concerned with is found as follows.

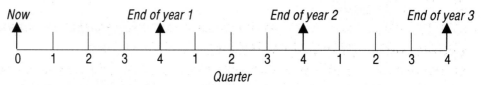

Number of time periods = 12 quarters

Annuity factor = 9.954

Present value of repayments = 9.954X

and x = $\dfrac{\$40,000}{9.954}$

= $4,018.49

Therefore, the equal amounts that must be repaid at the end of each quarter = $4,018 (to the nearest $).

(b)   (i) $44,994.56

       (ii)   10.787Y

       (iii) $3,290

Workings

(i)   In three years' time, the amount of money required to modernise the premises will be:

$40,000 \times (1.04)^3 = \$44,994.56$

(ii)   The instalments consist of a payment Y now plus an annuity of 11 payments at 2% per time period. The annuity factor at 2% for 11 periods is 9.787 and hence the present value is Y + 9.787Y = 10.787Y.

(iii)   The present value of $44,994.56 at time 12 discounted at 2% = $44,994.56 $\times$ 0.788.

$\therefore$ 10.787Y = $44,994.56 $\times$ 0.788

$$Y = \frac{\$35,455}{10.787}$$

= $3,290 (to the nearest $10)

(c)   Save and modernise later ✓

It costs less to save now and modernise later, therefore the retailer should be advised to do this.

89	D	No computer system knows exactly what you intended so can not make 100% accurate connections.
90	B	Microsoft Access is a database application.
91	D	Putting a value in the cell, such as 2,860, would mean that the cell was not updated to reflect later changes to the spreadsheet.
92	B	In Excel, placing the $ sign in front of a cell reference makes that reference absolute. When you move or copy a formula absolute cell references do not change.
93	A	The correct formula is =D28+D18. Although D18+D28 looks the same, because it has no = sign it is not treated as a formula. Both of the other options count sub totals as well the cost items.
94	B	Formulae, text and numbers can be entered onto a spreadsheet.
95	A	Option A shows the correct formula.
96	C	Option C shows the correct formula.
97	C	The formula would contain the COUNT function.
98	A	The absolute sign, '$', should be used on the row and column reference for the cell B15. Also using the '$' with the column references for C column will give the desired result.

Index

Review Form & Free Prize Draw – Paper C3 Business Mathematics (6/06)

All original review forms from the entire BPP range, completed with genuine comments, will be entered into one of two draws on 31 January 2007 and 31 July 2007. The names on the first four forms picked out on each occasion will be sent a cheque for £50.

Name: _____   **Address:** _____

_____

_____

How have you used this Interactive Text?
(Tick one box only)

☐ Home study (book only)

☐ On a course: college _____

☐ With 'correspondence' package

☐ Other _____

Why did you decide to purchase this Interactive Text? *(Tick one box only)*

☐ Have used BPP Texts in the past

☐ Recommendation by friend/colleague

☐ Recommendation by a lecturer at college

☐ Saw information on BPP website

☐ Saw advertising

☐ Other _____

Which BPP products have you used?

Text	☑	Success CD	☐	Learn Online	☐
Kit	☐	i-Learn	☐	Home Study Package	☐
Passcard	☐	i-Pass	☐	Home Study PLUS	☐
MCQ cards	☐				

During the past six months do you recall seeing/receiving any of the following?
(Tick as many boxes as are relevant)

☐ Our advertisement in *Financial Management*

☐ Our advertisement in *Pass*

☐ Our advertisement in *PQ*

☐ Our brochure with a letter through the post

☐ Our website www.bpp.com

Which (if any) aspects of our advertising do you find useful?
(Tick as many boxes as are relevant)

☐ Prices and publication dates of new editions

☐ Information on Text content

☐ Facility to order books off-the-page

☐ None of the above

Your ratings, comments and suggestions would be appreciated on the following areas.

	Very useful	Useful	Not useful
Introductory section (Key study steps, personal study)	☐	☐	☐
Chapter introductions	☐	☐	☐
Key terms	☐	☐	☐
Quality of explanations	☐	☐	☐
Case studies and other examples	☐	☐	☐
Assessment focus points	☐	☐	☐
Questions and answers in each chapter	☐	☐	☐
Fast forwards and chapter roundups	☐	☐	☐
Quick quizzes	☐	☐	☐
Question Bank	☐	☐	☐
Answer Bank	☐	☐	☐
Index	☐	☐	☐
Icons	☐	☐	☐

Overall opinion of this Study Text   Excellent ☐   Good ☐   Adequate ☐   Poor ☐

Do you intend to continue using BPP products?   Yes ☐   No ☐

On the reverse of this page are noted particular areas of the text about which we would welcome your feedback.

The BPP author of this edition can be e-mailed at: julietgood @bpp.com

Please return this form to: Janice Ross, CIMA Certificate Publishing Manager, BPP Professional Education, FREEPOST, London, W12 8BR

Review Form & Free Prize Draw (continued)

TELL US WHAT YOU THINK

Because the following specific areas of the text contain new material and cover highly examinable topics etc, your comments on their usefulness are particularly welcome.

Please note any further comments and suggestions/errors below

Free Prize Draw Rules

1. Closing date for 31 January 2007 draw is 31 December 2006. Closing date for 31 July 2007 draw is 30 June 2007.

2. Restricted to entries with UK and Eire addresses only. BPP employees, their families and business associates are excluded.

3. No purchase necessary. Entry forms are available upon request from BPP Professional Education. No more than one entry per title, per person. Draw restricted to persons aged 16 and over.

4. Winners will be notified by post and receive their cheques not later than 6 weeks after the relevant draw date.

5. The decision of the promoter in all matters is final and binding. No correspondence will be entered into.